Hiking guide to
Romania

'Tis a gift to be simple, 'tis a gift to be free,
'tis a gift to wind up where you ought to be

(from the Shaker folk song 'Simple Gifts')

Hiking guide to Romania

by Tim Burford

BRADT PUBLICATIONS, UK
HUNTER PUBLISHING, USA

First published in 1993 by Bradt Publications, 41 Nortoft Rd, Chalfont St Peter, Bucks SL9 0LA, England.

British Library Cataloguing in Publication data

A catalogue record for this book is
available from the British Library

ISBN 0 946983 78 X

Illustrations by Julian Drake
Cover photos by Tim Burford
Photos by Friso Spoelstra
Maps by Hans van Well
Typeset from the author's disc by Patti Taylor, London NW10 3BX
Printed by The Guernsey Press

This book is for my mother, and for Marlene, to show that it can be done.

Many thanks are due to many people, both in Romania and outside, including Patrice Vermeulen and family, Maria and Ioan Ciceu, Victoria and Isidore Berbecaru, Dan and Emilia Bărbos and all their friends and relations, Ina Postăvaru, Dr Paul Philippi, Mircea Costea, Vasile Vieriu, Emil Silvestru, Pepi Viehmann, Marius and Ana Sîntamarian, Mircea Pîrlog, Dan Jinaru, Maria and Ilie Urdea, Oana Lungescu, Catherine Treasure, Dr Jon Aves, James Brabazon, Helen Randle, and above all the Farcaş family. Thanks also to Hilary Bradt, and Patti Taylor, Hans van Well and Roger Jordan. All errors, of fact or of interpretation, are entirely my own.

You too can earn everlasting gratitude, dear reader, by sending corrections and updates to me c/o Bradt Publications.

ROMANIA

CONTENTS OF THIS BOOK

0 km 100

(Moldova)

(Ukraine)

Black
Sea

DOBROGEA

BUCUREŞTI

Danube

MOLDAVIA

WALLACHIA

TRANSYLVANIA

Braşov

Cluj

Sibiu

BANAT

(Ukraine)

(Hungary)

(Vojvodina)

(Serbia)

(Bulgaria)

Contents

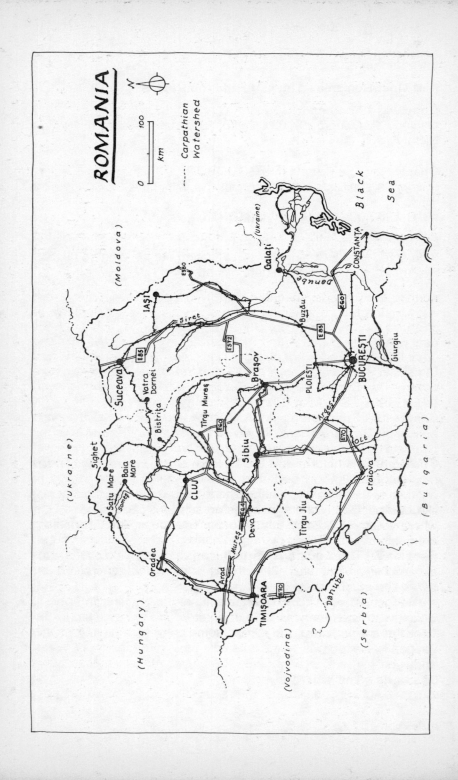

Introduction

The Carpathian Mountains

Although many people would not know quite where or what the Carpathians are, they would probably associate them with that inchoate *terra incognita* behind what was the Iron Curtain. They are in fact a continuation of the Alps, the backbone of that whole area north of the Balkans, starting not far from Vienna and running east into Ukraine before swinging south and west through Romania to finish on the Danube where Romania meets Serbia. This book will deal with the Romanian stretch of the Carpathians as well as a few other interesting areas for hiking in Romania; I will cover Poland and Ukraine in a separate book in 1993, and the Slovak Carpathians are covered by Simon Hayman's *Guide to Czechoslovakia* (second edition 1991), also from Bradt Publications.

In the future the Carpathians will increasingly be seen as the lungs of Europe, an area where people can genuinely get away from the concrete that has swallowed up the Alps and similar areas. However if hiking here is not like trekking in Nepal or Peru, where you spend most of your time in cultivated areas going from one village to another and constantly meeting the locals on the trail, neither is it like backpacking in the wilderness areas of Alaska or the Rockies, where you meet nothing but the occasional bear. The Carpathians are not totally untouched by human hands, and in particular you will meet shepherds almost everywhere you go, but they do offer a huge expanse of virtually unspoilt mountains where you can indeed see bears and much more.

The people are immensely hospitable and are delighted to welcome Westerners who take an interest in their country. In this book I offer a wide range of routes, some between monasteries and villages in the foothills, some in almost unvisited backwoods areas, and others in alpine areas with developed tourist facilities; there should be something for everyone.

Mitteleuropa and the death of communism

Geographically this area was known as Eastern Europe or Mitteleuropa and is now increasingly known as Central Europe as it draws closer to the west; Eastern Europe was always a misnomer, as Norway stretches as far east as Poland and Prague is a long way west of Vienna, and Mitteleuropa was more a concept or state of mind than a geographical entity, referring to the spirit of the multi-ethnic hotch-potch of the area, almost all at one time or another under the sway of the Austro-Hungarian Empire of the Hapsburgs; this initially combined a form of enlightened despotism with an unprecedented degree of centralised bureaucracy, before in 1867 handing over most of the eastern part of its territory to the less enlightened chauvinism of the Hungarians, who tried to impose their linguistic and cultural domination on all their newly subject races.

This broke up after the First World War, when there was an eruption of nationalist passions leading to the establishment of new countries such as Czechoslovakia and Yugoslavia. However after 1945 the situation returned more or less to what it had been, with Central or Eastern Europe under the sway of another empire and its stifling bureaucracy. This has now in its turn collapsed, and all the repressed ethnic tensions and passions are once more being unleashed with their original venom undiluted; we have already had terrible warnings of this in Yugoslavia and in Georgia. In Romania the province of Transylvania in particular, with its large Hungarian minority, remains a complicated patchwork of different cultures that give it much of its fascination.

In all these countries there is a sense of total economic dislocation and a fear of being overwhelmed by the developed economies of the West, although it was largely a desire for the goodies of the consumer economy that brought about the downfall of the communist system. Marx and Engels described this best in the *Communist Manifesto* (1848): 'The bourgeoisie, by the rapid improvement of all instruments of production, by the immensely facilitated means of communication, draws all, even the most barbarian, nations into civilisation. The cheap prices of its commodities are the heavy artillery with which it batters down all Chinese walls, with which it forces the barbarians' intensely obstinate hatred of foreigners to capitulate. It compels all nations, on pain of extinction, to adopt the bourgeois mode of production; it compels them to introduce what it calls civilisation into their midst, ie to become bourgeois themselves. In one word, it creates a world after its own image'. Ironically, it takes Marx himself to describe the death of Marxism.

In addition to the inherent conservatism of the communist (or more accurately Stalinist) system, there is also the spirit of conformism inherent in the Orthodox religious outlook, which stifles the development of private enterprise; people are conditioned in every way to wait for orders rather than to get up and go on their own. As a result many people want to do exactly that — get up and go to western Europe where they hope the system will give them a job and lots of money. There are widespread fears in the West of floods of economic refugees from the east (and from Africa) that will destabilise the whole of Europe; we must be honest with people and tell them of mass unemployment and immigration laws in the European Community, and that it takes more than consumer goods to make people really happy.

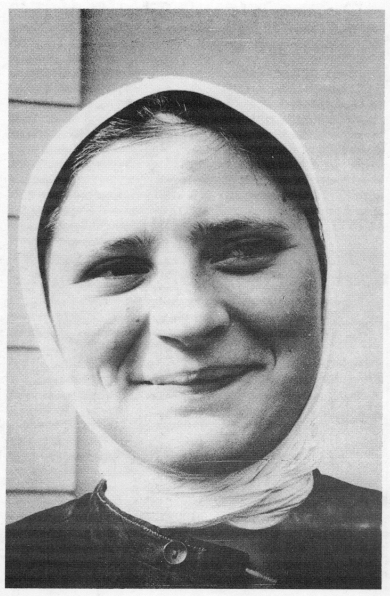

Novice nun

Part One

Romania — The Land and the People

Chapter 1

The Land

GEOLOGY

The Carpathian system is part of the Alpine-Himalayan chain, formed relatively recently in the Tertiary alpine orogeny, but there is as yet no explanation for the formation of the Carpathian-Balkan S-bend. The Carpathian system is as long as the Alps (1,300km, but with its ends on the Danube at Bratislava and the Iron Gates only 500km apart) but only half their height, making them easier to cross. They underwent Quarternary glaciation only in the Karkonosze, Tatras, Rodnas and the Southern Carpathians. The far older and lower remnants of the Hercynian mountains lie parallel to the north, running from the Vosges via the Ardennes, the Black Forest, and southern Poland to northern Dobrogea on Romania's Black Sea coast. For the most part the Carpathian chain is 35-40 kilometres wide, double that in the Parîng group and three times that in the Rodnas, and generally consists of three distinct bands, with Flysch (or turbidite) on the outside, young crystalline massifs in the centre and some volcanic ranges intruding on the inner side.

Starting from the western end the chain is divided into four sections, of which the third and fourth are in Romania:

1. The Western Carpathians, from the Vienna basin to the Hornad River, near Kosice — the widest, highest and most complex section, above all the High Tatras on the Polish-Slovak border, glaciated granite often covered with limestone.

2. The Central, Forest or Ukrainian Carpathians, from the Hornad River to the upper Tisa (or Tisza) River; lower sedimentary hills

providing major routes from Poland to eastern Slovakia and from Ukraine to Hungary.

3. The Eastern Carpathians, from the sources of the Tisa almost to Braşov, consisting of parallel ridges of sedimentary rocks (sandstone and conglomerates) to the east, a central crystalline schist zone with some resistant limestones, and to the west an inner zone of volcanic material. Between the volcanic and crystalline zones are eight main basins filled with fertile loess and aluvium, such as those around Miercurea-Ciuc and Tîrgu-Secuiesc.

4. The Southern Carpathians, from Braşov to the Iron Gates, are, with the Tatras, the only truly Alpine section of the Carpathians. Like the Alps, they underwent intense folding, followed by three later phases, including glaciation, that left platforms or *plaiuri* (paths), mostly to the west of the Olt valley. The Făgăraş and Retezat ranges are mainly hard crystalline rocks, and there are various areas of karstitic limestone. To the west the Banat mountains are largely sedimentary, with beds of coal around Anina.

In addition the Apuseni or western mountains (also known as the Bihor massif) block off the Transylvanian basin to the west, forming a rather awkward spur to the north of the main Carpathian chain. They consist of ancient crystalline rocks, Palaeozoic and Mesozoic sediments and recent volcanic material, and are a very complex area of irregular depressions and stranded massifs with meadow platforms or 'suspended plains'. There was erosion but no glaciation in the Quarternary, producing 'peri-glacial' forms. Above all, this is the main karst zone of Romania, producing many gorges, caves and potholes, while also tertiary eruptive forms give a 'haystack' form to the Munţii Metaliferi (Metal-bearing Mountains), where gold, silver and mercury have been mined for nearly 2,000 years.

Also in Romania, although not strictly part of the Carpathian chain, you will come across references to the following areas:

1. The Transylvanian basin — undulating hills of highly fertile Tertiary sediments such as clays, sandstone and loess. The lowest areas such as the Bîrsa country around Braşov and the Făgăraş depression were not drained until the Quarternary era, and there are still some peat marshes as a result.

2. The outer foothills of the Carpathians (or Sub-Carpathians) — mostly folded Tertiary sediments, with oil in Pliocene formations to the north of Bucureşti.

3. The Romanian lowlands — formed of loess east of the Olt, and of sand to the west. This is covered with chernozem or black-earth soils, very fertile agricultural land.

4. As mentioned above, the northern (or Romanian) Dobrogea (or Dobruja) forms the end of the worn-down Hercynian chain, with granite, limestone and schists dating from the Primary era, the oldest rocks in Europe, while immediately to the north the youngest land in Europe is still being formed in the Danube Delta.

GEOGRAPHY

Like Gaul, Romania is divided into three parts; it has three provinces, Wallachia, Moldavia and Transylvania, and is made up of almost equal thirds of mountain, central plateau and hills, and plains. Something under a third is covered with forest, and while on the subject, one third of the length of the Danube (1,075km) flows through Romania. Despite the building of a hugely expensive 64km canal to the port of Constanţa, the Danube is not heavily used for transport, but this may change with the opening of the Rhine-Main-Danube canal in 1992. Half of the total population of twenty-three million is urban, and an overlapping half lives in the plateau and hills. All these tidy figures would of course be changed if the formerly Soviet part of Moldavia (or Moldova) were ever reunited with Romania.

The country is very rich in natural resources; the black-earth plains of Wallachia and Moldavia yield large crops of grain, and the rest of the country is also very fertile, producing grain, maize, root and other vegetables, fruit and vines in abundance. Other areas are used for forestry and the mountain pastures are used for grazing sheep. Every rural household also has hens and often a pig.

There is a considerable oil industry, mainly around Ploieşti, coal mining in the Jiu valley and elsewhere, and mining for minerals in all the northern and western mountains. With its tourist potential as well Romania is a country with a good future ahead of it, if it can only organise itself.

Between 1930 and 1943 thirty-six zones, with a total area of about 15,000 hectares, were declared Nature Reserves; there are now 130, with an area of 75,000 hectares, and some, such as the Retezat and Apuseni mountains, the Iron Gates, and Mount Domogled, near Băile Herculane, are being promoted to National Park status. The reserves include caves, peat bogs, alpine meadows, and spruce groves, and several will be referred to in the following pages. However one area that will not be covered in a book primarily on walking in hills and mountains, but that you should know about, is the Danube Delta; this is 4,470 sq km (and 1,200 sq km in Ukraine) of water, floating vegetation and a little solid ground with a truly fantastic range of birds (up to one million, of up to 300 species), fish (110 species) and flowers (1,150 species). Under Ceauşescu, there were plans to reclaim 170,000 hectares of the Delta for agriculture and fish-farming, but these have now been abandoned; there has already been much pollution damage, and there is a risk of more damage from uncontrolled development of tourist facilities. The major channels are overcrowded with tourist boats and it can be a feat of considerable endurance to reach the true backwaters — this is an ideal place to have your own kayak.

The definitive description of the reserves is *Nature Reserves in Romania* by Pop and Sălăgeanu (Meridiane 1965).

CLIMATE

The Romanian climate is described as humid-continental or transitional continental-temperate, meaning essentially that it has hot summers and cold winters, with average precipitation of 637mm (about 1,300mm in the mountains) evenly spread throughout the year. Romanians think in terms of just two seasons, *iarnă* (winter) and *vară* (summer), although there are in fact the normal four seasons. Summer temperatures average 22-24° C and winter temperatures -3° C; in July Ruse, on the Danube, can reach 42° C, while in the mountains it can snow in any month and the Trans-Făgăraş Highway is only open from June to September or October. Snow can be a problem, drifting under trees and in gullies, until July, so summer and early autumn, in particular the September full moon, are the best seasons for hiking. Summer can be a good time to visit the German areas, which are then much more lively with many emigrés returning from Germany for holidays. Transylvania and the west have more precipitation than elsewhere; the southwestern climate has some Mediterranean influences, making it drier and warmer, and the north and northeast are sometimes affected by the *crivaţ*, a dry and icy wind from Siberia.

GREEN ISSUES

Oscar Wilde said anybody can be good in the country, but alas it is not so simple nowadays. As he also said, each man kills the thing he loves, and that is a very real problem for all of us who travel, particularly in the unspoilt parts of the world. The Romanians claim to love their mountains, but sadly they seem to be constitutionally incapable of carrying down the empty cans and bottles that they take up, and thus there are great piles of rubbish at the most popular camping spots. In addition communist industrial planning did far more damage than rampant capitalism or the EC Regional Fund have been able to, as seen in the Căliman mountains (see page 155) where an entire mountain has been mined for sulphur; the Padurea Craiului, in the Apuseni, where uranium was mined for the Soviet Union; at Copşa Mică, the notorious centre of the carbon-black industry, and in all the valleys flooded by dams. Rivers in which swimming and fishing are impossible include the Arieş below Cîmpeni and the Prahova below Sinaia.

However Romania is ahead of most Western countries in the sphere of reusing bottles and jars, with a deposit system in every food shop (an advantage of a state retail system). It is also active in public education on the dangers of deforestation, which happily is not yet a widespread problem, although Mrs Phillimore was well ahead of her time in 1912 in noting 'They have cut down all the forest to cultivate the ground and now there is not enough rain!' — and there are now fears that the paper industry may try to move into Romania. There is little in the way of unnecessary packaging, which is fortunate as there is little in the way of effective rubbish disposal; leave all unnecessary packaging at home.

As for *our* individual responsibilities, it is important to say that green tourism is a question not just of using biodegradable sunscreen and not littering, but also of attitude. You should be clear in your own mind just why you are travelling in the first place. We have great economic power which should be used wisely. If you take a package holiday or stay in 'international' hotels, the profits never reach the country you visit, whereas if you travel independently, staying in locally-owned establishments, travelling on public transport, buying food as you go and preferably not changing money on the black market, you are putting funds directly into the economy. In Romania the tourist industry currently has plenty of spare capacity, but in general you should consider travelling out of season if possible.

Remember that you are exploring not just a region but also a culture; try to learn the basic words of greeting at least, and take care not to behave insensitively, in particular by not dressing immodestly or showing physical affection in public, not taking unwanted photographs, and by respecting religious sites and artefacts. Try to repay hospitality fully, but not by showering money around; it is better to offer some reciprocal service, although simply taking photographs of people can be too much of an easy option.

The key advice can be summed up in the slightly hackneyed saying of the Sierra Club: Take nothing but pictures, kill nothing but time, leave nothing but footprints.

If you want to do some practical conservation work in Romania, working with local volunteers, the British Trust for Conservation Volunteers, 36 St Mary's St, Wallingford, Oxon OX10 0EU (tel 0491 39766) organises working holidays there, currently footpath repair work in the Bucegi mountains near Busteni and fencing in the Danube Delta.

NATURAL HISTORY
Fauna

In Britain the range of fauna is more limited than that in continental Europe due to isolation since the last Ice Age, and in recent years our wildlife has been decimated by modern intensive farming. In the mountains of eastern Europe there has never been anything but organic farming, and although there are some fairly exotic species, the real joy of hiking here lies in experiencing a largely unspoilt ecological system. The landscape is largely man-made, dominated by sheep-farming and forestry industries, but the wildlife has adapted well.

Among the more 'exotic' animals is the brown bear (*urs*/*Ursus arctos*), of which perhaps over 6,000 are still secure in their spruce forest hideouts. In fact Romania is over-populated with bears, while only three remain in Norway, a dozen in the French Pyrénées, and eighty in Italy's Abruzzi National Park. The male, weighing up to 315kg, has a range of up to 2,000 sq km, while the female has a range of 200 sq km; their tracks are similar to human footprints and and their legs are further apart than those of any other European animal. They hibernate for between three and five months in the winter.

The Romanians have a collective phobia about bears, taking staves, knives and fierce dogs into the hills and never going there alone or camping wild. I have some experience of Canadian bears and assure the Romanians that the only bears that actually want to eat humans, let alone those wrapped in plastic coats or tents, are polar bears, which are not found in the Carpathians. They are not convinced, and it is true that bears do take lambs and that they are dangerous when with their cubs in April and May. Many of the Canadian problems are due to the increasing familiarity of bears with humans, and as long as the Romanian attitude persists this is unlikely to develop here, although I am now hearing of bears raiding rubbish skips in Poiana Braşov. There is no need to hang your food high in the trees, although I would advise you not to have open tins of meat in your tent; I have in fact seen tents torn open by pigs searching for bread. Usually any bear you see will be as alarmed as you, and will leave a steaming pile as evidence.

There is slightly less talk of wolves (*lup/Canis lupus*); generally you are told that they live over the border in the Ukrainian Carpathians and only come south in bad winters, but there are many in the Romanian forests as well. In winter, especially in Bucovina, groups of *lupători* go out to hunt wolves and pose proudly for photos.

Also in the lower forests are wild boar (*mistreţ/Sus scrofa*), supposedly nocturnal and very protective of their young; but when I saw one in broad daylight it cleared off and left its young to fend for themselves. They can weigh more than 200kg — almost as much as a male red deer.

There are several varieties of deer, notably the red deer (*cerb/Cervus elaphus*), which lives mainly on spruce shoots and bark, shedding its antlers in March and April and rutting in September and October, when the hills ring with a mooing roar with a touch of chainsaw. In addition there are roe deer (*căprior/Capreolus capreolus*), small and elegant with a white rump, which feeds on ground bushes particularly at dusk and dawn, and ruts in late July and early August; and fallow deer (*cerb lopător/Cervus dama*), which is reddish-brown, with white spots in summer, and has a black stripe on its tail. They live in dense deciduous woodland and don't rut until late October.

In the higher, steeper forests (usually between 700m and 1,100m, although they can go as high as 2,000m) lives the lynx (*rîs/Lynx lynx*) which is rarely seen, although I frequently found their tracks in snow in the spring — their weight compressed the snow just enough for it to bear my weight as well. There are also wild cats (*pisică* as in pussycat *săbatică/Felix silvestris*).

Smaller forest mammals include the fox (*vulpe/Vulpes vulpes*), pine marten (*jder/Martes martes*), rock marten (*jder de stînca/Martes foina*), stoat (*hermelină/Mustella ermina*), weasel (*nevăstuică/Mustella nivalis*), badger (*viezure* or *bursuc/Meles meles*) and the red squirrel (*veveriţa/Sciurus vulgaris*), which can be black. One oddity is the raccoon-dog (*Cîine enot/Nyctereutes procyonoides*), which only came into Europe from Asia after the Second World War; it is nocturnal so you are unlikely to see it.

Above the forests most hikers are interested in the chamois (*capră neagră* (although not actually black) or *Rupicapra rupicapra*), which were reduced by hunting until found only in the Rodna mountains. It has now, however, been successfully reintroduced into other alpine areas. Generally the male is solitary while females stay in herds, and meet to mate in November; they have a whistling alarm call and a goat-like bleat, but generally they are not too timid, with a habit of standing on the skyline to see you off their territory. However I have seen chamois even in beech forest at below 1,000m altitude. There are also marmots (*marmotă*/*Marmota marmota*), which resemble big grey hamsters, hibernate for six months of the year and seem to keep their heads down more than their cousins in the Himalayas and Rockies; they live on the rocky floors of cirques in the Făgăraş while hikers tend to pass above along the ridges. Like the chamois, they have a whistling alarm call, but as their only predators are eagles, now rare, they don't need it much.

Also in the alpine zone, and also hard to spot, are the Alpine shrew (*şoarece de munte*/*Sorex alpinus*), which has a tail as long as its body at about 60mm each, and the snow vole (*Microtus nivalis*), which contrary to its name actually prefers sunny slopes, where it jumps from rock to rock.

  Other mammals of interest are European bison (*zîmbru*/*Bizon bonasus*), which disappeared from Romania in the 18th Century but has been reintroduced to reserves at Neamţ and Haţeg, the otter (*vidră*/*Lutra lutra*), the brown hare (*ieper*/*Lepus europaeus*]), which is of interest mainly because there are so few rabbits in Romania, and the souslik (*Spermophilus citellus*), a ground squirrel found on the steppes of Moldavia and Wallachia — a bit of a blob with little in the way of external features such as ears or tails.

In wet weather you will often see salamanders (*salamîzdră*/*Triturus montandonii*), a beautiful shiney black with orange spots. In the warmer south and west there are also newts (*triton*) and common lizards (*şopîrlă*/*Lacerta vivipara*), as well as tortoises (*testoasă*) and frogs (*broască*) such as *Rana temporaria*. The most common snakes are the adder (*viperă*/*Vipera berus*, found at over 2,000m altitude), the horned adder (*Vipera ammodytes*, almost one metre long), at the extreme western end of its range, and the (harmless) ringed or grass snake (*năpîrcă*/*Natrix natrix*), which has a more pronounced collar marking than its British cousins, and may also have two light stripes along its body.

There are many large birds (*păsările*), mostly above the treeline in alpine and moorland country, in particular the golden eagle (*acvila de munte*/*Aquila chrysaetes*) and the lammergeier or bearded vulture (*zagan* or *vultur bărbos*/*Gypaetus barbatus*), now very rare, and game birds such as the capercaillie (*cocoşul de munte*/*Tetrao urogallus*) — huge grey and brown birds with 'beards'. Also in the alpine zone

are the unmistakable ring ouzel (*mierlă gulerata/Turdus torquatus*),
dull black with a broad white crescent across its breast, and the
raven (*corb/Corvus corax*). Most striking in rocky areas is the wall
creeper (*fluturaşul de stîncă/Tichodroma muraria*) which looks rather
like a woodpecker but flies more like a butterfly.

In the woods are game birds such as black grouse (*cocoşul de
mesteacăn*, literally birchcock /*Lyrurus tetrix*), which has a red crest
and lyre-shaped tail, and the hazelhen (*ieruncă/Tetrastes bonasia*),
grouse-shaped with a long grey tail with a black band. There are
raptors such as buzzards (*şorecar/Buteo buteo*), sparrowhawks (*uliul
păsărilor/Accipiter nisus*), owl-like hen harriers (*vindereu/Circus
cyaneus*), eagle owls (*bufniţă/Bubo bubo*), Ural owls (*huhurez/Strix
uralense*), little owls (*cucuvaia/Athene noctua*) and smaller birds such
as white-backed woodpeckers (*ciocănitoare spatealb/Dendrocopus
leucotus*), great spotted woodpeckers (*Ciocănitoare/Dendrocopus
major*) (*ciocăni* meaning to peck or hammer, and having exactly the
lewd meaning you would expect), collared flycatchers (*muscar
gulerat/Ficedulla albicollus*), as well as jays, thrushes, tits and so on.
As elsewhere in eastern Europe there are decreasing numbers of
storks nesting on chimneys and telegraph poles. There are no gulls,
except on the coast.

There are 70 species of fish (110 in the Danube Delta), including
trout and rainbow trout (*păstrăv*), grayling (*lipan*), dace (*clean*),
barbel (*mreană*), bullhead or miller's thumb (*zglăvoacă/Cottus gobio*),
carp (*crap* (honestly) or *Cyprinus carpio*) and Crucian carp
(*Carassius carassius*), with many other species, including various
types of sturgeon (*morun*), in the Danube Delta. The *huchen* (Hucho
hucho) is endemic to the Tisa/Vişeu system in Maramureş.

Finally, on the insect front, there are mosquitoes at lower altitudes,
although of course no malaria, and often huge clouds of flies, which,
thankfully, follow you without crawling up your nose. By late summer
there are huge numbers of grasshoppers in the drier meadows,
usually feeding on animal droppings, but the most obvious insects
are the butterflies which flourish in great numbers on meadow
plants; I am not capable of identifying most of them, but there are
certainly purple emperors, swallowtails, black-veined whites and
peacocks.

Flora

Fortunately, in the Carpathians the main tree levels are generally
clearly defined, with oak woods along the outer slopes (especially on
the southern foothills of the Southern Carpathians and to the west

of the Apuseni), mixed oak and beech on the Transylvanian plateau, then beech from 400m to 1,400m altitude (and some up to 1,650m, for example on the south slope of the Parîng, when it comes into direct contact with the alpine level), with spruce mixed with beech from 1,000m and continuing to 1,700m (some only to 1,550m where hilltops have been cleared for pasture). The lower alpine zone, from 1,700m to 1,900m, is dominated by dwarf bushes, and above that is the higher alpine zone with grasses, lichen, moss and some creeping shrubs, gradually giving way to bare rock.

Increasingly the oak is being replaced by conifers, as man continues to modify the landscape; but although you may feel you are always walking in spruce and never seeing anything else, three quarters of Romania's trees are deciduous. In any case the conifers are never in the utterly deadening straight lines beloved of our own Forestry Commission; these are real, living forests, and although there is forestry activity everywhere there is remarkably little clear-felling.

Especially in the southwest, there are several types of oak such as common oak (*stejar pedunculat/Quercus robur*), Turkey oak (*cerul/Q cerris*), sessile oak (*gorun/Q petraea*), the nicely named fluffy oak (*stejar pufos/Q pubescens*) and the gîrniţa or *Q frainetto*. Mixed with beech (*fag/Fagus sylvatica*) are birch (mainly *mesteacǎn/Betula pendula*), sycamore maple (*paltin/Acer pseudoplatanus*), rowan (*scoruşǎ/Sorbus acuparia*), alder (*arin de munte/Alnus glutinosa*), hornbeam (*carpen/Carpinus betulus* and *C orientalis*) and others, particularly by streams. Other conifers mixed with the spruce (*molid/Picea abies* and *P excelsa*) are the common silver fir (*brad/Abies alba*) and larch (*zadǎ/Larix decidua carpatica*). Pines (*pin*) are rarer, although the Scots pine (*Pinus sylvestris*), Banat pine (*P nigra banatica*) and Arolla pine (*P cembra*) can be found; however the dwarf pine (*P montana*) is very common in the lower alpine zone, often forming almost impenetrable thickets which can viciously attack anything hanging off a rucksack.

In basic terms, pine trees have needles grouped in twos, threes or fives, silver fir has a very strong silver stripe on the underside of each leaf or needle, larch has needles sprouting in tufts from knobs, and spruce has smaller needles more densely packed, and cones which hang downwards and then fall.

In addition to the absence of chemical pesticides from mountain meadows, the great variety and abundance of flowers is due to the short growing season, which may be under three months a year, and causes them to bloom at about the same time. The maximum diversity of species is at about 1,500m, and above this the variety decreases. These meadow plants include clover, hawkweed, bistort, chicory, burdock, fritillary, buttercups and ox-eye daisy, and in the rougher mountain pastures gentian and *Crocus heufellianus* which erupts into a carpet of purple right up to the edge of the receding snow in the spring months. I was also fond of *Veratrum albinum*, the white false helleborine, which grows in the slightly damper meadows as a sheath of leaves wrapped around the stem, finally producing a terminal cluster of white, or greeny-yellow, flowers in July and August. This is very poisonous and easily confused with the great yellow gentian (*Gentiana lutea*), whose roots are used to make beverages.

Alpine plants include saxifrage, bellflowers such as *Campanula alpina* and *Campanula carpatica, Rununculus alpina* (alpine buttercup), *Primula minima* (least primrose), *Polyschemone nivalis (garofita Rodnei* or Rodna pink), *Dianthus callizonus* (Piatra Craiului pink), *Dryas octopetala* (mountain aven), and *Leontopodium alpinum (floarea de colţ* or *floarea reginei*, or edelweiss), as well as orchids, for example *Nigritella nigra* (the black vanilla orchid) and *Epipegium aphyllum*, sedges such as *Juncus trifidus* and the *Carex* genus, lichens, including *Cetraria islandica* and *Cladonia rangiferina*, and grasses amongst which are the *Poa* and *Festuca* (fescue) genuses and *Nardus stricta* (matgrass) and *Agrostis tenuis* (common bent grass).

Alpine and sub-alpine shrubs include *Rhododendron kotschyi (smîrdar)*, whose lovely pink flowers are harvested in mid-summer for herbal teas, *Vaccinium myrtillus (afin* or bilberry, whortleberry or blaeberry), with an edible black berry in mid-summer, *Vaccinium vitus-idaea (merisor* or cowberry) with red berries slightly later than the bilberry, *Loiseleuria procumbens* (creeping azalea), with tiny waxy oval leaves and tiny pink flowers in June and July, the heather-like *Bruckenthalia spiculifolia*, and *Juniperus communis* and *J siberica (ienupăr* or juniper).

In the Banat, on the southern slopes of Cozia and in gorges such as at Turda, there are many more sun-loving Mediterranean species, which are mentioned in the relevant sections. There is also a wonderfully rich flora in the Danube Delta.

Orthodox priest, Bucharest

Chapter 2

The People

As far as Romanians are concerned, the first thing you should know about their country is that they are not Slavs; the country takes its name from the belief that its population evolved from the fusion of the invading Romans with indigenous Dacians (the Daco-Romanian Continuity theory). According to this, when Rome withdrew in AD271, the bulk of the population remained on their farmsteads while the successive waves of the Age of Migrations (what we in Britain call the Dark Ages) washed over them — Goths, Huns, Avars, Slavs, Pechenegs and the like came and went or were absorbed, until at the end of the 9th Century the Magyars (or Hungarians) arrived under Arpad and colonised Transylvania. They still claim that the area was unpopulated when they arrived and that 'Vlachs' or Romanians only arrived, over the mountains from Wallachia to the south, in the 13th Century. Indeed there are still communities of Vlach shepherds in the mountains as far south as Greece. These two conflicting theories are used to this day to justify the two sides' claims to Transylvania, although the Magyars have been outnumbered there for many centuries. Although there are few totally unbiased historians writing in this area, the balance of probability seems to lie with the Romanian case. However it is not a subject to argue about; just agree with whoever you happen to be with.

In any case, Romanians see themselves as an island of Latin culture in a sea of Slavs. In fact they go too far in acting up to their vision of themselves as racy, temperamental fun-seekers in a world of stolid Slavs; they end up being chronically unpunctual and inefficient, and in any case they are not so unique: the Magyars themselves are also highly temperamental, voluble and impossible to satisfy, with in Hungary perhaps the world's highest suicide rate. Being 'a Latin race with a Turkish tradition' (in Wallachia and Moldavia, if not in Transylvania) this is the worst of worlds for women who find themselves appallingly exploited. I love the Romanians, above all for their open-heartedness and unlimited generosity, but their unreliability can be maddening, especially for those who haven't travelled in places like India to prepare themselves.

In western Europe, the general image of Romania has always been confused with that of Transylvania, its most colourful province, bringing to mind Dracula, both Bram Stoker's fictitious vampire count, and the real Vlad the Impaler, son of Dracul (a Wallachian prince but born in Transylvania), and a Ruritanian never-never world of chivalrous heroes and dastardly villains, all in wonderful uniforms. The uniforms are drabber now, but the Ruritanian image was not altogether dispelled by Patrick Leigh-Fermor's *Between the Woods and the Water*. More recently, though, the image has tended to be one of repression and poverty, villages being bulldozed by a megalomaniac dictator, and appallingly squalid orphanages. There is some truth in all this, but as usual the reality is less extreme.

HISTORY

The earliest historical accounts of the area that is now Romania tell of Greek settlements such as Istria and Tomis along the Black Sea coast from the 7th Century BC, and of a Dacian kingdom centred in western Transylvania, founded by Burebista (70-44BC) and brought to its peak by Decebal (AD87-106). It took the Roman Emperor Trajan two hard-fought campaigns during AD101-07 to defeat the Dacians, as recorded on Trajan's Column in Rome; Dacia was the last Roman province and the first to be abandoned to the barbarians in AD271. During the Age of Migrations many peoples swept in from Asia, diluting the Daco-Roman population, and there were only small local statelets until the Magyars began to move into Transylvania in the 9th and 10th Centuries, making it a province of Hungary, and bringing in Saxon colonists to guard the Carpathian passes from 1141. In 1241 the Golden Horde arrived, the precursor of regular raids by the Tartars and later the Ottoman Turks.

Moldavia and Wallachia only coalesced into feudal states in the 14th Century, and from then until the 19th Century the history of Romania is in fact the history of the three separate states of Transylvania, Moldavia and Wallachia. For all these states history was largely a matter of trying to keep the advancing Turks at bay, under great rulers such as Mircea cel Mare or Bătrîn (Mircea the Great or Old, 1386-1418) of Wallachia and Alexandru cel Bon

(Alexander the Good, 1400-32) and Ştefan cel Mare (Stephen the Great, 1457-1504) of Moldavia. The Turks defeated Serbia at Kosovo in 1389 and captured Mircea, who managed to buy his freedom, but had to accept Turkish sovereignty in 1417. In 1453 the Turks finally captured Constantinople, virtually bringing to an end the Byzantine Empire, and by 1456 were attacking Belgrade. It was the Transylvanian hero Iancu de Hunedoara (Hunyadi János to the Hungarians, also known as the White Knight), Regent of Hungary, who saved Belgrade, although he died of fever in the process, and his son Matthias Corvinus (Hunyadi Mátyás or Matei Corvin) became Hungary's great Renaissance king (1458-90).

Meanwhile Wallachia was ruled by a certain Vlad Ţepeş, son of Vlad Dracul (Vlad the Dragon), which led to his being called Draculea or 'Son of the Dragon'. He earned his name of Ţepeş (the Impaler) through his mastery of the art of terrorism, usually but not exclusively against his Turkish enemies. After his death in 1476 Wallachia finally became subject to the Turks; after Ştefan's death Moldavia basically went the same way, and Hungary collapsed after the battle of Mohács in 1526, with Vienna being besieged in 1529. As a result Transylvania was largely independent from 1540 to 1690, although nominally part of Hungary. Unlike Hungary itself, none of the Romanian provinces was actually occupied by the Turks, but they had to pay tribute. Between 1527 and 1556 Petru Rareş managed to achieve some independence for Moldavia, and in 1595 Mihai Viteazul (Michael the Brave) of Wallachia beat the Turks at Călugăreni, south of Bucureşti, and was able to seize the thrones of Transylvania and Moldavia from 1600 until his murder in 1601 by a general called Basta, who had clearly decided that enough was enough. This was enough to make Mihai one of the great figures of Romanian nationalism, although that was hardly his motivation.

Transylvania had something of a Golden Age during 1613-1629 under Gabriel Bethlen (Bethlen Gábor), an early enlightened despot, who enthusiastically promoted Protestantism but did nothing for the Orthodox Romanian peasants who continued to be repressed by the so-called Three Nations of Magyar aristocracy and self-governing communities of Saxons and Szeklers. The Turks were driven back after the second siege of Vienna in 1683 and the second battle of Mohács in 1687. In 1699 they recognised Hapsburg claims to Hungary and Transylvania. Wallachia and Moldavia were effectively ruled from the 1630s by families of Greek 'advisers' known as the Phanariots from their origins in the Phanar or Lighthouse quarter of Constantinople. From 1688 to 1714 Wallachia was ruled by Constantin Brîncoveanu, who led an artistic renaissance and himself developed a national architectural style. After his death (very nasty and brutal, having fallen out with the Turks) the Turks dispensed with the pretence of native rulers and directly imposed Phanariot princes who turned the screws even harder on the peasantry.

However the Turkish Empire was slowly decaying; in 1716 the Austrian Prince Eugen drove the Turks out of the Banat, which became part of the *Militär Grenze* or Military Frontier, where villages were effectively reorganised into garrisons, and during 1718-39 the Austrians also occupied Oltenia, the western part of Wallachia. In this period Swabians and Slovaks came to colonise the Banat, and the Uniate church was created to wean the Transylvanian peasantry away from Orthodoxy. In 1775 Austria annexed Bucovina and in 1784 crushed with appalling brutality a Transylvanian revolt led by Horea, Crişan and Cloşca, who had anticipated the principles of 1789. In Wallachia Tudor Vladimirescu led a revolt against Turkish rule in 1821, which ended with his murder but brought about the end of the Phanariot regime in 1824, when rule by native Romanians was restored.

As the Turks declined, the power of Russia grew; competing wih the Hapsburgs for the spoils of the Turkish Empire, Russia fought several wars with Turkey to set herself up as protector of Orthodox Christendom and incidentally annexed Bessarabia, the area of northern Moldavia between the rivers Prut and Dniestr. During 1829-34 Moldavia and Wallachia were occupied by a Russian army under General Kisselef, who implemented many positive reforms. In 1848 revolutions broke out all over Europe; those in Moldavia and Wallachia were put down by the Russians, but in Transylvania the situation was more complex. In the Apuseni mountains there had been since 1841 a low-intensity uprising against the Hapsburgs; in 1848 the Hungarians under Kossuth rose against the Austrians, but the Transylvanian Romanians under Avram Iancu were even more opposed to the Hungarians, their oppressors for centuries. By late 1849 both the Romanians and the Hungarians had been crushed, but there were concessions to the Romanians in 1863, and in 1867 the *Ausgleich* (Compromise) set up the Austro-Hungarian Dual Monarchy, whereby Transylvania, with Slovakia, Croatia and Vojvodina, became part of a Greater Hungary, while Bucovina, with Galicia and Ruthenia, was to be ruled by Austria. The result was the imposition of the Magyar language and culture and the further subjugation of the Romanians in Transylvania until 1918.

In 1859 Alexandru Ioan Cuza was elected ruler of both Wallachia and Moldavia, which were known as Romania from 1862; in 1864 Cuza abolished (in theory) serfdom, which led to his being forced to abdicate by the *boyars* (nobles) in 1866. The German Prince Karl of Hohenzollern-Sigmaringen was chosen to succeed Cuza as Carol I, and at the Congress of Berlin in 1878, ending yet another Russo-Turkish war, the Turks were forced to recognise Romanian independence and to cede northern Dobrogea, on the Black Sea, to Romania. In 1881 Carol became king, with Ion Brătianu as his prime minister, and Romania began to develop, with its oil industry particularly important. However nothing was done to improve the lot of the peasantry, and in 1907 there was a major uprising, put down with great savagery, as described in Liviu Rebreanu's *Uprising*. Romania avoided involvement in the first Balkan War of 1912-13, but joined the alliance against Bulgaria in the second in 1913 and won southern Dobrogea. Romania also avoided being embroiled in the First World War until 1916, when she came in on the Allied side. The alliance with Russia was a disaster as the generals refused to talk, the Russians claiming that among the first orders on Romanian mobilisation was one that no officer below the rank of major should use rouge!

The Bulgarians occupied Bucureşti and all Wallachia, and despite a desperate victory at Mărăşeşti in August 1917 Romania had to make peace in May 1918, losing southern Dobrogea to Bulgaria and the Carpathian passes to Austria-Hungary. With the collapse of the Central Powers, Romania opportunistically re-entered the war, having already reconquered Bessarabia after the October Revolution. By 1919 a Romanian army was occupying Budapest and gleefully revenging itself for centuries of Hungarian occupation of Transylvania; in the Trianon Treaty of 1920, Hungary lost half its population and two thirds of its territory, while Romania doubled in both, at last gaining Transylvania, with the Banat and Bucovina, and once again southern Dobrogea. Czechoslovakia and Yugoslavia were also created out of the remains of the Austro-Hungarian Empire.

This Greater Romania (12% larger than it is today), under King Ferdinand and his British-born Queen Marie (Carol had died in 1914) and governments of the Liberal and then the Peasants' parties, continued to develop economically, but the peasantry received little benefit, despite land reform in Transylvania which left the Magyar landlords feeling robbed. In 1927 Corneliu Codreanu founded the fascist League of the Archangel Michael, later known as the Iron Guard, which grew so powerful that in 1938 King Carol II (who had succeeded in 1930) established a royal dictatorship and had Codreanu shot 'while trying to escape'.

By 1940 the Iron Guard had assassinated four prime ministers and in that year General Ion Antonescu took power as *Conducător* or *Führer*, forcing Carol to flee into exile with his scandalous Jewish mistress Magda Lupescu; his son Mihai became a puppet king. In 1940, under pressure from Hitler, Romania was forced to cede Bessarabia and northern Bucovina to Stalin and then southern Dobrogea to Bulgaria and northern Transylvania to Hungary; this led to a revolt by the Iron Guard in Bucureşti in 1941 and their final elimination. Later in 1941 Romania joined Germany in its attack on the Soviet Union and reoccupied Bessarabia and Bucovina, pushing on to capture Odessa and Sevastopol and join the Germans in the disastrous siege of Stalingrad. Altogether 350,000 were killed or missing in the Russian campaign; meanwhile Jews and gypsies were being wiped out at home. When the tide had turned and Soviet troops were entering the country, Mihai took matters into his own hands with a royal *coup* on August 23 1944, arresting Antonescu, making peace with the Soviet Union and entering the war on the Allied side. Romanian troops fought alongside the Red Army into Germany, taking another 170,000 casualties.

Romanians still feel betrayed by the Yalta agreement of 1945 which delivered them up to Stalinist subjugation. After elections (probably rigged) in 1946 communists were dominant in the government of Dr Petru Groza and on December 30 1947 Mihai was forced to abdicate (although even now he is still waiting in the wings) and a Popular Republic was declared. In 1948 Gheorghe Gheorghiu-Dej took control of the Romanian Communist Party and set about creating a Stalinist state, with nationalisation in 1948, collectivisation from 1949, and the banning of the Uniate church in 1949, because of its ties with Rome. The Party changed course with massive purges of Stalinists in 1950-52 and pursued policies more independent of Moscow. This was accentuated after 1965 when Nicolae Ceauşescu succeeded Gheorghiu-Dej, making himself president in 1974. Although still part of the Comecon economic system, Romania made itself independent from Moscow in foreign policy, refusing to break with Israel or China, to support the invasion of Czechoslovakia or have Soviet troops on its soil. Ceauşescu also went all out to industrialise and to pay off all foreign debts by exporting oil and food, leaving virtually nothing for his people.

POLITICS

Romanian politics are, frankly, in more of a mess than in almost any of the other former Eastern bloc countries, largely because of the success of Ceauşescu and his *Securitate* secret police in stamping out all opposition. Thus there was no-one of equivalent stature to Lech Wałęsa or Vaclav Havel to lead an alternative government when the time came, and the eventual revolution was hijacked by a new generation of communists under a new name. As a result there has been little structural reform, above all to the economy, although prices have increased greatly, and the populace is increasingly cynical and disillusioned. There are even those who now regret the end of the Ceauşescu era and leave flowers on his grave, saying that then there was government action and no-one starved, whereas now it's all talk and there's nothing to eat. These people must have very short memories, I feel; but whereas for us, now able to travel freely, stay in peoples' homes and benefit from a highly favourable exchange rate, it may seem clear that freedom has come to Romania, it is a lot more difficult for people whose day-to-day lives have only got harder to feel that the deaths of the 'heroes of the revolution' were not in vain.

What exists now is something of a looking-glass world, in which the only east European state to undergo a violent revolution has changed the least, over two hundred political parties exist but there are no real democratic structures, a parliament meets everyday but takes no decisions, and real power is wielded by 10,000 miners. Where previously people queued not knowing if there was anything at the other end but knowing they could afford whatever there was, now they know there are enough goods but also that they cannot afford them.

The Revolution

Here begins a brief history of the revolution and events since, which I hope will put the above introduction and your conversations with Romanians into context.

The first tremor of the eventual earthquake was felt in Braşov on November 15 1987 when up to 10,000 workers from the Red Flag tractor factory rioted and destroyed the Communist Party offices in protest at reduced heating allowances, chronic food shortages, and the introduction of a seven day working week; the riots were suppressed with some loss of life.

In August 1988 the Cluj University lecturer Doina Cornea gained much publicity and support in the west for her protest against the proposals for the 'systematisation' of rural settlements (see page 106), and in March 1989 Silviu Brucan, a former ambassador to the United Nations and United States, and Corneliu Manescu, a former Foreign Minister, with others, protested in an open letter against increasing autocracy and were punished with internal exile.

In October 1989 an anonymous letter from a group called the National Salvation Front (Frontul Salvării Naţionale or FSN, pronounced FéCéNé) called on fellow delegates to the fourteenth congress of the Romanian Communist Party not to re-elect Ceauşescu as leader, but on November 24 he received the votes of all 3,308 delegates, presumably including the mysterious FSN members. On November 29 the gymnast Nadia Comaneci defected to the United States.

On Friday December 15 1989 protests began in the western city of Timişoara to prevent the internal exile of the dissident Hungarian Calvinist pastor Lászlo Tokes; from Sunday 17 the army and police were shooting on demonstrations, but on Wednesday 20, when 100,000 took to the streets, the army discovered that the protestors were not just from the Magyar minority as it had been told and began to fraternise and pull back its tanks.

The following day Ceauşescu returned from a ill-judged three-day trip to Iran to address a supposedly 'tame' crowd of 100,000 in central Bucureşti who began, at first quietly but with increasing power and conviction, to chant 'Ti-mi-şoa-ra' and the previous (and present) national anthem *Deşteaptă-te române* (Romanians awake). Ceauşescu gave up his speech in confusion while television screens went blank and police began firing on the demonstrators. Fighting continued all night and spread across the country, and the next day, after it became clear that the army had changed sides (it was announced that Defence Minister Vasile Milea had 'committed suicide'), Ceauşescu and his equally awful wife Elena fled by helicopter and hijacked cars; they were arrested the next day, December 23, in Tîrgovişte. In an attempt to end resistance by diehard members of the *Securitate* and the Ceauşescu bodyguard, the Ceauşescus were tried by a summary court and executed on Christmas Day. As it turned out, many of the desperate *Securitate* 'terrorists' were eventually to get their jobs back.

In any case fighting continued until after Christmas, being especially violent in Sibiu, fief of Ceauşescu's son Nicu. In all something over 1,000 people died, although the new government stuck to a figure of 60,000 for a long time. Even now facts and figures concerning the casualties and the fate of the *Securitate* are still kept secret by the government.

Initially, on about December 23, Corneliu Manescu was named as leader of a National Democracy Committee, but by December 26 it was the FSN that was naming a new government under its chairman Ion Iliescu, a Communist Party Central Committee member until 1971, and new Prime Minister Petre Roman, director of Bucureşti Polytechnic and son of a former army chief of staff and Minister of Telecommunications. Food rationing, the death penalty, systematisation and the registration of typewriters were at once abolished, and political parties, abortion, contraception and conversations with foreigners were permitted, among other measures.

On January 6 1990 the French journalist Alain Jacob was the first to publicly suggest that it had all been a cunningly disguised *coup*; General Militaru, the FSN Defence Minister until February 16, claimed the FSN had been in existence for six months. The rough consensus now is that there was a genuine popular revolt, but equally that there was a *coup* at the top, perhaps partly pre-planned; most people now speak of a 'so-called revolution'.

On January 12, a day of mourning for the martyrs of the revolution, there were the first demonstrations against the presence of former communists in government; the FSN responded by banning the Communist Party, which rather missed the point, and Roman pledged not to lead the government after elections then scheduled for April. The FSN had already reneged on a promise not to run as a party in these elections. To be fair there were few people available with any administrative experience who had not been obliged to join the Communist Party, and the former dissidents such as Lászlo Tokes, Silviu Brucan and Doina Cornea were all resigning from the FSN, calling it 'the Communist Party repainted'.

On January 27 the first local elections were held in Timişoara, where the 'Front for Romanian Democracy in Timişoara' was determined to maintain its identity as the true fountainhead of the revolution; however the elections somehow resulted in the same people as before being re-elected under the FSN banner. What was already known as the 'old FSN' of the revolution was being elbowed aside by ex-communists.

Supporters of the revived 'Historical Parties' (the National Peasant Party, the National Liberal Party, and the Social-Democratic Party) demonstrated in Bucureşti on January 28, demanding more involvement in government, and counter-demonstrators were joined next day for the first time by 5,000 miners from the Jiu valley to save the FSN from this 'considerable psychological pressure'.

Again on February 18 there were more demonstrations in Piaţa Victoriei when government buildings were sacked and Iliescu began talking of a anti-democratic putsch; again 4,000 miners arrived overnight on special trains from the Jiu valley to lay into the protestors. Working and living in appalling conditions, the miners had been given a 15% pay rise (after 35% had been promised), free work equipment, 30 days holiday and retirement at 45 instead of 55, to buy their loyalty.

From March 16 to 21 there were ethnic riots in Tîrgu Mureş which left up to eight Magyars dead; these are still unexplained, but there are suspicions that it suited the government to stir up nationalist emotions (Divide and Rule) and to have an excuse to re-establish a secret police, now called the Romanian Information Service. On April 22 the trial of the Ceauşescus was at last shown in full on television; from April 22 to June 13 Piaţa Universităţii in Bucureşti was occupied by 4,000 students still protesting against former communists in power, and from April 30 some began a hunger strike.

National elections were held on May 20 1990, with an 86% turnout. The FSN won 66.5% of the vote for parliamentary deputies and Iliescu won 85% of the vote for president; the actual voting was held to be fair by observers, but the FSN won by dominating the media and promising a naïf electorate a painless transition to a market economy.

On June 13 the police moved in to clear the Piaţa Universităţii; again there was widespread rioting and the next day 10,000 miners, directed by plain-clothes agents, arrived to deal with the *golani* and *opozanţi* (hooligans and oppositionists). By the time they left on June 16 there were at least seven dead, and 296 treated for head injuries and broken bones. Again they had been summoned by Iliescu, talking of averting an Iron Guardist fascist coup, and justified by Roman who blamed 'gypsies and black marketeers' and a 'hard-core of die-hards, linked with the most suspicious parts of society: speculators, smugglers and pimps'. Before leaving they sacked the headquarters of opposition parties which had refused to accept the election result, and went on one last rampage through the gypsy quarter.

The European Community expressed its 'shock and disappointment', the United States suspended non-humanitarian aid, and the *Independent* commented 'Slowly but unmistakably, the pigs are turning into humans'. On June 20 Iliescu was inaugurated as President in a ceremony boycotted by the United States ambassador. From June 18 until August 2 Marian Munteanu, President of the League of Romanian Students, was held in 'preventative detention' after being beaten by the miners and then detained in hospital.

There was now peace until minor demonstrations when food subsidies were cut in November 1990. In April 1991 staple foods such as bread, sugar and cooking oil doubled in price, the exchange rate was halved, from Lei 35:US$1 to Lei 60:US$1, while pay was increased across the board by the equivalent of US$28 per month to compensate, and a reshuffle brought opposition leaders into the government. As a reward for following approved economic policies, US$1 billion of aid was granted by the International Monetary Fund. In early September 1991 the price of petrol doubled, in preparation for further raising it to international levels once an exchange rate for the leu had been decided on; at this point it would cost the equivalent of two days wages for a gallon of petrol.

After a period when people had reacted to increased hardship with increased cynicism, while prices and unemployment doubled in ten months, the dam broke and these same miners at last turned against their patrons and went on strike on September 24, rioting in Bucureşti, ransacking the parliament building, calling it an irrelevant talking-shop, and leaving three or four dead. Their call was 'Iliescu, your time has come', but it was Roman who took the fall and resigned on September 25, although he remained in charge until the crisis was over and a replacement chosen. He spoke of it as a 'putsch of a communist type coming from below' and said he 'would not be prime minister in a country where corruption reigns'; in a land of passionate conspiracy theorists rumours began to circulate that, for instance, he˙had been the victim of manipulation by Iliescu or other conservatives in order to block a plan to make the leu immediately convertible, just as privatisation and land reform, both demanded by the IMF, had also been blocked. In any case the miners, ignoring the call of their leader, Mirion Cosma, to return quietly home, had shown that they had the power to overthrow governments without offering an alternative; the World Bank called off credit talks; and the phrase 'Vin minerii' (the miners are coming), like the bogeyman, began to be used to frighten bad children.

The new Prime Minister was Theodor Stolojan, a former Finance Minister and then head of the privatisation agency, and not a FSN member. He said that the miners episode 'doesn't matter' and 'was just a point in our transition', while Iliescu was talking of the need for a 'government of national openness'. By November the EC was ready to begin exploratory talks on associate EC membership, but US 'Most Favoured Nation' trade partner status would not be possible until after further free elections, due in mid-1992, with free access to the media for all political parties and proper controls on the security services.

On December 8 a referendum was held on the constitution finally proposed by parliament, which was technically a constitutional assembly. Seventy-five per cent of the voters, ie just over half of the electorate on a low turnout, voted to approve proposals for a presidential democracy (although the president will continue to have too much power and an unhealthily close relationship with the prime minister), with a mixed economy and respect for human rights. The referendum was accepted as fair by the opposition, although there was evidence of some people voting for other members of their families.

At the end of January 1992 it was announced that Romania, Moldavia, Ukraine and all the other countries around the Black Sea were planning to create a trade bloc. Local/mayoral elections were held on February 9 and 23, with the opposition coalition, the Democratic Convention, winning in Bucureşti and other cities, and the FSN (now beginning to fragment) winning in the villages, in the usual post-communist pattern.

Presidential and parliamentary elections were held on September 27 1992, with the main contenders being the FDSN or Democratic National Salvation Front, led by Iliescu (still sounding off about foreign speculators, capitalists and over-hasty reform), the FSN proper, led by Roman and presenting itself as a more modern pro-reform party, and the Democratic Convention alliance whose presidential candidate was Professor Emil Constantinescu, Rector of Bucureşti University, standing for a market economy with a social contract. Iliescu was beset by scandals such as his manhandling of a journalist, dioxin dumping, and sanction-breaking supplies of oil to his communist buddy Milosevic in Serbia, and also by the effects of cuts in subsidies for energy and staple foods (and the imposition of VAT on luxury items); but the desire of the conservative rural population for stability and continuity and its distaste for the untested city-slickers of the Democratic Convention outweighed the desire of the more educated and liberal part of the population for change and faster reforms. The fact that Michael Jackson chose to launch his Heal the World charity in Bucureşti and to visit an orphanage with Iliescu just days before the elections may also have helped! The minor parties declined to form a minority government, so Iliescu appointed a government of technocrats and civil servants under Prime Minister Nicolae Vacaroin, head of taxation in the Ministry of Finance, supported by an unacknowledged and unholy alliance of the FDSN and the ultra-nationalist and ex-communist parties.

THE ECONOMY

There is a widespread feeling that the Romanian economy is stuck in stagnation, without any major structural changes, other than some very limited privatisation, having been implemented since the revolution of 1989. However, when people look at the effects of rapid economic reforms in Poland and the former Soviet republics, many are grateful that they are proceeding more carefully. In any case there is no doubt that times are hard, as prices, particularly of energy, are rising sharply and salaries are not. (If Romanians ask what your salary is, it's the monthly figure they want.) In 1991 the average salary was something like L6,000, then worth about US$160, per month, and the pension was L5,000; by 1992 the average monthly salary was L15,000, then worth only US$40, and the dole was L9,000. (See Chapter 3, part 1, *Before you go*, for more on prices and exchange rates.)

Private enterprise is widespread but very small-scale, mainly in the form of stalls and caravans at stations and similar places selling imported chocolate, sunglasses and so on; there are numerous private travel agencies specialising in coach trips to Istanbul, a popular destination as Bulgaria and Turkey are almost the only countries Romanians can visit without almost unobtainable visas and hard currency. As times get harder, more and more Romanian women are going for 'working' holidays in Istanbul, where they are much in demand, it seems, and picking up horrid diseases. At the same time Romania is full of Moldavians coming by car or even in coach parties to sell sugar, make-up, combs, torches or anything else that might be available in Moldavia but not in Romania.

Restructuring of industry has proved very difficult, with both the bureaucracy and the labour unions blocking streamlining, for instance of a paper mill with 4,000 staff where only 800 are needed. By March 1991 unemployment had risen to at most 200,000 in a population of 23 million, and was expected to rise rapidly to 1.5 million, with traumatic effects; Romanians find it impossible to believe that we survive for years on end with unemployment of two million plus, but the difference is that there is almost no unemployment benefit in Romania — the extended family is expected to cope. The attitude that was institutionalised under communism of 'They pretend to pay us, we'll pretend to work' (*Ei se fac că ne plătesc, noi ne facem că muncim*) endures, and given the Orthodox and communist tradition of always waiting for orders and not thinking or acting independently, it will take some time for this to change; the more free-thinking Saxons are leaving, and the entrepreneurial Jewish and Armenian communities are too small to have much effect. Even so I have met many young Romanians who are desperate to start up in business, to achieve a Western lifestyle; the main problem is that it is impossible to raise capital without something like a house to set against it as security, and even if the banks were more willing they in fact have virtually no funds and charge 80% interest for what they have. There has been some limited privatisation, with vouchers distributed to 16 million people to be exchanged for shares, rather than the Thatcherite principle of selling everything off to the highest bidder.

It is ironic that just three months work in Germany would earn enough to set up a decent business in Romania, or for a farmer to buy a combine harvester from the IMA or state Farm Machinery Enterprise, and that with a few months inflation the assets of a new business are soon worth far more than the initial loan in any case. There is another catch-22 in that to go into business an *autorisaţie* (authorisation or qualification) is needed, but it's impossible to get this for anything new or innovative as of course these things are not taught in colleges; so more bribery is required. However there are new private establishments such as the Romano-Americane and Hyperion Universities in Bucureşti, and new state universities, formerly Institutes of Higher Education, such as that in Sibiu are offering newer subjects such as tourism and ecology.

In fact it seems to me, if not to most Romanians, that lack of labour mobility is at the heart of Romania's economic problems; in a system where most people have been allocated to jobs they don't want, it's hardly surprising that productivity and quality are so low. Bad pay is also an issue, and lack of materials; the results, as seen by foreign travellers, are that jam jars chip when opened, bootlaces break after one day, shoes are made with eyeholes that don't match up, and there are never enough light bulbs or washers. Romania and Albania are the only European countries not being spoken of as possible EC members, although Romania is potentially wealthier than Spain.

These figures encapsulate the changes in the Romanian economy since the revolution, although they are already out of date and it is in any case hard to compare these with unreliable communist figures: in 1990 investment was down 35% (partly because of the abandonment of nonsensical projects), industrial production was down 20% (partly due to the end of the six-day week, with meat products the only increase), GNP was down 11% at US$1,227 per capita per annum (expected to grow again from 1993), exports were down 42% (largely due to agricultural produce being kept for the home market), but imports were up by no less than 48%, although they also fell in 1991. Industrial production began to rise in early 1991, but in the year to June 1992 it fell by another 32%, with unemployment at 5.9%. Inflation in 1990 was 65%, rising to 300% in 1991, but it is down to 200% in 1992.

MINORITIES

The population of Romania is 23 million, of whom perhaps two or three million are Ţigane (or gypsy), two million are Magyar (or Hungarian), probably fewer than 20,000 now are Saxon (or German), with about 200,000 others such as Jews, Serbs, Slovaks and Russians. The balance are ethnically Romanian (or Vlach). The minorities live mainly in Transylvania and the Banat, with the Magyars and Germans concentrated in certain areas and the gypsies spread more thinly, as well as in Bucureşti.

The Transylvanian **Magyars** are the focus of a particularly intractable ethnic squabble, although thankfully a fairly quiescent one at the moment. Transylvania was of course a major part of the kingdom of Hungary for many centuries, the homeland of their great leaders Iancu Hunedoara and Matthias Corvinus (Hunyadi János and Mátyás Corvin to the Hungarians) and then 'the symbol of Hungary's defeats, the lost mountainous soul of their land' after 1918, when Romania doubled in population and area and Hungary lost half its population and two-thirds of its area. This still rankles in Magyar hearts, and some still dream of recreating a Greater Hungary, despite the fact that Transylvania's Magyars have long been outnumbered by Romanians (certainly since the 18th Century) and are separated from their fellows in Hungary by several hundred kilometres of Romanian-populated territory. There is no realistic chance of this happening, but it remains a potential source of trouble, with strong support in the Hungarian-American community, as ignorant as that of Irish Americans for NORAID. The Transylvanian Magyars are far more secure in their cultural identity than the Saxons, many being barely proficient in Romanian by the time they do their military service, and there is no real movement to emigrate to Hungary, partly because Hungary does not have the economic attractions of Germany. In the cities there are mixed marriages between Magyars and Romanians, but the villages are largely separate, with the Magyars having the best land in the plains, as the Romanians see it, and the Romanians keeping sheep in the mountains.

There are in fact two Magyar groups, of which the 700,000 or so Szeklers (Hungarian *Székelyek*) are the more interesting. It is unclear whether they came from Hungary itself, or whether they settled on the western approaches to the Eastern Carpathians when the Magyar tribes first moved west from Central Asia in 896, or indeed if they were some entirely different race which became totally magyarised. In any case they are now held to speak the purest form of the language, having been least affected by the Turkish conquests. In addition Magyars from Hungary began to move back eastwards into Transylvania, where there may or may not already have been Romanians (Vlachs or Wallachians); at the latest, these arrived from the south over the Carpathians in the 13th Century. The precise timing of these population movements is the source of the debate over which group has prior claim to Transylvania, which of course can never be resolved and is largely irrelevant to the current situation.

Until 1918 the Hungarians ruled Transylvania with a heavy hand, imposing their language and culture as also in Slovakia and Croatia (the reason that so many Romanian boys are named after Roman emperors such as Trajan, Claudius and Hadrian is that it was impossible for these names, reflecting the Roman ancestry of the Romanians, to be magyarised). After 1918 it was the Magyar landlords who suffered most from land redistribution, and since then there has been some official pressure on the Magyar culture and language leading to bad relations between Bucureşti and Budapest. During 1952-67 there was a Magyar Autonomous Region which never contained more than 35% of Romania's Magyar population while the proportion of Magyars within the region was never more than 79%; it was not greatly missed in itself but its abolition was seen as a sign of official lack of interest in minority rights. Under the new FSN government the right noises are being made but there are also signs of a communist style 'Divide and Rule' policy, as seen in the aftermath of the Tîrgu Mureş riots of 1990. There is still petty harassment such as the confiscation of Hungarian magazines, even on cookery, at the border. In any case, the Magyars rightly feel entitled to a Hungarian university and official status for their language.

The most interesting of the minorities is the **German** one, and in particular its Saxon section: just as the Minoan civilisation was wiped out by one volcanic eruption, so too the 850-year-old Saxon civilisation is vanishing in the space of just a couple of years. Catch it now or regret it for ever.

The first Germans were invited to colonise the areas guarding the Transylvanian passes in 1143 by the Hungarian King Geza II, and although they were in fact of Mosel-Frankish origin they were for some reason known as Saxons. (There is an alternative theory, as related in Browning's *The Pied Piper of Hamelin*: 'And I must not omit to say/ That in Transylvania there's a tribe/ of alien people that ascribe/ the outlandish ways and dress/ on which their neighbours lay such stress,/ to their fathers and mothers having risen/ out of some subterraneous prison/ into which they were trepanned/ long time ago in a mighty band/ out of Hamelin Town in Brunswick Land,/ but how or why, they don't understand'.) Their dialects, which vary depending on the village and (in Agnita) even on the gender of the speaker, are still easily comprehensible to the people of Luxembourg and the Mosel area, but fortunately the language learnt in school is standard Hoch-Deutsch, and they all speak fluent Romanian too.

Over the centuries the Saxon community prospered as farmers and merchants, and were allowed to govern themselves, from seven main towns, the Siebenbürgen (or Siebenstühlen, meaning Seven Stools) of Hermannstadt (now Sibiu), Kronstadt (Braşov), Schassbürg (Sighişoara), Klausenburg (Cluj), Mühlbach (Sebeş), Mediasch (Mediaş) and Bistritz (Bistriţa) — the isolated group around Bistriţa were known as the Obersachsen or upper Saxons, and the others were known as the Niedersachsen or lower Saxons, and also as the Specksachsen from their habit of keeping *speck* or pork fat in a church tower in readiness for a siege.

They developed a distinctive style of architecture, with fortified churches to protect them from the frequent raids of the Tartars and then the Turks, and rows of equally fortified houses with arched gateways onto the street. In the 18th Century they were joined by the *Schwabs* or Swabians who were invited by Maria-Theresa's government to settle in the Danube plains of the Banat, newly cleared of the Turks and drained, as well as other minor groups in the Semenic mountains (the *Böhmer*), around Abrud in the Apuseni (the *Bergland Deutsch*), around Vişeu in the Maramureş (the *Ţipţeri*), around Sibiu and elsewhere (the *Ländler*) and in Bucovina.

Under the Hapsburgs and also for the first years of Romanian rule the German communities were generally content with their lot, but there was a change after the Second World War when the German population was generally victimised for supposed pro-Hitler sympathies (although Romania had herself entered the war on Germany's side), and in January 1945 75,000 men and women between the ages of 16 and 45 were taken to the Soviet Union for slave labour until 1950. All their animals and most of their land was confiscated, and Romanian *kolonisten* moved into their homes; from 1954 the rest of their land was taken for collectivisation, together with the smithies and saddleries built up by them. Because their land was confiscated before the main round of collectivisation, it was not restored to them on decollectivisation, so that they now see Romanians and Ţiganes owning their ancestral land. So now there is *kein vertrauen mehr*, no more trust between the Germans and the Romanians; each year from 1975 the West German government paid about 8,000 Deutschmarks a head for 10,000 exit visas, bringing a total of about 140,000 to Germany. A population that had peaked in the 1930s at about 650,000 within the present frontiers of Romania and was around 390,000 in the 1950s and 1960s, after some post-war repatriation of Germans from Bucovina and Dobrogea, fell to 200,000 by the time of the 1989 revolution.

As soon as the revolution opened the borders, a mass exodus began, and within two years the German population had fallen to about 25,000, although it is hard to make accurate estimates. Virtually all those with children have left, and almost all those who are eligible for German pensions have also left; very soon only those who are too old to uproot themselves will remain, and they will not last forever. Many regret the need to go, but they say that while the Ceauşescu years were bad for them, at least there was *Ordnung* then, whereas now there is anarchy and *Ţiganerei* on all sides.

In the Schwab areas their houses have tended to be kept safely as holiday homes or have been sold as weekend homes to Romanians from Timişoara; in the Saxon areas, meaning above all the Sibiu/Braşov/Sighişoara triangle, the houses have often been stripped bare and vandalised by the Ţigane (I didn't want to believe it, but I have seen it) unless they are kept locked up and cared for by neighbours, who often keep a dog in the yard and from time to time sleep there themselves — keeping alive the Saxon defensive traditions. The churches and graveyards are always kept meticulously well as long as there is one old lady left to take care of them, but as each family goes it concretes over its graves, and eventually the churches do fall into ruin. A few of the best churches,

such as Biertan (Birthälm), Prejmer (Tartlau) and Harman
(Honigberg), have been restored, probably with German money
although no-one really knows, and there is the prospect of European
Council money for Viscri (Deutsch Weisskirch) and other places, but
in general the fabric of the many other villages will unravel. If you
want to see the future, you could visit the area around Țigmandru
(Zuckhantel) north of Sighişoara, which was evacuated by the
German army in 1944 in preparation for a last stand against the Red
Army. Very depressing. (Generally I am talking here of the Lutheran
villages of the Saxons, but there are also *Adventisten* or Seventh Day
Adventists, who worship on Saturdays and have other strange
habits, and the Schwabs, who are Roman Catholics.)

The Romanians left behind in these villages are finding that all the
craftsman and managers are gone and that the years of communism
have left them unable to take any initiatives or to give rather than
receive orders. The Germans meanwhile start life in Germany at the
level of the *Gastarbeiters* without any technical knowledge of
anything more complex than a 1950s tractor, but being hard-working
Saxons they soon catch up and within a year or two have overcome
any doubts and are ready to stay there permanently. Generally the
Tracht or traditional costume of each village is abandoned once a
family moves to Germany, so you should arrange to be in a Saxon
village on a Sunday to see it before the custom is totally lost.
Generally the married women wear black, with apron, shawl and
scarf, but the unmarried girls are dressed up gaudily to be shown off
to the eligible young men, in the Saxon colours of blue and red,
maybe (depending on the individual village) with apron or waistcoat,
and an elaborate high head-dress or *Borten* decorated with baubles
and long streamers. In the Schwab area the *Mädeltracht* involved
crossbraces, a black velvet choker, and up to eight petticoats;
however these villages really are empty already. Men nowadays tend
to wear a suit, but there is often a heavy leather coat with an
embroidered back; they used to wear round black hats but I never
saw these. *Tracht* is worn only for church, if then; at other times the
Saxons may be identified by the blue workman's aprons that they
seem to wear at all times, and by their tendency to be taller and
fairer than the Romanians and more likely to have glasses. Say
'Grüss Gott' if you think someone is Saxon, and 'Bună ziua' if not.

While the Romanians tend to characterise the Germans as very
worthy people but rather stiff and dull, I have always found them
very friendly and hospitable, and thankfully less obsessed with
forcing *țuica* down my throat; this is partly because there are so
many 'empty nesters' there now, couples approaching retirement
whose families are already in Germany. However Mrs Gerard in the
1880s found them less pleasant: 'The Saxon peasant is stiff without

dignity, just as he is honest without being frank...the besetting fault of this whole Saxon nation seems to be an immoderate spirit of egotism'.

There has always been plenty of aid from Germany for the *Volksdeutsche*, another source of bad feeling, and now the German government is willing to spend far more on aid (sending, for instance, minibuses to take children to the few remaining German-language schools) in an attempt to persuade them, in particular the million or so still in the former Soviet Union, to stay put and not return to add to the strain on the Fatherland; but in the case of the Siebenbürgisch Saxons the critical mass has clearly gone and the community is no longer viable. By contrast there is apparently a German community of 200,000 in Hungary which is totally assimilated and happy.

Of course, after the exodus, there will also be an increase in tourism from Germany to Romania, so that the Siebenbürgischen Karpatenverein, founded in 1880 to open the first mountain cabanas, may be re-established, perhaps as a branch of the Deutsche Alpenverein, and a Tourist Route is being established; already the roads are full of German cars in the summer as Saxons and Schwabs return to their old homes, and this is much the best time to visit, although access is not too hard at any season.

I describe some Saxon villages in more detail in the section starting on p282; see also the relevant sections on language and religion.

While the numbers of the Germans have declined recently, the numbers of **Ţiganes** or gypsies have shot up dramatically, perhaps to three million, and distrust and resentment of them have increased. Indeed relations between Romanians and Ţiganes are now a more serious problem than those between Romanians and Magyars, as many of the Ţigane community really do show absolutely no interest in getting along with the conventional society of the majority of Romanians. That's not to say that they live by crime, but it is a mystery just how they do live. In some gypsy communities the women are not allowed out to work, in others the men consider it beneath them to work, so the women turn their hands to fortune-telling and so on. In the large settlement outside Răşinari the traditional occupations were as broom and basket makers and as garbage collectors in Sibiu; they also sell mushrooms and wild fruit in markets, and traditionally make stills for ţuica; however the most traditional and respectable occupation for gypsies, as in Hungary, is as musicians or *lăutari*, and the most successful have huge bourgeois homes in Bucureşti. The majority of Ţiganes, though, live in hovels on the outskirts of towns, and although they now have a deputy in parliament they continue to be treated as second-class citizens, and in 1992 there are increasingly frequent reports of virtual pogroms against them.

The Ţiganes often look just as if they had arrived from India the day before; many of the men are very dapper dressers, with sharp haircuts and neat moustaches, a good jacket and trilby; they stroll down the street with their womenfolk following a few paces behind, in skirts of amazingly life-enhancing primary colours, often pregnant or carrying a baby. While gypsies generally are oppressed by the establishment, their women are even more oppressed by their men, not being allowed to walk in front of a man or a horse, and being married and set to child-bearing in their early teens.

Only 10% of the Ţiganes can truly be said to be nomadic now, but they are still a race of wanderers, often to be found congregating at railway stations. They are a people of the plains, hardly ever found in the mountains, so this may be your main contact with them. There are large numbers in Bucureşti; in addition many are heading illegally for Germany and other western countries, giving Romania an appalling reputation among people who cannot distinguish between Romanians and Romany. After riots in Rostock and other towns in 1992 it was planned to repatriate 50,000 Romanians, mostly gypsies, from Germany, together with a £12m aid package to create work in Romania, where 40% of the unemployed are estimated to be gypsies.

The **Jews**, like the gypsies, were victims of the Nazi Holocaust and Israel then paid for exit visas as Germany did for the Saxons, so that there are now no more than 150,000 left in Romania, of a million or so before the Second World War and half a million immediately after. There were two Jewish communities in Romania, the Sephardim of the Danube who spoke Ladino, a derivative of Spanish (see Elias Canetti's *The Tongue Set Free* for a magical account of growing up in this community in Ruse, on the Bulgarian bank of the Danube), and the Ashkenazim, the true Central European Jews who spoke Yiddish, a derivative of German with Hebrew. These lived above all in the north, in Bucovina and Maramureş, and across the border in Galicia and Ruthenia. Alas, anti-semitism is hardly extinct, especially in Bucureşti. Petre Roman, the first FSN prime minister, is Jewish, and like those I met, a great linguist.

The **Armenians** formed a similar community of exiles, having reached Moldavia by the 13th Century and Transylvania by the 18th Century. They now live in isolated pockets in, for example, Suceava, Dumbraveni, Constanţa, Brăila and Gherla.

Also in the north there are perhaps 70,000 **Ukrainians** or **Ruthenians**, mostly of the **Huţul** people, but also **Boyks** and **Lemks**, who moved here when the whole area was under Austrian rule. There are also about 45,000 **Russians** mainly in Dobrogea and the

Danube Delta, as well as near Suceava; these are mainly Lipoveni 'Old Believers' who were being persecuted by the Tsarist regime, and now work as fishermen in the backwaters of the Delta, with a formidable reputation, even by Romanian standards, as boozers.

There are slightly smaller numbers of **Serbs**, perhaps 40,000, living in the Banat, where they settled after fleeing from Turkish territory in the 18th and 19th Centuries, and also about 18,000 **Slovaks** brought here as colonists at the same time as the Schwabs; newspapers in both these languages are published in Timişoara, although they are increasingly integrated into the Romanian culture. Fifty thousand Schwabs and Serbs were forcibly moved from the border zone to the Bărăgan steppe south of Brăila after the Second World War, but were allowed to return after 1972. Also, in 1951, the Greeks of the Danube ports such as Sulina were given four days to leave Romania. There are also small numbers of **Turks** and **Tartars** still in the area of Constanţa, where Romania's only mosques are found. There were migrant communities of Bulgarians who came to farm onions on fallow land, but this has now largely ceased.

RELIGION

As elsewhere in the world, religious differences in Romania tend to run along ethnic lines, with the Romanian majority being almost entirely of the Romanian Orthodox creed. A minority of Romanians adopted the Uniate (Greek Catholic or Eastern Rite Catholic) church, concocted by the Austrians from 1692 to combine Orthodox rites with allegiance to the Pope, together with some doctrinal differences; the Uniate church played an important role in the rediscovery of Romanian culture but was banned by the communist regime in 1948 as it was regarded as untrustworthy, whereas the Orthodox church was firmly under their thumb; many Uniates were jailed and their families denied further education.

In Mrs Gerard's day, the 1880s, 'the average village *popa* (Orthodox priest) was simply a peasant with a beard'; under Ceauşescu the priest was a tool of the state, but after the revolution he was often the temporal as well as the spiritual head of the village until the local elections of February 1992, as many of the communist mayors had vanished. Now up to 1,000 new churches are said to be under construction, and there are hopes that this groundswell of religious feeling could be the saving of Romania, but only if it can inspire the people to action rather than a simple acquiesence as in the past. Certainly I have never been into a single home that did not have a religious calendar on the wall, and most had icons hanging as well, usually with an embroidered scarf draped over it in memory of a dead relative. The Uniate church has also been revived, with five new bishops, two new seminaries and the return of 25 of the 2,600 churches claimed back. The more familiar Western Rite or Roman Catholic church and evangelical protestant groups such as Youth with a Mission are also furiously recruiting people who respond 'not because they want to be Christian, but because they want order in society.'

The more mystical Orthodox services are based on chanting, with beautiful harmonies, and people frequently crossing themselves and responding 'Ah-meen', whereas the Lutheran services of the Saxons are more static apart from serious German chorales sung to the organ, and the Hungarian Calvinists tend to have fire and brimstone preaching. (There are also Hungarian, Schwab and Ländler Roman Catholics, who are little different from those further west.) One Orthodox speciality is the *toaca*, calling the people to church with complex rhythms on a wooden board (either hanging below the bells or carried clockwise around the church) or on a metal plate shaped like an octopus. Geoffrey Moorhouse writes in *Apples in the Snow* of this as 'not the mathematical method of the English campanologists, taking their exercise with rope and wheel, but a tintinnabulation of jangled bells, with a clopping of wood for counterpoint, and an ominous booming for requiems and days of reckoning'.

In the Lutheran and Calvinist churches men usually sit in galleries with the women sitting in order of seniority behind the priest's wife, and the children in front under her watchful eye. In Orthodox churches, particularly in the Maramureş, men stand in the nave or pronaos, while women crowd into the porch or narthex and stand outside, with ears to the walls if loudspeakers have not been fitted; in front of the altar is the screen or iconostasis, with perhaps four main icons separating three doors, the central one being used only by the priest and being opened and shut at key stages of the service.

There are four main groups of churches that are of particular interest to visitors, firstly the Painted Monasteries of Bucovina, secondly the wooden churches of Maramureş, thirdly the Brîncoveanu era monasteries of Wallachia, and finally the fortified churches of the Saxon villages; all of these are covered by hiking routes in this book. On maps produced in the communist era they are often disguised as a 'medieval architecture monument' or 'peasant citadel'. As a rule the monasteries (many of which are actually nunneries) are open at normal hours, but churches are usually kept locked and you will have to ask around for the key; the advantage of this is that you will get a guided tour, and perhaps a bed for the night. Don't be shy, the keyholder will be happy to show you around, and no payment is required.

Part Two

Information for Visitors

Street barber, Bucharest

Chapter 3

Planning and Preparations

BEFORE YOU GO

At the time of writing visas are still required for entry to Romania, and as there is little likelihood of Romanians being allowed visa-free travel to the West (the whole nation being regarded as potential economic migrants) this is unlikely to change soon, alas. The cost in 1992 is £24 for the British and as usual less (up to £21) for other nationalities. Again as usual cheques and credit cards are not accepted. Visas are available at the border but at double the cost. If travelling on a package holiday you will be on a group visa and won't have to worry about this. Visas are obtained from the Romanian Embassy at 4 Palace Green, London W8 4QD (tel 071-937 9667) (only open Monday to Friday 1000 to 1200) in 48 hours, and at 1607 23rd Street NW, Washington, DC 20008 (tel 202-232 4747/48), and 333 Old South Head Road, Bondi, Sydney, NSW (tel 02-365 015/305 718). There is near-total ignorance about visa extensions, but these can in fact be easily obtained from *Judeţ* (county) police headquarters or at Str N Iorga 7 in Bucareşti. Four-day transit visas are also available.

However, compulsory exchange has been abolished and foreigners' rucksacks tend not to be searched, so actually entering the country is now much simpler than before. Compulsory exchange was an absolute disaster for anyone planning to spend a lot of time in the hills, where it is impossible to spend much money — I once went for a month without paying for a bed. You should decide in advance whether you plan to change your money through official channels or on the black market, as obviously travellers cheques and Eurocheques, much the safest way of carrying your wealth, are only accepted by the banks (often only open in the mornings), and even there take quite a while to process. Dollars and Deutschmarks are most in demand, and you should certainly carry some in small denominations for times when it's not worth cashing a travellers cheque. I personally would not use the black market in a developing country that I cared for, as the economy needs my hard currency more than I need the relatively small savings, but you can legally make everybody happy by changing dollars with friends somewhere between the two rates. The moneychangers hanging around outside major hotels are, of course, crooks who will take your money and run; it's safter to change with the *maitre d'* of a restaurant, for instance. In 1992 the first private exchange counters began to appear, dealing only in cash, of course. In any case you will have to change some money at a bank to get a *buletin de schimb* or exchange certificate, without which you may have to pay *valuta* or hard currency for planes and some hotels.

The economy has supposedly now been de-dollarised, so that rather than being charged vast sums of dollars for a hotel room you will now simply pay, in Lei, about ten or fifteen times the rate for Romanians. Before the revolution there was also a parallel currency of Kent cigarettes, which then lost its importance but will probably take off again as inflation bites. Until late in 1991 the largest banknote was for L100 (about £1) — for the first time in my life I had too much money to fit into my wallet; you'll need a money-belt. Now there are also L500 and L1,000 notes, which of course are still not big enough. Was some monetarist taken literally when he told the new government not to print money?

Generally you have to pay 1% for travellers cheques, but some building societies will provide them free to account holders or buyers of travel insurance. Cash usually costs 0.5%, but some banks charge a flat fee which is better if you want large sums. Romanian lei are not legally available abroad but can be bought at a discount in Berlin and Debrecen, for example; keep them well hidden as you cross the border. If you have a credit card it's worth bringing along in case you lose everything else and need to buy an air ticket home or want to stay in a very expensive hotel or hire a car. Generally credit cards are not much used in Europe; even at major German stations you can't buy a rail ticket with plastic — it seems that the tradition is to carry vast wodges of cash or to use a banker's draft, or of course a cheque (now available to individuals even in Romania).

In mid-1991 the pound sterling was worth about L100 at official rates and L300 unofficially (the US dollar was worth about L65 and L200), but the official rate was being increased to nearer the unofficial rate to squeeze out the black market; at one point in

February 1992 the official rate was L590 to the pound, more or less keeping pace with inflation, and the black market rate just L600; just a week later the official rate was down to L350 to the pound. By mid-1992 the pound was worth L700, before dropping to L650 on sterling's exit from the ERM.

In early 1992 accommodation in mountain huts cost about L50, while the motel-style cabanas cost from L200 to L500; museums cost L10-20, a loaf of bread from L10 to L20 (or L35 from private bakeries), a kilogram of cheese about L500, and a kilogram of tomatoes L50 in season. Bananas appeared for the first time in 1992 at L300 a kilogram, and Turkish jeans at L3,000 a pair. Inflation and removal of subsidies will continue to force all of these upwards.

Very basic **Tourist Information** is available at 17 Nottingham St, London W1M 3RD (tel 071-224 3692), and at 573 Third Avenue, New York, NY 10016 (tel 212-697 6971) but not in Australasia. The London office has a very Romanian concept of opening hours, but is theoretically open on Monday, Tuesday, Thursday and Friday from 0930 to 1730. The Bucureşti office of ONT-Carpaţi at Bdul Magheru 7 (tel 145 160) is not bad for an organisation which is primarily concerned with selling tours for hard currency; if you haven't been able to get the key *Invitation to the Romanian Carpathians* booklet of hiking maps from the London office, as it is frequently out of print, you may be able to get it here in Romanian, or French, German or English. The Braşov tourist information office has closed, with an inadequate replacement in the lobby of the Carpaţi hotel, but Cluj, Sibiu and Suceava have better offices. The national office goes under the name of Officiul Naţional de Turism or ONT-Carpaţi, and county offices are called Officiul Judeţean de Turism (OJT); however these are now being privatised and will concentrate more on selling trips to the seaside or the spas. County maps are worth getting hold of where available, from the OJT.

In Bucureşti there now some English-language news-sheets, available free in hotels and airline offices, which allow you to keep up with local politics and news.

GETTING THERE

Unless you are going with a package group, flying to Bucureşti may not be the ideal option; generally it means flying with TAROM, surviving Otopeni airport, and then backtracking a bit to get into the Carpathians. TAROM, which flies daily from London Stansted and four times weekly from London Heathrow (with Tupolevs and BAC 1-11s, which are genuinely believed to be the latest British technology, although Airbuses and Boeing 737s are now on order) taking three hours to Otopeni, is a pretty primitive airline, accustomed to cattle-trucking the masses around and not customer-friendly; particularly in August they are very likely to overbook so be sure to check in as early as possible. There's no vegetarian food, and unless you're lucky seating will simply be 'smokers to the right, non-smokers to the left'. Otopeni, Bucureşti International Airport, is equally primitive, although there is a lot of building work going on. For some reason you may get a fairly intimate body search on arrival, but not on departure. It seems that all the British ski charters arrive at the same time, so that immigration takes ages, and luggage retrieval even longer.

However, whereas in 1991 it was not possible to find a cheap fare from London to Bucureşti, certainly not with more than a month's validity, things have begun to get better in 1992: STA are quoting £180 return with six months validity (with TAROM). You could also try Friendly Travel (tel 081-566 9040), Russian-Romanian Travel (tel 081-741 4507) or Romanian Holidays (tel 0707-330 209) who in early 1992 are all quoting about £190 for one month validity, £220 for three months, and £330 for a year, and £170 on a summer-only charter to Constanţa, with discounts for groups and registered charities working in Romania. There is also a weekly flight from Manchester to Bucureşti.

There are more cheap flights to Budapest and Vienna, from where you can take cheap trains directly to the Banat and Transylvania; alas, cheap flights to Yugoslavia are probably not an option at the moment, but Austrian Airlines and Lufthansa are now flying into Timişoara. If you are planning to see more of eastern Europe, Budapest, Vienna and Prague are all good node points. Dan-Air to Vienna was (until its takeover by BA) a good option, costing £149 to £174 via STA for twelve months in 1992, or £139 to £165 via Campus if under 35. From Vienna Airport (*Flughafen Schwechat-Wien*) you can get a bus direct to Bratislava in Slovakia and avoid the expense of Vienna. Fares to Prague are coming down fast: for summer 1993 Campus are offering student charters for just £129 return.

At the time of writing it was worth considering an Inter-Rail ticket, if under 26, as this gave you free travel on all the railway systems of Europe, including Romania's. However, 1993 is the last year this will operate (price £249). From 1994 travellers should ask about the Freedom Pass or Euro-Domino ticket. A full-price rail return from London to Bucureşti, valid for two months, cost £358 in 1992. It would be cheaper to go to Vienna (Eurotrain return, for those under 26, valid for two months with unlimited stop-overs along the way, £169, full-price return £203 in 1992, taking just over 21 hours via Ostend), and rebook there, although you would lose some flexibility, and eastern European fares are increasing.

Eurolines (tel 071-730 0202) will take you by coach to Budapest (summer only) for £149 for a six month return (£139 for those under 25) in 1992. There are coaches onward from Budapest to centres of the Magyar population in Romania such as Cluj and Tîrgu Mureş. There are now increasing numbers of private coaches, in particular from London to Prague and Poland, and from Athens and Istanbul to Bucureşti.

Other agents to try for cheap air (or coach) tickets are New Millenium (tel 021-711 3328/3379/4306), Intra (071-323 3305), Trailfinders (071-937 5400/938 3939/938 3366), Sunquest (081-749 9933), New Horizons (0756-798066), Liftjet (0827-713060), Bridge the World (071-911 0900), and STA and Campus around Britain (London numbers respectively 071-937 9921 and 071-730 3402).

Companies organising walking tours to Romania are High Places, The Globe Works, Penistone Rd, Sheffield S6 3AE (tel 0742-757500) (in which I must confess an interest), Sherpa Expeditions, 131a Heston Rd, Hounslow, Middlesex TW5 0RD (081-577 2717), Ramblers Holidays, Box 43, Welwyn Garden City, Herts AL8 6PQ (0707-331133), Exodus Expeditions, 9 Weir Rd, London SW12 0LT (081-675 5550), Explore, Frederick St, Aldershot, Hants GU11 1LQ (0252-319448), including the Delta, and the French Terres d'Aventures, 12 r St Victor, Paris 5e (010-33 4046 9522/4329 9450), which also runs a nine day cross-country skiing trip to Maramureş.

Other companies taking groups to Romania (excluding those listed in the Skiing section or just doing package holidays on the coast) include Romanian Holidays (Tours and Travel) Ltd, 34 Burrowfield, Welwyn Garden City, Herts AL7 4SR (tel 0707-330209), and Friendly Travel Ltd, Research House, Fraser Rd, Perivale, Middlesex UB6 7AQ (081-566 9040).

Of all these Sherpa is the only one which does not peddle the myth of Bran being Dracula's castle, which gives them maximum credibility in my eyes.

In addition the British Trust for Conservation Volunteers, 36 St Mary's St, Wallingford, Oxon OX10 0EU (tel 0491-39766) organises working conservation holidays in Romania.

GETTING OUT

Buying a rail ticket out of the country is now relatively straight-forward, with no need to use hard currency. The office on Piaţa Unirii in Bucureşti is computerised and doubtless the most efficient — go early to avoid the queues. If you wish to take a specific train, perhaps with a couchette, it is worth buying a timetable for L55, but this is not foolproof — due to the crisis in the Romanian tourist business two of the three trains between Romania and Poland were cancelled, so that I had to change trains in Hungary and would have done better to rebook there in local currency. There are now also private coaches to Budapest, Istanbul, Sofia and Athens, usually found near the Gară de Nord in Bucureşti.

WHAT TO TAKE

As Saint-Exupéry said, 'He who would travel happily must travel light'; you should take the standard 20kg airline allowance as your absolute maximum, bearing in mind that you gain a kilogram when you put a litre of water into your bottle, and that food in eastern Europe tends to come in heavy glass jars; dispose of as much packaging as you can before departure, but this may not be possible with what you buy after arrival. I find that a Body Shop plastic bottle carries enough shampoo for several months, and soap can be carried in a film canister. In eastern Europe basins never have plugs, so take a squash ball or universal plug if this is important to you.

Specifically for hiking, you should remember the six essentials of map, compass, matches (and maybe a firelighter) in a waterproof box, first-aid kit, extra food and extra clothing. A knife, spoon and mug or bowl are also pretty important. Wood fires are becoming environmentally unacceptable nowadays, even in Romania where there seems to be no shortage of wood; if you want to cook, take a stove but plan your fuel supplies in advance, as Camping Gaz is hard to find in eastern Europe and cannot be taken by air, and petrol is in short supply. Personally I don't bother for three to five day trips in summer.

With regard to clothing, the key principle is that of layering; in the mountains the weather can change suddenly, or you might finish a long hot climb by reaching a ridge and walking into a cutting cold wind. Modern lightweight breathable materials such as GoreTex make this easier, but you can apply the principle just as well with normal everyday clothes, a T-shirt to soak up sweat, then a shirt and thin pullovers for warmth topped by a cagoule to protect against both wind and rain — in modern terminology wicking, insulation and shell layers. You will need waterproof trousers as well, and the jacket or cagoule should have semi-waterproof pockets sealed by Velcro or a zip under a storm flap. Wear jeans at your peril, as they take days to dry. I find army-surplus fatigue trousers ideal, with a map pocket on the lower thigh, an adjustable waistband to allow me to lose weight on a long trip, and very fast drying properties; you can also buy similar trousers from companies like Rohan, at much higher prices. Shorts are perfectly acceptable except perhaps for visiting churches. A fleece jacket is wonderful for warmth but is neither wind- nor water-proof. There are some mosquitoes at lower altitudes, so be sure you have a shirt with long sleeves.

Good boots are essential for rough, rocky or wet terrain, or long cross-country routes; light boots or tennis shoes might be acceptable for easy walks without a heavy load, and are kinder to sensitive terrain as well as being useful to change into at the end of the day. Take a spare pair of bootlaces (also useful for drying laundry and so on) if you're likely to need them, as Romanian laces break on day one.

To carry all this you need a backpack or rucksack — above all make sure you have a padded hip belt, and pity the poor eastern Europeans who have to carry all their load on their shoulders. Ideally you should carry 50% of your load on the hips — any more and you slip out of your shoulder straps, even with a chest strap. Nowadays there are also likely to be straps to adjust the balance of the load for uphill or downhill work, away from the body going uphill, and closer to the body downhill. At airports wrap the hip belt backwards around the pack, do it up in reverse and tuck away or tie up any strap ends, both to stop them getting caught in conveyor belts, and to delay anyone wanting to sneak a look inside; a small padlock is also useful, although more as a deterrent than as a real barrier. No rucksack is really totally waterproof, so you should keep clothes and the like in plastic bags. Romanians have to swathe their packs in plastic sheeting, as their equipment is far worse than ours.

Unless you plan to stick to the areas such as the Bucegi and Făgăraş where there are plenty of cabanas, you will also need a tent, and again don't wait till you get to Romania before buying one. Unless making a winter trip you won't need an especially warm sleeping bag, but a camping mat is always invaluable.

A camera should be as robust as possible — I have destroyed several in the past by travelling on rough roads; remember not to sit behind the rear axle of a bus. A telephoto lens renders binoculars or a telescope unnecessary, but otherwise a 35mm compact camera is ideal. Nowadays some compact cameras incorporate a limited zoom lens. You will need a spare battery for a long trip, and you should take enough film; ASA 200 and 400 film is not available, and the only slide film is poor quality made by ORWO of East Germany (now taken over by AGFA). There is a lot to be said for the view that if you take photographs you don't really appreciate the scenery.

With all this you should have insurance, available from most travel agents and insurance agents. One policy I have recently spotted is Activcard from General Accident, Pithleavis, Perth PH2 0NH; this covers high risk sports, such as mountaineering, climbing, pot-holing, hang gliding, parachuting and paragliding, and for Europe premiums are from £18 for five days to £35 for 25-31 days, with extra weeks costing £5 up to a 90 day maximum. West Mercia Insurance Services, High St, Wombourne, near Wolverhampton, WV5 9DD have cheaper policies excluding climbing. Normal hill-walking should be covered by a standard policy, and if under 35 the cheapest (not necessarily the best) may be from Campus Travel (£8 for a month, or £16 covering personal baggage). Having done this you should remember to carry a pocket diary with a list of numbers of insurance policies, travellers' cheques, passport, credit cards etc, as well as the addresses to which you intend to send postcards.

HEALTH AND HYGIENE

For the traveller health is of course closely related to fitness, but you should not let yourself be daunted by this, as most people humping a backpack around Europe are already basically fit. Keep to a good easy rhythm, with reasonably long strides, and remember that hiking is above all a matter of mental discipline; if you want to get up that mountain, you will, although you may not be fit for much the next day. If in a group you may be obliged to keep up with the group and with daily targets, but the independent hiker can go as slowly as he/she desires. In any case some walking or cycling before leaving home will help; although modern boots do not need much breaking in, it is still helpful to wear them for a few days before departure. Contrary to much medical advice, I am a believer in lancing my own blisters before bed, with a needle sterilised in a flame. Keep your feet clean and dry, and your toe-nails short, and with modern boots you should in fact have few problems.

You should also remember to have your teeth checked and bring your tetanus jab up to date. other jabs for travel in eastern Europe are not necessary, but if in doubt contact your local health centre, MASTA (Medical Advisory Service for Travellers Abroad), at the London School of Hygiene and Tropical Medicine, Keppel St, London WC1E 7HT (tel 071-631 4408), or any of the vaccination services run by British Airways, Thomas Cook, Trailfinders and others.

The United Kingdom has a reciprocal health agreement with Romania entitling British visitors to free basic treatment — an NHS card may be useful, and take an E111 form if travelling overland through EC countries. To call an ambulance dial 061. In any case basic advice can be obtained at a pharmacy (*farmacie*); a health centre is a *policlinic* and a dental surgery a *cabinet stomatologic*. Doctors are very over-worked (about one to 10,000 rather unhealthy people) and their surgeries are the most smoke-filled places I have been in Romania. (In eastern Europe heart disease rates are a third higher than in western Europe, as 45% of energy intake comes from fat, as against a WHO recommendation of 30%, and at least half the male population smokes, as against a third in western Europe.)

Prevention is better than cure, but you will need a basic first aid kit: sterile needles are available from that well known high street chemist for about 10p each. Obvious things are sticking plasters and dressings, pain-killers, anti-septic cream and throat lozenges, as well as tubular bandages to support sore ankles and knees.

Tap water is safe and bottled water available (it's said that the best mineral waters are those that begin with B, such as Biborteni, Borsec and so on), but stream water must be presumed to be dilute sheep urine: use Puritabs or Sterotabs, from high street chemists and camping shops, or boil water for five minutes. Do not throw food scraps, or any other rubbish, into streams; all rubbish should be taken out, or failing that burnt; burying litter is a waste of time as animals will dig it up. Dig a ten-centimetre toilet hole, at least 100 metres from any water or path, and fill it in afterwards; then wash your hands.

Diarrhoea is the classic traveller's ailment; if it happens, avoid alcohol, fatty and spicey foods, and milk products. Rice and potatoes are helpful. Replace lost fluids with treated or bottled water, or preferably with a rehydration (electrolyte) formula — one litre of water with three teaspoons of sugar, one of salt, half of baking soda and three-quarters of potassium chloride (or dextrose and salt tablets). Dark orange urine indicates a lack of fluid. Bumblockers such as Lomotil only relieve the symptoms for the duration of a long bus journey, but they will not tackle the causes. Persistent diarrhoea can be treated with antibiotics (available over the counter in eastern Europe) but Hilary Bradt notes that Vibromycin can cause increased sensitivity to the sun, particularly at altitude, which may be an increasing problem if the European ozone hole grows. In general avoid alcohol when hiking, especially during the day. If it really is forced on you, wet your lips to taste it and hand the glass or bottle back. If suffering from constipation, boost your fibre intake.

Rabies is rare in Romania, with just ten cases in the third quarter of 1990, mostly in the north, which compares with 460 in Poland and

1,344 in Germany (mostly in eastern Germany), but with all those sheep dogs, not to mention bats, it can be a worry. It can be transmitted by scratches or even licks where the skin is broken, as well as by bites; get treatment at once, after immediately washing the wound, ideally with alcohol. Vipers can also be a problem, as there is no anti-venom, but in Britain at least more people die of bee stings than of snake bites. (Bees can be irritable in dull or humid weather.) There is no malaria, but even so bites and stings can turn septic, and clouds of flies can be intensely annoying — insect repellant may work, although I have little faith in it. It should contain at least 80% Diethyl Toluamide, but many do not.

I always wear a floppy sun-hat and only use sunglasses on snow; 70% of heat loss is from the head, so wearing a hat can stop your toes freezing, and a hat also protects the eyes, ears and the back of neck from sun and flies. Heat exhaustion is caused by over-exercising when the body cannot dissipate its heat quickly enough: symptoms are nausea, florid complexion, stumbling, lack of alertness, cramp and eventual collapse. Like exposure, it tends to affect those unaccustomed to being outdoors in extreme weather, the old, the unwell and convalescents. Don't wear or carry too much (young people should not carry more than a quarter of their body weight), shelter from the sun, remove excess clothing, apply cold wet towels to the limbs and head, and take salty drinks. Exposure is defined as 'a reduction in body heat usually caused by getting wet in cold or windy weather... Symptoms are unexpected or unreasonable behaviour, stumbling, lack of alertness, complaints of cold and tiredness, pale complexion and shivering which stops as the patient becomes colder' (NB). Again, do not wear or carry too much as this hastens exhaustion, and change wet clothing.

Altitude sickness should not be a problem at under 3,000m, although a few people might theoretically have problems if they rushed directly from sea level (or Bucureşti) to Bîlea Lac and rushed on up to the top of Negoiu or Moldoveanu (2535/2544m). If you do have headaches or nausea, wait before ascending further until you have acclimatised (aspirin may help), and if they persist go down and get medical advice — but you would have to be abnormally sensitive to have problems in the Carpathians. There is also a greater risk of sunburn and sunstroke at altitude — take care, wear a hat and don't confuse the symptoms.

Motion sickness could be a problem on Romanian roads; remember to sit near the centre of any vehicle, ie not behind the rear axle of a bus. Again, avoid alcohol and if necessary take pills 30 minutes before travel.

As for sex, my advice is don't do it; getting involved with an alien culture, which is what Romania is, is a minefield of potential problems, and many of the best educated Romanian women are desperate to get out of the country and settle in the west, by hook or by crook. If you must, bring your own condoms and other contraceptives from western Europe. The sex lives of Romanians are in fact very interesting; Ceauşescu saw the foetus as 'the socialist property of the whole society', and giving birth as 'a patriotic duty, those who refuse to have children are deserters, escaping the laws of national continuity'. Seldom can there have been a despot who meddled quite so intimately with every detail of his subjects' lives. Immediately after the revolution contraception and abortion, which had been banned since 1966 for any woman under 40 or with less than four children, and since 1972 for any woman under 45 or with less than five children, were permitted again, and one million abortions were carried out in 1990, all of them very quick, impersonal and sordid by all (Western) accounts. In 1991 there were one hundred a day in Braşov.

The impression one gets in the streets in springtime is that only Ţiganes have sex and get pregnant, but as summer goes by the number of pregnant Romanians goes up, showing that the Romanian saying about winter being good only for counting money and making babies still applies. However by 1992 it was clear that students and other young people were rapidly acquiring a more liberal attitude to sexual matters; hotels such as the Intercontinental

---

WEATHER STATIONS

It can be interesting to visit weather stations, which are found in just about every massif in Romania; most of the meteorologists chose their career at least in part as a way of opting out of communist society, and are genuine mountain lovers as well, so they make excellent company. The most convenient is perhaps that at Cozia cabana, just down the corridor from the room I slept in, but they can also be found on major peaks as high as Omu in the Bucegi (2,505m). As a rule there should be four men (I didn't meet any female meteorologists, although some men have their families with them) based at each station, but in practice there are often less; at Omu there was just one man, keeping awake by chewing on coffee beans.

Their duties involve five minutes of observation every hour, and then converting these into five figure codes and transmitting them by radio to the nearest main town, from where they are sent on to the Meteorological Institute in Bucureşti; they don't seem to do any analysis of the observations themselves, but apparently don't find the work tedious. Alas, weather forecasts on TV are incomprehensible to foreigners as they don't use standard symbols; one word which crops up a lot is *instabilitate*, usually meaning rain.

and Ambasador in Bucureşti are now infested with prostitutes, and kerb-crawling by 'tourists' from Greece, Italy and Turkey is becoming a problem. It is generally hard to discuss these things there, and even mildly bawdy jokes are not really understood, at least by women.

Homosexuality is not acknowledged or discussed.

AID

After the 1989 revolution the most striking images of Romania were those of the orphanages and the desperate plight of the many abandoned children in them who were treated like idiot beasts and left to decay mentally until they were fit for nothing but life-long incarceration in a mental home or 'Home for the Irrecuperable'. There was little affection shown, little mental stimulation and little hygiene. There was of course a great urgency to do something for the most desperate cases and there were many cases of inspired people moving heaven and earth to hire lorries and take vast amounts of toys, soap and baby clothes across Europe. However much of this went straight out of the back door of the orphanages and into the black market; in addition much aid, particularly from Germany, was simply driven into villages and dumped beside the road, where it was seized by one or two families with carts, leaving those at home in Germany feeling good about themselves but not actually doing any good.

The Romanian orphanage staff were baffled by this unexpected largesse, and took it all gratefully, but in the end their professional attitudes and skills were unchanged. Now that things are settling down somewhat and the orphanages all have toilets, the more professional charities are taking control and some long-term planning is now taking place, recognising that what is needed is not sticking-plaster aid of the blankets and cocoa type, not techno-overkill such as medical scanners without trained personnel or spare parts, not evangelism and bible-bashing, but rather training and development of local resources, and simple essentials such as sterile needles, contraceptives, and rubber boots so that children can get to school. Ultimately what is needed is economic growth to fuel government spending, so the more we can do to develop the tourist industry the better.

Large amounts of money have been raised (£8m by the Romanian Orphanage Trust, £4m by the Braşov Distress Fund, £100,000 by the Abbey National Christmas Appeal) and good work is being done; for example, Romanian nursery nurses are now being trained by the Romanian Orphanage Trust and by VSO's East European Partnership, and play therapists by the Comedy Store Fund for Sick Children. Addenbrooke's Hospital in Cambridge has a well-structured scheme for co-operation with the health authorities of Arad judeţ; orphanages are setting up their own bakeries to provide both bread and funds. For

£4,000, about the cost of taking a lorryload of aid to Romania, four Romanian nurses can be trained and paid for a year, which has to be a better use for your money. In addition existing structures, especially those of the churches, are being used more to provide effective targetting and follow-through and to provide information about what is really needed.

Romanians in general are slowly getting involved: Ion Tiriac, Boris Becker's coach, has set up an orphanage in Braşov and run television advertising which may not raise much money but is a useful first stage in awakening consciences. Efforts are being made to encourage Romanians to adopt, or even just to take orphans for weekend visits, to give them a little love and show them the world outside. After the Bacău dam tragedy there was an appeal for aid for the 100,000 homeless, whereas in the Ceauşescu years a disaster of this type would simply have been hushed up. However there are no votes in health care, and neo-communist 'divide and rule' tactics will make things worse for the dispossessed.

One can, of course, ask just why these problems arose in the first place: the flood of orphans in Romania was essentially due to Ceauşescu's policy of boosting the labour force by banning abortions and contraception, and forcing women to have families, when in many cases they could not afford to bring them up. There are few social institutions in Wallachia and Moldavia due to the Ottoman tradition and the lack of a native bourgeoisie, and social solidarity was further eroded by communism, so many babies just had to be abandoned. It is interesting that Romanians don't adopt when it is generally taken for granted that everyone needs children to look after them in their old age; I can only assume that the extended family copes with childless people better than it copes with unwanted children. Abortion and contraception were legalised immediately after the revolution of 1989, but an IUD still costs a month's salary on the black market; obviously the key to the orphanages problem is to provide long-term family planning. In the 18 months after the revolution 10,000 babies were adopted by foreigners, but half of these were under six months old, ie probably coming directly from the mother rather than from an orphanage. In July 1991 adoptions abroad were temporarily halted, and in February 1992 strict new regulations were introduced, to stop sales (for up to US$5,000) to infertile western baby-boomers, who had stampeded to Romania as the only source of white babies, boys as well as girls, for adoption.

Another aspect of this sorry saga is of course the question of HIV, spread by the widespread re-use of needles for 'micro-transfusions' of 15-20 cubic millimetres of blood intended to give a boost to new-born babies; almost a third of children tested in hospitals and orphanages in Bucureşti and Constanţa are HIV-positive, and half of all Europe's child AIDS cases are in Romania. Although there has been a wave of compassion in the west for Romanian AIDS babies, this is perhaps partly a way of forgetting the less 'innocent' gay men and drug users dying of the disease at home. In Constanţa in particular there is great work being done, largely in association with medical staff from Edinburgh, but this is still barely spoken of in Romania. There is some very dodgy AIDS drug testing going on in Romania that would not be permitted elsewhere; efforts are being made to stop this, but corruption will find a way.

GUIDEBOOKS

There are only a few good guidebooks to Romania, and only one of these, at the time of writing, dates from after the 1989 revolution; this is *Where to go in Romania* by Harold Dennis-Jones (Settle Press 1991), and although it shows many signs of the haste with which it was put together and published (in particular he gets the words for departure and arrival the wrong way around), it is clearly written by someone who has known and loved the country, and its music, for many years.

The Rough Guide to Eastern Europe (ed Dan Richardson, Harrap-Columbus 1988), which despite its title only covers Romania, Hungary and Bulgaria, is the most reliable general guide, although I find the way its background information is divided into *Basics*, before the main descriptive chapters, and *Contexts*, after them, rather awkward to handle. A volume on Romania alone is due in late 1993.

Eastern Europe on a Shoestring (David Stanley, Lonely Planet, second edition 1991) is the quintessential Inter-Railer's book, covering the whole of eastern Europe in one volume, which inevitably makes it too sketchy to be much use anywhere. American US$25-a-Day books (Fodor, Frommer, etc) and the French *Guide du Routard* give similarly rapid overviews; *Eastern Europe — a Traveller's Companion* by Phyllis Méras (Houghton Mifflin 1991) appeared too late for me to use, but it seems a bit better, as a guide to the towns. Nagel's Encyclopedeia-Guide is a very detailed cultural bible; Richard Bassett's *Guide to Central Europe* (Viking 1987) has a chapter on Transylvania which takes a similarly highbrow approach, dealing almost entirely with architecture and good meals.

There are also Romanian-published guides such as *Romania, a guide book* (Meridiane 1967) and *Romania, a tourist guide* (The Publishing House of Tourism 1974) which give detailed descriptions of towns but don't cover the mountains at all.

There are some excellent accounts of the area by 19th Century and pre-First World War travellers, such as *Transilvania, its people and products* by Charles Boner (Longman 1865), *From Carpathians to Pindus* by Tereza Stratilescu (Unwin 1906), *The Frontier Lands of Christian and Turk* by JH Skene (London 1853), *Hungary and Transilvania* by John Paget (Murray 1850), *The Land Beyond the*

Forest by Mrs Emily Gerard (Blackwood 1888), and *In the Carpathians* by Mrs Lion Phillimore (Constable 1912), the last three particularly recommended.

More recent travellers' accounts include Patrick Leigh-Fermor's wonderful *Between the Woods and the Water* (Penguin 1987), *Romanian Journey* by Sacheverell Sitwell (Batsford 1938; Oxford Paperbacks 1992), both accounts of Romania's Ruritanian swansong of the 1930s, as well as another *Romanian Journey* by Andrew MacKenzie (Hale 1983), *Travels in the Balkans* by John Higgins (Barrie & Jenkins 1972), *Berlin to Bucharest* by Anton Gill (Grafton 1990), three accounts of cycling trips, *In Another Europe* by Georgina Harding (Hodder/Sceptre 1990), *Stealing from a Deep Place* by Brian Hall (Heinemann/Minerva 1988), and *Transylvania and Beyond* by Dervla Murphy (John Murray 1992, one of her best), and two journeys in search of folk music, *Raggle Taggle* by Walter Starkie (Murray 1964, perhaps with a record of Starkie playing his fiddle) and *Walking Good* by Peter O'Connor (Weidenfeld 1971). *Danube* by Claudio Magris (Collins-Harvill 1989) is a slightly Chatwinesque collection of trivia and philosophising with high-class straight travel writing.

Of the few foreign novels set in Romania, the best known is of course Bram Stoker's *Dracula*, which is wonderful in its way, although less of the action happens in Transylvania than you might expect; others are *Le Château des Carpathes* and *Mathias Sandorf* by Jules Verne, *Memoirs of an Anti-Semite* by Gregor von Rezzori (partly set in northern Bucovina, now Ukrainian), *The Dean's December* by Saul Bellow, and Olivia Manning's *Balkan Trilogy*, which hardly get out of Bucureşti.

Contemporary Romanian writing, notably by Mircea Eliade, and that of Eminescu, the national poet, is available in translation from Forest Books, 20 Forest View, Chingford, London E4 7AY (tel 081-529 8470/0384) ('the window to eastern Europe').

Geography text books include *Romania, a Profile*, Ian Matley (Pall Mall 1970), *The Geography of Romania*, T Morariu *et al* (Meridiane 1969), *Mountains of Europe* by Kev Reynolds (Oxford Illustrated Press 1990) and a whole shelf of books by the excellent David Turnock (mostly from Routledge). Two excellent but academic books from the University of California Press cover village life and folk customs: *Transylvanian Villagers, three centuries of political, economic and ethnic change* by Katherine Verdery (1983), and *The Wedding of the Dead* by Gail Kligmann (1988).

There are many books (and more appearing all the time) on the background to the revolutions of 1989, such as *Writings on the East* (New York Review of Books), *The Wilder Shores of Marx* by Anthony

Daniels (Hutchinson 1990), *The Other Europe* by Jacques Rupnik (Channel 4/Weidenfeld 1989), *Romania, Politics, Economics & Society* by M Shafir (Pinter, 1985) and *Eastern Europe 1939-89, the 50 Years War* by Patrick Brogan (Bloomsbury); and on the revolution itself *Spring in Winter, the 1989 Revolutions* edited by Gwyn Prins (Manchester University Press 1990), *Revolutions in Eastern Europe* by Roger East (Pinter 1992), *Revoluţia Română în Direct* (the transcripts of the TV revolution, in Romanian), *Without Force or Lies, Voices from the Revolution of Central Europe in 1989-90*, editors WM Brinton and A Rinzler (Mercury House, San Francisco 1990), *Kiss the Hand You Cannot Bite (the Rise and Fall of the Ceauşescus)* by E Behr (Hamish Hamilton 1991), *The Life and Evil Times of Nicolae Ceauşescu* by J Sweeney (Hutchinson 1991), *The Rise and Fall of Nicolae Ceauşescu* by Mark Almond (Chapman 1992), *With God, for the People* by Laszlo Tokes (Hodder & Stoughton 1990) and the spring and summer 1990 editions of *Granta* (Penguin). *Downfall* by George Galloway MP and Bob Wylie (Futura 1991) is an irrelevant load of whitewash.

See chapter 4 on Hiking for details of maps and guides to specific hiking areas; in addition there are rather coffee-tableish books on the Maramureş such as *Terre Magnifique des Carpates* by Patrick and Christiane Weisbecker (Chêne 1983), *Maramureş, Monografie*, editor Ioana Niculescu (Editura Sport-Turism 1980), *Zona Etnografica Maramureş* by Mihai Dancus (Editura Sport-Turism 1986), and *Ţara Lemnului* (Land of Wood) photos by Francisc Nistor (Editura Sport-Turism 1983), the first in French and the others in Romanian; and German books on the Saxon communities such as *Die Siebenburgische Karpatenverein* (Wort und Welt, Thaur bei Innsbruck), *Siebenbürgen, ein Abendländisches Schicksal* by H Zillich (Blauen Bucher 1956) and *Kirchenburgen in die Siebenbürgen* by Hermann and Alida Fabini (Hermann Böhlwas 1986).

Many of these will only be found in Romanian or major United Kingdom copyright libraries or occasionally in second-hand shops; you could also try the library of the School of Slavonic and East European Studies, in the University of London's Senate House on Malet Street, which is open to all with a genuine interest. More recent books can be bought from Collets at 129-131 Charing Cross Road, London WC2H 0EQ (tel 071-734 0782) or at other major bookshops.

WOMEN TRAVELLERS IN ROMANIA

Women travelling in Romania by bus, train or car, stopping in towns and cities, are generally little more at risk of unwelcome attention than men, provided they wear nothing less than a T-shirt and Bermuda shorts and do not flaunt money and jewellery. I have been attacked by gypsy boys on two occasions, in exactly the same place on a Transylvanian country road. This had nothing to do with my sex and everything to do with Romania's worsening economic situation and the decline of law and order; these particular boys apparently attacked every passing stranger.

Nevertheless, a woman traveller, particularly if she is alone and wearing a rucksack and walking boots, is an object of curiosity. Old-style chivalry is alive and well in Romania's educated classes; you may well have your hand kissed rather than shaken, and people think it odd that a woman should carry a rucksack. In the countryside, where women routinely carry heavy loads and work long days in the fields, if anyone travels it's usually the men, and for business.

It's unusual for women to dine alone — I often found people staring as I ate alone whilst reading a book, and a young Romanian widow told me she found it hard, without a man present, to get service — and drinking alone in a bar will invite suspicious looks. In Cluj in 1989, I came across a women's restaurant called 'Intim' and was warned that nice girls didn't go there. Amusingly, I found it full of elegantly dressed women taking a break from shopping, who, seeing my short hair, long shorts and T-shirt, advised me kindly that this restaurant was for women only.

The lot of Romania's women has improved slightly since the revolution, with the legalisation of abortion and the provision of contraception. (You should take your own contraceptives and sanitary protection, remembering that HIV has now entered the adult population, particularly around Black Sea resorts.) Yet the Western woman's comparative financial and social independence still surprises. A constant question is 'Are you married?' A negative answer may well be greeted with surprise, sympathy or disapproval from women and with increased interest from men. Saying (truthfully or otherwise) that your husband is at home invariably prompts a question such as 'How come he let you out?'!

Before the revolution, I found hitching a key part of Romania's rural transport system, used by local women and men of all ages, with an established system of payment per kilometre, in cigarettes, coffee beans or even money. Since the revolution, however, life is no longer as safe and it is advisable to take local advice before sticking your arm out.

Wild camping, though permitted, is frequently considered unsafe. In a field one night in western Romania, I was woken by a policeman asking me to move my tent to a school playground, warning of 'bad people' and wolves. It is good practice to ask a woman or the priest (*popa*) in any village for a safe place to camp. I have found this leads to offers of beds, barns, or camping places in gardens, ruined castles or churchyards.

Romanians will warn you constantly of the dangers of women travelling without men. Ultimately, you will have to decide for yourself how much of their advice is sound, and how much is based in cultural conditioning.

© Catherine Treasure 1992

Kissing the image of Christ, Sibiu

Chapter 4

In Romania

THE ROMANIAN LANGUAGE

Anyone with some knowledge of Latin or Romance languages such as Italian, French or Spanish will be able to function fairly well in Romania and will have no problem with most notices — a pleasant island of normality amidst so many Slav and Magyar languages. German and Hungarian are spoken by the minorities, there are still traces of the pre-war cultural links with France, and English is of course the language that everyone wants to learn now, so most people should communicate adequately. However Russian, which was forced on the school population in the communist era, has made minimal impact.

By and large the building block approach works fairly well, and there's no need to learn too much grammar; living in a multi-cultural society, Romanians are used to the concept of foreign languages and of people not being fluent in their language, unlike the Poles for instance who really don't make much effort to work out what you're saying. First though you must tackle the accents and pronunciation; ş is pronounced *sh* as in *ship* and ţ is *ts* as in *bits*, ă is like the *e* of *father* or *Bitte* (or *u* as in *but*), and î (formerly â) is like the final *e* in *intelligent*, spoken rapidly. Before e or i, c is pronounced *ch* and ch is *k*; before other letters c is hard, like *k*, which doesn't exist in Romanian except in *kilometru* etc. Others are generally as in English, but with an Italianate lilt. Stress is generally on the final syllable if the word ends in a consonant and on the penultimate syllable if it ends in a vowel; the terminal i is not pronounced but softens the preceding syllable. To help you get into the habit, I have throughout used the Romanian spelling *Bucureşti* rather than the English

Bucharest. A few words are almost impossible for English speakers, such as *cîine* (dog), *pîine* (bread), *mîine* (tomorrow). In Maramureş there is a tendency to eliminate the final syllable of many words and to speak more sibillantly, saying *zin* for *vin* (wine).

Nouns have three genders, masculine, feminine and neuter, as in Latin, but there is no need for the traveller to worry about these, as long as you realize that forms can differ. As a rule the definite article (*the*) is tacked on to the end of a word, generally as *-ul, -l, -le* or *-a*. Plurals are *-i, -ii,* or *-e* without an article, or *-lor* or *-le* with the definite article. In addition there is a more emphatic definite article *cel, cea, cei, cele,* as in *Ştefan cel Mare* (Stephen the Great) or *cel mai mare* (the biggest). The indefinite article *un* or *o* precedes the noun (and any adjectives).

Verbs are conjugated so do not need pronouns (I, you), but these can be used for emphasis. You will always be referred to by the formal *Dumneavoastră*, but less formally 'you' is *tu, voi* or *dumneaţa*. Others are *eu* (I), *el* (he), *ea* (she), *noi* (we), and *ei, ele* (they).

Vocabulary is largely derived from Latin, with a substantial overlaying of Slavic words such as *deal* (hill), *tîrg* (market) and *prieten* (friend), with some Turkish words such as *han* (inn), *cioban* (shepherd) and *musafir* (guest). Some French words such as *apropo* (sic) (regarding, concerning), *déjà* (already), *vis-à-vis* (opposite), *pardon* (sorry) and *merci* (thank you) have also been incorporated into the mainstream language.

See also the Food and Drink section for vocabulary.

Cabana (mountain hut) and stîna (sheepfold) are such basic hiking terms that they are not even italicised in this book.

Some useful words and phrases are:

Basics

Good morning	*Bună dimineaţa*
Good day	*Bună ziua* (can sound much like the French *Bon jour*)
Good evening	*Bună seara* (often reversed)
Good night	*Bună noapte* (often reversed)
Cheers!	*Să trăieşti!* (The standard hikers' greeting)
Cheers!	*Nuroc!, La mulţi ani!* (Long life!)
Yes	*Da*
No	*Nu*
Sir	*Domnul*
Madam	*Doamnă*

Miss	*Domnişoară*
(I) thank you	*Mulţumesc*
(We) thank you	*Mulţumim*
Please	*Vă rog (Vă rog frumos* — pretty please, honestly)
Goodbye	*La revedere, Sanitat*
Bon voyage	*Drum bon* (literally Good road)
What does it cost?	*Cît costă?*
Do you speak English?	*Vorbiţi englezeste?*
I don't understand	*Nu inteleg*
I don't speak Romanian	*Nu vorbim românеşte*

Directions

(To the) left	*(La) stîngă*
(To the) right	*(La) dreaptă*
North, south, east, west	*Nord, sud, est, vest*
Straight ahead	*Drept înainte*
Here	*Aici*
There	*Acolo*
This/that	*Acesta*
(Is it) far?	*(Este) departe?*
Where is/are..?	*Unde este/sînt..?*
Is there..?	*Există..?*
Hotel	*Hotel*
Campsite	*Popas, camping*
Tent	*Cort*
Railway station	*Gară*
Train	*Tren*
Bus station	*Autogară*
Bus	*Autobuz*
Daily	*Zilnic*
Departure	*Plecare*
Arrival	*Sosire*
Crossroad	*Răscruce*
Road junction	*Intersecţie, bifurcaţie*
Bridge	*Pod*
Church	*Biserică*
Key (for church)	*Cheie*
Citadel	*Cetate*
Hospital	*Spital*
House	*Casă*
Museum	*Muzeu*
Car	*Maşină*
Tram	*Tramvai*
Trolleybus	*Trolibuz*

Link words

And	Şi
But	Dar
Or	Sau
With	Cu
Without	Fără
If	Dacă
Now	Acuma
Today	Azi, astăzi
Yesterday	Ieri
Tomorrow	Mîine
To	La, spre
Via	Prin
For	Pentru
What/how	Ce
When	Cînd
Above	Sus
Below	Jos
Enough	Destul, gata
After	După, peste
Big	Mare
Small	Mic
Very	Foarte
Many	Mulţi
More	Mai (mult)
Less	Mai puţin
Good	Bun
Bad	Rău, prost
True	Adevărat
Fast	Repede
Slow	Încet
Open	Deschiz
Shut	Inchiz
Strong	Tare (alcohol or muscles)
Heavy/difficult	Greu
Easy/light	Uşor
Beautiful	Frumos
Wonderful	Minunat
Sure	(De)sigur
Single/alone	Singur
New	Nou
Old	Vechi, bătrîn

Verbs

| Stop! | Stai! Ajunge! |

To buy	*A cumpăra*
To sell	*A vinde*
To exchange	*A schimba*
To want	*A vrea* (I want *vreau*, we want *vrem*)
To go (on foot)	*A merge (pe jos)*
To depart	*A pleca*
To arrive	*A sosi, ajunge*
To wait	*A aştepta*
To see	*A vedea*
To sleep	*A dormi*
To eat	*A mînca*
To work	*A muncă, a lucrare*
To have	*A avea (am, ai, are, avem, aveţi, au)*
To be	*A fi (sînt, eşti, eşte, sîntem, sînteţi, sînt)*
It is necessary	*Trebuie* (invariable: *eu trebuie să plec* I must go)
It is possible	*Se poate*

Living

Bed	*Pat*
Room	*Cameră*
Shower	*Duş*
Bath	*Baie (Băile* spa, *Baia* mine)
Water (hot/cold)	*Apă (caldă/rece)*
(Too) expensive	*(Prea) scump*
Cheap(er)	*(Mai) ieftin*
Money	*Bani*
Bill	*Notă*
Shop	*Magazin*
Bottle	*Sticlă* (also means glass (material); *pahar* means glass (receptacle))
Married	*Căsătorit*
Child	*Copil*
Boy	*Băiat*
Girl	*Fetiţa, fată*
Man	*Om*
Woman	*Femeie*
Tired	*Obosit*
Ill	*Bolnav*

Hiking Terms

Cave	*Peştera*
Cliff	*Colţ*
Cloud	*Nori*
Crag	*Stînca*

Field	*Cîmp (Cîmpulung* meadow, literally long field)
Fog	*Ceaţa*
Forest	*Codrul* (the most popular sheepdog's name)
Gorge	*Chei*
High	*Înalt*
Hill	*Deal, măgură (deluros* hilly)
Hollow	*Aven*
Hut	*Cabana* (also signal box)
Ice	*Gheaţă*
Lake	*Lac (lezer, tăul* tarn)
Landscape	*Priveliste*
Ledge	*Poliţa*
Marsh	*Mlăstina (mlăstinos* marshy)
Meadow	*Poiana* (also glade or clearing)
Mouth	*Gură*
Pass	*Pas*
Pasture	*Păsune*
Path	*Poteca, traseu*
Peak	*Vîrf, pisc*
Precipice	*Prăpastie (prăpăstios* steep, pessimistic, violent)
Rain	*Ploaie*
Ravine	*Rîpă*
Ridge	*Creastă (coasta* in the north), *coamă*
River	*Rîu*
Rock	*Piatra* (also stone or crag)
Saddle	*Curmatură, şaua*
Sheep fold	*Stîna*
Side	*Latura*
Slope	*Panta*
Snow	*Zăpadă*
Spring	*Izvor, izbuc* (mineral spring *Borcuţ, izvor mineral*)
Steep	*Abrupt*
Stream	*Pîrîu* (also brook, creek)
Summit	*Culme* (also crown, peak)
Swollet	*Ponor*
Valley	*Valea*
Village	*Sat*
Wandering	*Hoinaresc*

Wood	*pădure* (the source), *lemn* (the product

Numbers and dates

One	*Un, una*
Two	*Doi, două*
Three	*Trei*
Four	*Patru*
Five	*Cinci*
Six	*Şase*
Seven	*Şapte*
Eight	*Opt*
Nine	*Nouă*
Ten	*Zece*
Eleven	*Unsprezece*
Twelve	*Doisprezece*
Thirteen	*Treisprezece*, etc
Twenty	*Douăzece*
Twenty-one	*Douăzece şi un*, etc
One (two) hundred	*O (două) suta*
One thousand	*O mie*
First	*Primul, prima*
Second	*Al doilea, a doua*
Third	*Al treilea, a treia*, etc
Half	*Jumăte*
Quarter	*Sfert*
Monday	*Luni*
Tuesday	*Marţi*
Wednesday	*Miercuri*
Thursday	*Joi*
Friday	*Vineri*
Saturday	*Sîmbătă*
Sunday	*Duminică*
January	*Ianuarie*
February	*Februarie*
March	*Martie*
April	*Aprilie*
May	*Mai*
June	*Iunie*
July	*Iulie*
August	*August*
September	*Septembrie*
October	*Octombrie*
November	*Noiembrie*
December	*Decembrie*

A few obvious mistakes

Because the language is so similar to Italian, I found myself initially saying e instead of şi for 'and', and da for 'there' as well as 'yes' and 'but'; alt means 'other', not 'old'. Other sources of confusion are sigur (sure) and singur (alone), a mînca (eat) and a muncă (work), and suta (hundred) and satu (village) (remember the town of Satu Mare or Big Village). I couldn't remember the difference between deschiz and inchiz until I thought of 'des res' and remembered that it's desirable for a shop to be open, especially in Romania.

If you want to learn more there are a few books available: Teach Yourself Romanian by Y Alexandrescu and D Deletant (Hodder 1992), Colloquial Romanian by D Deletant (Routledge 1983), and Romanian Conversation Guide (Hippocrene Language Studies).

Magyar (pronounced Modyor)

There isn't room for more than a few phrases of Hungarian or Magyar: yes igen, no nem, please kérem, thank you köszönöm, cheers! egeszegedre!, How are you? Hogy van?, where is..? Hol van..?, How much is it? Mennyibe kerül?, station palyaudvar (abbreviated to Pu).

German

Similarly in German, traditionally the lingua franca of eastern Europe: yes Ja, no Nein, please Bitte, thank you Danke (schön), cheers! Prost!, Hilf Gott!, Greetings Grüss Gott, How are you? Wie geht es?, where is..? Wo ist, How much is..? Wieviel kostet..?, station Bahnhof, key Schlüssel.

ACCOMMODATION

Until 1989 it was not possible for foreigners to stay in private homes in Romania and most tended to come on package tours either to the Black Sea coast or to a ski resort, and not stray much further afield. Although the tourist infrastructure has hardly developed since then, it is now far easier to travel freely and to stay where one wants. In addition to hotels in the resorts and towns, there are about 150 cabane or mountain huts, more than 155 campsites, most of which also have small huts, usually for two people, which I refer to as cabins or camping cabins (these are also known as camping maisonettes, chalets and bungalows) and you can camp wild in the hills. There is also, of course, the hospitality of the Romanian people themselves to be taken into account. The ONT produces maps of cabanas and campsites.

The Intercontinental Hotel in Bucureşti is like any other international hotel and charges prices to match, from US$130 in 1990. Other three star hotels in Bucureşti, and the Carpaţi in Braşov, the Alpin in Poiana Braşov, and the Hotel Tuşnad in Băile Tuşnad, charge (in 1992) between L10,000 and L16,000 for a double room; other hotels in towns charge about half this, and prices on the coast and in Maramureş are still less. Many hotels are obviously part of the tourist economy and therefore very expensive by local standards; however by international standards they are not too extortionate and might be justified if a rest from hard travelling is needed. Even so, hot water will be intermittent, light bulbs dim, and do not expect to have your boots cleaned here. In any case as the hotels are privatised and deregulated, and if the crisis continues in the Romanian tourist industry caused by the absence of the East Germans who were its mainstay, there will be wider variations in price. At some point there will also be new private hotels.

Slightly cheaper than hotels are the *hans* or tourist inns, sometimes also called motels, mainly on major roads or in places like Bran, which can be useful in need. They can also offer good Romanian, rather than international, cuisine.

If you plan to spend time in the mountains, or indeed anywhere outside the towns, you will need to rely on camping and on cabanas for accommodation, and although generally basic the warmth of the welcome, at least in season, will generally make up for this. Broadly, the cabanas can be divided into two groups; firstly those with access by road (or by cable-car) which tend to be bigger modern buildings with bars and restaurants, and higher prices, and secondly the genuine mountain huts, much smaller and simpler, often with outdoor toilets and no electricity, and costing about half as much. Like the 'simple' Youth Hostels in England and Wales, these are places that transmit the true spirit of the mountains but are threatened by the forces of progress and profit.

Like the hotels, the cabanas (German *Schützhutte*, or Hungarian *Turistahaz*) are being privatised, ie taken away from the OJTs or county tourist offices and trade unions etc. Prices have already risen from about L15 to L50-100, and in one case (Nedeia) to L220, more than one tenth of the monthly salary of a waitress there; foreigners now have to pay ten to fifteen times as much as Romanians. No wonder there is a crisis in the tourist industry. Those in Poiana Braşov were, in 1991, part of the now-defunct dollar economy, starting at US$25, but it is possible to escape to the 'real' cabanas at the top of the cable-cars.

In addition to the cabanas, there are refuges which provide a far lower grade of shelter and are generally best thought of as a convenient spot to pitch tent in the hope of some company, rather than as a place to sleep in normal weather. One exception is that at Cînaia, in the Cindrel mountains, which is a cabana in all but name and the absence of a bar or cooking; other than this, refuges are free. There are also cabanas for *vînǎtori* (hunters), and others belonging to private clubs, which may be able to offer you accommodation, or at least camping facilities.

The Romanians love to camp by water, and in summer almost every stream and lake is lined with cars and tents — the area around Plaiul Foii, between the Piatra Craiului and the Fǎgǎraş, is perhaps the best example. This is natural, given the legal open access to the countryside and the lack of facilities in the official campsites (*Popasuri Turistice*), which in any case tend to be near the main roads and towns. To my mind, there are only two good reasons for paying money to camp in a wide-open country such as Romania: firstly for hot water and decent washing and toilet facilities, and secondly for the security to leave one's belongings for the day or evening. On both these counts the official Romanian campsites fall down, and they can also be relatively expensive; in particular when I return to Sibiu I shall be camping in the oak woods outside rather than inside the campsite. Almost all campsites have camping cabins to rent, for two or more people, which usually cost about the same per head as a cabana. Some cabanas, such as Obîrşia Lotrului, in fact have no other accommodation, and they can also be found at some hotels. There are also private campsites now beginning to appear, but they are caught in a cleft stick of wanting to provide better facilities than the official sites, but being unable to afford anything unless they first open up with minimal facilities. Wherever you camp in Romania there will always be a dog barking long after dark; even on top of a mountain the noise will carry from a stîna several kilometres away.

There are also private rooms now available in homes on the coast and in places like Braşov, Sibiu, Sibiel, Bran and in Bucovina. In 1990 these could theoretically be booked via the OJT tourist offices for about L5,000, or you may be approached at railway stations with offers of rooms for about US$7-10; the EXO agency has a room-finding service in Braşov (Str Postavarului 6; tel 44591/43975) and Sibiu (Str Doljului 2, near the station; tel 821 960). In small villages you won't need an agency to find somewhere to stay, but you should take great care not to abuse the great hospitality of the country people. They are unlikely to accept payment, although presents are appreciated in the unlikely event that you can squeeze any more into your backpack.

Other possibilities are student rooms in July and August, usually booked through the office of the BTT (Youth Travel Agency) in major towns, and rooms in spas booked through a central office, usually near the tourist office, which theoretically involves a stay of a week or so including meals, but which may now be subject to negotiation. It is also possible to stay in monasteries, which is very popular with Romanian families seeking a bit of tranquility, but which usually requires advance planning.

TRANSPORT

Naturally you will wish to travel under your own steam as much as possible, but it will occasionally be necessary to resort to technology to cover large distances and reach the more interesting areas. Public transport in Romania is quite easy to cope with, although not as fast nor as frequent as in western Europe. During the Ceauşescu era trains and what buses actually ran were hideously overcrowded due to the near total lack of fuel; but that is generally history. (City buses were mostly methane-powered, with balloon-like tanks on the roof, as they still were in Suceava in 1991.) If you haven't travelled in the Third World you may still find buses rather overloaded, but it's not something that ever occurs to me.

Most local travel is still by bus, and almost all long distance travel by train — there are internal flights, but only a tiny minority of Romanians can afford these, and car ownership, though rising, is still low, with costs preventing most drivers from using their cars other than locally. Even so they practise assiduously the art of freewheeling and turn on headlights well after dusk because of inadequate batteries. (If you see a car with its lights on in daylight it will almost certainly be Hungarian.) Current rises in fuel prices are bound to reduce the numbers of cars on the roads and make hitching harder.

Trains

The rail passenger has a choice of paying more to travel fast or less to travel more slowly (useful if you want the journey to last overnight) or of course to get off at a local stop. Fast trains are known either as *accelerat* or *rapid* (international trains being more likely to be *rapid*), and overnight fast trains will carry cheap couchettes. Slow trains are known either as *cursa* mainly on branch-lines or as *personal* on the main lines, and on the electrified main lines they can in fact rattle along moderately quickly. They basically stop everywhere but once in a while will miss out a halt for no obvious reason — always check that it will stop at your destination, although no foreigner is actually likely ever to want one of these middle of nowhere halts. If going anywhere other than a major city, sit towards the front of the train, as often the only name board is on the station building and may be unlit.

In Romania as in most of Europe, particularly the east, they operate a seven-day timetable with engineering work carried out throughout the week (less being needed due to the lower speeds). This means that all timings contain a considerable margin for delay. For a chronically unpunctual nation, trains and buses leave remarkably punctually, especially from their originating points. Ironically though, while the slow trains only stop for a minute or so, the fast trains have to stop for three or four minutes to allow passengers to find the right carriage for their reserved seats. Fast trains are only slightly more likely than slow trains to have lights after dark — the ticket inspectors (your ticket will always be inspected) work by torchlight. Clearly it's not hard to sleep at night. Most passenger compartments are non-smoking and smokers go into the corridor or lobby area to light up, but for some reason it is felt to be acceptable to smoke in *nefumatori* (non-smoking) double deck carriages (only used for slow trains) and on the narrow-gauge trains. There are additional trains in July and August, mostly running across the country to Constanţa and Mangalia on the Black Sea.

Timetable boards will list two columns of trains under *sosire* (arrival) and *plecare* (departure), giving the train type and number, its destination, its line (counted outwards from the main station building), and perhaps the duration of its stop in the station. Most fast trains require advance booking and a seat (or couchette) reservation, usually most easily bought either when you arrive at a station or at an *Agenţia de Voiaj CFR (Căile Ferate Române —* Romanian Railways) in major town centres (not usually open at weekends). Trains do not run at regular intervals throughout the day, as in the west; there will be a wave of trains leaving major centres early in the morning and until about 0830, and then there is often a gap until about 1400, when people start to leave work. Naturally this pattern is less rigid at intermediate stations. One can normally rely on there being several trains through the afternoon and evening, and there sometimes seem to be as many night trains as day trains — for instance at Băile Herculane there were, in 1991, five fast and three slow trains passing through betwen 0100 and 0500, and five fast and seven slow trains between 1000 and 2230.

Left-luggage offices are widely available, charging, in 1992, L30 (L60 if 'voluminous') and L40 per 24 hours. Otherwise station facilities are limited, although private snack caravans are taking over the forecourts.

The rail network has been influenced by the country's history: Transylvania has a good network built by the Hungarians, but there are few lines through the Eastern Carpathians between Transylvania and Moldavia, which were the border between Hungary and Romania, and Maramureş was cut off by the advance of the Soviet border after the Second World War until the Salva-Vişeu line was built, largely by volunteer labour. In these areas buses may be more useful than trains. For some reason, down the eastern side of the Apuseni there is a chain of totally unimportant little towns such as Razboieni, Teiuş and Vinţu de Jos which happen to be major rail junctions; you may get heartily tired of these places.

Buses

Bus services are gradually extending their range so that instead of just feeding traffic in and out of one major centre, they can now occasionally be used to reach the next major town as well. Tîrgu Mureş is particularly well served by buses, as it is only on a fairly minor rail branch and a narrow gauge line. It has the only bus station (*autogară*) that I came across that is comparable to the better Turkish ones, with separate arrival and departure platforms and a large hall. Being a centre of the Magyar population, it has three buses a day to Budapest as well. Timetables at the *autogarăs* only list the final destinations, so you may have to enquire about other places, with pen and paper so that the times can be clearly written down.

There are an increasing number of private bus companies appearing, both internally and to Hungary. Most of these use the *autogarăs* and can be discovered by means of posters there. Those from Bucureşti mostly depart from near the Gară de Nord, to places such as Rîmnicu Vîlcea, Tulcea, Tîrgovişte, Focşani and (every few hours) Istanbul. There are also international buses from Constanţa to Istanbul (daily) and Varna (four per week). Tourist coaches tend to call at hotels, such as one leaving the Hotel Nord, Bucureşti, at 1400 on Fridays and 0800 on Saturdays to Sinaia, Braşov and Poiana Braşov, returning on Saturdays and Sundays. At a time (June 1991) when the rail fare from Bucureşti to Braşov was L175, the coach fare was L160. Other useful services run from Braşov to Tîrgu Jiu (L240) via Făgăraş, Rîmnicu Vîlcea and Horezu, and to Budapest (L1,000) via Cluj. However, there is a general economic adjustment underway, and some services may be suspended as unprofitable, such as those from Braşov to Rotbav.

Morning peak buses start running around 0430, and in some cases the last bus can be as early as 1630, although this is now less common. At intermediate stops you should of course buy a ticket from the driver, but I often found myself being told to just take a seat and have a free ride. Not wanting to delay people, I usually agreed quickly enough. In Maramureş and Bucovina, I generally found that buses would stop wherever they found me; in other parts they tend to insist on your being at a bus stop. Anywhere in the country people will flag down mine or works buses (usually built on a lorry chassis); sometimes money will change hands, sometimes not, especially in the case of a foreigner. These are the only buses that allow smoking; as Romanians are constitutionally allergic to fresh air, this can be a bit much.

In towns you will find urban buses, trams and trolley buses, and should buy tickets in advance at kiosks, and cancel them on boarding. From August 1 1991 fares in Braşov were L6, with a L150 fine for ticketless travel. It can be hard to find a ticket in the evening, but this should not be a problem. Nor did I ever have problems taking luggage on to a Romanian bus, although theoretically there is a charge over 15kg.

When bus and train fares increase tickets are usually corrected by hand, but as fares are generally posted you won't be ripped off. Fares are based on distance, with a substantial discount for longer journeys. In 1992 train fares were about L2 per kilometre up to about 150km, and then declined progressively to less than half that rate; bus fares were generally less.

Hitchhiking

The next transport option, frequently overlapping with bus travel, is hitchhiking. In the Ceauşescu era, when buses were few and far between, this was more common than it is now, and it was normal to pay slightly more than the bus fare for the journey, for the added comfort and speed — never mind that you've waited half an hour and are going to be set down miles from anywhere! Kent cigarettes were said to be essential for procuring rides; they are much less important nowadays, but may reappear as times get harder. Payment is usually refused from foreigners, and in fact you may find yourself being forced to stop for some free ţuica. Outside Maramureş and Bucovina, where every vehicle, including horsecarts, would stop to offer a lift, I found it helped greatly to accentuate my obvious foreignness by putting on glasses, hanging my camera on my shoulder, and making my high-tech rucksack visible to approaching drivers.

As elsewhere in continental Europe it is possible to tell where a car is from by a two-letter Judeţ code on the numberplate — TM for Timiş, BV for Braşov, MM for Maramureş and so on. Seat belts are not generally worn, lights are turned on as late as possible despite unlit carts and drunkards on bikes on the roads, and it is not unusual to go the wrong way down one-way streets — all of which will have to change if Romania is to come into harmony with the EC. Main roads are called *Drum Naţional* or DN, lesser roads are called *Drum Judeţean* or county roads, local roads are called *Drum Communale*, and everything else is a *Drum Forestier*, even if not actually in a forest. You will see a lot of these DFs when hiking, but would be best advised not to drive on them. Many of the local roads will also be unsurfaced, and there are potholes everywhere.

Cars are still generally Dacias — a Renault 12 clone produced on the cast-off French production line. At first these were just 500cc sewing machines on wheels, but the current 1400cc models are quite reasonable vehicles. Like Rolls-Royces they are worth more used than new, due to a five-year waiting list. Recently a similar deal has been struck with Citroën to produce the Oltcit on what was the Visa production line. Equally ROMAN trucks are produced in the Moldavian town of Roman under licence from MAN, who else. There is also a home-produced four-wheel drive vehicle, the ARU, and an ever-increasing number of old German cars, many of which are illegally exported after failing the German or Austrian roadworthiness test; because of this the import of cars over eight years old was banned in 1992. Virtually all road transport was still state-owned in 1992, under names such as ITA, Autotransport, and International Reef Transport (possibly meant to mean Beef Transport, as these are refrigerated lorries), but this probably made the drivers more rather than less inclined to give lifts to all and sundry. With the closure of Yugoslavia there are now many Turkish trucks heading for western Europe; be warned that these may be searched thoroughly for drugs at borders.

Car-hire and taxis

Currently hire cars are Dacias and Oltcits, but this is changing. From June 1991, Hertz rates were US$18 per day plus 25 cents per kilometre, plus petrol coupons at 80 or 85 cents per litre (before the September 1991 fuel price rises) for normal or super fuel — these give the right to jump the often lengthy queues for fuel, and can also be bought at the border road crossings. Due to the risk of theft, you should remove windscreen wipers when you leave the car.

In addition to the state-owned taxis, there are an increasing number of *Taxi-Privat* — fares rose from L7 to L18 per kilometre after the September 1991 price rise, but as the price is still well below international levels it's likely to rise again. There are also now appearing MaxiTaxis (or Combinats), a shared taxi minibus or a *dolmuş* by any other name, for instance linking Baia Borşa to Borşa.

Flying

If you really are in a hurry you may choose to fly, although there is nowhere in the country that is more than an overnight train trip away, and as elsewhere in the world surface travel is the only way to see the country. Domestic flights leave from Băneasa airport, nearer the centre of Bucureşti than Otopeni, the international airport, and better served by local buses and trams.

From March 1991 TAROM, the state airline, required foreigners to pay for internal as well as international flights with *valuta* or hard currency, at an exchange rate of their own devising. What used to be fares of L780-800 to the further corners of the country became US$42-48, giving rates of between L16.66 and L18.57 to the dollar, at a time when the official rate was L60 and the unofficial rate three times that. This was clearly a retrograde step when the economy was supposed to be moving towards greater openness and convertibility and away from rip-offs of this sort, so I hope that it was reversed as the economy was 'de-dollarised'. Be warned, however.

FORESTRY RAILWAYS

In 1948 there were 752km of narrow gauge railways in Romania, which had been cut to 590km by 1978; since then I'm sure the distance has been cut by much more, perhaps even by half. Lines have closed for various reasons such as dam-building and floods, and been converted into forestry roads, but the economics of using wood-burning steam locomotives for forestry work continue to be perfectly sound, so there is no reason why some should not survive. They all have an early-morning train taking the loggers up to their work, then various trains of logs coming down and finally in mid-afternoon a train bringing the men back again. They are all operated by the *Căile Ferroviale Forestiere* (Forestry Railways), with Class 764 (640mm gauge) tank locomotives mostly built in Reşiţa, but also in Reghin, Bucureşti, Budapest and Berlin, some before the First World War and others as recently as 1985.

The best known are those from Vişeu de Sus to Coman and from Covasna to Comandau and the Vrancea mountains. The line to Coman, near the Ukrainian border in Maramureş (see page 136), carries not just foresters but also soldiers (and their pigs), hikers and kayakers (and their kayaks) and in theory even has tickets. It was built in 1933, and now has a 40km main line, and a 12km branch southeast to Jhoasa. The scenery of the Vaser valley is lovely, but the train goes so slowly, taking five and a half hours to cover the 40km, that you might find your attention flagging.

The Covasna line, and its inclined plane, are described on page 186 with the hiking route; it was built in 1883, and was once linked to the 167km of the Nehoiu system to the south, now closed.

There is also a stretch of forestry railway still operating north from Secu in the Căliman mountains (see page 155/6), although threatened by dam building. There may well be other lines still working on the eastern side of the Eastern Carpathians, south of Piatra Neamţ, around Comăneşti and west of Adjud. There is certainly a metre-gauge line from Piatra Neamţ to limestone quarries at the entrance to the Bicaz gorges.

Other forestry lines may still be working along the southern slopes of the Carpathians, especially in the long valleys north of Piteşti; the line from Tismana to Tîrgu Jiu (see page 254) is still in place, but doesn't look especially active. There is also a line north from Moldoviţa in Bucovina to Argel and the Huţul country (see page 151). There was also a network around Satu Mare in Maramureş, running southeast to Arduşat and Şomcuta Mare, and northeast to Negreşti-Oaş and Bixad; there are still passenger services on the latter section.

I have also come across disused forestry lines in the Oituz, Siriu and Orăştie valleys; these are now of interest only to industrial archaeologists, and there are bound to be many more. There are two splendid illustrated books in German on the forestry railways: *Mit Dampf Durch die Karpaten, Waldbahnen in Rumänien* by Florian Hofmeister (Bayerisches Eisenbahnmuseum, Munich 1986), and *Wälder und Dampf* by Rudolf Reichel and Hans Hufnagel (Otto Novacek, A-3003 Gablitz, Linzer Strasse 64, Austria).

In addition to the forestry railways as such, there are also diesel-powered narrow-gauge lines operated as part of the main CFR system; in addition to the Bicaz line mentioned above, there is also a line just to its west, from Topliţa to the mineral water plant at Borsec, and an extensive network in the centre of Transylvania, running from Lechinţa (near Bistriţa) and Miheşul de Cîmpie via Tîrgu Mureş to Băile Sovata, the lines from Sibiu to Vurpăr and Agnita, the 94km line up the Arieş valley from Turda to Abrud (see pages 297, 307 and 310), a shorter one just to the south from Alba Iulia to Zlatna, and other shorter lines.

To round off this subject, it is also worth mentioning that main-line steam power is now essentially extinct, although I did see one steam loco working at Satu Mare; however there are sidings full of pensioned-off steam locos outside Oradea, Cluj, Galaţi, Bucureşti and other major towns. There is a rail museum not far from the Gară de Nord in Bucureşti, and a static display of locomotives at Reşiţa Nord station. There are also reports that Ceauşescu's £3m private train, which was kept secret from his own people, is to be made available for tourist charter.

FOOD AND DRINK

Keeping healthy for hiking

I shall first discuss the theory of what one should eat and drink for ideal health and performance, and then turn to what is actually available in Romania, which is not quite the same thing.

Energy comes from four sources: protein, alcohol, fat and carbohydrate. Protein will only be used for energy when other sources are exhausted, therefore you need take in only the body's basic requirement of about 1-1.5g per kilogram bodyweight. Beans, white meats and dairy products are suitable sources. Alcohol is not a suitable energy source either as it is only broken down slowly, by the liver, and it also intoxicates. Generally alcohol and hiking do not mix well — even if you just have a couple of drinks in the evening, the effects on your legs will be obvious in the morning. Only a few hundred grams of fat will be consumed by a hearty day's exercise, and as men have a fat store of 12-15kg, and women of 15-20kg, you need make no particular effort to boost your stocks.

Therefore we are left with carbohydrates as our main energy source, most easily obtained from foods such as cereals, bread, pasta, bananas, potatoes and rice. This can be topped up with refined or sugary carbohydrates such as jam, chocolate or other foods containing sugar; however consuming large amounts of refined sugary carbohydrate just before or during exercise may actually cause fatigue as its rapid absorption can cause insulin to be released into the bloodstream with a consequent drop in blood sugar levels. For sustained hiking you need three times your normal carbohydrate intake.

You also need to replace **fluids** lost through sweating, an inevitable consequence of muscular activity. Make sure you drink at least half a litre (say a pint) at the start of the day, and then keep yourself topped up as you go — don't wait until you're thirsty, and drink more in the evening; in hot weather it's worth having a water-bottle by your bed as well. Roughly speaking you should take a pint for every 10°F every 24 hours, if you still know what pints and Fahrenheit are — ie if the temperature is 80°F you should take eight pints of fluid a day. Water is obviously ideal, but you can also add some carbohydrate such as fruit juice. However this will slow the rate of absorption, so keep it dilute.

In addition B vitamins are needed for energy metabolism — these can be obtained from fruit, vegetables (particularly pulses), cereals, nuts, and fish or white meat. Iron is also needed for oxygen transport — best obtained from meat, eggs, pulses and green vegetables, nuts, seeds and cereals. If possible take this with orange juice or some other source of vitamin C to aid uptake.

And now the reality

In eastern Europe as a whole, 45% of energy intake comes from fat, as against the 30% recommended by the World Health Organisation; there is generally little fresh fruit and vegetable available out of season, so for instance the average Czech eats 337 eggs and 90kg of meat per annum, as against 139 eggs and 54kg of meat in the United Kingdom. In Romania the situation was far worse under Ceauşescu, but it has now improved somewhat. If you travel to enjoy cuisine, Romania may not be the place for you for the time being, but it is quite possible to eat reasonably well in season, especially if you like pork. Even as a vegetarian I was perfectly happy for four months; it was only when I reached Slovakia and then Poland that I suddenly remembered the concept of choice, faced with the problem of having more than one type of jam to choose from.

In the 1930s Romanian cuisine was famous; although this was the period when Bucureşti was known as the Paris of the East, it was not merely a copy of Parisian cuisine but an individual and creative blend of this with eastern influences. Under communism this was thrown away in the familiar process of levelling down, and then Ceauşescu's mad rush to pay off the country's foreign debt led to all Romania's agricultural surplus and considerably more being exported, above all to the Soviet Union. This ultimately led to the Romanians being laughingly described as 'the vegetarians of eastern Europe' by their fellow eastern Europeans, for whom vegetarianism is a fate worse than starvation. Virtually all meat was exported, leaving only *slănină* or bacon fat, which fortunately the Romanians are very fond of, often taking a slab for a picnic or to eat at work. Tourists, particularly those on package tours, were however spared all this and were well fed to hide the realities of Romanian life from them. One of the government's first acts after the revolution was to stop these food exports, so that there was again meat in the shops, together with pots of jam and so on, still with Cyrillic or even English export labels. (Labels show what could be the date of manufacture or a sell-by date — who knows?) There was also a flood of food imports from countries such as Egypt and Turkey, which means that now there is some limited choice in the shops. And of course Coke and Pepsi are everywhere.

However as prices rise the problem now for the Romanians is to afford their food. As ever it is the city dwellers who suffer most, while those in the country or with relatives there will always be able to procure supplies. In any case winter is hard; even in April the only vegetables available were radishes, spring onions and potatoes, although from then on through the summer things got better and better, with new fruits and vegetables on show every time I went to a market. Chocolate and jam are widely available but trail mix, dried fruit, peanut butter, dehydrated meals and so on should be brought from home.

Those who actually choose to be **vegetarians** may find life rather dull if they decide to eat in restaurants to any great extent, as they will be limited to omelettes, *frites au gratin* or *cașcaval pané* (cheese fritters) for most of the time; but in summer there are plenty of vegetables available, and pasta and so on, if you have a stove, and if not it is quite possible to survive on eggs, fruit, salad, biscuits, bread, cheese and jam, although I admit that when hiking I got through a pot of jam a day (at British prices, too). Soups will usually be made with a meat stock, or worse.

Romanian **meal times** can seem a bit mysterious; as most city people work from 0600 or 0700 and come home by 1500, they tend to eat their main meal then, with just a snack in the evening; this is reflected at some cabanas which do not serve lunch until 1400. However in the country the tendency is to eat the main meal in the evening, after a full day's work.

What does however happen all through the afternoon and evening is **drinking**; from about 1400 onwards the bars will be busy with men (not, as a rule, women) drinking beer from bottles (or, in Saxon areas, from glass steins) or the dreadful firewater or plum brandy (or vodka) called *țuica*. This is the national drink, which will be thrust upon you everywhere; being 60° alcohol and often cut with medicinal alcohol, it does not mix well with hiking or any other normal use of the legs. Alcoholism, especially in the rural areas, looks set to be Romania's greatest continuing problem and will probably take one or two generations to dry up; with smoking, it was in many ways the natural response to the despair of the Ceaușescu years, but it remains firmly entrenched. In any case it has been a constant feature for at least the last century or more, and is seen as a natural feature of peasant life. The waste of human talent and energy is appalling.

The Saxons, although less prone to fully developed alcoholism, are great vine growers and until their mass exodus produced good quality wines, mainly white; however their *weinbergen* or terraces are now largely abandoned, making ideal level camping spots. Wine is also produced in Dobrogea and other areas, notably a sweet red dessert wine called Murfatlar. The fact that Bulgarian Cabernet is now the most popular red wine in Britain shows the potential for a well planned and marketed wine industry, but this is unlikely to be realised without the Saxons' expertise and drive (although in 1992 a good Romanian Pinot Noir had reached Sainsbury's shops in Britain). The Hungarians fancy a tipple of *bitter*, like a herby red vermouth, as well as *vermut alb* or white vermouth, and all races drink beer, although this can be hard to find in the shops. Perhaps the best is from the Reghin brewery, perhaps the only one to keep for more than three days, which can make it almost impossible to find beer except at weekends.

In Maramureş and Cluj you should be given an apple juice, usually lovely, with your meal in restaurants, and in Bucureşti and other major cities *Ness* is popular; this is not loch water but rather Nescafé, served hot or cold. Tea or *ceai*, pronounced chai as in India and elsewhere, is available almost everywhere; in cabanas in particular it will always be incredibly sweet and not necessarily available on demand, as it is stewed on the stove and not made with an electric kettle. Shops that once specialised in mineral water now also serve sickly sweet fruit juices such as mango and orange, which are also served in the *cofetărie* or *patiserie* which often provide the best snacks in Romania. The key vocabulary to master here, after pointing out your choice of cakes, is *farfurie* or *paquet*, meaning plate or packet, although staff often assume that a sticky cake such as a *Carpati* is for consumption on the premises while a *pateuri cu brînză* or cheese pastry is to be taken away. If you want something sweet this is the place, as there is rarely any dessert in restaurants.

Just as *cofetărie* tend not to sell coffee, Romanian **restaurants** tend in fact to be nothing more than beerhalls, and should be avoided by those looking for a proper meal in a pleasant setting. This may be found in a hotel restaurant; otherwise you can try an *autoservire*, a functional cafeteria-style restaurant found in most major towns, or a lacto-vegetarian restaurant, although these are hardly less likely to be glorified beerhalls and usually serve plates of salami, even if they do not actually cook meat. (You may also find the odd Lactobar, serving yogurt drinks and cheese pastries, among other things.) Here and there you may find a place that calls itself a pizzeria, but in my experience the pizza is hardly ever available. In any case Romanian pizza is made with salami and no-one will ever understand why you want it without.

In summer every shop moves out onto the pavements and the barbecue season gets under way, with *micî* or *mititei*, the local version of hot dogs, icecream, and of course beer the most popular items.

Sheeps' cheese and *mămăligă* (maize mush, or *polenta* to the Italians) are above all associated with the lives of the shepherds in the hills and are covered in detail on page 108.

Other dishes are listed below:

Pîine, pită	Bread
Prăjiturî	Cakes
Plăcintă	Pancake, like Indian deep-fried breads (also *Plăcintă cu brînză/cu mere* cheese/apple pie, and *clătiţă* fritter)
Pateuri cu brînză/cu mere	Cheese/apple pastry
Gogoşî, langoş	Doughnuts
Gem	Jam (also *dulceaţa* for very good jam, traditionally served in a glass with a spoon, and *marmeladă* for a low quality blend of fruits)
Miere	Honey
Zahăr	Sugar
Îngheţată	Ice cream
Iaurt	Yogurt
Smîntînă	Sour cream
Unt	Butter
Brînză	Cheese
Ouă	Eggs
Omletă	Omelette
Jumărî	Scrambled eggs
Ochiurî	Poached eggs
Ouă fierte	Boiled eggs
Ouă prăjite	Fried eggs
Peşte	Fish
Carne de porc	Pork
Carne de vacă	Beef
Pui	Chicken
Mezelurî	Sausages
Micî, mititei	Spicey sausage-like burgers
Salam	Salami
Slănină	Bacon fat
Tocană	Goulash
Sarmale	Cabbage leaves stuffed with mince
Supă	Soup
Ciorbă	Hungarian soup with sour cream
Legume	Vegetables
Ghiveci	Mixed stewed vegetables
Ardei	Peppers

Cartofî	Potatoes
Orez	Rice
Castraveţî	Cucumbers
Ceapă	Onion
Ciupercî	Mushrooms
Fasole	Beans
Mazăre	Peas
Roşii	Tomatoes
Salată	Lettuce, salad
Varză	Cabbage
Vinete	Aubergine
Fructe	Fruit
Caise	Apricots
Mere	Apples
Pere	Pears
Piersicî	Peaches
Strugurî	Grapes
Vişine, cireşe	Cherries
Băuturî	Drinks
Lapte	Milk
Ceai	Tea
Cafea	Coffee
Apa (minerală)	(Mineral) water
Bere	Beer
Rachiu	Brandy
Vin (roşu, alb)	(Red, white) wine
Sifon	Soda water
Limonadă, citronadă	Lemonade
Suc (de fructe)	Fruit juice

FOOD FOR FREE

In the most literal sense it is possible to live for free by relying on the generosity of the Romanians, but this section is not about that. Rather it is about the fruit and other goodies available in the countryside and the use which the Romanians make of them.

The most obvious of these are the berries, particularly wild raspberries and strawberries, which are especially sought after. Take some sachets of sugar if you want to make the most of them. The *frag* (pronounced fraj) or wild strawberry (*fraise des bois*) is absolutely tiny, but very sweet. It is found generally in July on low plants in the lighter parts of woods, usually beech, and the best way to find the berries is to work slowly uphill looking for tiny spots of very bright red. I am told that in the uranium mining area around Baița the *frag* are much larger, probably because the earth is warmer rather than because of some mutation. *Zmeură* (wild raspberry) is even more popular, both with people and, I gather, with bears too as they prepare for hibernation. The fruit is ripe in August and September, bigger berries on tall stalks, also in open woodland as a rule, and along the verges of roads.

Above the tree line there are large patches of *afin* or bilberry, also called blaeberry or whortleberry, which flower in April and May and bear small shiny black berries all summer. These are harvested and sold in markets mainly by Țiganes; on the north side of Pietrosul in the Rodnas the *afin* patches seemed to me almost like Sri Lankan tea plantations, with armies of women at work, using a small box with comb-like teeth across the open end to remove the berries in bulk. Other berries are *ienupăr* (juniper), also a dwarf bush above the tree line with small blue-black berries and spiky leaves (used against warts), *agrise* or wild gooseberries, which I found only by the roadside near Vatra Dornei, and blackberries (*mur*), which grow in fantastic quantities and to fantastic sizes especially in Maramureș. The leaves of wild mint, *frag, afin*, and *smirdar* (Rhododendron kotschyi) and wild rose flowers are collected for herbal teas. Herbal remedies can also be found in markets; it seems that even in Roman times the Dacians were noted for their skill in this field.

Plums are grown all over Romania mainly for making *țuica* or plum vodka, but in the warmer southwest in particular they seem to grow everywhere, and what's more, to be left to rot as often as not. I felt no guilt about helping myself from the ground, and they really do taste good. If you want to enjoy the fruit without any moral dilemmas, you could join the fruit-picking rambles organised by the Suceava OJT tourist office. Apples do not seem to be amazing, and there is no distinction made between cookers and eaters.

Even more popular than the fruit are the astounding variety of mushrooms that erupt in the woodlands after summer rain. There are a lot of obviously unsafe red puffballs, but you should not assume that the others are safe; in 1991 there were mystery illnesses among the many weekend mushroom collectors. I had the luck to join a group of French *cèpe* lovers whose judgement I could trust, but you should take care if you do not have expert knowledge. At weekends buses and trains are full of people with bulging bags of mushrooms which they take home to dry for winter stews.

Fishing is popular, notably for trout in the mountain rivers, and for pike in the Danube Delta; you should enquire at the local OJT or at the *Judeţ* Association of Amateur Fisherman and Hunters, at Str Isaccea 10, Tulcea, about permits and closed seasons.

In addition there are many mineral springs that are worth sampling (see the section on spas).

LIVING THERE
Shopping

The key to happy shopping in Romania is to forget about the concept of choice, and simply to take what's available without fussing. Generally things are cheap enough for us not to make this too difficult, although jam and chocolate are almost as expensive as in Britain, and with the current inflation other products might start to catch up as well. Availability is even more of a problem with things like shoes, which, almost inevitably, will be in most sizes except yours. The quality of many products is also awful, so bring whatever you are likely to need. Food shops generally open from 0800 to 1200 and from 1600 to 2000, while department stores open from 0900 to 2000; in villages the midday break may be longer, but even this may not be enough to allow them to get their farm work done, especially at harvest time.

Shops are also constantly closing for *inventar* or for deliveries, which is annoying. As a rule most food shops will take back your bottles and jars and return your deposit, but they can be awkward, particularly in city centres, and only take back what they have sold you themselves. In bookshops and department stores you will usually find the system found only in Foyle's Bookshop in London, of choosing your purchase, paying for it somewhere else, then returning with a chit to collect your goods. In cities like Braşov there are now many import shops selling things like fruit juice and beer from Egypt and Turkey, sunglasses, baseball caps and similar consumer tat; they are always busy.

There are still queues, and it can be hard to understand why in

Honey

In many towns you will find *Apicultura* shops, which stock everything to do with bees except honey (*miere*) itself; these serve the many bee-keepers profiting from the great variety of flowers all over the country. Honey itself however is hard to find, unless you ask around in the villages, preferably equipped with an empty jar. If you are lucky and in the right place at the right time, though, you may meet some bee-keepers in the hills and be able to sample their products. Just as shepherds take collective flocks into the hills, so too all the bees from a village will be loaded into a lorry trailer, really a mega-hive, and taken up into the hills in July to escape the heat of the plains (usually about 36°C); by August the nectar is finished and the bees return to the plains. Honey is made on the spot with a hand-powered centrifuge, and because of the great interest of bears in honey it is necessary to have a dog and to keep a fire burning all night.

this age of relative plenty. They are most commonly for bread because everyone insists on buying it at the same time and in vast quantities; in addition bread is often only sold through a hatch opening on to the street so that everyone has to wait outside the shop. In addition people are willing to queue for better quality, as fruit and vegetables in particular are not of the uniform good quality that we take for granted from our supermarkets. In general peasants' stalls will have longer queues than the mostly state-owned shops; remember that you will be expected to have your own carrier bag. Ticket queues usually move fast enough, and if you run out of time you can pay for first class.

Working hours

Working hours tend to be on the early side, generally from about 0600 to 1400 in factories and maybe two hours later in shops and offices, so if you have to visit an office, do this in the morning. This makes it possible to be a 'serialist' or afternoon student, which is a popular option. Retirement age is 50, which leads people to think of themselves as old at that age, and in fact they do tend to look quite battered; Romania is, I think, the only country I've been to where people have consistently thought I'm younger than I am.

Postal service

Many people both inside and outside Romania have no faith in the postal system, but in 1991 I always found it very efficient, delivering letters to and from the UK in five days, about half what it took in the bad old days when the *Securitate* doubtless checked every item. In 1992 it was much worse, with many letters going astray; important messages should be sent only by postcard (found mainly in post offices and hotels), as these cannot be suspected of containing dollars. I suspect that the problems are mainly in Bucureşti, and would recommend the use of *Poste Restante* in Braşov or somewhere similar, which I found very good. The usual rules apply for *Poste Restante* — underline the surname, leave out unnecessary titles and initials, and make sure the name matches your passport. You will have to pay for a stamp.

Sending a parcel abroad can be a trial of endurance, involving taking it, unsealed but in a cardboard box if possible, to a *vama* or customs post in the outskirts of major towns (Bdul A Vlahuţa in Braşov, or at the station in Sibiu), to be told what can and cannot be sent. They will be able to seal it up and fill in the paperwork, and then you just have to pay a pretty minor sum of Lei. Aerogrammes are not available, but you can buy pre-paid postcards and envelopes at post offices which can easily be made up to international rates. In 1992 international postage cost L60, or L30 for postcards, and letters to the UK should be addressed 'ANGLIA UK', even if going to Scotland or Wales.

Telephones

In the remoter villages the telephone system is very basic, with no dialling at all; the caller speaks to the operator who will make the connection and call back when this is done. After 2200 calls go direct to the police in the main town. (Under Ceauşescu calls could only be made between 0800 and 1300, and between 1700 and 2000.) In the towns local calls can be dialled, but trunk calls have to be made via the operator. Public phones (many of which are out of action) can only be used for local calls (L1 for 13 minutes), and trunk calls must be made from a telephone office, usually next to the main post office (in 1992 costing up to L12 per minute, half-price from 2000 to 0700 and on Sundays and festivals, and L160 per minute to the UK, with a minimum of three minutes). Although there are television relay towers on many hills, there are no microwave links and all calls go through the wires, so call quality is not great.

Addresses

Romanian addresses can be remarkably simple, in the villages where houses just have a number and no street name, or remarkably complex, with addresses such as 'Str 23 August nr 4, Bloc 2, Ap 17, Sc A, et II' in the horrible blocks ringing every town, listing street, block, apartment, staircase, and floor. Every town has a *Cod* or postcode, which is followed by the *Judeţ* or county, except for Bucureşti which is simply divided into sectors. *Bdul* is short for *Bulevardul* and *Str* for *Stradă*. In many towns many of the street names have been changed since the revolution, and street maps, where available, are unlikely to have caught up with this. Romania has adopted the general continental habit of naming streets after **dates**, which in Romania are written day first — Liberation Day was 23/08/44, which would be 44/08/23 in Hungary or Czechoslovakia.

Costume

There is an amazing variety of costume in Romania; whereas in Bucureşti people can look as stylish and trendy as anywhere in Europe (I even saw male students with ear-rings), in many small villages you will still see old men in the *costum naţional* of white trousers and smock with an embroidered sheepskin waistcoat or *cojoc*, with strong regional variations, of course. Most people dress in something in between, with older men in the country wearing Turkish-peasant style pinstripe suits or the standard eastern European fake leather jackets, older women wearing skirts, aprons and headscarves, and the young wearing jeans, tracksuits and rather bad imitations of American T-shirts, with words like *Ralley, Saffari* and *Cazino*; I even saw one that had *Hugo Boss* on the front and *Iron Maiden* on the back. Some Marks & Spencer shirts are made here and you may see some that have fallen off the back of a lorry along the way. In addition there is the familiar Third World mix of uniforms of all kinds.

Music and crafts

Similarly in the sphere of music there is a divide between Bucureşti and the rest of the country; apparently in the capital there is war between the 'heavyists' and the 'hip-hopists', but in the country all you ever hear is *muzică populară* or folk music blasting out of radios and cassette players, and wherever there is dancing this is what you will hear, particularly the more up-tempo Serbian-influenced music of the Banat (played *cu foc*, with fire), which drives people to paroxysms of hip-wriggling and foot-stamping. Folk-music snobs (ie the few city folk who are interested) see Banat music as 'vulgar' rather than 'popular', but I think it's just as valid in its way, although I get fed up with the 'fa-la-la' refrains. Wallachian dancing is more in the traditional *horă* or round dance style, linking at arms length and showing off the fanciest footwork possible. In Transylvania dancing is more likely to be polka-style boy-and-girl stuff; they say that where Wallachia and Moldavia go in for yelling and stamping, Transylvanian music is more tuneful and emotional, especially the *doina* or bluesy singing of Maramureş and Bucovina.

Traditionally music for weddings and dances is provided by gypsy musicians, but they do not play gypsy music as such; Romanian, and particularly Transylvanian, folk music is infused with gypsy and Hungarian elements, but is distinct from them and in fact is one of the glories of Europe, as was recognised even before 1904 when the composer Béla Bartok began to collect and publish it (*Romanian Folk Music*, M Nijhoff, Den Haag 1967).

There are now popular folk music tours by groups for whom performances are laid on, but you are just as likely to catch authentic music at weekends, market days and festivals in the smaller villages. If you want a tour, one contact is Silviu Ciuciumiş, The Doina Foundation, Aarhuispad 22, 3067 PR Rotterdam, Netherlands ((31-10) 421 8622).

There is a clear contrast between the emotional call-and-response of the Orthodox church and the solid four-square hymns and chorales of the Saxons; it is also worth mentioning the *colinde* or Christmas carols of Maramureş, with their homely lyrics such as 'Holy Mother, please don't weep/ You'll have diapers aheap/ In warm clothes your son to keep'. Classical music is also important in Romania and has been well supported by the state; the great national composer was George Enescu (1881-1955), the great conductor Sergiu Ceilibidache, and performers include pianists Dinu Lipatti and Radu Lupu and soprano Ileana Cotrubaş. Other composers such as Bartok and Xenakis were also born in what is now Romania.

Other folk crafts flourish; in particular the best woodcarving is found in Maramureş and Gorj Judeţs, in addition to the barrels made by the Moţi in the Apuseni. Ceramics are good, especially the blue Hungarian style from Corund (sold from stalls at Bîlea Lac), Wallachian pots from Horezu (painted with a goose feather), and the burnt black pottery from Marginea in Bucovina. It is now hard to find carpets (made to be hung on the walls and draped over chests and beds) made with traditional dyes rather than screamingly bright modern colours.

Museums

Museums usually open from 1000 to about 1800, and almost all are closed on Mondays. Most major towns will have an ethnographic museum, dedicated to the study of local costumes and customs (as opposed to an ethnological museum, which deals with those of other races), which is quite likely to be open when it's meant to be. Some even have English or French captions. Skansen-type open-air museums of vernacular building styles are also popular, as all over eastern Europe.

Housing

Housing, while not amazing, is adequate, except for the Ţiganes who are a separate problem. Town living is mainly in apartment blocks which are cramped and frequently have no phone and unpredictable hot water; however the daily power cuts of the Ceauşescu era are in the past. In the country most families own detached houses, still crowded but with one room, the *casa mare* or big room, set aside for receiving guests, with heirlooms and dowry on display. It's always been traditional to build a home for newly-weds, but in the last few years there has been a craze for building new houses, mainly because collective farming made it a bad idea to put any money into land or animals. Frequently families have demolished half their existing house to rebuild on the same site. Unfortunately there is rarely enough money to finish the job properly. These houses usually have a cooking range, like an Aga but less sophisticated, and are heated by large tile-covered wood-burning stoves. Washing machines, if you ever get invited to use one, are hardly labour-saving devices, as you have to change the water every four minutes. Most houses have fridges, and almost all have televisions. These have greatly changed lifestyles; but statistics show that Romania is still lagging far behind Poland and Hungary in ownership of such appliances.

Television

Romanian television (which you will see in many cabanas and campsites, as well as in private homes) is pretty dreadful, but for a country which only had three hours of television a night before the revolution, 2½ hours of it on Ceauşescu's glorious achievements, it's wonderful. The 1989 revolution was perhaps the first television revolution, effectively starting when Ceauşescu's speech was taken off the air and then coming live from Studio 4 in the Television Centre which was a focus of the fighting; and broadcasting the Ceauşescu trial and execution was seen as crucial. Since then, control of television has been the key to the FSN's control of the country; 'news' programmes would be called propaganda if they weren't so dull, generally a recitation of official delegations and meetings with occasional statements from opposition parties. This was epitomised on the day of the Soviet *putsch*, when the first five minutes of the main news bulletin were taken up by a statement by President Iliescu, followed by a dubbed interview that Prime Minister Roman had given to French television and then statements from all the other parties agreeing that it was a bad thing. After 23 minutes there was a tiny clip of film from Moscow, then lots of reaction from foreign statesmen, all agreeing that it was a bad thing too. After 50 minutes there was the first mention of an attack on the Indian Embassy in Bucureşti by terrorists, two of whom were killed by the *Brigada Anti-Terrorista* of the Romanian Information Service, whose leader was interviewed wearing balaclava and ski mask.

Advertising is new and still amazingly inexpensive, so it is possible to make nationwide lost property announcements and so on.

Romanian-made programmes feature large hand-held microphones, obviously prepared questions and no autocue; not surprisingly people are more interested in *Dallas* and American films, and Bulgarian and Serbian television are also popular where they can be received (mainly in mountaintop weather stations). In Bucureşti, Braşov and Ploieşti there is a second channel, which carries the BBC World Service News and the French TV-5 Europe, and in fact started up before the revolution (it is too easy to assume that progress only came with the revolution), and there are a few hours of Hungarian and German programming per week. Satellite television is greatly sought after now, superseding videos which were used as a form of *samizdat* before 1989, but are now simply used for watching pulp Hollywood films.

Sport

The national sport is soccer, dominated by two pseudo-amateur Bucureşti teams, *Steaua*, the army's team, and *Dinamo*, formerly run by the *Securitate*. Ironically these are the only teams with crowd trouble. Nine of the current national team are now playing in western European teams, notably the captain Gheorghe Hagi, 'the Maradona of the Carpathians', now with Real Madrid. Rugby is also popular, although there is of course no sign of it in the summer; many of the national team were killed in the revolution, when the Olympic shooting team also distinguished itself. Nastase and Tiriac are famous in the world of tennis, but that is hardly a sport you'll see much of in Romania.

One particularly interesting sport is *Turism-Sportif*, which is a blend of mountain orienteering, rock climbing, and theoretical tests of knowledge of flora and fauna, geology and first aid. There are many clubs (half a dozen in Braşov alone) and competitions in all the main mountain areas; there is also conventional orienteering in the lowlands. If interested, one person to contact (if you speak Romanian) would be Tovan Liviu, at the Refugiul Salvamont, Petrosani (see the section on the Parîng massif); I also noticed a summer school at Muntele Mic.

The police and law and order

The police have better things to do than play football, as crime is a serious problem now; although there is less street crime than in Budapest or Warsaw, as the consumer goodies of the West are dangled ever closer but made harder to reach by the country's economic restructuring, there is more frustration, less well repressed, than ever. There is also something of a moral vacuum as the country moves from a situation where everything was banned unless specifically permitted to the reverse, and the police themselves are unsure of their powers or which laws they are still supposed to enforce. At the same time the Ţigane are generally supposed to believe that democracy means they can do what they want and take what they want, and there is a general distrust of them as their numbers increase.

The ports of Constanţa and Galaţi have always been mafia towns, but now entire cargoes are vanishing to be sold in the former Soviet Union. Violent crime *per capita* is four times the British rate, largely due to the alcohol problem: according to Mark Almond of Oriel College, 'During the rule of Nicolae Ceauşescu, government propaganda against non-Romanians helped foster animosity towards the ethnic communities living in the country. But rivalries between ethnic Romanians, from village to village, are also common, and it is not hard to find tensions within a single village community. The perils of *ţuica* and the strains of life dependent on the whims of the weather and the caprices of distant government often break out in violence'. I saw this when I was attending the dedication of the site of a new monastery in Maramureş, and the shepherds of the next village took the opportunity to pursue a dispute over grazing rights that had already led to the road between the villages being torn up; at once half the congregation set off to join battle and repel the invading flocks.

The police are generally recruited from those doing their **army** service, which since the revolution has been reduced from 16 months for all males to 12 months, or just nine months if going to university. Only the élite trains in the mountains, and the majority don't even do any basic yomping or survival training; nevertheless it is generally reckoned that time in the army is a good thing, turning boys into real smoking, drinking men, and of course the soldiers were heroes of the revolution. Nevertheless they can be seen working on the railway line and doing similar slave labour.

HIKING

It is hard to define the differences between trekking, hiking, backpacking and similar terms, and these definitions vary in different parts of the world. For me a trek is either an organised expedition with porters and guides, or simply a hike of a length that isn't usually necessary in the Carpathians, although of course if you wanted to carry the required weight of food you could link together enough routes to keep going for weeks on end. Rambling really just involves day walks which are, for me and in the Carpathians, not nearly enough to feel that I have got away from civilisation. Hiking seems to cover the area between these two extremes, and that is the name I have chosen for this book; backpacking is a mainly American umbrella term for all these activities, although it implies a degree of self-sufficiency.

Hiking in the Carpathians is not at all like hiking (or trekking) in the Himalayas or Andes. The distances are less and the altitudes lower, and you are almost always in a man-made landscape dominated by forestry at the lower altitudes and sheep above that. Yet in spite of this it is not the hiking from village to village, mainly along busy and obvious valley routes with occasional passes, that characterises trekking in Nepal or Peru; you are in fact on your own much of the time and can genuinely feel you are getting away from it all. Carpathian routes are mainly ridge routes in moorland or alpine scenery, with relatively few hard climbs to go up to a pass only in order to come down again; this makes them seem higher than they often are, although there are no glaciers or eternal snows. In fact Moldoveanu in the Southern Carpathians (or Transylvanian Alps) of Romania is 2,544m, just lower than the Tatras at 2,655m; to put this in context, Mont Blanc is 4,807m, Kala Pattar in Nepal is 5,545m, Kilimanjaro, the highest peak in Africa and perhaps the highest most of us are likely to hike, is 5,895m, and Everest is 8,863m. In practice you will spend most of your time here hiking between 1,500m and 2,200m, which is well above Ben Nevis (1,343m, or 4,406 ft) and Kathmandu (1,400m), although I do also describe a few routes between monasteries and villages at lower altitudes. One metre is 3.28 feet, so 2,000m is 6,560 ft.

A lot of this hiking will be in forests, usually beech or spruce, and above this you will be in open moorland or downs country, with relatively few genuinely alpine zones. Almost all the paths are pretty good, although often no more than sheeptracks; in an exceptionally wet year there were a lot of trees toppling over and blocking paths, but the only really muddy stretches I found were in cow-farming areas of the Transylvanian plateau. With the exception of the northern Harghita mountains there are none of the peat bogs that so bedevil walking in Scotland and the Peak District.

Hiking is well established in Romania, as in the other former communist states, which encouraged it as a cheap and healthy outdoor activity for the masses; in fact the word *turism* is more or less synonymous with hiking. There are marked paths in almost every mountain area, and also between the Bucovina monasteries, but in fact the only ones that are at all heavily used are those in a few popular areas well-equipped with hotels and even ski-lifts (above all the Bucegi, Piatra Craiului, Făgăraş, Retezat and Apuseni). In these areas you will meet many Romanian hikers in the summer months, particularly students from mid-July onwards. Before 1989 there would also have been many East Germans here, but now they are either unemployed or seeing the West. (The Black Sea resorts in particular were a convenient meeting place for families separated by the division of Germany.)

Romanian hikers are not usually too concerned about covering great distances; they tend to move from one *cabana* or mountain hut to another maybe half a day's walk away, largely because their equipment is so poor. Tents are not especially portable and clothes and rucksacks are not waterproof, and when I bought a pair of Romanian boots they began to fall apart within a fortnight; in particular no eastern European rucksack has a hipbelt, and they all seem to use old seatbelts for shoulder straps — quite possible as seatbelts are never used in cars. These equipment problems mean that winter hiking is out of the question for the Romanians, even without the national paranoia about bears and wolves, which is far more than a local version of our own ramblers' fear of bulls. As the hiking classes are also the chattering classes, they are likely to speak English or French and also to be interesting company. Although Romania is not exactly a Third World nation, its people are like those of most Third World nations in that they cannot conceive of doing anything alone, much less going into the mountains alone, so they are usually in groups. Clubs such as *România Pitoreasca*, the *Club Alpin Român* and the *Clubul Alpin Florea de Colț* (Edelweiss Club) own their own huts in very popular areas, and there are also numerous hunters' huts as well as the standard tourist cabanas.

In other areas, particularly out of season, you will meet absolutely no-one other than a few shepherds, and will find very few huts or facilities. There are very few Westerners in the mountains; generally you will find French and Italian tourists in good hotels in the cities, a sprinkling of Inter-Railers passing rapidly through, and Transylvanian Germans returning to visit their old homes. The French in particular, having a traditional cultural association with Romania, have been more adventurous than the British, coming especially for caving and hang-gliding in the Carpathians.

Trail markings, maps and hiking directions

Routes are generally marked, as I have said, but the efficiency varies from place to place; in principle Romanian trails are marked with red, blue and more recently yellow stripes, crosses, dots and triangles (the main ridge route usually being marked with red stripes), painted on stones and trees and sometimes on special poles; junctions may be unmarked or there may be a display of arrow signs giving hiking times. Romania being Romania, some of these are only painted on the wrong side, so that you have to climb into the trees to read them. As so many shepherds and foresters work in the mountains, there are tracks criss-crossing everywhere; I spent up to ten minutes an hour looking for the right route when I was in the Eastern Carpathians in May and June; as the weather got better and I

Mountain rescue

This is provided by an organisation called Salvamont, which can be contacted through the town hall or *primăria (consiliu popular* before the revolution) in twenty-five towns near the main mountain areas. There are basic Salvamont refuges located particularly on the high ridge of the Făgăraş range which are open all year and are manned from May 15 to September 15 by volunteers who come up for ten day stints and spend their days out patrolling the mountains; of course Salvamont is also very busy in the ski season. Rescue is free, being funded mainly by the government, but equipment is minimal, with even first aid cupboards having limited stocks and very few radios available. I was interested to notice that the Băile Herculane Salvamont group is offering five hour guided walks in the surrounding hills, which doesn't seem to happen elsewhere.

Local Salvamont groups and hiking clubs, often sections of a factory's Sports Association, are also responsible for marking paths, and some do it better than others; generally the most touristed areas have the best marked paths. The marking was originally undertaken by the Pioneers, the communist equivalent of the Scouts, which officially no longer exists, although groups of schoolchildren may continue to be involved where there is an enthusiastic teacher. There is a volume of maps of all the marked areas, *Asaltul Carpaţilor, Acţiunea Patriotica-Pioniereasca* (The Assault on the Carpathians, Patriotic-Pioneer Action, 1985 Consiliul Naţional al Organizaţie Pionierilor), which of course has minor errors; this is hard to find unless you meet one of the enthusiastic teachers mentioned above.

moved to more touristed areas this became less of a problem, but nevertheless I feel it is worth giving fairly detailed instructions to save you these problems, particularly if you try to go in the other direction to that described. I must stress, though, that the timings given are generally the result of just one visit and are of course likely to vary with the weather, my load, my state of mind and fitness and so on; they are net timings, excluding all stops of more than a couple of minutes, whereas the timings on signs and in the *Invitation* (see below) seem to include a healthy margin for stops and delays (those in the Apuseni are especially generous). In addition, I was hiking alone and on business; anyone with company and on holiday is bound to take longer, and experience will tell you how much longer. The compass bearings given are uncorrected, ie just as they appear on the compass, which of course need correction before transferring to maps.

Once in a blue moon, you'll find a sign with a map, but in Romania these almost never show where you actually are so can be rather hard to make sense of (and if it did say 'you are here' it would probably be moved!). At least north is usually at the top. Generally Romanian maps are unreliable, including those in the Tourist Office's *Invitation to the Romanian Carpathians* booklet which I refer to throughout as the *Invitation* and which you should try to procure, either in English, Romanian, French or German (the appropriate edition should be available from tourist offices, but they are frequently out of print). Not only does this get routes wrong and give conflicting information on things like altitudes, but it is also appallingly printed so that the ink runs when it rains; but it's all there is in many areas.

There are also hiking maps of some areas, almost always available only in other areas — the rule is always to buy any map as soon as you see it, and perhaps even plan your hiking according to the maps to hand. The *Munţii Noştrii* ('Our Mountains', also available in German as *Unserer Berge*) series of hiking guidebooks present an opposite problem in that they are available nation-wide, but only a few titles are available each year due to bottlenecks in the publishing industry — in 1991 these were on the Muntele Mic-Ţarcu, Semenic and Gutîi ranges, all published in 1990, and there were no new titles in 1992. Romanians are quite used to buying each year's offering as it appears and saving it for later use, but that's not much use for the visitor, although at between L7 and L16 they are incredibly cheap for us and worth buying just for the maps, which are generally very good. Some hikers use maps from the Hapsburg period (in Transylvania) which are topographically accurate, but don't use Romanian names. The most accurate road maps are in *România, Atlas Rutier*, edited by GenMaj Ing Dragomir Vasile *et al* (Editura Sport-Turism, about 1982). You should buy a map of the country before going there; my favourite is the Kümmerley + Frey *Romania and Bulgaria*, which covers everything from Budapest to Istanbul.

CYCLING

There are few places that you cannot tackle with a mountain bike in Romania, barring only the truly Alpine ranges of the Făgăraş and Retezat massifs, the Piatra Craiului ridge and perhaps the peat bogs of the Harghita, and Romanian law or custom gives open access to the mountains, via the many forestry and shepherds' tracks leading there. In general the roads of Romania are acceptable for standard touring bikes, although they may be littered with animals and broken glass, but to penetrate into the maze of *drumuri forestiere* I would recommend a mountain bike or one of the better hybrid 'town and trail' bikes now appearing. Even if you do not dream of riding along mountain crests there are some great rides possible along major forestry roads such as those from Cerna Sat to Cîmpu lui Neag, along the southern edge of the Retezat, and from Rînca to Obîrşia Lotrului across the Parîng range. Mountain biking would also be the best way to get to all the remoter villages of the Saxons and Magyars, or the further corners of Maramureş and Bucovina, although some of the tracks used by cows rather than sheep can get very muddy. In general my route descriptions refer to walking, but almost all of them are equally practicable by bike with the exceptions given above, and the area around Siriu (page 191) where there are many washed-out tracks. You will also have to lift the bike over many fallen trees — spruce doesn't have very deep or strong roots. You should be prepared to carry all spare parts and tools, as well as camping gear, with you; Romanians do use bikes locally, but there are few shops and fewer proper repairers. Major towns will usually have just one shop, dealing with cycles, motorbikes, camping equipment, and frequently car spares as well; in Braşov the Velo-Camping-Sport shop is out to the east at the junction of Calea Bucureşti and Str Carpaţi. Naturally you won't find **Shimano** parts or the like here.

Buses do not have roofracks, but there is no problem putting a bike on to a local train, although it is not much done; the Romanian Tourist Office suggests travelling first class as trains can be very crowded. One great advantage of taking a bike to Romania is that you can simply turn right out of Otopeni airport and head north, away from Bucureşti.

There are good accounts of cycling in Romania by Brian Hall, Georgina Harding and Dervla Murphy (details on page 57), as well as in Bernard Newman's *Blue Danube* (Herbert Jenkins 1935), an article in *New Cyclist*, summer 1990, and briefly in Josie Dew's *The Wind in my Wheels* (Little Brown 1992).

HORSES

The reasons why the Carpathians are attractive for hiking apply even more to pony-trekking except in the few truly alpine regions; it is wide open country once above the tree line, and there is free access and free grazing just about everywhere. However as yet there is nothing of this type happening in Romania, although there are plans afoot.

In Negrişoara forestry cabana to the north of the Căliman range, a former male nurse from the Camargue has set up Europe's only school for equestrian guides to take young Romanians and train them to work in the tourist industry; they have worked against great odds to build the school for themselves with next to no resources. As well as moving boulders and stones to make space for a *manège* fenced with logs, they have built stables, a sauna, no less, and a very wild cross-country course through the woods, totally unlike Badminton; but they still have no saddles, so the students, who had never ridden before, now do everything bare-back and with great panache. They have learnt French and in theory should be learning English too, as well as mountaincraft, first aid, principles of marketing and business and so on, to equip them to deal with Western tourists, whether on foot or on horse. As the first batch qualify the plan is to start pony-trekking, and in winter *ski-cheval*, either taking a cart uphill and skiing down, or actually dragging skiiers behind a horse, first in the Căliman and then in even more suitable areas such as the Apuseni, as well as taking groups into the neighbouring countries. The aim is definitely to protect the environment as much as possible, by zoning various activities in appropriate areas — ultimately the aim is to welcome mountain bikers, walkers, anglers and so on, to stay in new cabanas scattered around among the trees.

The horses used are Huţuls, from the Bucovina-Ukraine border area; these are ideal mountain horses, supposedly able to see with their feet and needing very little water during the day. They are said to be related to the *takhi* or Mongolian wild horse (also known as Przewalski's horse), which has two chromosomes more than the regular horse.

Although currently in the Negrişoara cabana (see page 159 for access from the Căliman) there is a strong possibility of a move to bigger premises in Bistriţa-Năsăud judeţ; a safe contact address should be Robert Rigal, c/o Rus Gabriela, Str V Nascu 35, 4500 Năsăud, Judeţ Bistriţa-Năsăud, but allow plenty of time.

Otherwise there should in principle be pony-trekking from the state stud at Rădăuţi (on Str Bogdan Vodă, south of the town centre) to the Bucovina monasteries, but my latest information is that this has not managed to get off the ground yet, due to all the usual problems of inertia in the Romanian system. However you can go here to ride on the premises, as also at the Black Sea resorts of Aurora and Saturn, and at the Echitaţie cabin in Poiana Braşov, where they have 24 Lippizaners as well as some Huţuls; here they specialise in providing horse-drawn sleigh rides for the package tourists, of course. However I gather that some of the British ski companies are now boycotting the sleigh rides, either because of cruelty to the horses or because of accidents (cruelty to the customers).

In general though, in Romania the horse is used almost exclusively for hauling carts and dragging logs; it is very rare indeed to see one being used either as a pack animal or for riding, and donkeys are equally rare. Almost every horse will carry a red tassel against bad luck, and sadly some are blinded in the left eye to prevent them from being frightened by road traffic — so much cheaper and easier than using blinkers.

In *Between the Woods and the Water* Patrick Leigh-Fermor spends much of his time on horse-back, but this is not a book about riding; *Vagabond* by Jeremy James (Pelham 1991) is a better account of actually riding through eastern Europe. Of course, if you can put up with the extreme tedium of the scenery, the Great Plain of Hungary is the place to go for holidays on horseback, organised by IBUSZ, the national tourist office; ORBIS in Poland is also active in this area, but their holidays tend to be based on a stud rather than travelling.

CAVING

Caving is immensely popular in Romania, which has many great cave systems and prides itself on its major part in the development of the science of speleology. This is largely due to one remarkable man, Emil Racoviţa, who was born into a noble family in Moldavia and was sent to the Sorbonne to study law, but switched to biology. After taking his doctorate, he was a member of the first purely scientific expedition to Antarctica with Amundsen on the *Belgica* in 1897, which was trapped in ice for eighteen months, with all the crew being given up for dead. He then became the first scientific diver, and pioneered the use of photographic slides. In caves in Majorca he discovered new insects and founded the new discipline of bio-speleology. When in 1919 the Upper Dacia University was founded in Cluj, Racoviţa was invited to teach zoology but insisted on having his own Speleological Institute, which was founded in 1920. Ultimately he became Rector of the University and president of the Romanian Academy with other honours, dying in 1947.

The Racoviţa Institute has done sterling work in discovering, mapping and studying the many caves of Romania, and establishing cave science worldwide. However by 1956 the Institute had been transferred from the University of Cluj to the Romanian Academy, based in Bucureşti, and there was only one member of staff left in Cluj. The entire Academy's budget is just one tenth of that of the Romanian Information Service, but the Institute has in recent years been able to rebuild. It remains the focal point for caving in Romania and should be your first contact if planning an expedition there; the Cluj University Caving Club and the SAS (*Societa Ardeleana Speologica* or Transylvanian Speleological Society) are also based in Cluj.

An environmental law is due in 1993, which among many other

things would acknowledge a move from caving being seen as a sport, with points scored for speed and technical difficulty, to an exploratory activity, concerned with science and conservation. The law will be close to United States practice, with three categories of caves (defined as being over five metres in depth); category A, much the same as the present cave reservations, will be closed and totally protected, category B will be show caves such as Scarişoara, Chişcău and Meziad, and category C will be the rest, almost 11,000 caves (so far) which can be visited without permission. However to bring equipment in to the country you will need an official letter from the Institute allocating a local club as your host; you will make friends for life if you leave this club some of your equipment, as even batteries are prohibitively expensive these days. Emil Silvestru, the Director of the Institute, is immensely helpful and keen to encourage visitors; contact him at the Institut de Speologie 'E Racoviţa', str Clinicilor 5, 3400 Cluj (tel 951-15954).

There is plenty of scope for new exploration; for instance in the Sighiştel valley, just east of Dr Petru Groza in the Apuseni, where there are 200 caves still to be mapped, or in the Valea Fieri, east of the Padiş plateau, also in the Apuseni, which includes the Humpleu cave with Europe's second largest chamber.

The longest system in Romania, at least 42.5km in length, is the Peştera Vinturilor or Vintului (Cave of the Winds), just east of Şuncuiuş between Cluj and Oradea, but the last information I had was that the lock had been changed and even the Racoviţa Institute didn't know who had the key, although there were plans to build a proper gatehouse. The deepest cave in Romania at 405m is at Tăuşoare in the southeast of the Rodna massif. This is one of the two caves in the world to have mirabilite crystals, and also gypsum flowers. The Apuseni are full of caves, of course, as well as the citadels described in that section; other areas worth investigating are the south side of the Mehedinţi (including a network of over ten kilometres formed by four underground rivers that is the seventeenth longest in the world), the Moneasa or Codru-Moma massif, west of the Apuseni, the Valea Strei in the Sebeş mountains, the southern Retezat and Jiu valley (dolomitic limestone), the Piatra Craiului (where there are deep vertical caves), the Cioclovina, Ohaba and Tecuri grottoes near Hunedoara, and Dobrogea.

On the other hand, if you don't want to spend your time exploring but would rather simply visit well lit and managed caves you would be better off visiting those at Aggtelek in Hungary, at Postojna in Slovenia (visited by 25 million people since 1818) and in the Moravian Karst in Czechoslovakia. The only Romanian show cave that is up to Western standards of presentation is Meziad, in the western Apuseni. Some of the others that I mention elsewhere are

Scarişoara and others in the Apuseni (pages 295-305), Comarnic in the Banat (page 314), Peştera Ialomiţei in the Bucegi (page 213), Polovragi and Peştera Muierii to the south of the Căpăţînei mountains (page 249) and Huda lui Papară in the Trascău (page 310).

If you want to have a look around some caves, remember to take a torch or flashlight, preferably on a headband or hardhat. Remember that it is actually quite an energetic activity; take some food and water, and also warm clothing. The definitive book (in French) is *Grottes de Roumanie* by M Şerban *et al* (Meridiane 1961).

SKIING

Although hardly comparable with the Alps, skiing is well established in Romania, serving both Romanians and foreign package tourists. The industry was built up in the 1960s and 1970s largely for foreign business; this slumped in the 1980s, but now everyone is going all out to compete with the Bulgarian industry, and with the natural friendliness of the Romanians officially unleashed, after the years when every conversation with a foreigner had to be reported to the *Securitate*, this is now one of the most enjoyable skiing destinations, as well as one of the cheapest and least spoilt.

The general view is that Romanian skiing is fine for beginners and intermediates but less demanding of experienced skiiers; the Romanians counter this by claiming that their red runs are in fact equivalent to French black runs and their black runs are even better. However the *Good Skiing Guide* says of a run at Poiana Braşov that it is 'graded black only because it is not prepared, it has one moderately steep pitch towards the end, and it is used as a downhill race course'. Doubtless the top grade skiers will still head to the Alps, but the attractions of Romanian skiing are more to do with friendliness and of course value for money.

If you come on a package, you will almost certainly be in Poiana Braşov, the main purpose-built ski resort, although some companies also go to the 19th-Century resort of Sinaia. There are other resorts in the other massifs, notably Păltiniş which is to Sibiu what Poiana Braşov is to Braşov; these are generally used only by Romanians and have just a few ski-drags — another type of experience altogether. Snow has been in short supply for the last eight years, but was apparently very good early in 1992; generally there should be about 50cm of snow from December to March and average temperatures of -4°C in the resorts.

For the 1991-92 season prices for a week's package were between £154 and £299, from Falcon, Enterprise, Intasun, Inghams,

Crystal, Balkan Holidays, Duggan Holidays, Friendly Travel and Romanian Holidays (and from Belfast, Balkan Tours), as against £190-500 in Switzerland, and you will also have to pay £60-74 for a skipack, including lessons, £28 for a Poiana Braşov lift pass, and about £25 for insurance. Extra lessons are £8 per hour in a group, and the instructors speak good English and are not as stuck-up as those in the Alps. Heli-skiing is now available for about £25-30.

As usual in Romania it is impossible to get accurate or consistent figures for altitudes and distances, but to enable those of you who are intimately acquainted with other resorts to make comparisons, in **Poiana Braşov** (base altitude 1,020m, highest skiing 1,802m) there are 2,780 beds, 8,650m of cross-country trails, and at least ten main pistes, including two green or nursery slopes (near the Sport and Teleferic hotels), at least two blue runs, four red runs and two black or difficult runs. The longest (3,820m with a drop of 540m or 650m) is a blue run, confusingly called the *Drumul Roşu* or Red Road, and the black runs are the *Valea Lupului* (Wolves' Valley), 2,860m with a 775m drop, and the *Subteleferic*, 1,000m with a 280m drop.There are two cable-cars, the *Teleferic* to Kanzel, about 2,440m long with a rise of between 630 and 730m (0900-1700 Mondays excepted), and number II from the Sport Hotel to Postavarul, about 2,805m long with a 737m rise (0900-1630 Wednesdays excepted), and a two-person gondola to the Cristianu Mare cabana, 2,050 or 2,096m long with a 646m rise, (0900-1630 Tuesdays excepted). There are up to ten chair-lifts and drag-lifts, all singles except for the Camelia. In the summer of 1991 the cable-cars cost just L40 (and even less for early and late runs), but by the 1991-92 ski season the gondola cost L500 and the chair-lifts L100; at weekends when the Romanians rush to the slopes, there can be a wait of up to two hours for the cable-cars.

Whereas those skiing in Poiana Braşov have to take a bus to my favourite Transylvanian town, Braşov, those skiing in **Sinaia** can actually stay in a real town, although it may take slightly longer to reach the slopes, unless you stay in the Hotel Alpin, formerly the Cota 1400, 600m above the town at 1400m. See page 207 for brief details of the town. The cable-car from the town to the Hotel Alpin takes seven minutes, and from there there is another climbing 600m more to Furnica (Cota 2000), and a single chair-lift to Cota 1950, as well as a twin chair-lift from Furnica down to the Valea Dorului beyond. The cable-cars are closed for maintenance on Mondays, although they may open by lunchtime, and the chair-lifts on Tuesdays. There are ten or eleven pistes, including two black runs, 14km of easy cross-country trails, and a 1½km luge track.

Just north of Sinaia is **Buşteni** (see page 207), a much smaller resort at 880m better known as the centre of Romanian climbing, with a cable-car up to Babele on the main Bucegi ridge, and another from there down the other side to Peştera, both closed on Tuesdays. The Babele area seems to be littered with ski-drags. A bit further north is **Predeal** (see page 203), at 1,032m, which has fifteen pistes, eight blue, five red (one floodlit) and two black, and an easy 2.5km cross-country trail. There is a cable-car from Clăbucet-Sosire to Clăbucet-Plecare, 1,730m long with a 400m rise, and three or four chair-lifts. At Cioplea there is a 70m skijump dating from 1934.

Away from the Bucegi, there is skiing at **Păltiniş**, 32km southwest of Sibiu at 1,450m in the Cindrel mountains (see page 275), where there is often snow from November to April. The resort was founded in 1894 for fresh air cures, and the first ski competition was held in 1914. Now a gondola is being built to Vf Bătrîna (1,911m) to serve a new 3.8km piste opened in 1989; currently there is just a chair-lift up Vf Onceşti, 1,050m long and rising 241m. Currently accommodation is in the Casa Turistilor (179 beds) and the cabana (60 beds), but there should be new hotels opening by 1995. In 1991 ski lessons cost just L60 per hour, but you mustn't expect all the instructors to speak English here.

Further to the southwest there are various climatic resorts each with one chair-lift, such as Vf Parîng Mic, Muntele Mic and Semenic (see pages 271/2, and 315). Borşa on the north side of the Rodnas (pages 135/8) is similar, while other resorts such as Stîna de Vale, Arieşeni, Vatra Dornei, Durău, Bîlea, and also Izvoru Mureşului near Gheorgheni, Izvoarele and Mogoşa in the Gutîi mountains, Muntele Băişorii southwest of Cluj, Moneasa west of the Apuseni and Balvànyos near Băile Tuşnad all have the odd ski-drag and perhaps a cabana for accommodation.

Another possibility might be to join a French company such as Terres d'Aventure (tel 4329 9450) or Allibert (Rte de Grenoble, 38530 Chapareillan, tel 7645 2226) for *ski du fond* or cross-country skiing in Maramureş and Bucovina.

CLIMBING

Climbing or *alpinism* is popular in Romania but there is almost no equipment available, as it all comes from Poland and Czechoslovakia at great cost; the way to instant popularity is to donate equipment to Romanian climbers. Currently there are, I believe, about 50 bolts on five routes, mainly in the Turda and Bicaz gorges.

The centre of climbing in Romania is Buşteni, between Sinaia and Predeal, and the *Club Alpin Român* has private huts at Coştila and Valea Alba (where there is a 900m conglomerate cliff, the highest in

Europe, among others) just to the west in the Bucegi massif; these are normally kept shut, but turning up at the weekend could be a good way to make contacts. There is also good climbing in the western part of the Bucegi massif, on Bătrîna and Turnu Seciului.

Here and in the Piatra Craiului (on the Diana Towers, Ciorînga, Călineţ and Padina Inchisa), Retezat (on Peleaga, Bucura II, Iudele and Slăveiul) and Făgăraş ranges climbing is on mountains, but all over Romania there are also many gorges (*cheile*) that provide good cliffs for technical climbing, mainly on limestone, such as the Turda gorges in the Arieş valley, the Bicaz gorges, the Crăciun (meaning Christmas) gorges in Deva judeţ, the Nerei gorges, perhaps the most spectacular in Romania, near Sasca Montana in the Almajului mountains in the south of the Banat, and around Vadu Crişului, between Oradea and Cluj, and around Polovragi and Băile Herculane. Another interesting area is the Buila massif and the Cheii valley cliffs, 30 kilometres west of Rîmnicu Vîlcea and rather reminiscent of the Piatra Craiului.

A useful book of climbing routes and maps is *Drumuri spre Culmi — Trasee alpine în Carpaţi* (Ways to the cliffs — climbing routes in the Carpathians) by Walter Kargel, Editura Sport-Turism 1988.

OTHER SPORTS

There is very little to be said about **water sports** in Romania, other than in the Black Sea resorts where it is possible to rent windsurfers, as also on Lac Herăstrău in Bucureşti. The key to a really worthwhile visit to the Danube Delta is definitely to bring your own kayak or inflatable dinghy, in order to get deep into the backwaters and see the unspoilt flora and fauna that have largely deserted the most touristed areas. Elsewhere in the country the Bistriţa river (in western Bucovina) in particular is becoming popular with Czechoslovak canoeists, but again the key is to bring your own equipment, which probably entails coming by car. Particularly in the Apuseni, where there has been a seven-year drought, low water levels have been a problem, as well as the pollution of the Arieş and other rivers. In other areas, such as the Parîng, streams offer impressive amounts of white water, but the large number of trees fallen across them pose problems to those who don't duck in time.The Dîmboviţa river, between the Piatra Craiului and Iezer-Păpuşa could also be an excellent kayak descent.

There is also nothing to be said about activities like **paragliding and hang-gliding** in Romania which does not apply everywhere else, except that the sports are virtually unknown (unlike in Czechoslovakia and Poland), and that before launching you should be quite sure where you plan to land, as there really are a lot of trees in the Romanian Carpathians. In summer a cart will go up to each stîna perhaps twice a week to collect cheese and dirty laundry, if you need help taking equipment up, but there are not many ski-lifts outside the Bucegi and other skiing areas. However with more modern paragliders it is possible to fly with a folding bike on your back, which gives total mobility!

See also the reference to Turism-Sportif on page 91.

COUNTRY LIFE

In the plains of Wallachia and Moldavia, and a considerable part of the Transylvanian plateau, farming is still largely in large-scale cooperative farms of the communist type (always with lots of free-range geese and hens) even though there has been decollectivisation; however in the mountains where you are likely to spend most of your hiking time, the economy is still almost entirely a peasant one — if synchronised scything were an Olympic sport, Romania would hold the gold medal. Horses (and some buffalo in Transylvania) are generally used for ploughing and hauling carts, rather than tractors, but almost no-one seems to have caught on to the idea that one can also ride horses. Most mountain farms are small and largely pastoral, with fields being used mainly for growing hay; a village's cows and sheep will usually be taken collectively to graze in the hills, the cows returning at night and the sheep, and shepherds, staying in the hills for the whole summer. The sheeps' milk is made into cheese in the sheepfold while the cows' milk is used for drinking and for yoghurt; as a rule, when you are offered milk it will be heated to sterilise it, although if the cow doesn't come into contact with others this may be thought unnecessary. Sheep are grazed on any open grass in the mountains apart from a very few areas they are barred from, and just about everywhere else is used for forestry, so that virtually wherever you go will be a largely man-made landscape; but there are many things worse than open moorland or alpine meadows.

Between the hay and cow fields and the higher meadows where the sheep graze are the forests (6.5m hectares of them, 27.5% of Romania's area), in which you will spend plenty of time; there is logging all over Romania, but as a rule I found it was remarkably unintrusive as there is not a great deal of clear-felling. Generally it's a matter of constantly thinning out trees of a certain size, so there are cart tracks everywhere in the woods, which is one reason why trail markings are so necessary. Particularly in the north much of the hauling of logs is still done by horsepower; there are also steam-powered forestry railways in some areas (see page 76). As elsewhere there is a gradual shift underway from beech and other deciduous species towards more and more of the faster growing spruce. There are still many forestry cabanas (or *canton silvic*) for accommodation when working in a particular area, but these are used less with the development of motorised transport, usually something like a portakabin mounted on a trailer behind a tractor. You might be able to sleep in these cabanas, but don't count on it; it is more tactful to pitch a tent nearby. A *pepiniera silvica* is a tree nursery; these tend not to be too big or intrusive.

You will also see dams in all the mountain areas, still being built at a furious rate where money permits; most of the major rivers systems such as the Bistriţa, the Mureş and the Argeş have series of dams on them, and the Danube itself has been dammed jointly with Yugoslavia at the Iron Gates both to tame this wild stretch of river and yield 2,140MW of *Hydroenergetica* power. Most of the schemes now under way are smaller, more local projects, but they are still changing the landscape on all sides. There are also microhydro stations that do not need a dam but simply work from the flow of a river.

Mains water is very rare; as a rule water either comes straight off the hillside or from a well. Toilets tend to be of the dry privy variety and paper is usually provided in private ones. Outside almost every house is a bench where old women spin all day and families sit in the evening to talk to everyone who passes. Unfortunately television is now taking over as the main entertainment, as virtually every village has now been electrified.

COLLECTIVISATION AND SYSTEMATISATION

Almost everyone who goes to Romania has heard the dreadful stories of villages being bulldozed and peasants being rehoused in dreadfully inadequate blocks of flats; thankfully this had barely got started before Ceausescu's fall, as once the Danube-Black Sea Canal was completed in 1984 his attention and resources were diverted by his plans for the Centru Civic in Bucureşti and his determination to repay all foreign debt.

Collectivisation was introduced from 1949, supposedly 'voluntarily' at first, but after 80,000 arrests it was enforced, with peasants surrendering all property to the collective farm except for their house, one cow, one sow, three hogs, ten sheep or goats and unlimited rabbits and poultry, all on a plot of 0.2 or 0.3 of a hectare. In addition to Collective (or profit-sharing) Farms, renamed Cooperativă Agricolă de Producţie (CAP) in 1965, there were State Farms

(Întreprindere Agricolă de Stat or IAS), model or experimental farms which paid their workers a salary, and also independent Farm Machinery Enterprises (Întreprindere pentru Mecaniizarea Agriculturii or IMA). Production declined steadily, so that in 1985 the tiny private sector (under 5% of land area) produced 29% of the country's fruit, 14% of its meat, and almost 20% of its milk. To increase the available land, in order to export yet more food and speed the elimination of the country's foreign debt, and also 'to wipe out radically the major differences between towns and villages; to bring the working and living conditions of the working people in the countryside closer to those in the town', so that 'the community fully dominates and controls the individual', the systematisation plan was drawn up.

This was to involve the demolition of 8,000 out of 13,000 villages by the year 2000 (affecting eight million people or a third of the population), with the remaining 5,000 villages being grouped around 558 agro-industrial centres or 'new towns', which were to provide more towns in remoter areas and to relieve existing large cities. These plans were scaled down before long so that *only* a quarter of the country's villages were to be abandoned, with all repairs and new building henceforth banned in these. By 1985 only one new town had been named, which was in fact the mining centre of Rovinari in Gorj județ, and by the revolution only 24 had been named. Counties took differing approaches to the plans, with the Maramureş permitting repair work on outlying farms and the Banat allowing reoccupation of houses abandoned by emigrating Schwabs. The only villages to be actually resettled and demolished were in the Ilfov Agricultural Sector, just north of Bucureşti's Otopeni airport; elsewhere there was some tidying up around the fringes of villages, which probably meant moving on the gypsies. The scheme aroused world-wide protests from the likes of Prince Charles, the real-life Ambridge, and Doina Cornea, a Cluj University lecturer later important in the early days of the revolution, and led to the foundation of Operation Villages Roumains in Brussels in June 1989, part of what was called 'the most remarkable humanitarian campaign of the 1980s'. Remarkable it may have been, but it was other factors that held up the project, as noted above.

Since 1989 80% of agricultural land has been returned to private ownership (and thus frequently to strip farming), which has been quite a windfall for those families that had moved to the cities and for the many villagers who now commute to work in factories. Already there is more livestock production, which will mean more natural fertiliser, of course; however artificial fertiliser is unaffordable, and machinery is still owned by the state IMAs and too expensive to hire or buy until farmers' associations have been formed. Most farms are worked by elderly couples whose families are in the cities (mostly attracted by the communist industrialisation programme), so productivity is unlikely to rise for some time. In the long term, Romania's agricultural potential is immense, as the land is highly fertile and well-watered.

Life in the stîna

To the Romanians, the shepherd or *cioban* is a symbol of their national folklore and guardian of their heritage. There are at least 15 million sheep in the country, every one of them spending the summer in flocks of about 500 in the mountains; each flock is based at a *stîna* or sheepfold, a very basic hut in a clearing with a *strungă* or milking enclosure of hurdles which is moved every few weeks in good weather or weekly in bad. Whereas in most other countries sheep are reared for wool and meat, in Romania these are seen as by-products and the real purpose of the flock is to produce *brînză* or cheese.

Thrice daily the flock, usually of Turcană sheep, is herded into a small section of the *strungă* and then passes through flap doors to be milked by hand under a low shelter and reach the main section of the *strungă* — this takes about 80 minutes. (At lower altitudes there will be goats mixed in with the sheep; they produce more and better milk, but they are less disease-resistant and need water throughout the day.) The milk, in a large cauldron, has *kaarg* or rennet (an enzyme from the lining of a lamb's stomach) added to cause the fat to separate, and after 45 minutes the *baci* or head shepherd begins the cheese-making process by rolling up his sleeves and ever so gently, in fact rather sensuously, pressing down on the mixture. The more solid part, the *caş dulce*, is scooped into the *crinta*, a large wooden bowl, to drain and is then wrapped in muslin and gradually has all the remaining liquid squeezed out of it by a flat stone and a long wooden lever with the *baci* sitting on the end. Eventually it will be put into sacking and hung up to dry for a couple of days, before being collected by cart. (Other varieties of cheese such as *caşcaval* (like Gouda, usually smoked, and less salty than normal *brinza*, *şvaiţer* (ie Swiss, but more like a Brie) or *burduf* are generally made in factories nowadays, and *topliţa* has never pretended to be anything but a processed cream cheese.) The *zer* or whey, the left-over liquid, is drained as well to yield *urdă*, rather like cottage cheese, which the shepherds themselves live on, together with *mămăligă* or maize mush, the traditional peasants' food, made by simply cooking maize flour with water in a cauldron, until it can be turned out on to a board as a solid block and sliced like bread.

I find *urdă* quite wonderful, and as it only keeps for a couple of days it can usually only be found in stînas. If you are particularly lucky the shepherds will wrap the *urdă* in *mămăligă* and bake it in the ashes as *bulze*. The remaining almost fat-free liquid is used to wash and sterilise the tools, and then fed to the dogs. (This is in fact a remarkably hygienic process, with all tools and muslin washed every time they are used and always kept hanging up rather than being put on a table; it is important to conserve water in the stîna, as they are always sited a certain distance from a spring to avoid polluting it.)

Shepherds work all summer for about L5,000 per month, but they have a reputation for being rather better-off than one might expect: in the Ceauşescu era and even nowadays there has been a ready market for black-market lamb. Apparently they all have very good houses (although there was a general mania for rural house-building in the Ceauşescu era when there was no incentive to invest in agriculture) but nevertheless they are always desperate for cigarettes. If you smoke, keep yours well hidden.

Each sheep owner will provide a dog for the collective flock, and these dogs are the worst problem for anyone walking in the mountains. Of course they come from broken homes, spending the winter in the family and the summer in the mountains, but the real problem is that they are totally undisciplined and are in fact encouraged to be aggressive. Romanian sheepdogs have absolutely nothing in common with our familiar collies that round up sheep on the fells, directed by whistling from the farmer sitting in his Land Rover; here the shepherd does all the work and the dogs exist only to drive off bears and wolves. Romanians in general, and shepherds in particular, have a deeply engrained paranoia about bears, which do indeed take the occasional lamb but offer no threat to humans outside the cubbing season. Because of this fear you will often be advised to camp at a stîna, and it is well worth visiting a few stînas to see their life; generally the shepherds are very friendly and hospitable, although there are exceptions.

FESTIVALS

In Romania traditional folklore and festivals are as living and meaningful as anywhere in Europe, but it has to be said that even here they are now in decline. Although many festivals are tied to the great feasts of the Orthodox church and are celebrated nationwide, others have pagan or secular origins and are usually more local. It is very hard to give any specific dates for festivals, as these depend not only on the Orthodox calendar, but also on the weather and the progress of the agricultural seasons; in 1991 the spring was very wet indeed and all festivals were about two weeks later than usual.

Both types really start with the spring, around Easter (*Paşte*). This, the great feast of the Orthodox church, is determined by the Julian calendar and is usually in April (on the 18th in 1993, May 1 1994, April 23 1995, and April 14 1996, by our Gregorian calendar), coinciding with fertility festivals celebrating the beginning of ploughing and agricultural work. These can centre on decorating the plough, or on celebrating the first ploughman of the year, who is of course chosen in advance, although he generally tries to resist his fate (or fête); the best *Tînjaua* or first ploughman festivals should be in Hoteni on the first Sunday in May, and in other villages of the Mara valley in Maramureş the preceding week.

Soon afterwards come festivals connected to the departure of the flocks of sheep to the hills in early May; there are Measurement of the Milk festivals (*Măşurisul Laptelui, Ruptul Sterpelor*, or *Sîmbra Oilor*) in many places about three days after the sheep have first gone to the hills. The best known is at Măgura Priei northwest of Huedin, but I particularly enjoyed the one just north of Hodac on the first Saturday of May (see below), and there are others at Borlova, near Caransebeş, at the Huta pass between Oaş and Maramureş, generally on the first Sunday of May, and at Bogdan Vodă in Maramureş on the second Sunday. There are others in June (at Sirnea, near Poiana Braşov) and July (near Săcele), which are too late to be anything but tourist events. Having traditionally gone up to the mountains on St George's Day, the flocks return either on the birthday of the Virgin on September 8, or on her christening day, September 12.

In June the first harvest fairs and *Nedeias* take place. The *Nedeia* is an institution dating from at least 1373, when shepherds were away with their flocks not just for the summer as nowadays, but also for the winter, when they would take the flocks south as far as Greece, and so had little time to meet anyone or have any kind of normal social intercourse; as they could not go to people, the people came to them, with inhabitants from a wide area meeting on an open hilltop for a market and festival. The extreme example of this is the *Tîrgu de Fete* (Girl Fair), nothing less than a marriage market where families would parade their worldly wealth in the hope of attracting a fine upstanding young shepherd for their daughter. This aspect has sadly vanished now, but the fairs are still great popular festivals.

The most famous *Nedeia* is at Fundata, above Bran, which is especially mobile in date (theoretically on the last Sunday of July but in my experience usually in early September), and others are at Avram Iancu (the lesser known one, south of the railhead at Vaşcău in the Banat) on the second Sunday of June, at Polovragi in mid-July, the small Tîrgu de Dat at Calineasa (near Scarişoara) on about July 13 (see below), the Girl Fair at Munte Găina (near the better known Avram Iancu, near the Arieş valley) around July 20 (see below), and the *Horă* (Round Dance) at the Prislop pass between Maramureş and Bucovina, on the second Sunday of August, although it was cancelled in 1991 due to the *han*'s burning down.

Also in June, on the 24th, is *Sînzîene* or the feast of St John the Baptist, with fires lit on hilltops the night before, and wreaths thrown on to roofs by people calling out 'Hai Maria la Sînzîene!'. In August there are several more modern festivals of music and crafts, as well as the Feast of the Assumption or Dormition of the Virgin on the 15th (*Adormirea Maicii Domnului* or *la Sfînta Maria Mare*, 'Great St Mary's', as opposed to 'Little St Mary's', her birthday in September); this is celebrated above all at Tismana where there is a music and crafts festival, but also at Moisei (in Maramureş) where there is a pilgrimage to the monastery, and by special church services in most villages.

In August and September there are harvest festivals, but these are particularly hard to pin down owing to the vagaries of the weather, usually being scheduled for the first Sunday after the harvest; some examples would be the Cherry Fair in Brîncoveneşti, north of Reghin, which should be on the first Sunday of June, a festival at Lainici, between Tîrgu Jiu and Petroşani, on the first Sunday after the harvest, another at Negreşti-Oaş on September 1, and the Onion Fair in Asuajul de Sus in western Maramureş around September 14. In early August there are also less traditional festivals of music and dancing at Călimăneşti (near Cozia) and Ceahlău.

October is a busy time for weddings, as there is plenty of new wine and little farm work. Things go a bit quiet until the run-up to Christmas; December 6 is best avoided as every family then traditionally slaughters a pig at dawn, and spends the day turning it into sausages and bacon. Pigs know what's about to happen to them, and the squealing is appalling. *Colinde* or traditional carols are still sung, but other Christmas customs are dying out. The National Day is December 1.

A village the size of Hodac has no less than seven flocks of sheep (and goats), each of 400-500 animals, so the **Measurement of the Milk festival**, on the first Saturday of May, takes place on seven sites in the hills about an hour's walk north of the village. The flocks will have gone into the hills two or three days earlier to feast on the new green grass, and now return in order to establish which are the most productive animals this year and how the cheese will be divided between the owners' families. The sheep are penned and then each of the 40 or more families take their sheep and milk them. The milk is measured by pouring into jugs of one litre (*cumpana*), then half a litre (*galata*), a quarter litre (*fortai*) or one eighth of a litre (*potoriţa*), which are all poured into a communal tub, to be made into cheese on the spot in the usual way (see page 108). Each litre of milk entitles that family to 24kg of cheese over the season (also called a *cumpana*), and any cheese left over at the end of the season is the shepherds' to sell. After all this has been noted down and agreed, it's time for lunch, with the cheese made in the previous days being produced, with the *caş* and *urdă* made that morning, made that morning, and plenty to drink. After which everyone climbs onto the carts and is taken home. People were very keen to explain that this was unique, being an 'economic festival', but I felt that most agricultural festivals could be said to be economic in origin.

A little known local festival is the **Tîrgu de Dat** at Calineasa, between Padiş and Scarişoara in the Apuseni (see page 300); the name is a pun, meaning the Festival of Trading both goods and blows, as this is one of those festivals traditionally given over to settling old scores, particularly over grazing rights. The rules are that no knives are allowed, and murder should generally be avoided, but other than that anything goes — sticks, stones, socks full of sand. In fact nowadays the festival is pretty tame, although it could of course flare up as it often did in the communist era; when I was there the buying and selling was quickly done and almost everyone was wandering around with new rakes and scythe shafts, which are in great demand at that time of year. Then everyone got on with the business of eating, drinking and dancing; lorries full of beer and meat for barbecuing can reach this hilltop quite easily from the Poiana Horea to IC Ponor road just to the east. There is no Moţi music as such, so the band of two clarinets and a drum play fairly standard up-tempo *muzică populară*, with plenty of jazzy improvisation on set phrases. The dancing is the standard shuffling in circles and turn your partner, with plenty of scope for incompetents and drunks. All great fun.

The **Girl Fair** on the 1,486m top of Munte (or more properly Muntele) Găina, on about July 20, is very well known and a major tourist event nowadays, in total contrast to Calineasa. Traditionally this was the meeting place for people from Zarand (noted for their ceramics), the Apuseni (woodworking), and Bihor (grain), and an opportunity to find brides outside the closed mountain communities. Since about 1983 much of the action has moved from the mountain-top to the village of Avram Iancu below, easily reached by bus from Cîmpeni, where there is a museum in the birthplace of the leader of the 1848 revolution, and crowded fields full of market stalls and tents. This is the place for buying imported T-shirts or having your fortune told by gypsies who use budgerigars to pick the appropriate cards.

Many people get no further than this, but the real action is still on the mountaintop; those who are really serious hike or drive up the night before and camp or sleep in cars to be ready for an early start, although the traditional dawn chorus of massed *tulnics* or alpenhorns now happens at midday for the television cameras. (I gather that the Swiss alpenhorn can produce more volume, more notes, and harmonies as well.) Many more people walk or drive up the 8km *drum forestier* in the morning, and large numbers also come on foot and horse along the ridges to the west. There is a permanent concrete stage for organised displays of dancing and concerts by the biggest names in Romanian popular music; there is remarkably little alcohol here, and the Romanian Information Service has its troops here (unarmed) to keep an eye on things. There used to be 50,000 people at the festival, and if the cultural chief of Alba county has his way and forces all the market stalls to come up the mountain, this may happen again.

SPAS

Romania has an amazing variety of spas and health resorts, which date from Roman times and are still one of the great strengths of its tourist industry. There are 2,000 mineral springs, a third of the European total, and 160 spas or 'balneo-climatic stations', of which fourteen are in the 'international circuit'.

There is an amazing variety of waters — alkaline, chlorinated, sodium-, iodine-, magnesium-, sulphate- or iron-containing, carbogaseous, and radioactive — mostly on the western fringe of the country and along the volcanic ranges of the north and the Eastern Carpathians, as well as thermal springs and *mofettes* venting carbon dioxide and sulphured hydrogen gas, all of which can be prescribed for specific ailments, or just for a general toning up. Spas are also now moving into complementary medicine with treatments such as acupuncture, ultrasound, electrotherapy, ultraviolet light baths, plant essence bathes, and sapropelic muds, and drugs such as Pellamar and Gerovital H3 have been developed to slow ageing. In addition many resorts, by the sea or in the mountains, are climatic resorts, with particularly beneficial combinations of ozone, ions and aerosols which can be recommended for specific conditions. These places are likely to be useful to hikers as they tend to have campsites. Usually the waters are free and you'll do yourself no harm by sampling as you come across them, although in theory you should take the cure for two weeks twice a year for two or three years running; in areas such as Maramureş you will also find mineral springs in the countryside, usually under a kind of summerhouse. It's not a good idea to put mineral waters into a plastic water bottle; use a glass bottle if possible.

Băile Herculane (the Baths of Hercules, where he rested after his labours) is the best known of the Roman spas and was also one of the most fashionable of the Austro-Hungarian spas in the 18th and 19th Centuries. Other Roman spas, now much less well known, were at Călan, Turda and Geoagiu Băi.

Among the best known spas are Băile Felix, Băile Tuşnad, Borsec, Covasna, Sîngeorz-Bai, Slănic, Sovata and (my favourite) Vatra Dornei, and the leading climatic resorts include Borşa, Buşteni, Cheia, Lacu Roşu, Semenic, Sîmbăta and Stîna de Vale, as well as the leading ski resorts such as Poiana Braşov, Paltiniş, Predeal and Sinaia.

The palace, Bucharest

Part Three

Romania Guide

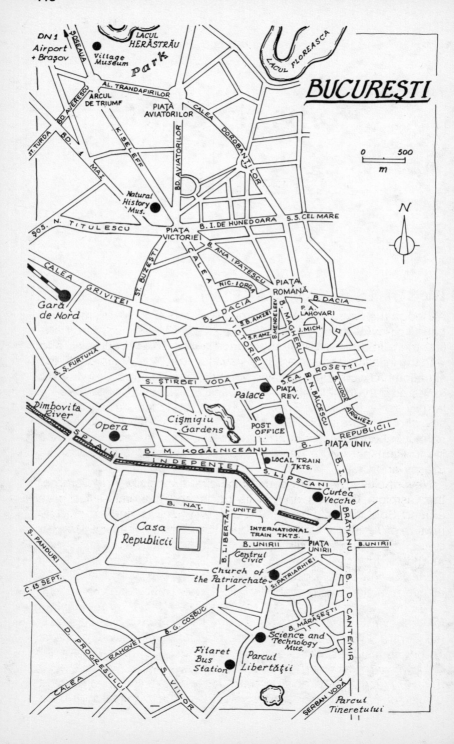

Chapter 5

Orientation

BUCUREŞTI (BUCHAREST)

Although the name of the city comes from the word *bucur*, meaning happy or joyful, in my opinion Bucureşti is best avoided; when I was first there in 1991 it barely functioned, like a Third World city, and with the inflation and economic dislocation that have set in since, the situation has worsened; it is also horribly humid in summer. Whereas in the country people have been able to resort to barter and to be largely self-sufficient, in Bucureşti money is all that is available, and so without corruption (far more widespread than before the revolution) and access to the black market it is hard to survive. Real life in Romania is not here, it is in the country and in towns like Braşov and Cluj.

Nevertheless there are compensations, especially in the area of the Cişmigiu Gardens and to its north and the embassies area around Bdul Dacia, where there are leafy streets and an eclectic mixture of *Jugendstil*, 1930s and Venetian Gothic/Byzantine/Moorish styles of architecture, with wonderfully ornate *portes-cochère* such as that of the Iraqi Embassy on Bdul Dacia. There are also small Orthodox churches, mostly from the 18th and 19th Centuries, dotted all over the city, which are fun to dip into in small doses.

Another architectural sight that has attracted a great deal of interest over the last few years, though for all the wrong reasons, is the Centru Civic, one of Ceauşescu's most megalomaniac projects. Three monasteries, about a dozen churches, and up to 20% of the old town were lost when the Uranus-Antim district was cleared (using the 1977 earthquake as a pretext) for redevelopment as modern blocks of flats flanking a ceremonial boulevard (just longer and broader than the Champs-Elysées), with at its western end the mammoth Casa Republicii (House of the Republic), supposedly the second largest building in the world after the Pentagon. It was a phenomenal act of vandalism, but it could have been worse, as can be seen simply by looking at the rear of the blocks of flats, far uglier than the fronts, which remind me more of Canary Wharf than of anything else. In the end the church of the Patriarchate (1658) was spared and other churches were actually moved, while as the flats and shops are occupied and the fountains come to life the area begins to seem more human. Piaţa Victoriei to the north of the centre is also far uglier.

Getting there

Almost all **trains** use the Gară de Nord, providing easy interchange if you don't want to stop at all. Other stations are used only by local or seasonal trains. The Gară de Nord is an awful introduction to the city, and for many people to the country. It is squalid and overcrowded, and although there is a Tourist Information office opposite platform 1, it is no use at all unless you want to change money.

International **flights** use the Otopeni airport, 16km north just beyond the ring road on the main DN 1 to Ploieşti and Braşov, while domestic flights use the Băneasa airport just south of the ring road on the DN 1. City buses, tram 5 and night bus 414 from Piaţa Unirii go to Băneasa, and express bus 783 (fare L25!) runs every 30 minutes from Piaţa Unirii via Piaţa Victoriei and Baneasa to Otopeni.

The main **bus** stations are at Filaret (in an old railway terminal south of the Centru Civic), Băneasa (near the domestic airport) and Obor (at a suburban rail terminal to the east of the centre, not that close to the Metro station of the same name); however it is far easier to arrive than to leave by bus.

Once safely arrived, the easiest way to get around is by the Metro (see map), confusing at first with its dim lighting and poor signposting, but very handy once you're used to it: just feed a L10 coin into a slot to enter and travel anywhere. Rucksacks are not allowed, but I had no problem with mine, although it gets very busy around 1600. In 1992 I was at last able to find street plans and public transport maps, needed only for reaching the suburbs.

Where to stay

There is a considerable number of hotels, from the Intercontinental downwards, almost all expensive and uninteresting; those near the Gară de Nord are generally cheaper. Private rooms are not yet widely available here, as Bucureşti is not a city like Prague or Budapest in which travellers tend to linger, but you may be offered rooms for about US$15 at the station.

Camping is not too convenient here, with the main site at Băneasa (at km 10.1 on the DN 1 between the two airports) being used as a camp for Somali refugees. Other sites are at Vlăsia 22.5km to the northwest on the DN 7, and nearby at Buftea 25km out on the DN 1A and the Ploieşti railway line (with about 15 stopping trains per day, taking 30 minutes) by a lake and near the 19th-Century Ştirbei palace, six kilometres beyond the Brîncoveanu palace of Mogoşoaia, 'the most important civil building of its period in Wallachia', which is a worthwhile excursion from Bucureşti in its own right. There may also be sites to the east at Cernica, by a lake on the DJ 301, three kilometres from km 9.3 on the DN 3 (three kilometres from the 17th-Century Cernica monastery, 'among the greatest complexes of this kind in the country'), at Pasărea, north of Cernica, two kilometres from the DN 3 (km 18) by Lake Pasărea (with the 19th-Century Pasărea monastery and museum reached by boat across the lake), and at Călugăreni, about 30km south on the DN 5.

What to see

Fortunately, the city is laid out on a clear north-south axis which makes it easy enough to find places of interest; to the north this axis is the Şoseaua Kiseleff, running south from Băneasa to the Piaţa Victoriei; from here it continues as the Calea Victoriei, with the road successively called Bdul Ana Ipătescu, Bdul General Magheru, Bdul N Bălcescu, Bdul I C Brătianu and Bdul Dimitrie Cantemir running parallel as far as the Centru Civic to the south. Other great cities have a river as an axis, but the Dîmboviţa has here been driven underground or canalised as it passes through the city; however there is a chain of attractive lakes in the parks to the north.

At the north end of Şoseaua Kiseleff, near the Băneasa station, is the Casa Scînteia ('Spark House'), which seems to be a Stalinist counterpart to Ceauşescu's Casa Republicii in the Centru Civic, but is in fact the base of the entire state publishing industry. Behind it are the Feudal Arts and Popular Arts Museums. To the east of the Şoseaua is the Herăstrău Park and Lake, with the famous Village Museum (Museul Satului); this is the biggest and best of the many open-air museums of vernacular or popular architecture in Romania. If you are going to be spending time in villages all over Romania you needn't feel guilty if you miss this, but if not you should try to see it, particularly the wooden churches from Berbeşti and Dragomireşti in Maramureş. The Şoseaua continues south past the Arc de Triumpf, a war memorial reflecting Bucureşti's pre-war idea of itself as the

'Paris of the East', and passes between the Geological Institute Museum and the Grigore Antipa Museum of Natural History (with a huge collection of butterflies, and a new Wallachian Ethnography Museum behind it) to the Pia a Victoriei.

Continuing south down the Calea Victoriei, you will pass at no 141 the George Enescu Museum of Music in the fantastic *fin de siècle* Cantacuzino palace (partially open in 1992 after restoration — Enescu's wife was a Princess Cantacuzino, but they in fact lived in a small house in the garden), and at no 107 the National Folk Arts Museum, before arriving in the large and irregular Piaţa Revoluţiei beside the Hotel Athénée Palace, which was the centre of the pre-war smart scene described in Olivia Manning's *Balkan Trilogy*. To your left are the Athenaeum, the main concert hall, and the former Central Committee Building of the Romanian Communist Party, and to your right Ceauşescu's Palace and the Congress Hall. In the southern part of the square are the National Art Gallery to the right/west and the FSN's headquarters to the left/east. Just east at

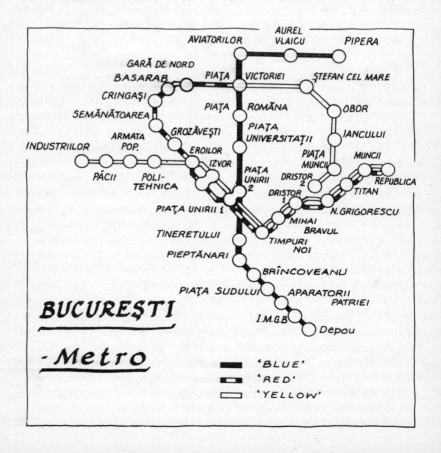

Str Rosetti 8 is the Theodor Aman museum, the most accessible of the various memorial houses of notable artists dotted around the city.

Continuing along the Calea Victoriei there is the Creţulescu church on the right, built during 1702-22 by Brîncoveanu's daughter and her husband Iordache Creţulescu (or Kretzulescu), with an unusual fresco of the Apocalypse (note that the church on Str Kretzulescu, just north of the Hotel Athénée Palace, is known as the Biserica Alba or white church). Behind this, to the west, are the lovely Cişmigiu Gardens, and to the south on Calea Victoriei is the Post Office; note that Poste Restante is cunningly hidden at the Officiul PTTR No 1, down Str Matei Millo around the corner to the left behind the PO, *not* the Poste Restante on Str 13 Decembrie (to be safe you should address mail c/o Poste Restante, Officiul PTTR No 1, Bucureşti). Further south on the left side is the Romanian History Museum, in the former Post Office building of 1900 (opposite the excellent CEC Savings Bank building of 1896); after years of glorifying the Ceauşescu regime it now gives up in the 1920s, and also displays the national treasury. Behind it is the Stavropoleos church, dating from 1730.

Further east are the Curtea Veche (Old Palace), the remains of Vlad Ţepeş's 15th-Century palace, and its church. Nearby, also on Str 30 Decembrie, is the Hanul lui Manuc, a genuine 19th-Century *caravansarai* built by an Armenian merchant called Manuc, rather in the style of a Tudor coaching inn. Just south of here is the Piaţa Unirii (hub of the Metro system and site of most of the main department stores), leading to the Centru Civic, the Patriarchate, and the adjacent Parliament building. A fair way south of the Piaţa Unirii is the Parcul Libertaţii (Liberty Park), with Science and Technology Museums, and the Parcul Tineretului (Youth Park), with the Cemetery of the Heroes of the 1989 Revolution, immediately beyond it.

Returning to the north up Bdul I C Brătianu, etc, you will pass Strada Lipscani, the nearest Bucureşti has to a bazaar area, and come to Piaţa Universitaţii. The Bucureşti Municipal History Museum is on the southwestern corner (also with a lovely *porte-cochère*), St George's church and the Coltea hospital (1704) on the southeastern corner, the University on the northwestern corner, and the Intercontinental Hotel and the National Theatre on the northeastern corner (if there is a play on directed by Andrei Şerban or Alexandru Darie, see it). To the north, just before the Piaţa Romană, is the main ONT-Carpaţi tourist office at Bdul Magheru 7, open from 0730 to 2000, to 1500 on Saturdays and to 1400 on Sundays, most unusually for Romania. (There should in theory also be a tourist information office at Otopeni (0700-2200), and others in the major hotels.) Further north at Bdul Ana Ipatescu 21 there is an astronomical museum (Monday to Friday 1000 to 1600) and observatory (Tuesday and Friday 2030 to 2230, for a different kind of evening activity, although there must be too much artificial light to see much).

Practical information

Other than the department stores around Piaţa Unirii and other shops along the main avenues, you may also find useful the Comturist shop ('the dollar shop') at 9 Str Episcopei (an unmarked mansion opposite the junction with Str Nicolae Golescu, open Tuesday to Friday 0800-1600 and Saturday mornings and Monday afternoons) useful; this is officially for residents only but you should be able to get in if you don't look too disreputable. Unlike the Comturist shops in hotels this does sell more than just liquor and cigarettes. There are also good markets north of the Ion Creanga Theatre on Str P Amzei and to the east of Piaţa Unirii. Beware thieves with razors homing in on foreigners particularly in the posh shops along the Calea Victoriei.

The British Embassy is at Str Jules Michelet 24 (tel 111 634/5/6), but its library and newspaper reading room are now at a new British Council office at 14 Calea Dorobanţilor, apparently run by an Austrian who speaks less than perfect English. Both establishments keep British shopkeepers' hours of nine to five, and the library closes in late August. The United States Embassy is at Str Tudor Arghezi 7-9 (tel 114 593/104 040) with an American Cultural Centre, also shut in August, on Str JL Calderon (named not after the Spanish playwright but after a French photographer killed in the 1989 revolution), and the Canadian Embassy is at Str Nicolae Iorga 36 (tel 505 956). Australians and New Zealanders should go to the British Embassy. Embassies are guarded by the Romanian Information Service and if you've lost your passport you had better let the embassy know by phone that you're coming.

International rail tickets should be booked at Piaţa Unirii 2 (tel 134 008, open 0730-1900 Mondays to Fridays, and 0730-1230 on Saturdays), and internal tickets at Calea Griviţei 132 (tel 507 247) near the Gară de Nord, and Str Doamniţa Anastasia 6 (tel 132 644) near the Cişmigiu Gardens. Air tickets can be booked from TAROM at Str Brezoianu 10 (tel 163 346/152 2747, open 0800-1800 Mondays to Fridays) or around the corner at Str Doamniţa Anastasia 6 (tel 150 499), and possibly from LAR, mainly an Air Taxi firm, at Str Ştirbei Vodă 2-4 (tel 153 276) by the Palace. Foreign airline offices are mostly along Bduls Magheru and Bălcescu.

A few streets have been renamed, in particular Bdul Anul 1848 which is now Bdul I C Brătianu. In addition Bdul Gh Gheorghiu-Dej has become Bdul M Kogălniceanu, leading to Bdul Dr Petru Groza, now Bdul Eroii Sanitari; Bdul Republicii is also known as Bdul Carol II, Bdul Ilie Pintilie is Bdul Iancu de Hunedoara, and Bdul Dacia has now been extended to meet Calea Griviţei, which leads to the Gară de Nord.

Excursions

Other than the monasteries and palaces near the camp sites listed above, the only excursion in the immediate vicinity of Bucureşti is to Snagov 41km to the north, which is very busy on summer weekends. There is a long lake here with watersports available, and across it a 14th-Century monastery with the tomb of Vlad Ţepeş or Dracula. It can be reached by rail or by DN 1 and DJ 101B. On another lake 14km to the southeast off the DJ 101C is another monastery, founded in 1638, at Căldăruşani, which is harder to reach by public transport, although not too far from Grădiştea station. There are ONT coach trips that include these places (about US$12 each in 1990).

Longer excursions might take you to the old Wallachian capitals of Tîrgovişte and Curtea de Argeş in the southern Carpathian foothills. Tîrgovişte, 82km to the northwest, was the third capital, from 1396 to 1659, and the main sight is the Curtea Domnească (Princely Palace) on Str N Bălcescu, as well as a 16th-Century church and museums dealing with history (mainly Vlad Ţepeş again), printing, local writers and the painter Gheorghe Petraşcu. The Dealului (Hill) monastery, three kilometres north, was built in 1501 in traditional Wallachian style and is the burial place of the head of Mihai Viteazul.

Curtea de Argeş, 34 km north of Piteşti at the start of the Trans-Făgăraş route, was the second Wallachian capital, from about 1350 to 1396, but its greatest monument, the monastery church, was built by Neagoe Basarab in 1517. This is one of the most totally over-the-top buildings in Romania, with twisted or even contorted towers and an intricately carved exterior. It is said that Mestru Manole, Manole the master-builder, was stranded on the roof and forced to jump off, to stop him building anything comparable for anyone else. Where he landed and died a spring appeared which is still there. You can also visit the remains of the Princely Palace, with the small church of Sf Nicolae Domnesc from 1330 with frescoes from 1384.

WHERE TO HIKE

I would suggest Braşov as the ideal base, although if coming from the Hungarian border via Oradea it would be logical to stop at Cluj first. Generally I think it's fair to say that there is little of interest in

Bucureşti for people who are more interested in seeing the country and hiking in the hills than in doing a tour of Europe's capitals.

If you have only a couple of weeks available and want to spend a week of that hiking, particularly if you want to sleep in cabanas rather than camping, I would recommend either spending that week in the well-known and reasonably developed massifs south of Braşov, such as the Bucegi, Piatra Craiului and Iezer-Papuşa, or the Leaota if you prefer fewer tourists or somewhere less alpine for a day or two. These can easily be linked together on foot in a circuit of four or five days starting and finishing in Zărneşti, Predeal or Sinaia. Alternatively you could hike the length of the Făgăraş mountains, the highest and most alpine of the Romanian Carpathians, and either continue to the west or return from Sibiu through the Saxon villages.

The Retezat massif to the west is my favourite of the alpine areas, with a greater variety of routes than in the Făgăraş, and it can be visited in a few days on your way out of the country via Timişoara or Arad. The Ciucaş mountains would be a very pleasant route from Braşov towards Bucureşti or southeast to the Delta, taking just one or two days to visit.

Two less mountainous areas that are well worth making an effort to visit are the Painted Monasteries of Bucovina, in the northeast of the country, and the Delta of the Danube; the latter is a trip in its own right, but Bucovina can be combined with hiking in the Rodna or Căliman mountains, both much less visited than the mountains between Bucureşti and Braşov. From the Rodnas you can also continue into Maramureş, the *judeţ* or county in the far northwest which is one of the parts of Europe where folk customs have changed the least over the years. Other areas I particularly recommend for their human interest are the Saxon villages of the *Altenland* between Sighişoara, Sibiu and Braşov, and the Apuseni mountains to the west of the Transylvanian plateau, which are also a paradise for cavers. In all of these areas you can walk between villages in pleasant countryside with quite amazing quantities and varieties of meadow flowers. It is also easy to link together some of the fine monasteries on the southern foothills of the Carpathians, although more by bus than on foot.

Those who have more time, or who wish to get off the beaten track, have the whole chain of the Eastern Carpathians at their disposal — parallel ridges mostly covered in spruce where you will meet almost nobody but have a greater chance of seeing bears, deer and boar. However navigation is harder here than elsewhere, given the combination of poor maps and poor trail markings. I have described routes through the Harghita and Vrancea-Penteleu mountains, but there are many more areas to be explored. There are also the smaller and more scenic areas of Mount Ceahlău and Lacu Roşu, which can easily be visited in a day or two *en route* from Moldavia to Transylvania.

If you have an interest in archaeology, the Sebeş mountains, east of Haţeg, combine the chance to visit the fascinating citadels of the Dacians, whom the Romans had to struggle hard to defeat, with walking in wide open moorland to the east. Nearby are the Parîng, Lotru and Cindrel mountains which I have linked together in a route from Petroşani to Sibiu: the Parîng is the smallest and most easily accessible of the alpine massifs in the Carpathians, and the Lotru and Cindrel offer more open moorland walking in almost perfect solitude.

It is possible to link almost all of the routes given, but if you want to sample areas further apart, they are never more than an overnight journey distant.

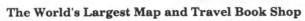

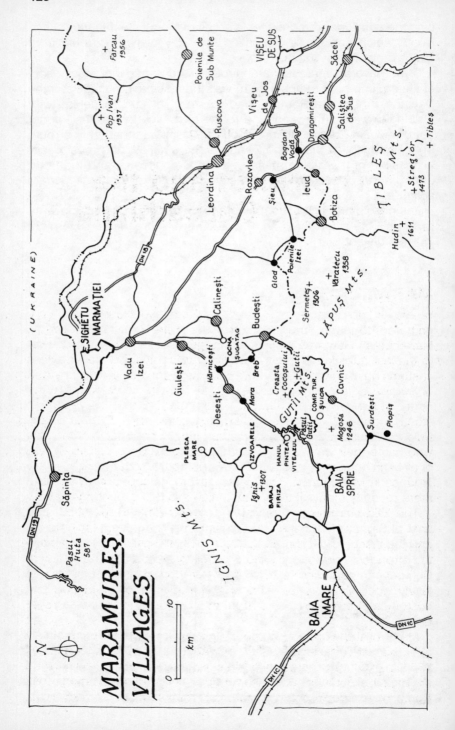

Chapter 6

The North and the Eastern Carpathians

MARAMUREŞ

Wherever two or more enthusiasts for Romania ('Roumaniacs') are gathered together, they will utter the catechism 'Were you in Maramureş? How was it? Has it changed at all?' Sadly the answer to the last question is these days likely to be yes, but nevertheless customs have changed less here in recent centuries than in any part of Europe except Ruthenia, the area of Ukraine immediately to the north. The Moroşeni or people of Maramureş have always been stoutly independent, keeping out the Romans, Huns, Gepids, Avars, Bulgars, Pechenegs, Cumans, Tartars and just about everyone else who came their way; they proudly claim to be pure Dacian, ie free of all Latin criminality and unreliability (in addition, there are very few Ţiganes in Maramureş). They were never reduced to serfdom, and more recently many of the villages also avoided collectivisation.

The 'Old Maramureş' consisted of four valleys to the south and east of Sighetu Marmaţiei (known as Sighet), the Iza, Mara, Cosǎu and the Vişeu, and it is the villages in and off these valleys that have the strongest enduring traditions of folklore and costume of any in Romania. In particular visitors come here to visit the distinctive and lovely wooden churches, and to see traditional woodcarving and costumes in everyday use (although more on Sundays than other days).

Many of the wooden churches date from the years immediately after the last Tartar raid of 1717, but others date from as far back as 1364, in exactly the same style; what makes them particularly striking are the tall slim towers and the rounded curves of the shingled roofs. Some have fine frescoes inside, but they tend to be very dark, without electric light. Like the painted monasteries of Bucovina, they have an organic strength that comes from fitting so well into their settings. They are kept locked but it is easy to find who has the key. On Sunday mornings, in villages without a modern church, there is a crowd of women listening outside and in the narthex or porch, while the men stand in the pronaos or nave, and people come and go throughout the service which can last for several hours.

In the afternoon the whole village promenades and with any luck there will be an open-air dance. The women wear flowered skirts, sometimes with heavy black and orange aprons, a black sheepskin jerkin and, always, a headscarf. Men wear black trousers, a white sheepskin jerkin with black pockets and trimmings as a rule, and a little straw pillbox hat which in villages like Budeşti are worn all day from a remarkably young age. The traditional costume differs from village to village; in Ieud for instance the mens' jerkin is black with green and blue flecks, in some villages men wear black sheepskin caps, and east of Borşa women wear red waistcoats. The jerkins are worn with sleeves in winter and without in summer, and can be reversed or folded neatly and carried on the arm. Women will only go out in skirt and headscarf, although some now pull a skirt on over tracksuit trousers.

The dances are very formally structured, with the first entry into the dance being treated as a sort of initiation; however girls are not permitted to refuse any invitation to dance without good reason. The dancing itself is not particularly spectacular here, generally being fairly simple polkas and so on; music is provided by two violins, a guitar and an accordion or bass. There are no dances during fasts such as Advent and Lent, but particularly good ones immediately afterwards.

We have a very great responsibility here to encourage the preservation of traditional customs without turning the place into a zoo or leading the young even more rapidly into 'Westernisation'; in particular we must encourage pride in the wooden churches because just about every village has outgrown them and built huge new concrete basilicas in Identikit Romanian Orthodox style, and there is a risk of the old churches falling into disrepair. This is a classic case of the need to 'step lightly' and spread the load of tourism over as wide an area as possible; I suggest an itinerary for a fairly gentle walk (an ideal warm-up if you've just left home) through lovely countryside between some villages in the centre of this area, but you should feel free to vary it as much as you like — almost all the villages are worth seeing. However you should be aware that Maramureş villages are very long and thin, as every house has its smallholding immediately behind; it can take an hour to walk through some villages, and you won't go much faster on a cart, so try to arrive directly in the centre. The hills are not particularly high, and in any case this route avoids the main crest of the Lăpuş mountains, part of the longest volcanic chain in Europe, starting in the Oaş region just west of Marmureş and continuing via the Căliman and Harghita massifs to Lacul Sf Ana beyond Băile Tuşnad.

There is some arable farming, but it is mostly pastoral, with fruit trees everywhere; there are also many small mines of non-ferrous metals and mineral springs. It is damper here than elsewhere in the country, with 140 days of precipitation per annum.

Getting there

The capital of Maramureş Judeţ is Baia Mare (Big Mine), an industrial and mining town south of the hills in the 'New Maramureş' (the nearby Lăpuş valley has also conserved much of its folklore, and there are fine churches in Surdeşti (the tallest of the wooden churches) and Plopiş); it is reached by train and bus from Satu Mare and Cluj (with through trains from Oradea and Bucureşti). Buses go onwards from the *autogară* adjacent to the rail station (two kilometres west of the centre), and from the Oaş Depression to the west (another 'folkloric' area), to Sighet, the chief town of 'Old Maramureş'. Sighet also has through trains from Bucureşti via Braşov but it is better to get off at Săcel or Vişeu de Jos rather than going all the way to Sighet.

Nevertheless, Sighet is an interesting place, if not as exotic as 20 years ago when John Higgins makes it sound like somewhere in the North West Frontier Province of Pakistan: 'I have rarely been in a fiercer town. Most of the men had guns slung over their sheepskins; the women were swaddled about with unidentifiable textiles and never spoke... It was not a town for the faint-hearted'. Mrs Phillimore also found it 'wonderful and mysterious like a place seen in a dream'; nowadays it's worth visiting for its Ethnographic Museum and its open air section east of the centre. From the *autogară* on Str Iuliu Maniu, near the rail station, buses run to all the local villages and west to Săpînţa and Oaş: Săpînţa is a compulsory stop for tourists in the area because of its 'merry cemetery' with its elaborately carved and painted headboards, and equally colourful rhymed epitaphs. It has recently been in the news because of a 'peasants' revolt', declaring itself a 'communist-free zone' and attempting to push ahead with land reforms.

Hiking directions

Although it is possible to walk between the villages in almost any combination you choose, I will describe one route starting at the Gutîi pass between Baia Mare and Sighet, and running east through Budeşti and Botiza to Ieud. It is easy to get here by bus, or by walking from the resort of Izvoarele in the Gutîi (or Ignis) mountains to the west; however I found that the Tatarului gorges, north of Izvoarele, the only andesite gorges in Romania, are now a construction site and will be submerged by a dam, and Pleşca cabana has been taken over by the workers. At the 987m pass (above the Mogoşa/Şuior tourist complex and cabana) is Hanul Pintea Viteazul (the Inn of Pintea the Brave, named after a famous outlaw whose coat of mail hangs in the Josan or Lower church at Budeşti), and a path marked with a red stripe heads east from the layby opposite. After about one kilometre the right fork runs to the left around a clearing, continuing as a track through beech and birch and then across a meadow towards the distinctive peak of Creasta Cocoşului (Cock's Crest, 1,428m).

Although the markings can be confusing, you should aim just to the left of the peak before turning to the right and up through beech (ignoring markings a little way off the path) and over rocks, to scramble up to the saddle just below the crest itself, with views of the villages scattered across the plain ahead. There is a 50-hectare reserve here, protecting various types of eagle and lichen as well as juniper and edelweiss. There is an easy route along the ridge to Vf Gutîi (1,443m) once you find the right route through the dwarf bushes; from here the main path runs southeast via Vf Gutîi Mic (also known as the 'Three Apostles') to the Neteda pass just north of the mining town of Cavnic. However I headed just south of east through dwarf pine and then a beech wood, into a meadow. Here I crossed the headwaters of a stream and picked up a *drum forestier* dropping steeply down through beech to fields and the road from Cavnic, about an hour from Vf Gutîi and five kilometres from Budeşti.

This is a large village at about 550m, but remarkably unspoilt; most of the roads are still muddy tracks, and many new houses are being built in the traditional style although on breeze block foundations and with asbestos roofs. In particular they still have the elaborately carved beam gates that are characteristic of this area, although also found elsewhere; they carry the motifs of the tree of life, the sun, a coiled rope (a symbol of continuity), the raftsman's pick and axe, flowers, birds and fir trees. There are two similar wooden churches, the Susan (upper) and Josan (lower), dating from 1595 and 1643 respectively, and a new church is planned as well.

I found it a delightful walk by road northwest from here to Breb, where there is a pleasantly ramshackle wooden church, and on through the fields and blackberry patches to the villages of the Mara valley (Hărniceşti and Sat-Şugatag are particularly worth visiting);

however my real route heads southeast from Budeşti and then east over a shoulder of the Lăpuş mountains, starting by turning left over the bridge below the Susan church, ten minutes up the Cosău stream from the Josan church. After following the left bank of this stream for an hour, turn left on to a bulldozer track, just east of some spruce and a bridge over a side-stream from the north. This climbs uphill to hayfields and you should then continue just north of east up a minor valley to reach after another hour or so the ridge with a cart track from the village of Baiuţ to the right. The track runs to the east over this ridge of fine open downs country and along a stony cart track for ten minutes to a saddle where it turns left to drop down past a stîna for ten more minutes to a clearing and site of a forestry cabana. From here there are multiple paths crisscrossing in the immature beech wood, but they all head north and then curve eastwards around the hill to emerge after 20 minutes at forestry marking 278, at a junction at the corner of the wood.

Although the right-hand track may well be more direct, I kept left to go via a *borcuţ* or mineral spring, along paths winding in a random way, but generally east-southeast down across a meadow. After about 12 minutes there is a junction with tracks forking both left and right, again both ending up in the village of Glod; the vague path to the spring runs just south of east and then drops steeply to the spring set discreetly on a hillside below the trees. From here the path drops down to cross a stream and turn left down the valley; after seven minutes it swings left at a junction by a cross and reaches the village of Glod after another ten. Opposite the *magazin mixt* is a path up to a wooden church in an orchard that claims to be a graveyard, all very rustic and peaceful.

From here there is a very minor road to Poienile Izei, but I took a short cut slightly to the south; continuing down the main street by a stream, I took a turning to the right after eight minutes, then kept left/southeast along the power line and turned right away from the stream after 14 minutes. The path climbed up into beech and then along a cart track along the right side of the valley to rejoin the power line and then the road at a low pass after about 24 minutes; from here it took 22 minutes down to the village of Poienile Izei (locally called La Poien'). There is a big new church here with the priest's house above, and below them, a wooden church with awesome frescoes on the left side of the narthex showing all the horrors of hell and the punishments in store for sinners, particularly females.

Returning to the centre of the village and turning right, you can follow the valley north for 1¼ hours to Şieu; it takes another 1¼ hours to walk the length of the village past the shop and wooden church, dating from 1760, to the Iza valley main road. There is a longer route continuing past the upper church for 30 minutes to turn left down the Valea Sasului to reach the centre of Botiza in 45 minutes. Again there is a new church here partially hiding the 17th-Century wooden church, apparently moved from Vişeu de Jos in 1899. The village is noted for its mineral springs and wood-carving, although there are fewer ornate gateways than in the villages around Budeşti. When I was first there local craftsmen were assembling a wooden church for the Romanian community of Caracas in Venezuela. Those with a genuine interest could call at the priest's house just south of the church; his wife has single-handedly rediscovered the authentic motifs and vegetable dyes of Maramureş carpets, motifs of animals, flowers and the *hora* and other dances in dark greens and browns, in a style rather similar to that of Lesotho, rather than the universal screaming red flowers that have taken over elsewhere. You might also wish to visit the Ruthenian village of Poenile de sub Monte, near the Ukrainian border, where they make very thick black and white blankets that are soaked for a week to make them fluffy.

From Botiza there is a road south over the Lăpuş mountains to Tîrgu Lăpuş, or north through Şieu to the Iza valley road; my route goes across the hills east to Ieud, site of two of the best-known wooden churches. This starts across the second bridge north of the village centre and heads uphill on an obvious farm track and then on a path across the last field to a ridge, although there is a lower route to the right. My path (not necessarily the most direct) dropped a bit, then climbed to the left of a farm before taking a very faint turn to the right where the track wheels left. This continues along another cart track and turns left at a sheep fold to reach a viewpoint over an absolutely enchanting valley of meadows and orchards lost between Botiza and Ieud, which would be a wonderful spot to camp. I went to the left through some coppiced beech and down another cart track to the valley, about an hour from Botiza. What looks like a track climbing up the other side is in fact a stream bed, but if you keep this on your left side you will reach a path around the head of the valley and go over the ridge to a smallholding; from here there is a narrow sunken lane which can be rather muddy (you can easily avoid this by walking through the fields alongside); very Devonian.

This reaches the rather dusty road in Plopşor, the south end of Ieud, after about 45 minutes more; it's several kilometres north to the centre, first the wooden Uniate *Biserică din vale* (church in the valley), built in 1717 after the last Tartar raid, full of icons on glass and also remarkably full of light. The priest here worked as a vet and undercover priest until the revolution while the Uniate denomination was banned; he is the son of Traian Bilţiu-Dăncuş, a well-known painter from Ieud, and grandson of a patriot of the same name.

There is a new Orthodox church to the north, and then to the right up a path opposite the hardware shop, the *Biserică din Deal* (church on the hill), the oldest in Maramureş, dating from 1364. The Ieud Codex, the oldest document in Romanian, now in the Academy in Bucureşti, was found here. Being close to the main road, these villages are visited by many tourists, particularly Romanians and Germans; most of the wooden churches have an explanatory notice outside in Romanian and German, but here, you will be pleased to hear, it is in Romanian, English and French. The many village children seem slightly corrupted by tourism, always demanding chewing gum and chocolate, but as usual they are very friendly and helpful once you get beyond this. The people of Ieud have many customs of their own; in particular they greet each other by saying *Laude-se Iesus* (Praised be Jesus!), answering *In veci, amin* (In eternity, Amen). For Lent and Easter this is changed to *Hristos o-nviat!* (Christ is risen!), answering *Adevărat c-o-nviat!* (Truly he is risen!). Then for three days at Ascensiontide they say *Hristos s-o înalţat!* (Christ has ascended!), and *Adevărat s-o înalţat* (Truly he has ascended). If in doubt at these times, just say *Adevărat*. Ieud people are noted woodworkers; it was a group of craftsmen from here who were brought to Bucureşti to restore the Han lui Manuc.

From here it is two kilometres north to the main road at Gura Ieudului (mouth of the Ieud) just west of Bogdan Vodă, formerly Cuhea but now named after Bogdan who went from here over the Prislop pass to found Moldavia. From here you can either go north to Vişeu and Poenile de sub Monte, west to Sighet, or east to a cabana beyond Săliştea de Sus and on to Borşa and the Rodnas.

Practical information

There is no hiking map of Maramureş as a whole, but there is a good English-language tourist map of the county, as well as hiking maps of the Borşa-Vişeu area and the Gutîi mountains. It doesn't matter which way you go between the villages, and there are usually plenty of people to ask the way. For some reason children all learn remarkably good French here, especially in the Iza area, and many of the older men here speak German from service in the Second World War.

THE RODNA MOUNTAINS

The Rodna and Maramureş mountains are the dominant massif of northern Romania, and as they stand between the wonderfully unspoilt folklorique area of Maramureş and the jewel-like monasteries

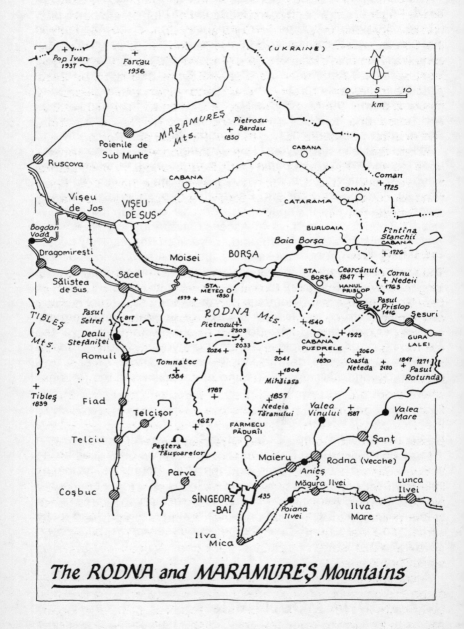

The RODNA and MARAMUREŞ Mountains

of Bucovina, they are ideally placed for tourism.

The central zone of the Rodnas is alpine, although not as extreme as the Făgăraş range, and it is surrounded by high moorlands which can be very bleak in winter, with long empty ridges running south to the Someş valley. To the west of the Rodna range is a limestone zone with Romania's deepest cave (Peştera Tăuşoarelor, 425m) and karst springs. I have been here several times and describe three possible routes, one through the wild and unpopulated Maramureş mountains from the forestry railway at Coman to Puzdrele cabana and Borşa, one from the western end of the Rodnas to Puzdrele, and one from Sîngeorz Băi north to Vf Pietrosul and Borşa.

At one time, the only chamois left in Romania were in the Pietrosul Mare reserve in the highest part of the Rodna range; however thanks to a very successful breeding programme they have now been reintroduced to the Făgăraş, Bucegi, Piatra Craiului, Vrancea, Parîng and Retezat massifs.

Getting there

The focal point of the area is the town of Borşa (675-700m), a very long thin town running into Moisei to the west, the mining suburb of Baia Borşa (Borşa Mine, not Băile Borşa or Borşa Spa, as shown on many maps) to the north, and the ski resort of the Borşa tourist complex 12km to the east. Buses from Baia Mare and Sighet usually run through to Baia Borşa, and the rarer buses from Vatra Dornei run to Vişeu via Borşa. There is a branch rail line from Vişeu de Jos to Borşa, terminating about two kilometres west of the centre, from where there are plentiful maxibuses to the centre and Baia Borşa. From Vişeu de Sus, on this branch line, there is the best known of the Romanian forestry railways, which is well used to taking passengers up to Coman on the Ukrainian border (see page 76).

Mrs Lion Phillimore, an Irish proto-hippy, vividly describes travelling through this area in a horse-cart in 1912: 'Borşa is a whitewashed little town with the smell of the East hanging about its streets and houses...beyond the folds of the green foothills that sloped together to the plains, black Pietrosul towered, lifting his gaunt bare head some 7,000 feet into the pale twilight sky.' Now that the Jews, who gave them that 'smell of the East', have gone, Vişeu and Borşa are somewhat less exotic.

Accommodation may be a problem, as the recently privatised *Han* at the Prislop pass between the Maramureş and Rodna ranges was burnt down in 1991 and may not have reopened, the *Han* in Moisei seems to be moving up to the pass south of the village and one of the Puzdrele cabanas has closed. However the *Han Butinarilor* in the Borşa tourist complex east of the town should be open for business as normal, and the hotels in Borşa and the tourist complex actually quoted prices in Lei rather than dollars in 1991, when this was not normal (L1,390 for the Iezer in Borşa).

Hiking directions

1. My first route begins with the train ride, painfully slow but very beautiful, from Vişeu de Sus to Coman, arriving there at about 1230; when I attempted to walk further east to hike down to the Fîntîna Stanchii cabana I was turned back by a sentry (just before the break-up of the Soviet Union), so had to walk back one kilometre to Catarama (you could get off the train here, but it might not actually stop, and in any case it's less trouble to go to the end of the line and walk back for ten minutes) and head south on a *drum forestier*. After walking uphill for 45 minutes and passing two small mines, the road kinks sharply left; from here it is possible to continue straight ahead up minor forestry tracks, mainly in stream beds, to the Vf Gîlu stîna (1,490m) and down to Burloaia, but it is simpler to follow the *drum* around to the left for about 20 minutes to the ridge (1,408m) where you should fork left on to a similar track and head down along a spur to the south.

This is all typical logging country, steep heavily wooded slopes often shrouded in cloud, with views of vast areas of the same terrain when the cloud clears. Eventually the track zigzags down into the Tişia valley (with a few short cuts at the bottom, only practicable going downhill) and reaches the valley road after about 90 minutes, ten minutes above Burloaia, the centre for all the small mines in the valleys above. This area is rich in non-ferrous metal ores, mainly polymetallic combinations of copper, lead and zinc. The mines are small and primitive in terms of technology and of health and safety — interesting to visit but not particularly safe.

It is also possible to walk in about an hour from Baia Borşa past the mines' 'flotation' plant and the Vinişoru valley with its mineral springs along the main valley *drum* to Burloaia. From here it is 3km to the southeast through Bucaţii to the last mine at Cornul Nedeii, just below some hairpins in the road, with a substantial short cut beside the stream. It takes an hour to walk up to the ridge route, just above the tree line and just below the summit of Vf Cornul Nedeii (1,763m); from here Fîntîna Stanchii cabana is 2km north, but I headed south into the large Cornedei (another version of Cornul Nedeii) reserve for black grouse (*cocosul de mesteacăn* or *Lyrurus tetrix*): the male or blackcock is black with a red crest and a lyre-shaped tail, and the female or greyhen is like a red grouse.

This is broad open moorland with good views to the Rodna range ahead: although you have to walk in through landscape scarred by

mining and logging, it is easy to put that behind you upon reaching
this splendid scenery. It takes 80 minutes along the track south, past
the site of the defeat of the last Tartar raid in 1717, to reach the
Prislop pass (1,416m), under a monumental archway with the *Han*
tucked away out of the wind to the west. This is also the site of the
well-known Prislop *horǎ* folk-dance festival, held on the second or
third Sunday of August. There are two buses a day between Vatra
Dornei and Vişeu which go over this pass.

In Mrs Phillimore's day this was a very dangerous road with many
robberies, but there were gendarmerie stations here and at the
Rotunda pass: 'Great mountains rose on either side, and a chaos of
steep hills and valleys spread out before it, while behind it the rough
grazing land stretched upward far into the distance to where on the
highest spot a beacon post was set, to mark the path...in winter. In
the moon's faint light the mountains loomed dimly, some bare and
gaunt, some sharply peaked, some covered to the top with dense
forest. They were alive too, strong magnanimous beings... Close to
the beacon post, a stunted pine stood alone and on its top bough
sat an eagle... Here, where in silence the mountain tops sang
together, problems and explanations seemed but ripples on the
surface of existence'. One might almost expect a Tibetan lama to
appear next.

The path, marked with a white triangle (which should really be a
red triangle) on a crash barrier, continues directly across the road
into the Rodnas. Before reaching some huts the path swings left to
join a track coming up from the road below to the east, and then
zigzags up into conifers. Once on the ridge this is a level easy
forestry track passing to the left of Vf Stiol (1,611m) and then out of
the trees on to more fine open moorland with the 'real' mountains
rising closer behind. To the right is a path to the top of the ski-lift,
but the main route continues along the ridge to the Şaua Stiol
(1,560m), with the Tǎul Hîrdau tarn and stîna to the left and a path
right, marked with blue stripes, to the top of the chair-lift and foot of
the ski-lift, with views of the Cascada Cailor (Horse's Waterfall) to the
west. Slightly further on a path marked with red triangles goes
steeply down to the waterfall itself and on down to the Borşa tourist
complex, and another path goes right to a stîna and to Puzdrele; the
main route up to the east-west ridge of the Rodnas, marked with
blue stripes, goes slightly to the left and climbs southwards. This
follows a cart track across the moor, then the right/east side of a
stream bed, passes below some slate scree to a small tarn and then
climbs up to a sign visible on the skyline at Şaua Gǎrgǎlǎu (1,925m),
probably under an hour from the saddle when the snow has gone.

From here there is plenty of good walking eastwards along the
ridge to Vf Ineu, the Rotunda pass and all the way to Vatra Dornei,

as well as a blue cross route south to Anieş in the Someş valley; to
the west the ridge route, marked with red stripes, runs along the
south side of Vf Cailor, unfortunately much less impressive than the
northern side. After 25 minutes this arrives at the Şaua Galaţului,
where the main ridge route continues to the south side of Vf
Galaţului to Şaua Laptelui (1,963m) and Tarniţa Bîrsanului (see
below). I took the turning right, marked with blue triangles, which
traverses along the side of a hill to the left and along a ridge, turning
left/west just after the unmarked path right back to the Şaua Stiol
and just before a viewpoint towards the tourist complex. From here
there is a choice of routes down to pass behind a cliff to the north,
and then swing north through dwarf bushes towards Vf Faţa Meisei
and drop down the last few hundred metres to the Puzdrele cabana
(1,540m) either on an old slate tramway, or on the blue triangle path
just to the right/north. It should take an hour or so from the saddle
to the cabana; this is a basic but very friendly hut, now privatised,
which has very little food available in April but should be better
stocked in summer.

    From here there are three routes down to the Vişeu valley and
Borşa; to the northwest is the *drum forestier* to the Gura Repezii area
of Borşa, to the north the steep direct path down to Poiana Borşa,
and to the northeast a less well-used path to the tourist complex.
The path north, marked with blue triangles, drops steeply through
thick woods for 35 minutes to reach a stream and an impressive
gorge; after three log bridges and 20 minutes it emerges into a field,
and then continues again along the right bank of the stream,
gradually turning into a village road and after 30 more minutes
arriving at the main DN 18 road by a bus stop and *alimentara* at the
east end of a long straight stretch of road, at about km 153.2.

The route to the tourist complex, marked with blue dots, starts above
the foundations of the old, demolished cabana northeast of the
surviving one, and begins with a considerable amount of rock-
scrambling and is then so poorly marked that you should certainly
not take this route late in the afternoon or whenever you're in a
hurry. If all goes well it should take about two and a half hours to go
around the west side of Vf Faţa Meisei and Vf Buza Dealului, arriving
down a farm track at the third house above the Han Butinarilor at the
bottom of the tourist complex (845m).

2. The second route starts at the Şetref pass (816m) at the western
end of the range, on the DN 17C south of Săcel and Moisei. Moisei
is the Romanian equivalent of Lidice in Czechoslovakia or Oradour
in France: at its eastern end is a circle of 12 statues by Vida Geza
(1972) in memory of 29 villagers massacred by fascists in 1944, and

the house opposite is a museum. The monastery south of the village is the site of a major pilgrimage on the feast of the Virgin Mary in August. Not far from the monastery, at the pass between Moisei and Săcel (705m), is a campsite and possibly now a cabana. Săcel has a station a long way east of the centre on the Moisei road. Meanwhile to the south of the Şetref pass are three villages called Salva, Parva and Romuli supposedly founded by Roman legionaries: the names very loosely mean 'Save the poor sons of Romulus'.

Joining a route from the Tibleş mountains, to the west, and south of Botiza and Ieud, head east on a muddy farm track, rather than the better track just to the north. After 18 minutes, where you might expect to go right or else steeply up ahead, there is a red stripe marking visible above to the left; climb hard up a sunken path for 22 minutes and then bear left along the edge of a beech wood and keep climbing for 20 minutes to reach a cairn on a hillock, hidden in the woods. From here the path goes down, zigs briefly right through a wood and drops sharply to cross a high saddle by the Capul Muntelui stîna where a direct, unmarked path from Săcel comes in from the left about 70 minutes from the pass.

The path climbs up the other side into conifers, forks left and then climbs as a cart track through fields to meet after about 30 minutes a path from Dealu Ştefăniţei now marked with blue triangles (at one time also marked with red stripes — confusing to say the least). The path continues for a considerable distance on the cart track above the Preluca cu Bulboci, an open glade slightly reminiscent of the *poloninas* or hilltop meadows of the Bieszczady mountains in southeastern Poland, continuing on the level where a path drops away right to a stîna. The track swings right to another stîna and then left at a fork below a shed and soon drops down through conifers, turning left on to a path as the track swings right 45 minutes from the Dealu Ştefăniţei junction. After crossing the end of the Preluca de sub Piatra the path swings left at a rather ambiguous arrow marker and begins to drop across a meadow and below some rocky crags. Here you have the first view of the alpine mountains ahead, a total contrast to the wooded hills and prelucas this far. From a stîna 75 minutes from the last junction, the path goes to the far left of the hut and drops steeply to a stream and a clear-felled area before Pasul Pietrii (1,190m), 20 minutes away. Here there is a dirt road from Moisei campsite to Romuli: if you wanted to hike up the road for about seven kilometres it might be possible to make a day-trip from the campsite to Puzdrele cabana.

The path continues up on the east side of the pass, forking left and then going up less steeply to the right into conifers; where the track turns right in a small clearing, the marked route continues straight ahead up a very minor path and climbs slowly and steeply for 20 minutes up to a meadow. From here the path goes right along the edge of a wood and almost south up to a junction sign just to the right/west of a tripod on the ridge of Vf Bǎtrîna (The Old Woman, 1,710m), at the junction of paths southwest to Romuli and Telciu, about 75 minutes from the pass. You are now above the trees and on to good open moorland, heading towards the peaks 400m above but also with views of the Tibleş and Maramureş ranges. The route follows the main ridge eastwards, passing three memorial crosses and reaching the Jneapǎnu ridge after an hour; if going north up to Pietrosul itself you can climb the ridge to Vf Gropilor and Vf Buhǎescu Mare (2,110m), but the main route follows the south side of this ridge for about 45 minutes to the Tarniţa 'La Cruce' (1,984m), to cross route 3 from Sîngeorz-Bǎi to Pietrosul and Borşa.

Heading southeast from here the route passes to the east of the rocky outcrop of Obîrşia Rebril (2,052m), with the very deep Repede valley to the left/east, and traverses around large basins on the east side of Vf Cormaia and Vf Repede, a fine pyramid- shaped peak of 2,033m, before heading east after about 50 minutes from a sign at the Şaua Între Izvoare (Saddle between the Springs) which claims that it is three hours back to 'La Cruce', and two hours on to Tarniţa Birsanului. In fact it took me two and a half hours, but only because of snow drifts which caused me a lot of problems; normally it should take 60 to 90 minutes. The path splits to pass either side of Vf Negoiasa (2,041m) and then goes over a small hill to cross a cart track running south to the Coasta Neteda *drum forestier* to Anieş. Fifteen minutes east of this track is Şaua Puzdrele (2,090m) on the south side of Vf Puzdrele and overlooking the lower peaks of Negoiasa and Repede, and ten minutes east of this the blue dot path to Puzdrele and the Borşa tourist complex turns left off the red spot ridge route. This runs along a spur for a bit and then drops down to the right into a rocky basin and down to the cabana and on as described above; the ridge route passes to the south of Vf Galaţului and after about two kilometres meets route 1 at the Şaua Galaţului, as described above.

3. This route starts from the rather run-down spa of Sîngeorz-Bǎi (435m), one stop along the branch line from Ilva Mica to Rodna Vecche, on the very attractive line from Suceava and Vatra Dornei to Salva and Beclean. Rodna Vecche has been a mining town since the time of Ştefan cel Mare and has long had an amazingly diverse population of Romanians, Hungarians, Germans, Slovaks, Ukrainians, Poles and Ţiganes. Mrs Phillimore described in 1912 how 'the river ran black from the silver and lead mines in the mountains'. Nowadays I gather that it has a particularly high suicide rate,

possibly induced by heavy metal poisoning from dust blowing from the mine lorries and making its way into the food chain.

The Statiunea or resort of Sîngeorz-Băi lies to the northwest of the village in the Valea Borcuţului (valley of the mineral spring); from the station turn right and then right up Str Izvoarelor (street of the springs). Here there are several hotels and cabanas (not the cheap mountain hut type of cabana), restaurants and shops, although quite a few of the shops seem to be one-person businesses that close for holidays in August. This is a shame, as there is a folk festival here in mid-August, but in any case there are a lot of men in national costume here at other times. There seem to be as many locals as visitors filling up their bottles at the springs, which gives the place a more homely atmosphere.

It is possible to follow blue stripe markings from the Statiunea up to the ridge to the west and then follow this north to the Rodnas, but I was recommended to take the next ridge to the east, from Cormaia. This turned out to have the advantage, for those who bridle at following markings the whole time, that the marked route takes you up on to the ridge and then abandons you to find your own way along it. From Sîngeorz-Băi I followed the main road northeast up the Someş for three kilometres to the Cormaia stream bridge, and then turned left past the site of a new private *han*, which is unlikely to be completed for years due to lack of funds. There is an asphalt road through Cormaia to a quarry and then an unmade road on for a total of just over eight kilometres to a turning right to La Farmecu Padurii and Cabana Cormaia; this is a small private cabana, closed on Mondays and Tuesdays, which probably caters mainly for day-trippers. There is another quarry five kilometres further up the main valley to the northwest, so it should be possible to get a lift this far.

The valley route continues, marked with red triangles, all the way to Vf Cormaia (see above); my route, marked with red dots, turns right past the cabana and then left after five minutes at the first stream (unmarked). At once the path turns to the right to zig up north through the woods and climb steeply up the right/east side of a meadow past two huts and then on a less clear path up the middle of the meadow, to a spring marked with a cross 37 minutes from the stream.

From here the path, largely unmarked, goes up to the left and climbs northwest to a ridge where it goes up between two 4WD tracks from their junction, past a small spring with log drinking troughs and above some scattered rocks, through meadow with an incredible quantity of grasshoppers and straight up to the main ridge — it would in fact be easier to forget the marked path, such as it is, via this last spring and instead to simply head for the ridge and climb directly upwards. From here the route passes a couple of saddles, steadily climbing although not as steeply as before; avoid the tempting sheep tracks along the east side of the hills and keep on finding your own way upwards into the dwarf pine zone. The route drops to the northwest with five small tarns on a shoulder to the right, passes a limestone cliff to the left and drops again to a saddle with some muddy little pools. Go up from here through a gap in a line of trees, where there is actually a red dot marking before a minor spring, and to the right of a highish peak.

After this the route passes to the left/west of the ridge with exposed strata and tors, and then to the right dropping below some rockfalls, but not following the main tracks down to a stîna below. It passes through some patchy spruce and above the stîna, then past some springs to a major saddle at the head of a basin to the east, and then past a smaller valley to the east. It passes through some spruce and scattered rock outcrops to arrive at the top of a virtual cliff above a stîna in a cirque, almost directly opposite Vf Mihăiasa (1,804m). A sheep track goes up around the edge of the cirque, with a brief push through dwarf pines, passes below a saddle to the west and then eastwards up to a ridge overlooking the last major cirque to the east. Red dot markings appear out of nowhere here, and soon there are also junctions with red and yellow cross markings from the Anieșu Mic valley to the right/east. Soon after the remains of a stîna or cabana and scattered rockpiles the path crosses a stream and reaches the sign at the Șaua Între Izvoare on the main Rodna ridge route (see route 2 above). It took me five and three-quarter hours net to get here from La Farmecu Padurii, which is probably about right for about 15km. The route described (so vaguely) is simply the one I took, following sheep tracks for much of the way; you could very easily find alternative routes, probably more to the western side of the ridge, but in any case you will feel miles away from civilisation for almost the whole length of this ridge.

From the Șaua Între Izvoare it took me an hour and a quarter to reach 'La Cruce', passing Vf Repede to the west and the deep basin of the Repede stream to the east, as described in route 2 above. Signs here tell you that access is forbidden to the 5,800-hectare Pietrosul Mare reserve (since 1980 a UNESCO Man and Biosphere reserve, like the Retezat and the Danube Delta, part of a project to establish just what the natural state of various environments is in order to then measure man's impact; it also protects chamois and various endemic plant species), but they neglect to say that you are permitted to use the trail marked with blue stripes which starts here. To begin with there are indeed markings but no actual path down through a rockfall, after which for a while there seem to be neither markings nor path as you make your own way left up to the ridge on a gravelly path to arrive at the Curmătura Buhăescu, north of Vf

Buhăescu (2,119m), after half an hour. The path climbs steeply on up the ridge to the north, crosses to the right below a minor peak and rejoins the ridge, climbing more easily to the summit of Vf Rebra (2,221m) after 26 more minutes. From here the path descends in rocky zigzags, with some easy scrambling, for 17 minutes and then climbs more easily, reaching a junction after 20 minutes and continuing to the left, with some steps and railings, to reach the summit of Pietrosul, the highest peak of the Rodnas at 2,303m (properly Pietrosul Rodnei, to distinguish it from Pietrosul Bardău just north in the Maramureş range) after ten minutes more. There is an automatic weather station here, with some good flat slabs of stone on which to picnic while waiting for the cloud to clear; when it does the views are superb.

Returning to the junction, the well-used path down to Borşa turns sharp left and zigzags down a long way into a rocky cirque inhabited by chamois, to reach the Iezerul Pietrosului lake (1,870m) after 40 minutes. From here you can briefly follow the stream before crossing to the left of the weather station on the lip of the cirque and joining the 4WD track that runs all the way down to civilisation over 1,100m below. This runs to the northwest before taking a hairpin bend to the right, through vast areas of *afin* or bilberry bushes which look like an Indian tea plantation at harvest time. Below this is a spruce forest, actively logged despite being still in the reserve, and just after leaving the reserve, almost an hour from the weather station, you should keep left at a fork in the track. Keep right at a spring after six minutes, fork right another six minutes later — these are well marked with blue stripes, but the markings soon get worse as the track passes through lots of small fenced hay fields dotted with houses; I think I went temporarily wrong after 15 minutes by not going straight on by a very minor path when the track turns sharp right, but after 30 minutes the paths were reunited to take a left and a right turning in the outskirts of Borşa on to Str Avram Iancu and cross a wooden bridge on to the main road just east of the new hospital, opposite Str Republicii 65. Whichever way you go on this final stage, you can hardly go wrong as long as you keep going downhill and vaguely north, with the town always visible ahead.

Practical information

The map of the Rodnas in the *Invitation* is inadequate for hiking, and doesn't cover the Maramureş range or the route north from Sîngeorz-Băi at all; however there is a Maramureş County Tourist Map, available in English, which gives a good overview, and a map of *Trasee Turistice în zona Borşa-Vişeu* (walking routes in the Borşa-Vişeu area), which gives very good coverage of the Maramureş range and the main crest of the Rodnas as far east as Vf Gărgălău, but again not of the ridges south of the main crest.

BUCOVINA

Strictly speaking what we can now visit in Romania is only southern Bucovina, Stalin having annexed its northern half to Ukraine in 1944, together with Basarabia (or Bessarabia). Before this it was in many ways the most oriental part of Europe, very much part of the heartland of the Ashkenazi Jews. There are exceptionally evocative accounts of growing up in northern Bucovina in the writings of Gregor von Rezzori (not himself Jewish): 'The Bukovina, today an

The BUCOVINA

almost astronomically remote province in southeastern Europe,...is probably one of the most beautiful areas in the world...rocky peaks loomed here and there from the green cones of the Forest Carpathians, and the poetic gentleness of the flowery slopes was all too deceptive in obscuring the wildness of the deep forests in which they were embedded...these tremendous, windswept black forests had at least as much character as the glacier-crowned massifs of Styria...beautifully canopied by the silky blue of a usually serene sky, the woodland was afflicted with melancholy, the melancholy of eastern vastnesses, creeping in everywhere.' Paul Celan, one of the 20th Century's great poets, was a German-speaking Jew also from Bucovina.

Bucovina, or Buchenwald, was the name adopted by the Austrians in 1774 when they annexed the region which at the time had no fixed name. It means 'beech wood' and indeed one of the strongest memories I have of the area is of the beauty of the beech woods as the sun shone through the new leaves in early May with an almost submarine translucency. (The hills north of Eger in Hungary are called Bükk, which means the same.) Of course the strongest memory is of the jewel-like monasteries of Bucovina, the external paintings of which are some of the greatest treasures of medieval art in Europe. As a development of the Byzantine style, it has been said that they 'far surpass traditional Byzantine art in scope, quality and imaginativeness, and constitute one of the most original contributions to European religious art of any time'. In addition to the originality of these huge bible stories, they are notable for the enduring brightness and freshness of their pigments, still not scientifically explained, and above all for the perfection of their settings in the landscape: what John Higgins calls 'the instinctive feeling for matching building with landscape: Voroneţ seems to lie in the arms of the woods and fields, and its brown, grey and beige tones blend with its surroundings whatever the season... The setting of Moldoviţa is even better. There is a spaciousness about it which Voroneţ lacks: the woods are slightly further away and the sky seems higher'. Georgina Harding describes them nicely as 'curled in on themselves like cats in the landscape', and talks of the deep roofs seeming to root them to the earth. It is very pleasant to walk between the monasteries, as the people are exceptionally friendly and the low wooded hills are not at all taxing.

The monasteries were founded by Ştefan cel Mare (called the Athlete of Christ by the Pope for his strenuous struggles against the Turks) and by his successors, in thanksgiving for their victories. His first was at Putna (founded 1466), and the last was at Dragomirna (1609). The frescoes were added from 1535 by local painters working with Byzantine masters and producing a rare fusion of the formalised Byzantine style with the verve and colour of folk art. The purpose of these frescoes was, of course, to provide a comic-strip education in religion and anti-Turkish propaganda for the illiterate peasantry, but part of the attraction for us is that they provide a picture postcard of their own medieval world. They have been well restored and are on the UNESCO World Heritage List. Most tour groups that come to Romania visit here, even if just brought up from Bucureşti for a 200km one-day coach trip; so it can get crowded.

Getting there

The main gateway to the area is Suceava, but the best base for the monasteries may be the town of Gura Humorului. Suceava is reached by express trains from Bucureşti and from Timişoara via Cluj, Vatra Dornei and Gura Humorului. It was Ştefan's capital and is now an industrial city of 86,000, although still set between the ruins of three hilltop fortresses. The main one is Ştefan's Princely Citadel (also known as the Scaun Citadel) off Str Cetaţii to the east, and there are also the Zamca citadel to the northwest and Scheia fortress to the west.

Nearer the centre are the ruins of the Princely Court, on Bdul Ana Ipătescu with the newly restored church of Sf Dumitru (built in 1535 by Voivode Petru Rareş, with a tower from 1561) behind it on Str Ştefan cel Mare. The museum is at Str Ştefan cel Mare 33, with art and natural history at no 23, and folklore at Str Ciprian Porumbescu 5 in the former Princely Inn. Other churches are the Mirăuţi (1390) on Str Mirăuţilor, New St George's (Sf Gheorghe Nou, 1514, with tatty external frescoes and better internal ones) at the Monastery of St John on Aleea Ion Voda, and the Invierii (1552) on the corner of Aleea Ion Voda and Bdul Ana Ipătescu. The tourist office is at Str N Bălcescu 2 (tel 987-21297 or 10944), with the TAROM and CFR offices, most shops and one of the hotels. The post office, market and shopping centre are behind to the north, between Sf Dumitru's church and the *autogară* at the corner of Str Armeneasca and Str V Alecsandrii, which leads north to the main rail station, Suceava Nord, passing the campsite off Str Ilie Pintilie. This is also the route to Dragomirna 14km north of Suceava, where there is a walled monastery founded in 1602 with internal frescoes, and a campsite.

Gura Humorului is smaller and more restful than Suceava, within easy walking distance of both Voroneţ and Humor monasteries. Its shops are more limited and, although the Suceava tourist office is quite good, the *Punct Turistic* here, on Str Avram Iancu, never seems to be open. There is a good ethnographical museum (closed Mondays) with captions in French. Accommodation is in the Ariniş Han (now *not* a cabana, if it ever was, and costing US$10 for foreigners in 1991) or the Voroneţ cabana just south of the bridge on the road to Voroneţ. There is plenty of space for free camping along the river here, as all over this area.

Hiking directions

My itinerary involves going by bus or train to Putna and then walking south to the Suceviţa, Humor and Voroneţ monasteries. Moldoviţa can be reached either by occasional buses over the Ciumîrna pass from Suceviţa, or by bus or train from Gura Humorului or Cîmpulung Moldovenesc, so you could if you wished go from Suceviţa to Humor via Moldoviţa and Gura Humorului rather than directly over the hills. There are all sorts of alternative routes and possible sidetrips in this area; it would be perfect for mountain biking.

Trains from Suceava and two buses a day from Gura Humorului meet at Rădăuţi, where the Bogdana church, seat of the Patriarchate before it moved to Suceava, is probably the oldest religious structure in Moldavia (1359-65). There is also a museum of popular technology, exhibiting agricultural machinery and the black pottery of nearby Marginea. From the rail station, west of the centre near the *autogară* and Tarancuta cabana, there are ten trains a day (one from Bucureşti) ambling around in the plains to reach the foothills at Putna, where there are village shops, a cabana and a campsite that knows all about dollars. This was the first monastery founded by Ştefan, who is buried there. It is unpainted, plain and strong, with a modern marble museum with fine 15th-Century embroideries and icons. Most of the fortifications are gone, but in its time this was the greatest cultural centre of Moldavia.

There are many trail markings here; in particular two red triangle routes seem to cross behind the monastery. You should follow blue cross markings from the station and ignore the red triangles (except initially if coming from the monastery); these run south down a village street to the east of the monastery, and then turn right at a stream and left over a bridge. The path follows the main valley mainly south-southeastwards, ignoring a turning to the left by a hut and small bridge after about 55 minutes, and then turning right to cross another bridge and then go on to the left. After another 15 minutes the route turns left at Canton Silvic 13, onto the *drum forestier* to Strulinoasa Sud, which passes various huts and turns left after 45 minutes at a small bridge, dwindling into a steep muddy pony track. After five minutes more go left at an arrow and southeast up into light beech wood to cross the main ridge after another ten minutes at Tarniţa Corbului; swing right along the hillside here, with a couple of forestry tracks coming in on either side, and go down parallel to a muddy track and stream. Another stream comes in from the east (ie if going the other way, keep left), and follow the muddy track which becomes a better forestry road running down a pleasant open valley. Almost an hour and a half after crossing the watershed you reach a bridge and a kiosk at the Suceviţa car-park, opposite the monastery.

This is very much a fortified monastery, nestling behind massive walls in the arms of the surrounding hills and seeming an organic part of its setting (climb the hill behind the graveyard for the best view of the complex). It was founded not by royalty but by Ieremia and Simion Movilă, in 1582, and painted in 1596, top to bottom, inside and out, on a base of green 'as intense as a lawn after rain'. The frescoes really are superb, with a Tree of Jesse on a dark blue background, the Virgin Mary and a frieze of ancient philosophers dressed in Byzantine cloaks (Plato with a reliquary of bones on his head as a *memento mori*) on the southern wall, the Ladder of Virtue, 'possibly the finest individual painting', on the northern wall (despite the immense overhangs of the eaves, the north walls of almost all the other monasteries are very badly weathered) and the Hierarchies of Heaven on the apse or east end, with rows of seraphim, angels, prophets, apostles, bishops and martyrs, all in order. The Last Judgment on the west or porch end was left unfinished supposedly because the artist fell from the scaffolding and died. Inside the smoke-darkened walls are covered with a religious calendar portraying the miracles or more usually the gory martyrdoms of the saints. Here too there is a fine museum of religious art.

There is a *han* with camping cabins 500m east, from where six buses a day run to Rădăuţi; the only buses passing the monastery itself are a couple to and from Moldoviţa and Cîmpulung Moldovenesc (leaving at about 0715 and 1545). There is also a good new private campsite three kilometres to the west, not too far beyond the point at which my route south to Humor starts — there is also a ridge route, marked with red stripes, from the 1,100m Ciumîrna pass 14.5km west of Suceviţa, but I gather this can be very overgrown. A third route, marked with blue stripes, runs along a lesser ridge to the east, starting along a *drum forestier* opposite no 99, just east of Suceviţa monastery, and finishing opposite Str 23 August no 54, just east of the centre of Gura Humorului, soon after passing the overgrown remains of a castle built against the Turks.

My route starts by a tiny shop and a bus stop, near the western village limits sign (as opposed to the '*Drum bon*' sign); it took 45 minutes on a horse-cart to reach the second forestry cabana, which would be over an hour on foot. From here the good *drum forestier* rapidly deteriorates into a stream bed and then makes a zigzag bend to the northeast and southeast while a small path continues due south. After about 50 minutes you will reach the watershed in mixed woodland, go down into a fairly young plantation and then fork right to join another stream bed track, with lovely mature trees to the right and immature planted trees to the left. One track comes in from the right but the route continues steadily down and southwards, and 16 minutes from the ridge at a junction from the left reaches a muddy *drum forestier* that gradually becomes more respectable. The valley opens out and after 22 minutes the route crosses a bridge into Poiana Micului, a very long village (keep right at the bridge if you go north). It took me an hour and a half to hike the length of this very linear village, and the same again to Mănăstirea Humor, also in a long straggling village of wooden houses.

Although its paintings do not quite match those of Moldoviţa and Voroneţ, Humor is one of my favourite places due to its incredible sense of peace and tranquility. It's a small unpretentious church without any real fortifications, founded in 1530 by Chancellor Toader (Theodore) Bubuiog, who is buried in the nave. The frescoes were painted in 1535 on a base of dark red, and the Tree of Jesse on the north wall has been badly damaged by rain and snow. The south wall bears a lively Return of the Prodigal Son and 24 scenes from the Hymn to the Virgin, composed by Patriarch Sergius of Constantinople after she saved the city from the Persians in 626 — the Persians are painted as Ottoman Turks, as if trying to reverse the result of the later siege in 1453. The west end, inside an unusual open porch, bears as usual a Last Judgment, with the Devil represented unusually as the Scarlet Woman. Again there is a calendar of saints and martyrs inside. It is possible to climb up the adjacent tower for a view of the church in its setting. Private rooms are now beginning to be available here.

From here it is possible to walk or hitch six kilometres down the road to Gura Humorului. Each day there are three buses to and from Poiana Micului and ten to Humor, although none before 5.30pm on Sundays, it seems. If however you are going direct to Voroneţ it is possible to bypass the town and walk into the hills to the west, although the locals were exceptionally unwilling to let me go that way late in the afternoon, such is their fear of bears and wolves (this in mid-May). If they are insistent you could claim to be going to Frasin, to the southwest. Just south of the monastery there is a fork to the right, marked with red crosses; take this road, turn right at the end and again right at the end of the village to go up a small valley. After 30 minutes turn left just before a small bridge to head south; soon the markings disappear in an area of logging, but it doesn't matter too much which way you go as you will soon dive back into lovely beech wood and in about 30 minutes from the bridge pick up the route on the ridge, marked as usual with red stripes. If you keep more to the right and go to the right/north along the ridge you will arrive after about 15 minutes at some rock outcrops, about 15m high, which can be climbed for a view above the trees.

Returning southwards, after about 15 minutes more the path runs into a meadow by a power line, with views of both Mănăstirea Humorului and Gura Humorului, and an obvious track down to the west side of the Humor valley. The path onward to Voroneţ goes to the right and south to the next hilltop ten minutes away and then down the left or eastern edge of a wood. It turns into the wood, fortunately well marked as there are plenty of other tracks around and ours takes a sharp turn to the right and then the left. It goes south into a side valley and emerges after about 20 minutes on to a track at the corner of a meadow, not really marked. After another ten minutes you arrive at the main road west of Gura Humorului, by no 138 and opposite no 133, and 100m west of a bus stop and the turning south to Voroneţ. From here you just have to follow the road for four kilometres, passing the cabana after one kilometre south of the bridge and then following red crosses through the village of Voroneţ, lying in another narrow valley.

Voroneţ, the 'Oriental Sistine', was built by Ştefan cel Mare in three months and three weeks in 1488, and painted internally in 1496-97 and externally between 1547 and 1550 under Voivode Petru Rareş. With its paintings on a base of azurite blue as distinctive as the blue of Fra Angelico or the red of Titian, this is the most visited of all the Bucovina monasteries. The porch was replaced in 1547 with a solid west wall to allow full scope for a massive Last Judgment that vies with the Ladder of Virtue at Suceviţa for the title of the best single painting, with the signs of the zodiac at the top, above the 'Deisis' or glorification of Christ and the pleas for mercy to God the Father of the Virgin, John the Baptist and the apostles, then Adam and Eve, Moses and the crowds of prophets, saints and bishops, above the scales of justice. The Turks, Tartars and other sinners lined up in limbo will doubtless be consigned to the flaming river of Gehenna where devils wait to drag them down to hell, while the saved jostle to get into paradise. The dead arise from their graves and all the wild animals except the doe and the elephant bring back the limbs they have torn off. The south wall is covered by the tree of Jesse, and the north, more weathered, with the Creation and Adam's contract with the devil — a popular legend. Inside are the usual saints and martyrs, and a portrait of the donor, Ştefan, and his family.

To return to Gura Humorului you can walk east along the right bank of the Moldova, past the cabana, Piatra Pinului Palaeontological Reserve and a rock carving of Ştefan cel Mare (I think) to the Ariniş han and a pedestrian suspension bridge across the river. (You can also get here by a path from Voroneţ over the Piatra Soimului, marked with blue crosses and supposedly taking four hours!) If you cross the bridge, turn right through the Dendrological Park (arboretum), cross the Humor River on to Str Primăverii and turn left on to Str M Eminescu, you will arrive, across a level crossing and a lorry park, at the Bucovina Restaurant opposite Str Avram Iancu.

You should also make an effort to see Moldoviţa. As already mentioned there are a few buses from Suceviţa and a few more from Cîmpulung Moldovenesc and Gura Humorului. There are trains on a branch line from Vama (meaning customs post), which connects with a narrow-gauge forestry line heading north to Argel and the Huţul country. Whichever way you go, you should get off at Vatra Moldoviţei, six kilometres south of Moldoviţa. It should also be possible to follow yellow stripe (or red triangle) markings from the bridge south of Putna monastery to Moldoviţa. The monastery and campsite are just to the north of the Vatra Moldoviţei crossroads; the monastery was founded by the Voivode Petru Rareş in 1532 and painted five years later. It is surrounded by six-metre walls, and the church is painted on a predominently blue and yellow base, with a Last Judgment (with Herod being dragged to hell by his beard) in an open porch as at Humor, and the Tree of Jesse, the Hymn to the Virgin and the siege of Constantinople on the south wall. Inside in the pronaos are paintings of the Virgin and the calendar of saints; in the naos is a fine iconostasis or screen, glowing blue and gold, and paintings of the donors, Petru and his wife Elena with their two children, with scenes of the life of Christ and the Military Saints. The museum contains Petru's throne and the much vaunted Golden Apple awarded in 1975 by the International Federation of Journalists and Travel Writers (FIJET).

The smallest of the painted monasteries is at Arbore, 11km west of Milisauti, between Suceava and Rădăuţi; there are late afternoon buses from both Suceava and Gura Humorului. You could walk or hitch from Humor via Solca, or walk following red triangle markings from Poiana Micului to Solca. It was founded by a general named Luca Arbore in 1503 and painted on a green base in 1541, with the Last Judgment and Siege of Constantinople on the south wall and scenes from Genesis and the lives of the saints on the west wall.

Practical information and moving on

There is an English language booklet describing the attractions of Suceava county with a very limited map, which mistakenly shows a road between Suceviţa and Poiana Micului. Vatra Dornei and the Căliman mountains, in the southwestern corner of the Judeţ, are

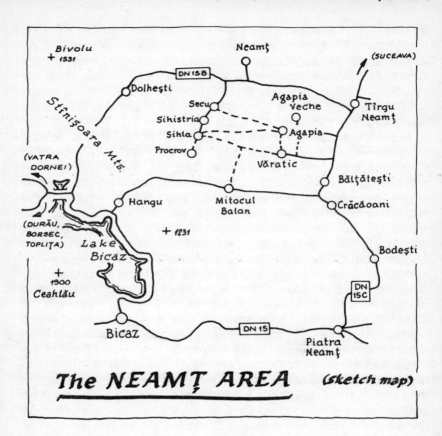

Bivolu
+ 1531

Neamţ

(SUCEAVA)

DN 15B

Dolheşti

Secu
Sihistria
Sihla
Procrov

Agapia
Veche

Agapia

Tîrgu
Neamţ

(VATRA
DORNEI)

Stînişoara Mts.

Văratic

Bălţăteşti

(DURĂU,
BORSEC,
TOPLIŢA)

Hangu

Mitocul
Balan

Crăcăoani

+ 1231

Lake
Bicaz

Bodeşti

+ 1900
Ceahlău

DN
15C

Bicaz

DN 15

Piatra
Neamţ

The NEAMŢ AREA   (sketch map)

covered in the *Invitation* and the next section of this book; the Rarău-Giumalău massif, between Vatra Dornei and Cîmpulung Moldovenesc, is also covered in the *Invitation*. I walked up the 14km road from Cîmpulung Est station (620m) to the Rarău cabana (1,520m), the multi-storey youth hotel type of place, with two-bed rooms; there was too much snow to take the red stripe route west to the Giumalău cabana and another at the 1,096m Mestecăniş pass, or east to the Slătioara Secular (ie centuries old) Forest of 50m high firs and spruces, with spurge flax (*Daphne cneorum*), spread between 800m and 1,300m altitude. I did manage to see the geological reserve of Pietrele Doamnei (The Lady's Rocks), 70m high Gothic towers of limestone with Mesozoic fossils. Then I walked on down the 11.5km road, marked with blue dots, to Chiril, at 740m in the Bistriţa valley just east of the Zugreni gorges and cabana. The DN 17B runs southeast to Lake Bicaz and Ceahlău (see relevant pages) through what John Higgins aptly calls 'one of the best areas of the Carpathians...bright green alpine meadows, cows fat on the lush grass the rains nurture, regular villages with blue Wallach houses and meticulously carved covered front gates...just as comfortable and gentle as the mountains close to Russia (in fact Ukraine) were menacing'. There is much local mine traffic, but hitching is hard and there are not many buses.

South of Suceava and east of Lake Bicaz lies another knot of monasteries and nunneries that are also well worth visiting, although less famous than the painted monasteries. The jumping-off point is Tîrgu Neamţ (German Market, although in fact it's never been a German settlement), between Suceava and Piatra Neamţ (German Rock, also never German) on the DN 15C; this is a fairly dull town with a ruined medieval hilltop citadel and modern rail and bus stations hidden in backstreets to the east of the centre (there is a branch line to Paşcani, although the *Rough Guide* specifically denies it, and a daily bus to Gura Humorului, with others to Suceava, Piatra Neamţ and Durău as well as to Agapia, Văratic and Sihistria).

Neamţ monastery, 17km west on the road to Durău and Ceahlău, is the oldest monastery of Moldavia and its greatest cultural centre, with an old printing house; the present church was built by Ştefan in 1497. There is also a bison reserve here, and mineral springs. Returning south to the main DN 15B and going a couple of kilometres west, you will come to an asphalted turning south to Secu, Sihistria and Sihla monasteries, much smaller hermitages built between 1602 and 1813 and tucked away in the foothills of the Stînişoarei mountains. The road has only recently reached Sihla, ten kilometres from the main road, and they are building a new guest-house, but they promise me there will still only be ten monks there. This is a particularly tranquil spot, built into the side of a cliff with the cave of Sf Teodora behind hidden among some weird outcrops.

From here you should follow a path marked with blue dots for two hours to the Văratic nunnery, founded in 1808. Both here and at Agapia the nuns, although vowed to poverty themselves, are allowed to live in houses built for them by their families, lovely vernacular buildings painted pale blue, with glassed-in balconies seemingly supported by all the firewood jammed in underneath. They are also let out to Romanians who come here for holidays. The monastery buildings seem very Mediterranean, painted gleaming white and set amid beautiful flower beds, while the church is much more incense-filled and devotional in atmosphere than most of the painted monasteries.

About seven kilometres north up a rough *drum* lies the similar Agapia nunnery, also big and bustling, surrounded by nuns' houses with flaps to protect the flights of steps from the snow, and with a han and a hotel above an *alimentară* outside. There is also a 30-

minute walk north to Agapia Veche or Agapia din Deal (Old or on the Hill, dating from 1644) (turning right at an unmarked junction after ten minutes) — this is totally different, a tranquil spot where the nuns can take time to notice you (when I arrived it was raining stair-rods and I was sickening for a fever; they took one look at me and sent me straight to the kitchen for much-needed soup). From the main monastery, as from Văratic, there is an asphalt link to the main road and you can return to Tîrgu Neamţ by bus; there are also paths to Secu and Sihla.

THE CĂLIMAN MOUNTAINS

With a main ridge of about 50km length and a maximum altitude of 2,100m, this is the main volcanic zone of the Carpathians, part of a chain running from Oaş to Băile Tuşnad; in particular the weird anthropomorphic rocks called the 'Doisprezece Apostoli' (Twelve Apostles), on the rim of the main crater (ten kilometres across) are a much-visited Natural Reservation. In general this is open country ideal for pony-trekking which should soon be available here (see page 97).

Getting there

My route runs from Răstoliţa, a minor station in the Mureş valley, with 14 slow trains a day, northwards to Gura Haitii, for a bus to Vatra Dornei, the main centre of the area, as well as a short link to the Negrişoara riding school. It is possible to walk north from Hodac, site of a Measurement of the Milk festival (see page 111), to Răstoliţa following blue cross markings over very pleasant easy hills with a familiar mix of meadows and woods, mainly beech.

Vatra Dornei is a very relaxed and stylish spa and climatic resort at 800m on the secondary rail line from Suceava to Beclean, the route from Bucovina to Transylvania. There are buses to and from Suceava, Botoşani and Iaşi to the east, Piatra Neamţ and Tîrgu Neamţ, Roman and Bacau to the southeast, Bistriţa and Dej to the west, and two a day north over the Prislop pass to Vişeu in Maramureş. It has two museums, one on Str M Eminescu opposite the post office and one by the spa or *staţie* buildings which are being nicely restored, and a dendrological reserve (or arboretum), hotels and the Runc campsite at km 146 just west on the DN 17. Vatra Dornei Băi station is most convenient for the *autogară* and shops, and from this station there are hiking signs onwards to the Suhard and Rodna mountains to the northwest and to the Rarău mountains to the northeast.

Hiking directions

The first stage of this hike is liable to be affected by the construction of a dam, which means that at the moment there is plenty of traffic to take you some of the way up the forestry roads, but that what's left of the forestry railway may soon be flooded; in any case this no longer runs up the Tiha valley, as shown in the *Invitation*, but does run from Secu up the Scurta valley.

From the Răstoliţa railway station, turn right along the left/south bank of the Mureş to join the forestry road from Poiana Iod and

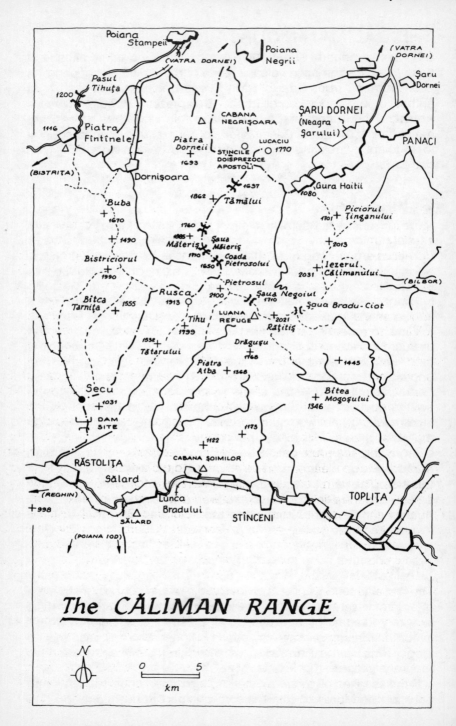

The CĂLIMAN RANGE

N

0   5

km

Hodac and cross the river by the old narrow-gauge railway bridge and continue to the right/east to the centre of the village, where the shop and *cofetărie* never seem to be open. Turn left here up the *drum forestier* and if possible get a lift up to the dam site or beyond; after four kilometres turn left off the route east, marked with blue dots, to a ridge route north from Lunca Bradului. The route north, marked with blue crosses and triangles, follows a *drum forestier* up the old rail line to the dam site and on above the future water level to Secu at the meeting of the Tiha and Scurta valleys. Here you may still see narrow-gauge steam locos working logging trains up the Scurta valley. Take the road to the right or northeast up the Tiha valley, marked with blue crosses, for about seven kilometres past some amazing berry bushes. At a forestry cabana a blue triangle route turns right to Vf Rusca, and my blue cross route continues just east of north for 50 minutes to the end of the *drum forestier*, and on uphill between the two valleys that meet here. From here the path is quite narrow but is not too steep for too long and only takes 25 minutes to climb through spruce to the main ridge.

This stony ridge track, marked with blue and red stripes, has been known as the Maria-Theresa road since Hapsburg times. Turn right to climb to a clearing below the double peak of Rusca (1,913m) and then around its north side; the path continues to climb to the dwarf pine level, with views of the Dorna valley to the north and Pietrosul and Măieriş ahead to the northeast. There is a clearing with a spring here which would make a slightly rocky camping place. The path swings south around the head of a valley, all pretty much on the level, passing another spring, and an hour after reaching the ridge arrives at a cross with picnic benches.

From here the route passes well below Pietrosul on the north side, and there is no clear or marked route up to the 2,100m summit from this side. The path continues easily on the level for 50 minutes to the 1,650m Coada Pietrosului saddle where it meets a circular route marked with red dots from Neagra Şarului and Gura Haitii via the Twelve Apostles (to the left/northwest) and Vf Cerbuc or Călimanul Cerbului (to the right/southeast), as well as a path marked with yellow dots that soon joins a *drum forestier* to Dornişoara.

Pietrosul is a pure black mountain that seems to absorb the sunlight and reflect none: it always seems as if there is a cloud over it. To reach the summit you should take the red dot path to the right down into the valley and then climb up the left side of the stream before swinging left up the ridge. Note that there is no longer a Negoiu cabana a bit further along this red dot path, although there is Luana refuge a bit further still, just before the Vt Răţitiş mine, which has taken off the entire hilltop, being solid sulphur. Apparently they are now using better French techniques, but the damage is done. The stream through Gura Haitii is also badly polluted.

From here you should follow the red dots left to the Twelve Apostles; this route passes to the east side of Vf Măieriş (1,885m) and along the western side of the main volcanic crater, passing various minor peaks before reaching Tămău (1,862m) about an hour and a half after leaving the junction. It continues across dry heathery moor with dwarf pines and other bushes, rather hard to follow at times, crosses a blue cross route from Dornişoara to Gura Haitii and climbs up a bit in young spruce to reach another picnic bench after roughly another hour. This would be a good place to camp; there is a spring about 50m below this to the right. The path climbs into a meadow (with gentians) and up after 22 minutes to a summit marker at the junction of the blue dot path right to Gura Haitii. The path swings leftwards here and then right to reach the Twelve Apostles in 13 minutes; these are huge monoliths on the skyline, and from most sides it is obvious why they are so called, as they really do look like heads bowed in prayer. Other famous anthropomorphic rocks in this area are 'Nefertiti' on Vf Tihu and 'Caesar' on Vf Tămău; I don't generally share the Romanian fascination with these things, but the Apostles are worth the detour.

The red dot path onwards passes quite a way below the Apostles on the east side, and just below a huge beetle-browed philosopher at the edge of the meadow to go through more dwarf pines to Vf Lucaciu and down to Neagra Şarului; however I returned to the summit marker and took the blue dot route down to Gura Haitii. This is a fairly narrow path down through young spruce for almost 30 minutes before it emerges at the top of a meadow and then hayfields (rather pastoral Swiss scenery) along the Piciorul Haitii ridge. The route here is fairly clearly marked on isolated trees except for the final stage where you should go to the right to then go down along the edge of some trees and then cross back to the left below a spring to pass through a wicket gate by a hut and then another by a sign and a bridge on the road, reached 40 minutes after entering the meadow. (I also once took a cart track to the left off the ridge to reach the valley road below Gura Haitii, but as it finished in a farmyard and I ended up climbing over too many fences, I suggest you keep to the marked route.)

Across this bridge is a *magazin forestier*, and to the left of it is the cabana of the Botoşani Ecologists' Club; they are great hosts, but are dissidents within the Romanian ecological movement as they disdain politics and prefer to concentrate on enjoying the great outdoors, and when resources allow introducing others to it. There are four buses a day to Vatra Dornei, at about 0700, 1430, 1700 and 2100, turning around about 100m down the left bank from the bridge.

It is also possible to go from the Twelve Apostles down to the Negrişoara valley to reach the School of Equestrian Mountain Guides (see page 97), but this is a very informal route. It begins a bit to the southwest of the Apostles by dropping for about ten minutes through bushes to an obvious saddle. Here the markings disappear, but the better of two possible routes seems to be to turn right and then go to the left around a hill, before gradually picking up a bigger path and ending up heading northwestwards down a stream bed to reach a *drum forestier* in under an hour. From here it takes about 15 minutes to reach Negrişoara cabana where the school is based. From here there are ten kilometres of good forestry road to Poiana Negrii, where there is an *alimentară* (closed on Thursdays). There is very little traffic, except for a milk lorry that goes down at about 0500! If you want to camp and wait for this, there is a good mineral spring in a 'summer house' 18 minutes down the valley from the cabana. From Poiana Negrii there are a few buses down to the DN 17 road and Vatra Dornei.

Just west of here, and north of Dornişoara, is the Tihuţa or Bîrgau pass (1,200m), perhaps the wildest stretch of road in the Romanian Carpathians, through dense forests thick with bears, wolves, boars and deer, the perfect setting for Bram Stoker's *Dracula*. There are also great views of Bucovina to the east, the Căliman mountains to the southeast, and the Rodnas to the northwest. Just beyond the pass are firstly the village and ski resort of Piatra Fîntînele, with some Roman road and a mineral spring, then Prundu Bîrgăului, site of an 18th-Century paper mill and of a log raftsmens' festival in October, and finally Bistriţa, which was the centre of a Saxon enclave; although they have now gone it remains an attractive town with 15th- and 16th-Century houses, churches from 1280 and 1560, and two museums.

CEAHLĂU

Ceahlău, the Magic Mountain, is thought of as the Moldavian Olympus, the Grand Old Man of the Eastern Carpathians, standing, according to Vlahuta, 'stern and solitary, the proud monarch of all it surveys, of mountains that look like molehills in comparison....as tall as a colossus lifting his head above the other mountains to watch the sunset'. It is said to have been the home of the Dacian gods, and even now every rock has a story (with names such as the Guardsman's Cap or the Shepherd's Stone). The mountain as a whole is more actively anthropomorphised than any other in the country. It is seen as a very special mountain, and one understands why when one sees its strangely weathered outcrops, and the way

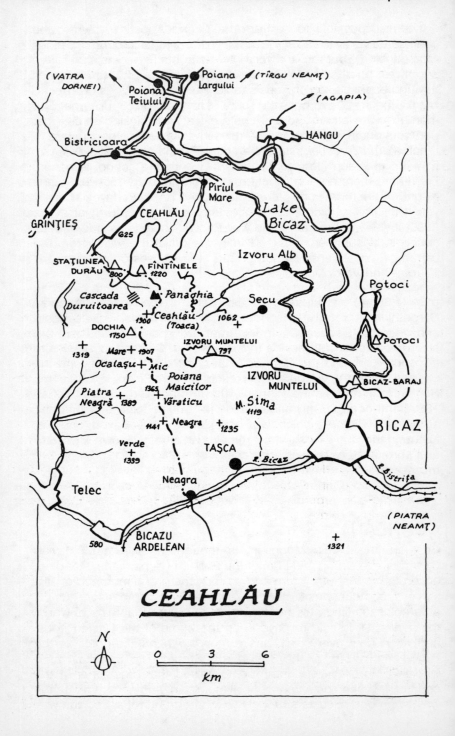

(VATRA
DORNEI)

Poiana
Teiului

Poiana
Largului

(TÎRGU NEAMŢ)

(AGAPIA)

HANGU

Bistricioara

550

Piriul
Mare

Lake
Bicaz

GRINŢIEŞ

CEAHLĂU

625

Izvoru Alb

Potoci

STAŢIUNEA
DURĂU   800

FÎNTÎNELE
1220

Cascada
Duruitoarea

Panaghia

Secu

POTOCI

Ceahlău
(Toaca)

1500

1062

DOCHIA
1750

IZVORU MUNTELUI
797

1319

Mare   1907

IZVORU
MUNTELUI

BICAZ-BARAJ

Ocalaşu   Mic

Poiana
Maicilor

1365

Piatra
Neagră   1389

Văraticu

M. Sima
1119

BICAZ

1141   Neagra

1235

Verde
1339

TAŞCA

R. Bicaz

Telec

Neagra

R. Bistriţa

(PIATRA
NEAMŢ)

580

BICAZU
ARDELEAN

1321

CEAHLĂU

N

0   3   6

km

it seems to dominate the surrounding landscape. In addition there is the more modern attraction of the artificial Lake Bicaz (or Lacul Izvoru Muntelui — Lake of the Mountain Springs), on which there are summer boat trips, for example from Bicaz dam (built 1950) to Pîrîul Mare landing stage below Ceahlău itself.

Geologically it is part of the Flysch zone, formed mainly of Mesozoic cretaceous sediments such as marl, sandstone, and especially conglomerates, which form great outcropping pillars. The flora is particularly stratified, with the beech level from 400-500m to 650-700m, an intermediate beech and fir level from there up to 1,000m, an intermediate fir and spruce level from 1,000m to 1,200m, the spruce level from there up to 1,700m, with dwarf pine, juniper and bilberry above that. There is also a reservation of larch (*Larix decidua var carpatica*) at 1,600m at Criminis or Polița cu Crini ('Lilies' Ledge', *crin* or lily being, I gather, the local name for the larch).

Getting there

The massif is conveniently placed between the Neamţ monasteries in Moldavia and the Szekler country in Transylvania, between the Tîrgu Neamţ — Borsec — Toplița road and the Piatra Neamţ — Bicaz — Gheorgheni road; buses run, mainly in the peak periods, from Piatra Neamţ via Bicaz and from Tîrgu Neamţ to Durău, the main resort on the north side of the massif, with a handy interchange at Poiana Largului at the north end of the lake, where there are less frequent bus connections to Vatra Dornei and Toplița, and a campsite. There are also some buses from Bicaz to Gheorgheni, passing through Lacu Roşu. The most convenient route therefore is one linking Durău with the road just west of Bicaz, which takes between ten and twelve hours according to the *Invitation*, but can in fact be done in eight hours. It will almost certainly be more practicable to spend a night on Ceahlău rather than doing the traverse in one day.

Hiking directions

Durău (800m) has an unreliable cabana and four hotels (Tourist Information in the Durău hotel), and a small hermitage (1835) beside a ski-lift on the Schitu or Hermitage stream; however there is really nothing to detain you, and it makes sense to press on at least as far as the Fîntînele cabana — this can be reached in 45 minutes from the bus terminal at the end of the road, following the red stripe route straight onwards. After five minutes swing left at the pumping station, and after five minutes more cross the minor road which winds around the eastern side of the massif; from here it is 35 minutes more up a steep track well marked and lined with tin cans for good measure. From this you will see that the map in the *Invitation* is not to scale, as it shows the road at least half way to the cabana. This hut is a three-storey chalet with a fine view from the terrace to Durău 420m below. It does have electric light but toilets are outside, unlit and without running water.

From here the red stripe route continues straight up the hill behind before swinging right along the hillside and up through spruce, parallel to a buried 20kV power cable. After almost half an hour the path (something between a path and a motorway) emerges above the trees on to a ridge and continues steeply upwards, with a view of the Panaghia rocks on your right. After another half hour you reach the dwarf pine level with a view of Toaca, the main peak if not quite the highest one, with the path continuing more easily up around the left hand side. After a total of 1¼ hours from Fîntînele you reach a flight of wooden steps up to the summit and then a meteorological cabana at 1,834m where even the roof is held on by cables. The views are great here, on a plateau between the two peaks. After another 20 minutes you come to the more substantial Dochia cabana at 1,750m, just over the eastern edge of the plateau with views and a ropeway for supplies southeast to Izvoru Muntelui.

From here, where you might be looking forward to an easy traverse around the left side of Ocolaşu Mare, the highest peak of Ceahlău at 1,907m, the red stripe markings in fact go down through the meadows and into the woods just to the right of an outcrop at the meadow's end, and continue downwards, with handrails, through massive columns of conglomerate, before continuing through the woods. After crossing a stream and turning right off the major path towards a stîna, the route continues gradually upwards again, and about 45 minutes after leaving Dochia cabana emerges into meadow and a great spot for a rest surrounded by outcrops. Again the route goes down, with handrails, between two huge cones of conglomerate, and 30 minutes after leaving the last meadow enters Poiana Maicilor right by a sheltered picnic table (big enough in fact to shelter a tent in need). From here the red stripe route turns left to follow a stream down to the Izvoru Muntelui cabana and the road to Bicaz; wanting to push straight on to Lacu Roşu I continued south following the blue crosses to Neagra.

This path runs along the top edge of the meadow before becoming less well marked — you should cross the next meadow to a sign, swing left along the right hand side of the hill to another sign on the skyline and straight on to the next black and white marker pole *just* visible at the end of the meadow. From here you head down, partly on a nasty little unmarked path through new growth, and then along the border line between young and old conifers.

Forty-five minutes after leaving the picnic shelter, you reach a saddle, and then go on up between a beech wood to the right and a felled area to the left before heading for a marker pole very well hidden in a clump of trees ahead to the left (just east of south). From here you can see the road to Neagra below to the left, and the path also goes down to the left (east of southeast) with the woods to the left, following occasional poles along the ridge until, almost exactly an hour after leaving the saddle, you arrive at a very muddy stretch just before the lower of two stînas and turn sharp right. Cross the track and follow the poles downhill for a quarter of an hour before fording a stream and turning left onto the forestry road. (In the other direction this turning is not signposted and it is difficult to spot the first marker pole in a field just after a copse of pines and a (mobile) sheep pen.) From here it took me 18 minutes to a bridge where a forestry road comes in from the left, and 32 minutes more to the main road, at a bus stop and *Magasin Mixt-Bufet*.

Although the map in the *Invitation* shows this trail actually going straight over Vf Văraticu, it in fact passes to the east of this 1,365m hill. I spent 30 minutes trying to find the blue cross trail at various points, but I hope it will be simpler for you with this guide. One variant worth thinking of, time permitting, would be to go from Durău to Fîntînele by way of the Duruitoarea waterfall, falling 25m in two stages on to the 'Ceahlău conglomerates': 'a wide curtain of milky foamy water, dropping from a tremendous height, is caught in a stone basin several metres above the valley and is poured down from there, spreading like a peacock's tail'.

LACU ROŞU AND THE HĂŞMAŞ MOUNTAINS

From Ceahlău and Lake Bicaz, the road to Transylvania follows the Bicaz River upstream through the spectacular Bicaz Gorges, where the road climbs 80m in a tight series of hairpins. Cheile Bicazului (Bicaz Gorges) cabana is at 855m in the heart of the gorges, with marked paths for walks of up to three hours in the limestone hills and gorges to the north. When I was here the bar of the cabana was packed with local boozers, but there was no wood for heating (in late May) so I was obliged to walk on for 2.5km (and 130m up) to the main resort of Lacu Roşu (Red Lake or Gyilksló), so called because of the red reflection of Mount Suhard to the north. The lake was formed in 1838 by a landslide from Suhard, and the resort has been built up on this dam and below it: it gives the impression of wanting to be a neat and tidy Swiss mountain resort, but alas it can't altogether escape from Romania. When I was there the Tourist Office had some useful-looking leaflets and maps locked in a case to which

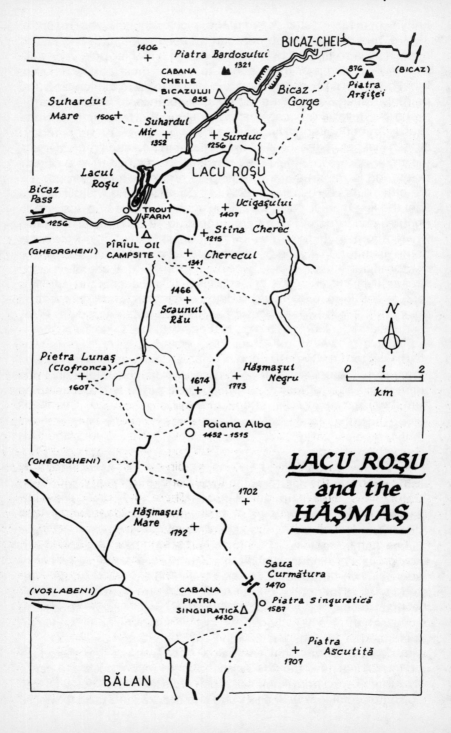

BICAZ-CHEI

1406
Piatra Bardosului
1321

CABANA
CHEILE
BICAZULUI   855

876
Piatra
Arșiței
(BICAZ)

Bicaz
Gorge

Suhardul
Mare   1506

Suhardul
Mic
1352

Surduc
1256

LACU ROȘU

Lacul
Roșu

Bicaz
Pass

1256

TROUT
FARM

Ucigașului
1407

Stîna Cherec
1215

(GHEORGHENI)

PÎRÎUL OIL
CAMPSITE

Cherecul
1341

1466
Scaunul
Rău

Pietra Lunaș
(Clofronca)
1607

1674

Hășmașul
Negru
1773

N

0   1   2
km

Poiana Alba
1452 - 1515

(GHEORGHENI)

1702

Hășmașul
Mare
1792

LACU ROȘU
and the
HĂȘMAȘ

(VOȘLABENI)

Saua
Curmătura
1470

CABANA
PIATRA
SINGURATICĂ
1430

Piatra Singuratică
1587

Piatra
Ascutită
1707

BĂLAN

they couldn't find the key, and the sign to the cabana was under the bridge in the river. It is mainly a summer resort but there is also some low-key skiing here.

Entering Lacu Roşu from the gorges one comes first to the post office and Vila Raza Soarelui, rather expensive compared to the cabana, with the Strand campsite and cabins opposite. In the centre of the resort one should turn right across the bridge to reach the Camping Turist and Suhard cabana, which is at 1,040m, 65m and 12 minutes above the resort by a path marked with a blue triangle, which continues up Mount Suhard and around to Cheile Bicazului cabana. Opposite the bridge, a forestry road heads southeast to the Bicăjel valley and the blue dot route to Şaua Varaşcău and Piatra Ghilcoş (or Verskö Nyereg and Gyilkoskö, all signs here being in Hungarian as well as Romanian). Continuing westwards up the main road, one comes to a few shops, the Tourist Office and private room service, and then the Restaurant Lacu Roşu and the start of the 3.5km walk, marked with a red cross, around the lake, much used of course by the tourists who come up here by bus and car. The forests are of the usual beech and spruce, with some fir, juniper and yew, and pine on the bare rocks of Suhard and Ghilcoş.

Hiking directions

The main route south, marked with a blue dot, starts at the east end of the lake at *Casa de Odinha* 14, opposite a boat hire and camping site; only the rear of the sign is visible from the road. This leads along the ridge of the Hăşmaş mountains, a karst and conglomerate massif on a crystalline base running parallel to the others of the East Carpathians, and over the watershed from the system of the River Mureş, flowing north and then west to join the Tisza in Hungary, to the system of the Olt, flowing south and through the Southern Carpathians directly to the Danube. There is a particularly fine section above cliffs with great views east into Transylvania, and Piatra Singuratică cabana is a small simple hut in a great setting.

The path sets off up the concrete steps, swings right past *Casa de Odinha* 17 and climbs steeply up into the woods to a cart track. A quarter of an hour from the start you'll turn right, and ten minutes later you'll come into a meadow and continue up, and then down, along its left side. Half an hour from the start there is a route left not shown in the *Invitation* and rather oddly marked with a blue dot with a white bullseye — the standard route continues along the foot of the cliffs, but I chose to take this route up a gully in the cliff (no climbing or scrambling required), and after seven minutes emerged into a beautiful bowl of sub-alpine meadow. The bullseye markings return north from here to Ghilcoş and Lacu Roşu, so I made my own way south over the edge of the basin, along a sheep track and southeast down into young firs. Swinging right and carrying on southwards I emerged, 40 minutes after leaving the bullseyes, at Stîna Cherec (1,215m) 230m above Lacu Roşu. Even if you don't emerge precisely at the sheep fold you are bound to arrive at a cart track marked (vaguely) with blue dots, on to which you should turn right/west. Eight minutes from Stîna Cherec this will bring you to the junction with the original blue dot route, also leading to the campsite at Pîrîul Oii (Sheeps' brook).

The route continues along the cart track left/south from the far side of this clearing, down into the woods, and after 12 minutes turns right to follow a power line uphill for 12 minutes. At the shoulder of the hill swing left, and two minutes further on fork left where a red dot route goes down to the right/west to the Pîrîul Oii valley. You immediately turn right and go uphill with a meadow to the right and woods to the left, before plunging into the conifers and climbing hard — although this is shown as a zigzagging route in the *Invitation* it is in fact a straightforward slog. Sixteen minutes of this will bring you to the clearing at the top, which you should cross keeping to the left, and continue southeast on the level in woods on the northeast slope of the hill, before rising to a ridge and continuing just east of south.

After 18 minutes turn right at a vague junction and at once right again on to a major cart track; three minutes later fork left. This is easy but boring in the trees: I stopped for lunch in a clearing planted with Christmas trees that were about six inches high in May 1991 — the clearing will probably have vanished by the time you get there! In any case, 23 minutes from the last junction the route turns right at a shoulder on to a very narrow, overgrown and undermarked path level along the hillside with views into a deep valley to the left. After nine minutes you emerge into a meadow just below a saddle to the right and turn left on to a slightly sunken cart trace (rather than a cart track) down the hill. Curving left across the second meadow brings you to a dead tree with signs on it in the middle of a field with sheep folds and huts to the left: this is Poiana Albă (White Meadow, 1,452m or 1,515m), reached in 18 minutes from the saddle and 3 hours from Lacu Roşu. This is the junction of the red stripe route northwest to Piatra Lunaş (Piatra Ciofronca) and Şaua Pîngăraţi (the Bicaz pass, on the road from Lacu Roşu to Gheorgheni), nine kilometres and three to four hours away; this means that Poiana Albă is somewhat north of its position on the map in the *Invitation*.

From here the route passes to the right of the sheep folds and up to the saddle and on across an open and not very well marked plateau, to the right of a hillock, then left up the left/east side of Hăşmaşul Mare (or Hăghihmasul), with a tripod on its 1,792m summit. The route takes the obvious route to the shoulder — after days of walking in forest, it's a great pleasure to be able to see where one is going! From Poiana Albă it took me 45 minutes to reach the ridge, and another five minutes (keeping to the right) to reach the highest point, with great views to the east. From here the route swings further right/west and after seven minutes turns left at a sign showing Piatra Singuratică as one hour away. This leads to the top of high open karst cliffs, windswept but with great views. At the far end of the clifftop meadows, head east-southeast to pick up the markers again and down the right side of a further meadow to Şaua Curmătura (1,470m), a big saddle with a sign announcing rather belatedly that you are leaving the Hăşmaşu Mare nature reserve and entering the Ossém reserve.

From here you should go right over the saddle, then left along the cliffs again and above the big rock — keep well above the spring to arrive (through broken glass and rubbish left by campers) at Piatra Singuratică cabana (1,430m) in about one hour fifty minutes from Poiana Albă. The 'Lonesome Rock' hut lives up to its name, sitting on a meadow ledge under tall rocky outcrops (see front cover); there is skiing here in winter but otherwise you may find this hut only open at weekends due to lack of visitors. It would be a lovely spot to camp, and in any case it takes under an hour to go down to the town of Bălan (or Balánbanya), while the red stripe route continues southwards along the main ridge to Poiana Tarcău, Crucea Condra and ultimately the Ghimes Palanca and Oituz passes.

The route down to Bălan leaves through the gate in front of the cabana to the south. Old blue stripe markings, leading to the south end of the town, disappear into the trees to the left and soon vanish in forestry workings; you should continue down with the red triangle markings to the bottom of the steep clearing where a cart track turns right/southwest. Very soon a narrow path with the newer blue stripe markings turns left off this.

This is the ridge route, as opposed to the red triangle route which leads down the valley to the north end of Bălan and which would be more convenient for the bus terminal. However it seems to me that the ridge route is an ideal gradient in both directions, except for the steep bottom section. It took me 45 minutes from the hut to where the path emerges behind a bench and a space for a tent at a junction of forestry roads, ten minutes from the main street along Strada Piatra Unică (a local name for Piatra Singuratică), which ends by a church and bridge, just north of a bus stop by a police station and small post office, and south of a good *alimentară*. Bălan is a Szekler town, dominated by a copper mine, and very little traffic goes beyond the mine.

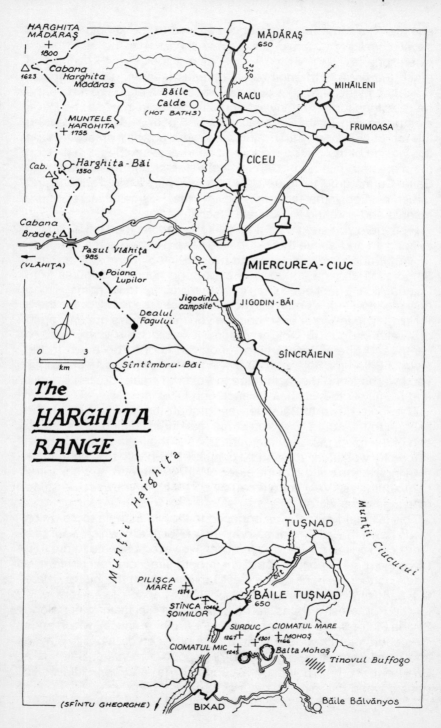

The
HARGHITA
RANGE

Moving on

The nearest station, known as Izvorul Olt (Spring of the Olt) is in fact in Sîndominic (or Csik Szent Domokos). As noted above, one could continue *ad infinitum* down the ridge from Piatra Singuratică, but I chose to go to the next town south of Sîndominic, Madărăş, and explore the Harghita mountains to the west. Equally one could go north to the Căliman range, or turn west at Ditrău to Lapuşna and Hodac.

THE HARGHITA MOUNTAINS

The Harghita Mountains form part of the volcanic chain to the western side of the Eastern Carpathians, with the young Olt valley separating them from the ranges to the east. As such they contain 23 mineral springs, as well as peat bogs. Although not spectacular, they offer a variety of scenery (ie open areas as well as continuous forest), but the main attraction is probably that, apart from the area around Harghita-Băi, they are largely empty of people; indeed the central section of this hike is not covered by the *Invitation* or any other easily available map, so that one has to blindly follow the marked route as far as possible. As some areas have been logged and the route obliterated, and as the weather was awful when I hiked the route, I cannot guarantee the accuracy of the timings quoted. However I took two-and-a-half days from Mădăraş to Băile Tuşnad, one of Romania's best known spas.

Getting there

It would be possible to start from the Sicaş pass to the north on the Gheorgheni (Gyergyós Szent Miklos) to Odorheiu Secuiesc (Odorheiu pronounced Odd-or-hey, Secuiesc meaning Szekler) road, or from the Miercurea-Ciuc to Odorheiu Secuiesc road which passes right over the middle of the range, but I chose to start at Mădăraş (Czik Madaras), on the railway line north of Miercurea-Ciuc. This may have been a mistake, as I never actually found the blue triangle route from there into the mountains, managing to stay just to the south of it all the way to the main ridge.

Hiking directions

According to the *Invitation* this route starts at the railway station at the southern end of the village, but there is certainly no sign of it there. It may run along a forestry road from the north end, or of course it may simply be unmarked. In either case a certain amount of enterprise and navigational skill is required of you. I ended up on the first farm track westwards to the north of the station, heading west across very flat and open farmland; although the mountains seem quite distant, at a steady speed of one kilometre every ten minutes they approach remarkably quickly. After 50 minutes (excluding time spent eating roast mushrooms and talking bad Romanian — them and me alike — with some Szekler cowherds, which made a change from *urdă* with Romanian shepherds) I ignored a path forking left and dropping into a valley; after another 17 minutes another track came in from the right, and two minutes later I turned left along the edge of the woods past a spring (which may or may not be the one shown on the *Invitation* map).

After another 15 minutes I forked right into a meadow, crossed a fence and started climbing, twice turning right to keep going westwards. After 25 minutes more I reached a small clearing at the ridge and then went down into the Mădăraşu Mic valley. After seven minutes the path ran into the dead end of a forestry road, and then eight minutes later this ran into a major forestry road by a bridge over the stream. This splits almost at once into two good roads; I took the right hand road which continued up the Mădăraşu Mic valley, past two usable huts. This is a lovely valley with lots of camping spots and white water, although not enough for canoeing.

After 40 minutes steady climb the good road ends at a turning space, and a more ordinary forestry track continues zigzagging up into moorland with a fairly nasty peaty surface. After 50 minutes, at the second hut, this track expires with only a very rough rocky track continuing, marked with the odd flash of white paint. To the left is a marshy bog, flowing south; I took a path up to a saddle to the right and a very boggy meadow. Across this in the southwestern corner I at last found a marker pole with a neat little roof but without any information under it. From here it is just six minutes, south and down a path to the right, to Harghita-Mădăraş cabana, at 1,623m together with a Salvamont hut and at least four private cabanas. There are two ski runs here, together with signs promising a blue triangle route back to Mădăraş, as well as a blue stripe route north to the Sicaş or Liban pass and south in 3½-4 hours to Harghita-Băi cabana, a blue circle route south and then west in 6-7 hours to Zetea and south-southeast in 4-5 hours to Vlăhiţa, and a blue cross path east in 5-6 hours to Racu.

After going back up the hill, the blue stripe route runs parallel to a cart track for 30 minutes until the blue cross route to Racu forks left. From here the track is very churned up and muddy; after 12 minutes a track dropped away to the right while I continued on the level and after another 12 minutes a minor forestry track also zigged down to the right, while the path continued on a blocked-off track and across two boggy and flooded clearings. Fourteen minutes further on there is a virtually unmarked junction to the right, bearing left over the shoulder and on gently up, bypassing some old fallen trees. Still a small path, it goes down to cross a stream and on level across a small meadow. Thirty-eight minutes after the last junction the track turns right on to another nasty muddy forestry track, and about ten minutes later, before a T-junction where this track plunges down into a valley, the original path continues above, swinging to the right/west and gradually up to go around the end of the hill after 20 minutes. After ten minutes more it passes a *very* basic shepherds' refuge with a water point five minutes further on, before again joining a forestry road. After 20 more minutes this arrives at a ropeway, from where a road goes down to the right (unmarked) to the bottom of a ski-lift, and a path takes a short cut on down from here to Harghita-Băi (Hargita-fürdó) cabana (disguised as a post office and bar) in ten minutes from the ropeway.

This is a large, rather gloomy, building, and once the bar is closed the young Szekler couple in charge are most friendly and hospitable. From here the road runs to the right and it is supposedly possible to reach the Miercurea-Ciuc to Odorheiu Secuiesc road in 40 minutes, although this seems a bit optimistic. To take the path (still marked with a blue stripe) you should turn left from the cabana and turn right at the corner of the road. After 300m this path goes straight across a double junction (to right and left) and then right, turning 90 degrees to an open stretch with views left. After 20 minutes the path forks right into the woods. Twenty and then another 15 minutes after this there are left turns before emerging into a meadow and passing to the left of a hut. Take the main track on from the bottom of this meadow to pass through the yard of Bradeţ cabana and cross the road about 1¼ hours after leaving Harghita-Băi cabana. This cabana seems to be as dull as most other cabanas and hostels on main roads.

Continue across the road on a farm track and fork left after five minutes. After about 12 minutes a disused version of the route continues straight ahead, but the main route is now to the left, following the power lines and then turning half-right to follow a fence. On reaching a zigzag road up to the right you can either follow this or just stick to the edge of the wood to the right; in either case you will reach, about 30 minutes after leaving the road, a marked tree at the hilltop. Here I managed to pick up the old route and ended up back at the power line — do not do this! Instead the path crosses the meadow ahead, via some marked trees in the middle and passing to the right of the shepherds' huts to go up right into the woods and bear left on to a cart track. After about an hour and ten minutes from the road this goes up to a ridge (keep right) and into Poiana Lupilor (the Wolves' Meadow). There are marked trees ahead and then to the right, and the path plunges back into the woods after 20 minutes, soon going up to the right.

This is easy going through nice mixed woodland, including one marked tree fallen across the path. A quarter of an hour after entering the woods there is a T-junction to the right by newly planted conifers, and then you should go straight on into the new growth rather than turning hard right. A track comes in from the left and then when you meet a cart track at right angles you should cross it to a minor path, lost in young conifers but soon climbing up to emerge in a meadow by some signs. From here the path actually runs northeast from the shepherds' huts in the middle to go into nice open woodland; the path runs east here with other routes crossing it, but it is reasonably marked and easy enough to follow, in fact developing into a sunken track, although it may be easier to walk alongside rather than in this.

After emerging on to a proper cart track this reaches a very well-built hut by a wide grassy area and a sign at the junction of the blue dot route to Miercurea-Ciuc Strand, about two hours away. This is Dealul Fagului (Hill of the Beeches) at which point one leaves Map 21 of the *Invitation* and heads into limbo. Apparently it should take 3-4 hours north to Bradeţ, and the same time on south to Sîntîmbru-Băi — I *think* my net time from Bradeţ to this junction was two hours and forty minutes (owing to constant snow it was very hard both to see across the large meadows, let alone to find my way out of them, and to take any decent notes), and I know that my time for the next stage to Sîntîmbru-Băi was only one hour and forty minutes.

The path is visible below to the south, a cart track passing through semi-open land and then crossing a ridge to go down into an area of blasted heath, where all the trees (and thus all the markings) have been cleared and the hydrology ruined. Eventually, keeping to or near the track, you will come to marked trees on the right, and 45 minutes from the junction swing right to a marked hut providing *very* basic shelter. Cross the road just beyond this hut to the right of the hairpin and bridge, go along the edge of the wood to a ford and then up into a wood to cross a clearing and continue on a tiny path that very soon becomes a decent cart track. About 25 minutes from the hut turn left and go up (you may hear logging trucks on a road to the right) to another blasted heath. The track curves right around to the southeast and up to a saddle with a big view to the east — nice if you can overlook the desolation immediately around you. From here it's a short walk up to the right/west to the wooden chalets that constitute the village of Sîntîmbru-Băi (Szentimrefürdó). Don't expect to be able to buy

anything here. At the crossroads in the centre the blue cross route
from Jigodin (a campsite at the southern end of Miercurea-Ciuc)
comes in via the forestry road — easy to follow but duller.

Going south from the crossroads, you will soon fork right onto a
'proper' path, almost like a municipal park, leading up to a campsite
full of cabins. To leave the village, turn left on to the road here and
at once right up a forestry track. After about half an hour this leads
into a long cleared area and goes down its left side. Again the
markings have all but vanished here; the correct route forks right
after ten minutes, crosses to the other side and then forks left to
lead south down the middle of the clearing. Keep right away from
the tracks down the left-hand side, and after about 20 minutes in this
clearing go left at a junction facing its far end. After 13 minutes, still
on a cart track, you will go over a ridge and down into trees,
emerging from them to cross another ridge after another 25 minutes.
About eight and 14 minutes later take turnings to the left; across a
stream to the right there is a fire tower where I was glad to sleep out
of the snow, but you should not expect it to be either empty or
unlocked. In any case there is only room for one inside. After
another 20 minutes the path rises up to another, collapsed, fire
tower and turns right. Eight minutes later a path marked with blue
and red triangles turns off to the right, presumably towards Baraolt
or thereabouts, and six minutes after this you should turn left on to
a minor track — if there are any markings here, they were hidden
under snow.

After another seven minutes there's a left turn where another path
comes in from the left. Go on along the top of the clearing (again
vanishing under new planting) and after ten minutes keep right
along the top edge. After another ten minutes turn left in a smaller
clearing. Then it's right after seven minutes, left after 13 minutes,
right after four more at a T-junction, and after quarter of an hour you
will arrive at the top of a clearing filled with new planting. Here you
turn 90 degrees right, to the south, and 18 minutes later emerge
from some rather English beech wood to follow the track across very
English parkland, briefly meeting a blue dot route. At the far end,
after a quarter hour, turn right at a muddy junction and then left up
into the woods. The path, which is very vague here, swings right and
then left/east down a clearing that starts like a formal beech avenue.
It continues through a wood and then more park-like meadow,
passing above a stîna (50 minutes after leaving the first parkland).
Ignore two left turns into the valley and then go left through the trees
at the far end to go along the right side of the next valley.

Twenty minutes from the stîna turn right at an old hut at Pilişca
Mare (*Invitation* Map 20), and fifteen minutes later join a blue cross
route trailing in from Uzanka, to the right: this is shown in the

Invitation as another blue stripe route but has sensibly been re-marked with blue crosses. So has the blue dot route onwards, down to Băile Tuşnad (wrongly marked as 'Tuşnad'), with a few vestigial dots remaining. If coming up from the valley, you should keep left at two unmarked junctions. After 54 minutes turn right at a T-junction then at once left. Five more minutes brings you to Băile Tuşnad (Tusnádfürdó) station — turn left to cross the railway and then back to the right to reach the station and beyond this the main road with bus stop and a turning to the right to reach the campsite (open from June 1), back across the tracks. The town, such as it is, is a bit further on to the right/south, at 650m altitude.

Moving on

Băile Tuşnad is, of course, a popular spa, with a few large hotels. The main excursion is eastwards to Mount Ciomatu and Lac Sfînta Ana (Lake St Anne): this is the only alpine volcanic lake in Europe and a noted beauty-spot. The path starts from the back road behind the Hotel Tuşnad and the Policlinic; follow this south parallel to the main DN 12 past the Apor and Mikeş springs and turn left. Naturally there is a road from the far side to reach the two cabanas here, which are very popular with Romanian students. Further to the east the road and more direct paths lead to Balta Mohoş, a 'moss-covered lake' in the next crater, the Tinovul Buffogo peat bog, the Puciosul cave (Peştera Puciosul) with carbon dioxide fumes on its floor, and the Balványos spa with its mineral springs, on the road from Bixad to Tîrgu-Secuiesc (Szekler Market), between the Oituz pass and Covasna.

To the west of Băile Tuşnad there is a short walk up (400m) to Stînca Soimilor — this starts not, as shown in the *Invitation*, from the blue cross route already described, but from the road on the right/west bank of the Olt a little further south.

From here the main road and rail routes run north and south along the Olt: *accelerat* trains from Bucureşti to Sighet and Baia Mare stop late at night (useful if you want a night on the move), but if you want to move on to Miercurea-Ciuc or Braşov in the daytime you'll need to take one of the half-dozen slow trains, or a bus. This gives you the opportunity of stopping at the Saxon citadels of Prejmer and Hărman (see page 283).

BRAŞOV

Although Sibiu (Hermannstadt to the Germans) was the chief town of the Siebenbürgen or Transylvanian Saxons, Braşov (Kronstadt) is a better base, nestling as it does right under the foothills near the junction of the Eastern and Southern Carpathians, just 2¾ hours by train from Bucureşti and virtually in the centre of the entire country. It is also well equipped with good shops, relatively speaking, and a good place to stock up and relax. Apart from its own attractions it is a good base for day-trips both to Saxon villages and to the mountains south of Poiana Braşov.

History

The Saxons began arriving here from Germany between 1211 and 1225, and the first documentary record of Braşov is from 1235. Unfortunately the Golden Horde of the Mongols arrived in 1241 and burnt down St Bartholomew's church and whatever else the Saxons had managed to build around it; as a result the nascent city was moved two kilometres south to its present site, tucked under Mount Tîmpa and more easily defensible. Here the present-day fortifications, and more, were gradually built up, with the various guilds each responsible for their allotted bastions. In 1364 Braşov was granted the right to hold an annual fair; the main church, the Black Church (or Biserică Neagra, or Schwarzkirche), was begun in 1383 and only finished in 1480 (between 1394 and 1690 there were 14 Tartar and Turkish invasions of Transylvania to delay the builders, with 40 earthquakes between 1530 and 1630).

The Lutheran Reformation arrived here in 1544 when the great humanist Johannes Honterus (1498-1549, a true Renaissance figure, but above all a geographer and cosmographer, who had brought printing (already established in Tîrgovişte and Sibiu) to Braşov in 1539) became the city's first Evangelical minister. (Leading Saxon families still have Latinised names such as Fabini and Philippi.)

The following centuries, with the Turks finally being driven back, were the peak of Braşov's fame and prosperity as it dominated the overland route to India, until finally undone by the opening of the Suez Canal. The Black Church contains a truly wonderful collection of over one hundred 17th and 18th Century Anatolian knotted carpets, mostly from Ushak and Gördes, brought back by the city's merchants and hung up in the church in thanks for another safely completed journey. Nevertheless the city was still in the wars from time to time; the fire which gave the Black Church its name was lit by the Austrian army in 1689, and the church was not finally rebuilt until 1772. Then came a major earthquake and more rebuilding which gave the city its present largely Baroque appearance.

Under communism many new factories were established and the largely German population was diluted with peasants, mostly from Moldavia, to boost the population to 330,000; it was briefly renamed

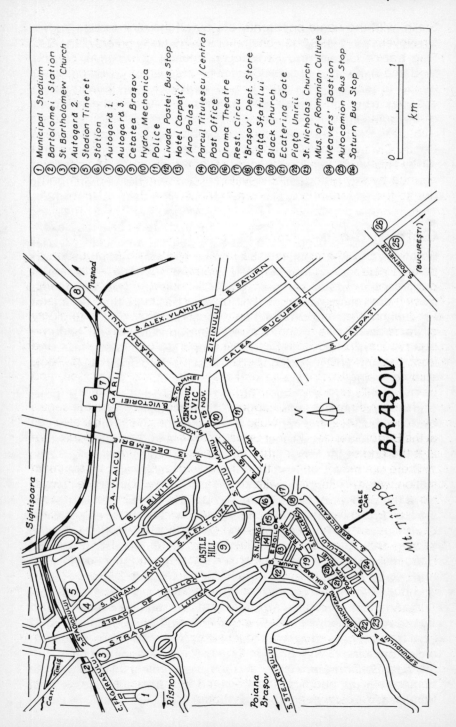

1. Municipal Stadium
2. Bartolomei Station
3. St. Bartholomew Church
4. Autogară 2.
5. Stadion Tineret
6. Station
7. Autogară 1.
8. Autogară 3.
9. Cetatea Braşov
10. Hydro Mechanica
11. Police
12. Livada Poştei Bus Stop
13. Hotel Carpaţi / Aro Palas
14. Parcul Titulescu/Central
15. Post Office
16. Drama Theatre
17. Rest. Circu
18. "Braşov" Dept. Store
19. Piaţa Sfatului
20. Black Church
21. Ecaterina Gate
22. Piaţa Unirii
23. St. Nicholas Church
24. Mus. of Romanian Culture
25. Weavers' Bastion
26. Autocamion Bus Stop
Saturn Bus Stop

BRAŞOV

Stalin, with the name apparently cut out of the pine forests above. On November 15 1987 demonstrations by 10,000 workers at the Red Flag tractor factory against reduced heating allowances, chronic food shortages and the introduction of a seven-day working week turned to riots which left the local Communist Party headquarters wrecked; although they were crushed these riots were the first signs of the crumbling of the Ceauşescu regime and they are remembered with pride. A smaller and more acceptable version of the Bucureşti Centru Civic was under construction just east of the city centre and will be finished before long; however the historic centre has not been harmed by any grandiose redevelopment schemes, perhaps partly due to the importance of tourism to the Poiana Braşov ski resort.

Getting there

Braşov is on the main electrified rail line north from Bucureşti to all points in Transylvania as well as Maramureş, Oradea and Arad; to put it another way, it is the spot at which lines, and indeed roads, from these places meet to be funnelled through the Bran and Predeal passes to the Wallachian plains. Therefore there are plenty of trains and buses to the city, including up to four trains and one bus per day to and from Budapest, in principle daily trains to and from Kraków and Warsaw, Berlin, and Vienna, Basel and Paris, summer trains to Constanţa and Mangalia on the Black Sea, and trains virtually hourly to Bucureşti.

The main station is near *autogară* 1, two kilometres from the centre by trolley bus 4 or an easy walk; trains to Zarnesti and Sibiu also call at the Bartolomei station near St Bartholomew's church and *autogară* 2 at the end of Str Lunga, the aptly named Long Street.

There are in fact no less than three *autogarăs*: No 1 by the main station, a tatty little place with no clearly defined departure quays; No 2 at Str Avram Iancu 114, by the Stadion Tineret or youth stadium (not the same as the Municipal Stadium just beyond, where city buses and trolley buses terminate), modern but under-used, only serving the Bran/Cîmpulung/Piteşti direction; and No 3 on Str Harmanului serving the Szekler areas to the northeast. No 2 is reached by bus 12 from Schei and the centre, bus 22 from Saturn, and bus 10 from the station; No 3 by trolley bus 1 from the centre.

In addition buses to Săcele and Predeal leave from the Autocamion factory on the Calea Bucureşti, across the main road from the Saturn bus terminal, reached by trolley buses 3 and 6 from the centre, bus 22 from Stadion Tineret (or trolley bus 5 or night bus 3N from Stadion Municipal), and the city's only tramline, No 101, from the station; and bus 20 to Poiana Braşov leaves every half-hour from Livada Postei near the central park.

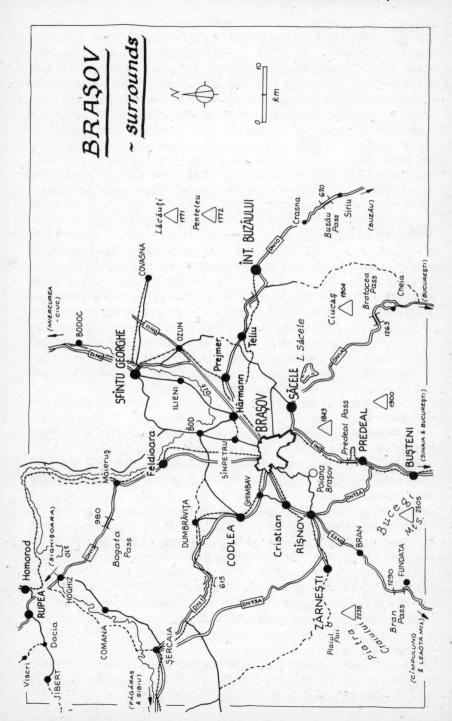

Where to stay

In the centre there are some of the best hotels in Romania, with prices to match, and some small but less expensive hotels; if you are on a backpacker's budget it would be worth staying at one of the cabanas or the campsite, all a slightly tedious journey out of the centre which would curtail your enjoyment of the nightlife if only such a thing existed.

Category A

The Hotel Aro-Palas or Carpaţi (both names are used), 9 Bdul Eroilor (tel 42840) is probably the best hotel outside Bucureşti, and better than most there. Used almost entirely by foreigners, its entrance is picketed by money-changers and assorted other pimps and touts, all looking interchangeably spivvy in their leather bomber-jackets and flash haircuts — these guys are not to be trusted. Once inside you will find useful things like Gordons gin at US$6 (but very likely no tonic), tourist information, car hire, or the *maître d'* in the restaurant who was a good contact for changing money. The restaurant serves a better class of omelette but can't be said to cater for vegetarians as such. Don't stay here unless someone else is paying and you want to try escaping from Romania for a night or two; in any case you're likely to be told it's full, although it has 307 rooms.

The neighbouring Hotel Capitol, 19 Bdul Eroilor (tel 18920), is similar but doesn't quite have the cachet of the Carpaţi.

Category B

The Hotel Parc, Str Nicolae Iorga 2 (tel 19460), the Postăvrul, Str Republicii 62 (tel 44330), the Hotel Aro-Sport, Str Sf Ioan 3 (tel 42840), behind its near-namesake, and the Hotel Turist, Str Iuliu Maniu 32 (tel 19464), are all smaller and more economical, especially the last two.

In addition there are 13 hotels 20 minutes away at Poiana Braşov, of which the Alpin is the best and most expensive, and the Ruia, Aluniş and Stadion should be the cheapest. These may soon be privatised which could make them more interested in lone travellers, but don't count on it. The only hotels with single rooms are the Caraiman, Piatra Mare and the Poiana. There are attractions such as swimming pools, saunas (L100) and massage (L500) available at these hotels.

Category C

The cabanas at Poiana Braşov are firmly entrenched in the tourist economy, as far as foreigners are concerned; the best deal I could find in 1991 was US$25 at the Poiana Ursilor (for one in a double room). However if you have time to catch the cable-car, or the energy to hike up, the Postăvarul and Cristianu Mare cabanas are genuine mountain cabanas with no nonsense about dollars. They are of course packed out in the ski season, and quite full in high summer too. There are almost no houses as such in Poiana Braşov, but private rooms are available for dollars at No 60, at the crossroads leading to the Hotel Alpin etc.

If you are coming from, or heading to, the south, the Dîrste campsite and Dîmbu Morii cabana are beside the DN 1 to Predeal, and while the campsite is ridiculously expensive, the cabana is a very pleasant and economical base if you don't mind making the effort to get there. The cabana is at km 158, with a small *alimentară, posta*, and bus stop, but only half a dozen buses a day between Braşov and Predeal, the last at 1850 from Braşov. Alternatives are to take a train to Timişu de Jos and walk back north for 15 minutes, or to take a Săcele bus (No 17 or 21) from the Autocamion factory, get off where it turns off DN 1, and hitch or walk 30 minutes south. In 1991 prices were from L95 to L125 each, and they even spoke some English.

To reach the Dîrste campsite you should take either a Predeal bus, or a Săcele bus as above and walk eight minutes south to km 160. The camp has hot water, security and so on, and in 1991 charged US$5 for one, US$8 for two, US$11 for three and US$14 for four to camp, or US$15 for a two-person cabin — these prices will now be in Lei. To camp wild, your best bet would probably be to take a Poiana Braşov bus and get off anywhere between Warthe and Zimbru/Cabana Junilor; there are pleasant walks signposted down again. In 1992 travellers were likely to be met at the station with offers of private rooms for US$7-10 or L2,500-3,000 — a new development that I haven't yet had a chance to investigate.

Where to eat

Other than the hotels (and functional *autoservires* next to the Capitol and Postăvarul hotels), Braşov has about four proper restaurants: the Cerbul Carpatin, in the historic Hirscher building (1545) on the main square, Pta Sfatului (Cerbul and Hirsch both meaning stag), which formerly had the reputation of being Romania's finest restaurant but has now rather fallen from grace; a Chinese restaurant on the same square which definitely is better than that in Bucureşti, and therefore is the best of its kind in Romania; the Panoramic at the top of the Tîmpa cable-car (closed Mondays), and a tourist restaurant with 'medieval atmospherics' in the former citadel or 'Cetatea Braşovului'. The Hotel Postăvarul has a pizzeria, and there is a lacto-vegetarian restaurant on Str Gh Bariţiu which serves meat. There are also several tourist restaurants at Poiana Braşov, such as the Coliba Haiducilor (Outlaws' Hut); I gather that most of the Poiana Braşov hotels cater surprisingly well for vegetarians (about L1,500 for three courses).

However Braşov does have the best *cofetarie* in the country, and my favourite pastries are sold on Bdul Eroilor, near the corner of Str Republicii — not the usual cream and chocolate confections, but savoury pastries with apple and nuts. Wonderful while chewing over mail from the post office opposite (open 0700-2000). It's also worth mentioning the wildly popular Turkish bakery on the corner of Str Republicii and Str Armata Română, which stays open late and does a roaring trade in the evenings.

What to see

The most important thing to do in Braşov is to walk around absorbing the Saxon townscape of the centre, starting with the main pedestrianised Str Republicii, and then to head southwest into the Schei quarter where Ion Tiriac grew up, around the Piaţa Unirii; in medieval times the Saxons did not allow Romanians to live within the walls, and this was where they built their homes. Strangely enough, it now looks like an archetypical Saxon town.

The most important single sight is the Black Church, an impressive hall church built between 1383 and 1480 and dominated by the Anatolian prayer rugs mentioned above. It contains an organ built in 1839 by Buchholzer of Berlin, the largest mechanical organ in southeast Europe with 4,000 pipes of Cornish tin (the largest pneumatic organ is in the Athenaeum in Bucureşti, with no fewer than 10,000 pipes). It also contains the second largest bell in Romania at 6,300kg (the largest also being in Bucureşti, at the Metropolitanate, weighing about 8,000kg); these details are not very interesting in themselves, but they illustrate the self-esteem of the burghers of Braşov and the real importance of the city. There is a display about the restoration of the church with captions in English. There are organ recitals at 1800 on Wednesdays, and daily in the summer.

For a total contrast you might wish to visit the nearby Sft Treime (Holy Trinity), an 18th-Century Orthodox church hidden down an alley off Str Gh Bariţiu, by the bus stop, or Sft Adormire (Holy Assumption or Dormition) down an alley off Pta Sfatului under an obvious neo-Byzantine cupola. Next to this is an alley leading to Pta G Enescu, with a very pleasant quiet *cofetaria*.

St Nicholas' church on Pta Unirii in Schei is the main Orthodox church of Braşov, built by various Wallachian voivodes between 1493 and 1564, with a belfry added in 1595, and 17th-Century side chapels. In its grounds is the first Romanian-language school (1761), with the first Romanian-language textbooks printed in 1581 by Deacon Coressi.

If you want to meet local Saxons, you should also visit some of the smaller Evangelical churches, where you can still see tweedy bourgeois ladies tending the graves and collecting their aid parcels. The most important is St Bartholomew's on Str Lungha, rebuilt in the late 13th Century, with a 19th-Century tower, and others are the Martinsberg on Dealul Cetăţii (Schlossberg or Castle Hill — key from Str N Filimon 12), the Blumenau on the corner of Str Iuliu Maniu and Str Cantacuzino, and the Obere Vorstadt on Str Prundului (Angerstrasse). The last has its Sunday service at 1800, the others all at 1000. There is also a Hungarian church on Şirul Scinteii, by the Liceul Şaguna.

The Casa Sfatului (Rathaus or Council House), in Pta Sfatului, built in 1420 with a tower from 1582, houses the County Historical Museum; in 1991 it closed for a year's restoration, but this could of course drag on somewhat. Just opposite on Str Mureşenilor is the Casa Mureşenilor, the home of the little-known composer Iacob Mureşianu (not to be confused with the poet Andrea Mureşanu, who wrote the words to the national anthem in 1848), which is equally unlikely to be open, sadly.

There are various bastions and bits of wall around the town, as well as the Ecaterina and Schei gates, from the 16th and 19th Centuries respectively, both leading into Schei. The best preserved bastion is that of the Weavers' Guild (Bastionul Ţesătorilor), built 1421-1436 and extended during 1570-73. This contains the Museum of the Birsenland Fortifications, small but perfectly formed, with some English captions; unfortunately one cannot go up into the wooden galleries — try Prejmer instead. Nearby is a well-preserved stretch of wall along the foot of Vf Tîmpa, where a pleasant promenade has been laid out with views of the old town, leading to the cable-car and paths up Tîmpa; the main path up is *very* easily graded with long zigzags, so the steeper path (marked with yellow triangles) at the northern end of the hill is much quicker.

At Bdul Eroilor 21 is the Art Museum, with a good representative collection of Romanian painters, and next to it a new ethnographic museum with a good collection of Saxon *Tracht* or costume, and some English captions — this may move to the building opposite the Cerbul Carpatin on Piaţa Sfatului.

Festivals

Braşov's annual festival is the *Sărbătoarea junilor* or Pageant of the Youths on the first Sunday of May, celebrating the annual waiving of the restrictions on the Romanians of Schei, when they were permitted to parade through the Saxon town, followed by dancing in a meadow.

Practical information

Briefly, these are the main post-revolutionary changes to street names: Pta 23 August is now Pta Sfatului; Bdul Gh Gheorghiu-Dej is Bdul Eroilor; Str Karl Marx is Str Iuliu Maniu; Bdul Lenin is Bdul 15 Noiembrie (commemorating the 1987 riots); Str 7 Noiembrie is Str Mureşenilor; Str 30 Decembrie (not to be confused with Str 13 Decembrie) is now an extension of Str Prundului; Str Alex Moghioros is Str Lucian Blaga; Str V Maiakovski is Str Sf Ioan; and Str Filimon Sirbu is Str Tiberiu Brediceanu. Eroilor, 15 Noiembrie and Iuliu Maniu also form a nice new post-revolutionary one-way system leading to the Centru Civic.

The ONT-Carpaţi tourist information office on the corner of Bdul Eroilor and Str Mureşenilor is now closed, leaving only a basic booth in the foyer of the Hotel Carpaţi, and an office in the Complex Favorit at Poiana Braşov. There is now a British Library on the north side of the Centru Civic.

Rail tickets can be booked at the *Agenţia CFR*, Str Republicii 53. *Poste Restante* is at the main post office at Str Nicolae Iorga 1. It is poignant to sit reading mail from home in the park by the post office with 24 graves of the heroes of the revolution. The university's engineering faculty building opposite is still proudly pockmarked with bullet-holes.

The main department store is at Str Nicolae Bălcescu 62, with a covered market beneath and an open-air fruit and vegetable market next to it, by the bus stop for the station. There are also sporting and hunting goods shops at Str Vlad Tepeş 12 and Str Republicii 16. The laundry service (*Spălat lenjerie*) at Str Michael Weiss 14 may also be useful; there is no problem washing clothes in Romania, but it's wonderful to get things properly dried. There is a UNIC supermarket on Str Muresenilor, and Bdul Griviţei is also a good shopping area.

The theatre ticket agency is at Str Republicii 4; the theatre itself at Pta Teatrului 1, naturally enough; concert hall at Str Mureşenilor 25; puppet theatre at Str Ciucaş 12; musical theatre at Str Operetei ('Operetta') 51; and major cinemas are on Bduls 15 Noiembrie and Griviţei.

Excursions

There are two main types of destinations near Braşov, the Saxon villages and the mountains above Poiana Braşov. The local Saxon villages fall into three geographical groups; firstly Hărman, Prejmer and SînPetru, to the northeast on the way to Covasna and Tuşnad, secondly Rupea, Homorod and Caţa to the northwest towards Sighişoara, (all dealt with in detail in the section on the Saxon villages) and Ghimbav, Cristian and Rîşnov to the southwest on the way to Bran, Zărneşti and the Piatra Craiului. Bran is described in the section on the Bucegi; Rîşnov has a 14th-17th Century fortified Lutheran church and the first Orthodox church built in Transylvania by the princes of Wallachia (1384) as well as a campsite at the start of the back road to Poiana Braşov, and Cristian has a 13th-Century church fortified in the 16th Century. I went to Homorod by train along the Olt valley, but it might be worth taking the road through the Munţii Perşani, in fact low rolling hills, with the Cabana Vînătorului at the Bogata pass (980m) in a large natural reservation with marked paths.

For the Poiana Braşov area, see Map 17 of the *Invitation*, and pages 207-209 of this book, where I describe an approach route to Predeal and the Bucegi rather than a day circuit. See also the section on skiing.

THE VRANCEA AND PENTELEU MOUNTAINS

In this relatively wild and un-touristy area of the southeastern Carpathians there are no cabanas or camp sites, making it ideal country for some wild camping and getting away from it all, although here as everywhere there are shepherds, foresters and meteorologists. There is also the added interest of a narrow-gauge steam-powered logging railway together with an inclined plane down to the plains, as it were. However it should be said at once that most of the rail network shown in the *Invitation*, Map 19, is now disused and converted to forestry roads. See below for more details of the railway. There is also a new *Hărta Turistica* of the Penteleu area, south of Comendău, published in 1991 by Editura Pentru Turism.

The route described is mainly on the main red stripe ridge route continuing from Lacu Roşu and Piatra Singuratică (see pages 165-167) to the north via the Ghimes Palanca and Oituz passes, and swinging to the southwest around the 'Carpathian curve' to the Southern Carpathians; anyone who feels adventurous can of course keep going the whole way along the ridge, or could try to trace the remains of the forestry railways that once stretched from Oituz in the north almost all the way to Nehoiu in the south, perhaps 80km.

The geology is mainly sedimentary, with gritstone, conglomerates, marls and clays rather than limestone: there is a main ridge running north to south through Lăcăuţi and Penteleu, with a large basin on the eastern side. At the far side of this basin, and well away from the

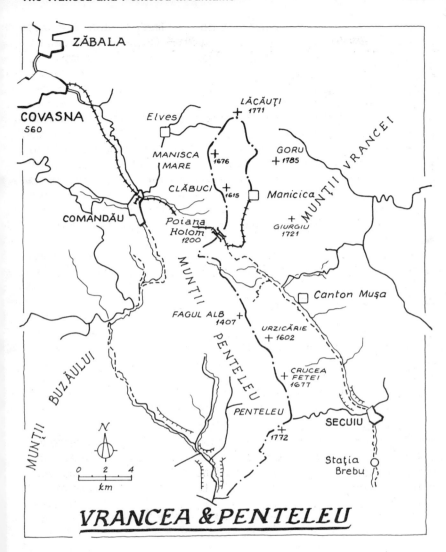

VRANCEA &PENTELEU

route described, are the Tisiţa gorges and the Putna waterfall, both natural reserves for chamois just south of the village of Lepşa. To the north of Lepşa and just west of the small resort of Soveja is the forestry reserve of Lepşa-Zboina on the south side of Mount Zboina Neagră, which contains 200-year-old beeches, 35m high and 1.2m in diameter, and spruce and fir trees up to 180 years old, together with two plant species that are themselves natural monuments: the globeflower or bulbucul de munte (*Trollius europaeus*) and papucul doamnei (*Cypripedium verticillatum*).

On the south side of Penteleu is the Milea Viforîta forestry reserve where there are the densest spruce groves in Europe, with up to 1,400m² per hectare, and some trees 34m high and 1.2m in diameter, as well as the rare orchid *Goodyera repens*.

Getting there

The main gateway to the area is the Szekler spa town of Covasna (575m), known as 'the resort of the thousand springs', and reached by a branch line from Sfîntu Gheorghe (Sepsi Szent György). You may be told at Braşov that there is only one through train, but in fact there are connections from most trains (via Hărman and Prejmer) at Sfîntu Gheorghe. At Covasna station there are quick bus connections into the town centre, so don't shilly-shally on the platform. Just to the north are the villages of Zăbala and Ghelinţa, with little-known fortified churches. There are good food shops in Covasna and buses roughly hourly to the Voinesti Spital (hospital) for the Popasul Valea Zinelor campsite just beyond. This is a pleasant valley full of strollers in tracksuits all here for some kind of cure or restful holiday.

It's about one kilometre further to the foot of the inclined plane, which is as far as the strollers get. It's a fascinating piece of living industrial archaeology, if one can say that, built in 1886 by a certain David Horn and Baron Groëder. It is 1,232m long, at a gradient of 1 in 3.5, and carries on its 1,450mm gauge wagons a daily total of 30 of the 760mm gauge wagons each carrying ten cubic metres of wood. These are brought from the forests above and transferred by the inclined plane to a lower line running parallel to the road to transfer sidings by the standard gauge line in Covasna. From here you should hitch a lift up the road to Comandău, the centre of the forestry and railway operations (and of military operations when this was the Hapsburg frontier — the name comes from the German Kommando, and the Oituz pass just to the north was the site of a First World War battle). You could walk up and indeed take a short cut left to Elveş and Lăcăuţi, but I saw no sign of the blue dot markings when I went up.

Comandău (at 1010m) seems amazingly muddy and primitive, but it does in fact have an *alimentară, cofetărie* and *restaurant*. Looking straight down the valley south-southeast you can have a fine view of Vf Penteleu 20km away. There is a Jewish cemetery here, but now all bar three Romanian families are Magyar — there are Romanian foresters, but they live in forestry cabanas and go home to their families elsewhere on leave. The Magyars live here and travel to work in a *dirzina* or lorry body on rail wheelsets, and if not too numerous you should be able to hitch a lift too; the line south is disused so leaving at 0700 this runs back towards Covasna before swinging around to the right and climbing over to the next valley. It's a very crowded, rough and noisy ride for 55 minutes to a spot called Manicica, southwest of Vf Goru. Alternatively you could hike up the valley road north to Elveş and then find the rough road to Lăcăuţi, marked with blue dots.

Hiking directions

From Manicica (or anywhere else the *dirzina* might stop) you must continue on up the railway line, which becomes increasingly disused, for about 40 minutes. No one likes walking on railway sleepers, but this is not too painful here. Then turn right on to a sheep track; after 23 minutes this is joined from the right by a disused railway track. This only continues for another five minutes before ending at the stream; from here you should go up to the right (briefly rather steep), crossing a *drum forestier* and reaching the ridge and the blue cross track remarkably quickly, in 22 minutes. From here, Şaua Gorului, 1,480m, you could turn right to reach Goru, the highest peak in the range at 1,785m, and the basin to the east, or, as I did, turn left and follow a cart track for half an hour to reach Lăcăuţi and the main ridge route. When you reach a better road, turn right for five minutes to reach the summit and the weather station; from here it should apparently take 12 to 14 hours to reach Herăstrău to the north.

To continue southwards, return down the road for 20 minutes to a rather small sign, where the blue dot route to Elveş and Covasna continues along the road, and our red stripe route turns left on to a decent path into relatively short conifers. Because of snow drifting under the trees my progress was rather slow here and timings are inaccurate. After 22 minutes I reached a clearing with a sign telling me that Poiana Holom was 3¾ hours ahead and Penteleu 12¾ hours ahead. Forty minutes later (having turned half-right or southwest out of the clearing and then gone down to the left along the side of a hill to the right) there was another sign telling me that Poiana Holom was now 2½ hours away and Penteleu 11¾ hours — that's right, it doesn't add up. Supposedly it should also take 2½ hours to go back uphill to Lăcăuţi, almost double what it took me downhill through the snow. After six minutes more the path passes through a cleared area — if in doubt keep right here. Then after another six minutes it passes through an abandoned stîna and seven minutes later reaches a spring and a ridge which currently has a good view, although it has been planted with young trees.

The path goes up into the woods, well marked for 22 minutes but then reaching an unmarked junction: do not follow the forestry markings of two red stripes to the right. The obvious path goes down and then up, reaching another viewpoint to the left/northeast after 20 minutes. From here you continue along a *drum forestier* on the side of a hill to the left, again with good views. After ten minutes another *drum forestier* comes in from the right at an unmarked junction and after 26 minutes (by a ruined hut) and seven minutes more the same thing happens twice more — this is an increasingly major route and increasingly badly marked before finally being totally unmarked. It is hard to be sure exactly where the direct path to Poiana Holom turns off to the left. Twenty-two minutes from the last junction I arrived at the Ursul forestry cabanas at a stream and the railway line I had come up earlier that morning — Poiana Holom is half an hour up the line from this point. With this dog's leg it took me just over four hours to get from Lăcăuţi to Poiana Holom, roughly in line with the times on the signs; the sign here says it takes five hours to go back uphill to Lăcăuţi. It's now only nine hours south to Penteleu, which again doesn't add up, via Vf Fagul Alb (White Beech Mountain, 1,407m), supposedly 3½ hours ahead although a forester told me he had once got there in 1½!

Poiana Holom, also known as the Deluşor pass, at 1,200m, is a meadow with a few forestry cabanas and nothing else; the *dirzina* returns through here at about 1500, if you want to make a day-trip of it. Heading on south as indicated by the sign you can take either route up through a logged area, and after 18 minutes turn right at an unmarked junction, then left and across a track, coming into a clearing after 12 minutes. Keep right of the sheep fold to follow the track along the ridge and down to the right. Eighteen minutes from here there is a very badly marked junction, particularly if going north; turn left and at once left again (going south) to head down to the south/southeast on what soon becomes a well-used forestry road, by a stream. After 25 minutes this crosses a bridge, and just before a second bridge your route turns off to the right. This path is largely hidden under moss, so keep an eye out for the markings. There is a short steep climb, a small clearing and then the route runs along the left edge of the woods opposite before going on up, as a smallish, overgrown but well marked path, to a ridge. Almost two hours from the bridge and three hours and ten minutes from Poiana Holom this brought me to Fagul Alb, with a summit tripod just ahead in the hilltop meadow. (There is another tripod further to the right, with wide views.) The marked route goes to the right, but very soon crosses to the left in, I think, the second dip it reaches, before a stîna to the right, heading for a tree with a red stripe hidden by a large wooden cross.

I camped here before moving on in the morning around various fallen trees. After 12 minutes the path enters another wing of the same big meadow and crosses it bearing slightly to the right. There is a painted arrow pointing uphill here, but in this area arrows do not have the same meaning as elsewhere: generally they indicate a less extreme turn than elsewhere. In any case there is almost at once a hairpin turn down left into the beechwood and the path continues merrily to the southeast as a broad and obvious track — it should be possible to cut out this dog's leg. Continue over the Şaua Gaiţa then up the left side of a wood to come into conifers and turn sharp right on to a path marked with forestry markings. Many of the trail markings here are confirmatory rather than navigational, meaning that they are painted on the tree parallel to the path, so that you see them as you pass, rather than on both sides at right angles so that you can see them as you approach. This is fine when following an obvious track on the ground but less so if not. As the number of fallen trees increased I veered away to the right around them and made my own way up to the ridge of Ciulianos (or Urzicărie, 1,602m), reached one hour after leaving Fagul Alb, turning left along the ridge to rejoin the marked route. This crosses diagonally to the left across a saddle in a clearing with a few dwarf bushes and heads southeast on a cart track along the ridge with views ahead to Penteleu.

After 33 minutes, after fighting my way around or over more fallen trees and passing through one small clearing, I came into a larger clearing where the path runs above the Bălescu sheep fold up across the side of a hill to the right with more good views ahead and to the left. The country continues to be rather open with few markings: half an hour from the sheep fold there is a marked stone at a saddle and 15 minutes later a spring, from where the path continues up, with the Pietrele Arse (Burnt Rocks) sheep fold below to the left. You should keep right (south or southeast), not taking any of the tempting sheep tracks down to the left, to finally reach the top of the obvious 'Dead Tree Hill' 20 minutes from the spring. Go down the east side of the hill and after 12 minutes on to a ridge at a spring thoroughly equipped with a mug, bench and table and a cross. This is a well-used and contoured route before turning into parallel sheep tracks up to a ridge and beyond it a 'proper mountain valley'. Don't take the sheep tracks down to the spring but keep up to a big rock with a clear marking and on up the valley. I passed two more marked rocks and then simply kept going up an unmarked small path overgrown with small trees — not easy with a pack. Thirty-five minutes from the spring with mug etc I reached a ridge in the cloud between two peaks and fortunately chose correctly to turn right up a very steep and rocky path with exactly one vague marking to reach the summit of Penteleu, at 1,772m, after another 21 minutes.

This is grazed right to the top, with only a few dwarf bushes and a very lively population of ladybirds all convinced that my pack would be covered in greenfly (Dead Tree Hill, as I called it, was, on the other hand, alive with dung beetles). Again there is a cartographer's tripod (or tetrapod, as they all have four legs). Below to the northeast is Lacu Roşu, another red lake, which should theoretically be on our red stripe route, but which must have been over the ridge above the sheep tracks after that well-equipped spring. There is a well-used but again unmarked path leading down to it along the northeastern ridge.

From here it is a very rapid descent and exit from the mountains: I left to the west, passing an automatic weather station and radio tower, and quarter of an hour later the main weather station. From here the red stripe path and both old and new 4WD roads run down together, passing above a stîna to the left at the Şaua Cernatul and then curving down to the left to reach it 34 minutes after the weather station; after five minutes more there is another, abandoned stîna where a *drum forestier* runs in from the left. After another seven minutes keep left at a junction with some red stripe markings; after another five minutes another *drum forestier* comes in from the left over a stream, and the road continues down from the coniferous level into beech, then birch and hazel as well — it gets less muddy, and there are some markings for short cuts going up the hill.

Fifteen minutes from the last junction you will reach a bridge over spectacular rapids, five minutes before turning right at a junction with a road, marked with a blue triangle, coming from the DAF Viforîta forestry site, eight kilometres up to the left/east, just below Penteleu. Going northwards, the red stripe route is signposted as DAF Cernatu. After seven more minutes this road reaches a disused cabana and the main Bîsca Mare valley; the route briefly goes north to reach a bridge and the main DAF Cernatu-Patacu road, which you should follow south, unless you would prefer to take the blue triangle route right/north and then westwards to reach the DN 10, the Braşov to Buzău road (see opposite). When I was here there was a lot of spectacular white water in the river, but it might not be so exciting outside the spring thaw season. There were also many anglers here.

Moving on

From here it is just over seven kilometres down the road to Varlaam, at the meeting of the Bîsca Mare and Mică rivers, and another dozen or so kilometres to the DN 10; after about two kilometres you reach a *magazin forestier* with the usual unpredictable opening hours, and the Gura Teghii village limits sign, although this village is in fact about two kilometres beyond Varlaam. Unfortunately when I was there the road was very badly washed out above Varlaam — it took me 15 minutes to climb around and there was no hope of a lift down the road. In spite of what could be a Dutch name, Varlaam reminded me of nothing so much as a small Himalayan village, with most of the houses on the wrong side of the river and linked only by pedestrian suspension bridges, and other houses terraced behind these houses, hills behind wooded hills. The omnipresent landslips, wash-outs and trees falling over because their shallow roots couldn't hold in the mud caused by two months of rain were also reminiscent of Kashmir and Nepal. It is a very attractive spot. The shop, *bufet* and bus stop are one kilometre beyond the confluence of the rivers, and I was able to catch a bus to Buzău at 1700, getting off at the junction with the DN 10 at the north end of Nehoiaşu.

To the north is Siriu town (508m), dominated by a new dam; given the geological instability of the area I wouldn't recommend sleeping beneath this or any other dam in this area, and my fears were, I think, justified by the Bacău dam disaster later in 1991. The Siriu dam has also drowned the hiking trails west into the Siriu mountains, so the next section begins further north up the DN 10 at Crasna.

THE CIUCAŞ MOUNTAINS

The final stage of the Eastern Carpathians, the Ciucaş range shows some beautiful lower woods and meadows and above them around Mount Ciucaş some weirdly attractive pillars and columns, almost reminiscent of Cappadocia in central Turkey. I have been here twice and found it most enjoyable, with very friendly cabanas and lots of open moorland walking. It can be treated as a loop from the DN 1A, the Bucureşti/Ploieşti to Braşov via Cheia road, or linked with the Siriu and Tătăru mountains to the east, as I have done, to provide a through route from the Vrancea/Penteleu area, and if desired you can continue west to Predeal (although the obvious route has been blocked), making at least two days hiking. While the Ciucaş area is well marked and geared up for tourism, the Siriu and Tătăru area is much wilder and you are virtually certain to have to find your own way in places until the marked route chooses to reappear, a situation complicated by the lack of a map of the area. Ciucaş is covered by Map 18 of the *Invitation*, but again there is a gap — less wild but harder navigationally — to the west before reaching Map 17.

Getting there

There is a daily bus service from Cheia to Ploieşti and Bucureşti, leaving southbound at 1100 (in 1991). Likewise from Braşov there is, as far as I know, just one daily bus from *Autogară* 1, by the railway station, to Valeni de Munte via Cheia. To reach the eastern

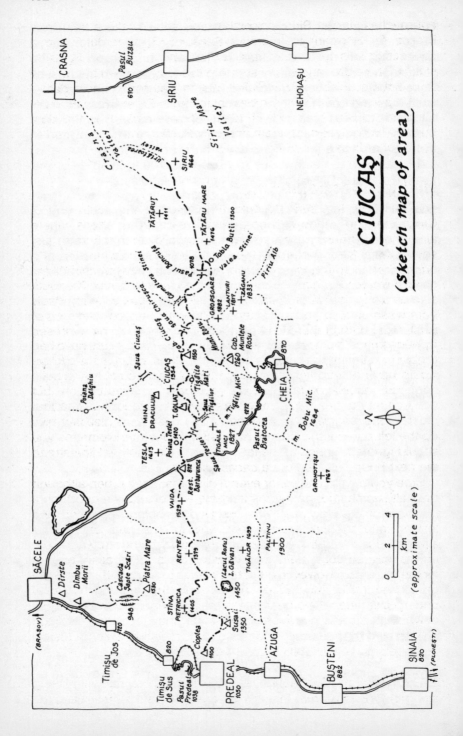

CIUCAŞ
(Sketch map of area)

approaches via the Siriu mountains, you should take a train from Braşov (or Hărman) to Întorsura Buzăului (Bodzafordulό) and a connecting bus to Crasna from a yard about 100m on from the station. There are reasonable shops in this logging town but no time to use them unless you actually want to wait for the next bus — stock up in Braşov, much the best place for it. From Crasna the DN 10 south to Siriu was still, in 1991, officially closed by the dam building works, although local and construction traffic continued to use it regardless.

Hiking directions

The bus from Întorsura Buzăului terminates at the south end of Crasna (a long village with no perceptible centre or shops, where almost every house seems to have a bread oven in the yard) just south of km 98 and north of the village limits, at the junction of a *drum forestier* to the west. Just to the north is a childrens' holiday colony, where you might conceivably be allowed to camp. The route sets off along this *drum forestier*, which in 1991 was suffering badly from wash-outs, in spite of extensive flood-prevention works on at least some of the tributaries upstream; it continued to be well used by pedestrians, both workers and hikers, but cyclists might have had problems carrying their steeds around the gaps. In any case cyclists would be unable to fight their way through the woods to the main ridge later on. Maybe the road will have been repaired by now, but don't count on it. In 1991 there was so much rain in this area that much of the work was left undone. In any case it's a pleasant hike up the left bank of the Crasna river; after about four kilometres you should ignore a bridge to the left and continue another kilometre to the next bridge, just before a *cabana silvica*.

Here you have a choice, or even a dilemma. The proper, although basically unmarked, path turns left here and provides a good route for most of the way up to the main ridge, before vanishing and leaving one to make one's own way for the final stage. The alternative is to continue further up the valley before turning south up the washed-out remains of a forestry railway, very easily graded for the most part. However when this comes to an end the final climb up to the main ridge is far harder and through much thicker undergrowth than the other route: it really is very hard work. In spite of which, this route is a quarter hour faster than the other, although it's not worth it unless you have a fascination with industrial archaeology. I shall briefly outline both routes below.

1. The 'official' route (although I found only one blue triangle marking along it) follows a *drum forestier* up the right bank of a stream, the

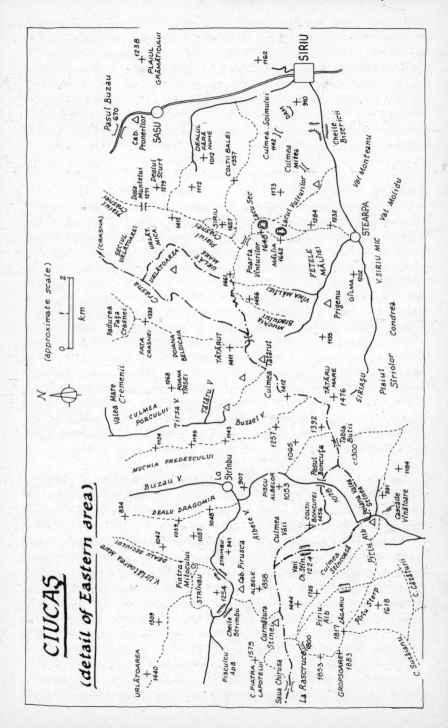

CIUCAŞ
(detail of Eastern area)

Urlătoarea, well equipped with modern weirs. There are also tautologous signs saying (in Romanian) 'Illegal cutting of wood is forbidden', which one ought to be able to work out for oneself. The track crosses to the left bank, makes a few zigs to reach some *frag* plants and then, just over 30 minutes from the junction, two derelict forestry cabanas in an overgrown clearing. This is where the trail dies: the valley splits into three, each with an unmarked path up it. As I knew I had to turn right/west along the ridge when I got there, I chose, after much deliberation, the right-hand route: it was by far the smallest, but it did show signs of having been used by sheep fairly recently. It was a typical sheep track running southwest and upwards; after 35 minutes it became too narrow and slippery, and covered with nettles, and I perhaps belatedly crossed to the left and went up into the beechwood to find a better path heading up to the south and then back to the southwest, up into spruce (and out of the *frag* zone), and emerging after 13 minutes into a large overgrown *poiana* on the main ridge, with a spring and drinking trough nearby.

Immediately above is a cart track marked with red stripes: take this to the right/west and at an unmarked junction head to the left/south of a stîna and into a valley lined on either side with spruce woods. Twelve minutes from the spring, with no warning other than a marked tree in the woods to the right, the path turns sharp right and climbs up steeply for two minutes before turning slightly left across a clearing and going down to the left on the far side of this ridge into mixed conifers, beech, elder and maple. Ahead is a big basin full of forest and also the alternative route; after ten minutes the path (unmarked again) reaches a saddle, then a rocky area and five minutes later an active forestry area at the head of the Siriul Mare valley to the south.

2. The more direct route continues up the Crasna valley for another kilometre or so before turning left across the next bridge. This is a very broad and grassy track, pleasantly disused and frequented by deer, which takes a couple of zigs uphill, and then continues south on the right/east bank where the track used to take a large sweep to the west. Soon after this is a spot where the ground, formed of *very* liquid shale, had been comprehensively washed out — I made my way up the stream bed for a while before crossing to a marshy plateau on the right and then crossing back to the path and continuing southwestwards past some old railway sleepers and axles. After another wash-out this route also dies; here I chose the left-hand valley and soon had to plunge into the trees to the left, to follow a vague sunken path, disused and almost totally blocked. This was very hard, sweaty work. Veering slightly left near a streamlet, after 20 minutes I reached a minor ridge and continued uphill over

broken rocks for five minutes before picking up a path at right angles: this is the red stripe route which leads, just to the right, to the active forestry area. If you continue down the forestry road south into the Siriul Mare valley, you will find more remnants of the old forestry railway, now blocked below by the new dam.

From here the red stripe path continues westwards (easy to follow although without many markings), and in ten minutes comes up into open downs country on a cart track which swings left to pass a stîna further to the left; twenty minutes after leaving the forestry area the track crosses to the right side of the ridge, with another stîna to the right, and after another six minutes passes just above a beech wood with superb views ahead to Vf Gropşoare, a high craggy ridge just to the south of Vf Ciucaş itself. Another six minutes on it passes a good spring and goes quickly through a beech wood to a saddle, continuing to the left along a sheep track above a cliff with views left to the Siriu Mare valley, and on along the top edge of more beech woods. Eighteen minutes from the saddle it reaches a stîna with about ten very vociferous dogs, and a cart track to the right side of a ridge in open moorland with some wind-stunted beeches. Quarter of an hour from the stîna the track reaches another damp beech wood with a couple of streams to be crossed and then a spring, coming in another couple of minutes to a junction to the right by a very solid well-kept hut. From here the cart track continues across moorland; it swings left around a hill and then zigs down to the right, so that a short cut would be possible. At another junction (Tabla Butii, c1,300m) a cart track comes in from the right and at once a path marked with red crosses plunges down into woods to the left. There is rumoured to be a Roman road running north into Transylvania via the Tabla Butii pass, but I didn't know this when I was there.

Here again you have a choice of routes, either down to the left and up the spectacular and narrow gorges of the Valea Stînei, taking two hours and twenty-five minutes to Curmătura Stînei, or a higher route through attractive woods and clearings, which took me just one hour and forty minutes. As the main red stripe route has been virtually unmarked to this point, although easy enough to follow, it is strange to suddenly find so many red cross markings on small metal plates nailed to trees on the route to the left, oddly mixed with a few red stripes: as elsewhere, I don't think that this is unconnected with the presence of a campsite at the bottom of this route. Commerce stretching out its tentacles, even here!

On the first route, after going downhill for ten minutes you should ignore an arrow seemingly directing you to the left; soon after two forestry tracks come in from the right, and then the route runs along a ridge (with some quite magnificent spruce) before dropping down by a fence to a road and a few cabanas to the left, including a *casǎ de vînǎtoare* or hunters' house where accommodation might be available. The Poiana Valea Stînea camping is also here across the river (left/south on the road to the cabanas, then right). The route into the Ciucaş massif proper, marked with blue stripes, takes the road to the right/north here, with the magnificent cliffs of the Pîrîu Alb to the left, and after ten or so minutes forks left at a small lake to head up the Valea Stînilor (or any other variant of the name) or valley of the sheepfolds. This is gradually squeezed up against the conglomerate cliffs to the left until one is often walking in the stream itself, or the stream disappears under an overhang. At its narrowest this gorge is only one metre wide but soon widens to make room for a small meadow and then continues further than you might have expected. At the top of the valley there can be a rather hard climb out of the woods over beech leaves on wet clay, just about the most slippery combination known to man, to reach a stîna and follow the blue stripe markings on up a small valley to arrive at a little pond and just beyond it at Curmǎtura Stînei (1,435m) rejoin the red stripe route, which goes *straight* up the hill to the left/west.

Sticking to the red stripe route at Tabla Butii leads you down the edge of the woods for twenty minutes to cross the *drum forestier* at the Boncuţa pass at 1,078m, and straight up the other side again with the beech woods to the left, and one large common silver fir to the right like a park cedar. After 17 minutes follow a cart track southwest into the woods, then after five minutes take a junction steeply up to the right and then after two minutes another to the left, crossing a cart track and zigging left past a clearing to reach another clearing in spruce trees. This is the end of the real climbing, 30 minutes from the pass, although the track rises easily for another eight minutes, after which it continues mostly fast and level on or near the ridge for 22 minutes. Then it emerges into meadow above the same stîna as above, with absolutely lovely views in the evening sun to the conglomerate peaks to the southwest. The track crosses to the right of the ridge and back to the left again to reach the pond at the junction with the blue stripe route from the gorge.

From here the red stripe markings continue on trees up the steep hill to reach a narrow conglomerate ridge with dead trees to the right. After about fifteen minutes cross a notch in the ridge rather than a saddle to the left and follow a sheep track along the side of a hill to the right, climbing steadily towards a marker pole visible ahead (weather permitting) on the saddle. Thirty-seven minutes from the pond there is a spring, using a metal marker pole as a water pipe; from here you should take not the tempting level sheep track but a vague cart track climbing steeply up to the saddle three minutes above. I camped here to enjoy both the evening view of Vf Ciucaş silhouetted against the sunset, and the stunning early morning view with the sun shining on to it from behind me. The sign on the saddle also acts as an Aeolian harp, playing tunes as the wind blows through it. According to this sign it should take two and a half hours back down to the Pasul Boncuta, although it took me one hour and fifty minutes net to come up. From here it is only 35 minutes on to the Ciucaş cabana (45 minutes according to the sign) so that one could leave Braşov on the 0824 train, get the bus to Crasna, leave there at 1040 and easily get to the cabana for the night.

Alternative routes from here head south (marked with red crosses) along the narrow crest of Gropşoara (1,883m) and La Lanţuri (1,817m), equipped with chains, to Cheia in four hours according to the sign. The route on to Ciucaş is marked with red stripes and crosses for the first ten minutes (crossing a gully and then following it down to the right) to the lower Şaua Chiruşca saddle in lovely pine meadows where the route from Vama Buzăului (meaning the former customs house on the former Braşov to Buzău road, although there is another former *Vama* nearer the border, south of Crasna) four and a half hours away joins from the right; from here the route is remarkably well marked with both red and blue stripes and crosses. The route continues easily along cliffs with views to the left and after 15 minutes turns left across open moorland away from a radio tower ahead to reach the cabana to the left in another five minutes. If going straight to Vf Ciucaş you could easily take an unmarked short cut over the hill to the left of the radio tower, rejoining the more level route from the cabana by a pond. The cabana (at 1,550m) is very simple and unpretentious, with a communal dorm, outside toilet, very friendly staff and an excellent map of the whole area, including the Siriu and Tătăru mountains to the east. As is often the case there are electric fittings but no power.

From here there are again two major choices, either to continue from the cabana southwards to the Muntele Roşu cabana and Cheia, or to pass through and over the Ciucaş massif and out to Babarunca cabana on the DN 1A north of Cheia, continuing if desired all the way to Predeal, and onwards into the Bucegi, Piatra Craiului, Făgăraş, and the whole way along the crest of the Southern Carpathians.

The path down towards Cheia, marked with a blue cross, drops rapidly away into the valley of the Pîrîu Berii; if you miss the short-cut path leaving the track at a hairpin bend, you will reach the stream at an abandoned hut and then turn right down the dry (with luck) stream bed. After about 30 minutes you reach a fountain and five minutes later a vague junction where the yellow stripe route leaves to the left. Continuing down the valley would bring you very easily to a forestry road and to the main road two kilometres from Cheia; I took the route to the left across the stream and up, not *too* steeply. Again there are cliffs to the right, and then the megalithic peaks of Turnu Caprioarei (Goats' Tower), and after 24 minutes the path turns a corner into a small meadow with attractive conglomerate outcrops and a view of Muntele Roşu cabana ahead with its large car-park. The path goes easily on through mixed woodland, after ten minutes the red triangle route from the north end of Gropşoare (close to my camping spot on the saddle) comes in from the left, and it's only four minutes more to the cabana at 1,260m. This is typical of cabanas on metalled roads, being really a concrete hotel with bar, restaurant, and a coach party being serenaded by an accordionist while they ate. On the other hand I did have a decent double room to myself, even if there was no hot water.

From here it is seven kilometres down the asphalt to Cheia at 870m, but much less following the yellow stripe markings. In just over half an hour you come to the DN 1A and head down a track to the right, turning left after just a minute, and arriving at the north end of Cheia five minutes later; if heading up, you should follow the path right into the conifers opposite an electricity sub-station. It takes five minutes more to reach the campsite (mainly cabins as usual) and another seven minutes to the hotel, two large chalet-style blocks also with camping cabins in the grounds. This is the centre of this pleasantly low-key resort and the place to wait for buses. At the road junction at the south end of the village is something that claims to be a *Bistro*. There is a bus to Bucureşti at 1100, which gives ample time to hike down from either of the cabanas. The road to the south, past the well-known nunnery of Suzana, is very attractive, particularly when approaching the mountains from the south.

The main alternative is to climb up into Vf Ciucaş itself (from 1,550m at Ciucaş cabana to the summit at 1,954m) and continue westwards to the main road. Either from the cabana or via the short cut past the radio tower, you should take the path marked with red stripes and crosses climbing up steadily to a junction under the Tigăile Mari (the Big Pans), where the red cross route continues left under the rocks with equally good views, and the red stripe route climbs up a conglomerate ravine to a small saddle about 35 minutes from the cabana. To reach the summit ignore the path to the left and continue up an eroded little trough of a path to reach, in another quarter hour, the grassy top, marked with a cross, and with views of row upon row of reddish conglomerate buttresses lining the radial valleys.

From here one path runs northwest and then down to the north to reach a *drum forestier* visible below and leading to Vama Buzăului; the red stripe route continues downwards on the south side of the ridge and seems to be beautifully graded, for climbing as well as descending, all the way to the Bratocea pass (1,272m, under two hours away) where it meets the highway between Cheia and Babarunca. Although it heads south for a considerable distance, this might well in fact be the best route if you happened to want to walk to Predeal. However after 20 minutes I turned right at Şaua Tigăilor (Saucepans saddle!) to rejoin the red cross route. Whichever route you choose you can safely ignore an odd marker pole above the Bratocea route.

The red cross route passes below some large outcrops to the north-northwest and soon became rather overgrown and wet with overnight dew, although the path is clear enough. After 25 minutes you will have dropped down to mature spruce without undergrowth and the path continues easily along the ridge before zigzagging down to a very overgrown clearing at Şaua Teslei 38 minutes from the junction, where a well-used sheep track comes in from the left, possibly from the forestry road in the Babarunca valley — if taking the red cross route in the other direction you should turn half-left at the marker pole in the clearing and find the path just to the left/north of the ridge, rather hidden in the trees. The path onward rises briefly to a ridge with mixed beech and spruce trees, and passes under a big outcrop to enter Poiana Teslei and cross a stream to reach a ridge and stîna. There is a sign to the *Izvor* or spring to the right here, and you should zig left off this to go down into the beech woods, with some fine mature trees along the ridge.

After 20 minutes you reach a junction and turn left on to a path now marked with a red stripe, not another red cross as in the *Invitation*: this runs down through tall beeches and after eight minutes turns on to a small path through a spruce plantation, where you may find more *frag* plants. In three minutes a path comes in from the left; keep right on a rather muddy sheep track through a beech coppice and more young spruce, to arrive after a quarter hour at the main valley *drum forestier* by a bridge. Turn right and almost immediately there is a sign-posted short cut left through a field to Babarunca cabana on the highway at 872m. There are camping cabins here, and a good restaurant/bar which doesn't seem to suffer too much from being a roadside stop. The cabanier grinds real coffee and sells bags of sultanas for hikers — the only ones I ever found in Romania. Wonderful!

From here it is only 27km to Braşov, or 18.5km to Cheia, which should be easy enough to hitch, although there is not a great deal of traffic. The blue stripe route west from here runs along a *drum forestier* starting from a bridge five minutes north of the cabana. Sixteen minutes from the main road there is a well-signed turning right to Vf Vaida and the valley of the Doftana (no connection with the Doftana prison near Ploieşti, the notorious pre-war equivalent of Moscow's Lubyanka). Take this past some forestry cabanas, cross a stream and turn right/north-northwest in the only remaining plot of mature beech and spruce. On a hot day this was one of the toughest climbs I had to tackle in the Carpathians; it was also where, very punctually on the first day of August, I found my first *zmeură* (wild raspberry), the favourite wild fruit of Romanians, both humans and bears. It took me some time to go through the mature trees, then young larch, beech and spruce, an overgrown clearing, and more mature beech, to the edge of a large *poiana*. From here the route goes uphill past a derelict hut to reach the hilltop in about ten minutes.

Here there are good views back to the east, and north-northwest to Lake Săcele; a further two minutes west-northwest across the downs bring you to the 1,529m summit of Vf Vaida, with views of the ranges to the west as well. Heading along the ridge to the northwest there is a sign on the saddle after just four minutes, but it is simpler to go left before this on to a cart track which goes down between two sets of trees to fork left about 12 minutes later. This ridge route, running northwest, is scattered with pine trees as well as the usual spruce.

After 17 minutes there is another fork to the left, and another after six more minutes. If you want to descend to the Doftana valley and then follow it to the DN 1A and Braşov you should go straight ahead here towards Santul-Vechi; I turned left again on the path signposted to Renţea cabana, although in fact this cabin has now been taken over by the military as a shooting lodge, and paths past it closed. This route passes the leftmost shooting butt and drops down into the woods to the right and then on in meadow with the woods to the right, before passing through a plantation of common silver fir for five minutes and finally coming down the left/south edge of a meadow to reach a forestry cabana and the junction of two unmade forestry roads, 18 minutes after the Santul-Vechi turning.

From here most route markings towards Renţea have been removed; the easiest route would certainly be to take the *drum forestier* opposite all the way up the Valea Ţigăilor (marked with yellow stripes) to meet the red and blue triangle routes from Renţea (which do still exist) just north of Vf Ţigăilor. Alternatively you could do as I did and turn off this route after five minutes, after crossing the Doftana bridge, at a yellow stripe marker pole, and then climb west-northwest up the very steep ridge on a cart-track starting by a tree marked V11 227 by the foresters. This took 15 minutes slog; at the top I went right before heading uphill westwards on a cart track along the ridge.

After an hour I reached the summit of Vf Renţei (1,379m). Renţea cabana is to the left straddling the head of a valley. If you continue north for roughly ten minutes you come to a path that leads either on to Săcele or back along the side of the ridge before dropping down to an unmade road complete with telephone line to the cabana. Just as when a fallen tree blocks a path, the local shepherds have established an alternative route through the woods behind the cabana; alternatively you could claim not to understand Romanian and hike straight through if you feel confident about fending off the dogs.

Then climb steeply up to the southwest to a stîna, and southwest then south along a level sheep track until reaching, 40 minutes from the cabana, a *drum forestier* and the red and blue triangle route to Lake Găvan (1,450m, also known as yet another Lacu Roşu), Susai cabana and Predeal, four and a half hours away. Turning right/southwest the route crosses a couple of streams, goes left across a clearing and climbs for thirty minutes, with a hill to the left, to a ridge and a junction with the red stripe route from Ciucaş via Bratocea and Predelus (see above). This leads to the right, signposted to Piatra Mare (Big Rock); although this is a very popular area for day hikes from the Braşov region, with quite a few cabanas and trails, you actually spend almost all your time here in thick spruce forests. As the route is never marked as it leaves clearings here, it is often hard to find the right turnings, despite now being in Map 17 of the *Invitation*. Near here I missed the direct route to Susai and Predeal, marked with a blue cross, and then the blue dot route from just north of Stîna Pietricica to Predeal. Therefore it did indeed take me just over four hours to reach Predeal.

Following the blue triangles and red stripes I reached a T-junction with a muddy forestry track in 50 minutes and turned right/north. After ten minutes this route crossed a very good gravel road on a saddle and after a short climb went to the left around a hilltop after another 30 minutes, to cross the overgrown clearing of Stîna Pietricica and a stream. This is the junction with the red cross route from Piatra Mare south to Susai, and in principle with the blue dot route to Predeal. The red cross route south runs generally downhill along the ridge in spruce and fir, and then rises gently to reach, after one hour, another *drum forestier* and the blue cross route at Şaua Pietricica. This is much closer than shown on the *Invitation* map to the junction of the blue cross route to Susai and the red cross route direct to Predeal — it took me just nine minutes, and then just four minutes more, on the red cross route, to join the main route down from Susai cabana, very busy with day hikers.

Almost immediately there's another junction, marked with blue crosses left/south to the Clăbucet-Plecare upper cable-car terminal — as shown on map 16 of the *Invitation*, not as on Map 17. Another 16 minutes down the main red cross route brought me to the lower end of that elusive blue dot route from Stîna Pietricica, and eight minutes up to Cioplea cabana at 1,110m at the top of B-dul Libertaţii, 25 minutes from central Predeal. This route from Susai to Cioplea is both a busy walking route and an active logging road, running parallel and crisscrossing; Cioplea is another roadhead cabana with a large car-park and a day bar.

Predeal is a busy resort in both summer and winter with a full range of shops (by Romanian standards). From the railway station five buses a day run to Pîrîu Rece and three a day to Trei Brazi, both cabanas in the hills to the west of the town (see the next section), and two a day to Găeşti via Sinaia and Tîrgovişte, as well as trains and buses to Braşov.

An attractive alternative would be to follow the blue triangle markings north rather than south from Stîna Pietricica to Piatra Mare and then down following the yellow stripe markings to Cascada Şapte Scării, the Seven Stairs Waterfall, a famous beauty spot, to reach the road at Dîmbu Morii cabana on the DN 1, which is worth considering as a good cheap base for visiting Braşov.

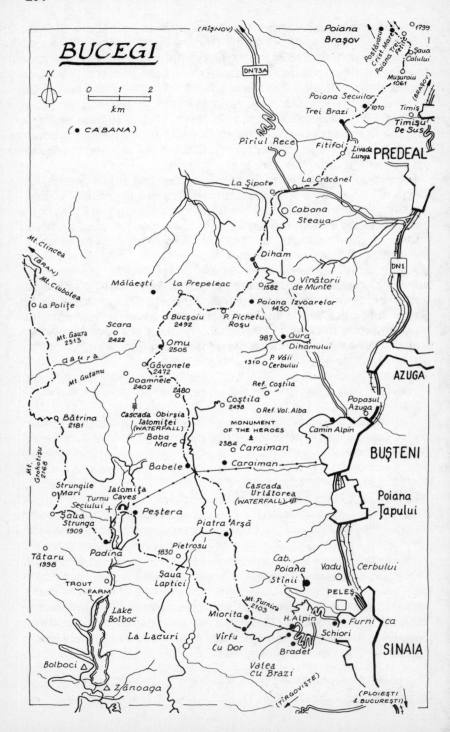

Chapter 7

The Southern Carpathians

THE BUCEGI MOUNTAINS

Of the three or four most popular mountain areas of Romania, the Bucegi are the closest to Bucureşti, just a couple of hours away, and therefore are particularly busy at weekends, especially around the cable-cars from the Prahova valley towns of Sinaia and Buşteni. They are also particularly well equipped with cabanas and refuges, and the sheep dogs are generally accustomed to tourists and well-behaved.

The most lyrical description of the Bucegi is by Vlahuţă, the bard of the Carpathians, and should ideally be read with Strauss's *Alpine Symphony* playing in the background: 'When you are high up here, you are seized by a vague restlessness as if you were ready to fly. There is something so magnificent and festive all around that you suddenly forget you are tired, hungry and thirsty, and refuse to sit down, gazing in amazement all around, breathing in the pure fresh air which seems to smell of snow; your eyes seem insatiably to scan the remote horizon, whilst a strange feeling of joy and pride makes you lift your head and look around as if you too had helped to create all this beauty and the hosts of mountains were singing a hymn of praise to you... Innumerable peaks spring up on all parts, unfolding and thrusting upwards in the clear air, as if ready to pierce the blue arch of the sky with their serrated crests. Looking down between them, the eye travels over the tops of dense forests in the valleys far below where clusters of human dwellings are scattered in white patches, some sparkling like bits of glass in the valley bottoms... That is how our towns must seem to the eagles soaring in their mighty realm'.

The massif is a sedimentary syncline, with Mesozoic gritstone and conglomerate above Jurassic limestone, especially in the Ialomiţei valley, on a floor of crystalline schists; much of it is a U-shaped plateau wrapped around the head of the Ialomiţei, and the only really high peaks and cliffs are at the northern end, well away from the cable-cars and ski areas to the southeast, which can be pretty sordid.

The flora is mainly beech up to 1,400-1,500m, mainly spruce to 1,600-1,700m, sub-alpine spruce glades and dwarf pine to 2,200-2,300m, and alpine tundra above that with dwarf species such as *Silene acaulis, Saxifraga moschata, Minuartia* and *Primula mininma* in small cushions adhering to the ground, as well as dwarf willow (*Salicetum reticulatae*) on the northern and northwestern slopes. In practice the forests are soon left behind and most of the walking is on open plateau with wide views.

There are now ten reservations in the massif, of which the main one, protecting all the northern and northeastern slopes, now covers 6,680 hectares, while others cover the Piatra Arsă forest of century-old firs up to 50m high, beech up to 45m high, and the rare orchid *Epipegium aphyllum*, similar forest near the Urlătoarea waterfall, the Peştera Ialomiţei cave and nearby Poiana Crucii, of which more later, the southern and eastern sides of Vf Zănoaga, an island of thermophilic vegetation on sunny Jurassic limestone slopes with a virgin grove of spruce above, an area of *Daphne blagaiana* on Vf Furnica and enclosed botanical reservations on top of Vf Omu (the highest peak in the Bucegi) and the Babele ridge, and a peat bog at the foot of Vf Lăptici containing *Salix myrtilloides* and *Salix bicolor*.

Among the more interesting fauna are about 150 chamois, in the alpine zone between Mount Jepii Mici and Mount Gaura, and deer, bears, boar, lynx and wolves, together with the white vulture (*Gyps fulvus fulvus*) and golden eagle. However as the mountains are so crowded with people for much of the year these do tend to lie low most of the time.

Getting there

There are cable-cars from Buşteni and Sinaia which provide the simplest means of access; the route I describe passes the upper terminals and so you can easily pick it up there, and indeed take a circular route to return by the other cable-car. However I chose to spend a day hiking down from Postăvaru (called Schuler by the Saxons), above Poiana Braşov, and passing close to Predeal, Romania's highest town at 1,032m; this was in fact one of the most varied days hiking I had in Romania, passing through almost all the most representative types of Carpathian scenery.

Sinaia, now one hour and forty minutes by train from Bucureşti, was the favourite royal resort and became known as 'The Pearl of the Carpathians'. The town dates from 1581 when St Nicholas' hermitage was founded, superseded in 1695 by St Catherine's monastery, founded by Michael Cantacuzino (head of the first Phanariot dynasty) in honour of St Catherine's monastery in Sinai, containing a stone which he had brought from there. In 1774 another hermitage was founded up the valley in Predeal. All traffic had used the Bran pass until a road (the present DN 1) was built up the valley and over the Predeal pass to Braşov in 1846. In 1875 Romania's first king, Carol I, chose Sinaia as the site for his summer palace (completed 1883), and in 1877 the railway was built. Whereas previously the valley had only a thousand or so inhabitants, it now began to develop a sizable tourist trade, although initially this was confined to the summer and also limited because Transylvania, so close to the north, was a foreign country.

Much of the architecture, such as the Casino, now the *Centru de Amuzament*, is in Côte d'Azur style, but there is always a suspicion that it is mocking its own pretensions, taking its cue from Carol's own Peleş castle which is a glorious pastiche of Bavarian mock-Gothic in the style of Ludwig. Having been appropriated by Ceauşescu as a private palace and then closed due to dry rot, Peleş is now open as a museum and well worth seeing, although only open from 0900 to 1500 Wednesday to Sunday. The Palace and Caraiman Hotels retains their Edwardian elegance and are worth experiencing, and I have also heard good things of the Hotel Intim, just above the monastery on Str Furnica, which leads to Cota 1400; there are a few other major hotels, as well as the Piscu Cîinelui, Schiori, Poiana Stînii, Brădet and Valea cu Brazi cabanas and Vadu Cerbului han and campsite, just north at km 127 on the DN 1. Tourist Information is at Bdul Carpaţi 19.

Buşteni, just to the north in the Prahova valley, is the climbing capital of Romania, and the start of the cable-car route up to Babele and down to Peştera; not all trains stop here, but if you can get here it is a smaller and more relaxed base, with the Hotel Silva at the cable-car terminal on Str Industriei, the Hotel Caraiman and the Caminul Alpin cabana up Str Valea Alba just north of the station, as well as the Azuga campsite just north.

Hiking directions

I have no hesitation in using technology to get me up a big hill to the starting point of a hike, so I began this one by taking a bus to Poiana Braşov and then the first cable-car up Postăvaru. You can of course hike up following red or blue cross markings, if you have the time. From the upper terminal the main path goes uphill, marked with a blue stripe, to the summit of Postăvaru and down to Timişu de Jos in 3½ hours, and down the steps and zigzag path to the right/west to reach Cristianu Mare cabana (at 1,704m) in eight minutes. This is a genuine mountain hut and not at all connected with the tourist economy of Poiana Braşov. From here I headed south, just to the right of the path down from Postăvaru, following yellow stripe markings and keeping left after two minutes when this route splits to also go down to the Postăvaru cabana, ten minutes below.

After five minutes of walking downhill an unmarked path comes in from the right; the route runs along the side of a hill to the left, with views over hills just over 200m below. After a brief rise it enters Poiana Trei Fetiţe (Three Girls Meadow) at 1,620m (for once, I'm in a position to say that the altitude of 1,720m given in the *Invitation* is definitely wrong); there is not much of a meadow here, but rather a small hilltop clearing ten minutes from the cabana, from which the yellow stripe route heads down to the left/southeast. This is a steep drop, zigzagging down over nasty slimy rocks and through firs for 22 minutes, before passing over a small beech-covered hillock and becoming less slippery and more sandy and overgrown; although there are still frequent fallen firs, the trees are mainly beech and silver birch.

After 45 minutes there is a good view west to the cliffs of Muchia Cheii at a point where there is a stretch of cable to help climb over a conglomerate outcrop a couple of metres high at 1,210m altitude. The path continues down with more fallen firs among the beech woods to reach a crossing with a path, marked with a red triangle, from Rîşnov in the west to the Timişu de Sus rail halt to the east. The actual saddle is not reached for another eight minutes, and then the path climbs a bit and runs along the Cărbunarea ridge. This is a broad path through light beech wood with some Austrian pines, in places running parallel to a muddy forestry track, and after a quick half-hour reaches Poiana Secuilor at 1,070m, and, five minutes later, the cabana of the same name, with a junction with a yellow triangle path coming in from the village of Timiş de Sus and going on to Rîşnov. Another quarter-hour along the main track brings you to the Trei Brazi cabana (1,128m), at the end of a road and bus route from Predeal. Naturally this is less of a real hikers' cabana than that at Poiana Secuilor; however camping is not permitted at Poiana Secuilor, while a fenced camping area is provided at Trei Brazi.

From here you have the option of crossing the road to take the blue triangle path to the Pîrîu Rece cabana (1¾ hours), also linked by bus to Predeal, but the direct route to Omul and the Bucegi turns left and follows the road for eight minutes before turning right at the end of the *poiana* and climbing steeply for 16 minutes to a junction where all three paths are marked with blue crosses; turn right here to follow the good path to La Crăcănel. You are already just one minute from the top of Vf Fitifoi (1,287m, in the heart of the woods), where you fork left/just west of south to go down the ridge for 20 minutes. This brings you to a natural gas wellhead and a hut, and five muddy minutes later, to the Predeal to Rîşnov road, particularly praised by Sacheverell Sitwell, where you turn right. Looking south here you have a good view of the climb awaiting you into the Bucegi massif.

Although the *Invitation* describes this route northbound (Map 17, route 3), I can't see any point in climbing up Postăvaru unless you actually want to base yourself in a cabana up there and not reach Braşov until the next morning; but if you should do this route in reverse you should take the cart-track leading up a broad avenue rather than the better *drum* more to the east. Even if heading south you should consider whether to hike from Postăvaru or to start from Predeal. If the latter you can either follow a path marked with a blue stripe up the Joiţei valley, not too far south of Predeal station, to this point; or take a bus from Predeal to Trei Brazi; or take a Predeal to Pîrîul Rece bus as far as La Şipote, the point 500m or five minutes walk to the right/west (and 20m higher at 1,110m), where a *drum forestier* turns left/south signposted to Diham and marked with red and yellow dots.

However you get here, this is the start of the real approach to the Bucegi massif. After nine minutes a path comes in from the right as the *drum* swings left, and the red dot path turns to the right; Steaua cabana at Forban, to the left, is not a public cabana, although you might well be able to find a bed there in season. Take the path, now running through typical low-altitude deciduous woodland — ash, common silver fir, beech, elder — with many streams, mostly crossed by log bridges. After 17 minutes an active *drum forestier* comes in from the right; after following this south for 100m over a bridge the path turns to the right up a minor forestry track that zigs up for five minutes to a *poiana* with a view north to Postăvaru. The yellow cross markings go straight ahead to Mălăieşti cabana, and our red dot path bears left on a gravel track to climb to Diham cabana at 1,320m after another 20 minutes. A path marked with a blue cross turns right here to Mălăieşti cabana, taking 2¾ hours in summer and, apparently, double that in winter.

You should continue south following the little red dots, following the track for four minutes and then turning right along a lesser cart track with views of both the Bucegi towering over 1,000m above and of the Birsenland depression below to the northwest. After 13 minutes there is a path left to Poiana Izvoarelor cabana (Meadow of the Springs, another highly original Romanian name) and after another 13 minutes, traversing easily around a hill to your left, you reach the end of the red dot route at Pichet Roşu, from where you can continue to skirt the foothills of the massif to reach the railway at Buşteni, or turn right to head west along the northern slopes of Vf Bucşoiu to find a spot from which to launch an assault on Omul.

This route, marked with red stripes, is forbidden in winter, as almost all routes around Mălăieşti seem to be. It starts by climbing steadily on conglomerate rocks and then levels out a bit, crossing three ravines that still had snow in them in July. After 45 minutes there is a short sharp climb to a minor ridge where you head left into dwarf pine and reach after two minutes the final junction to Mălăieşti, your last chance of refuge if you don't feel like assaulting Omu today.

According to the sign here it takes 3½-4½ hours to Omu cabana, although the sign at Pichetu Roşu reckoned 3½-4 hours from there; in fact it took me under two hours from here, although it would have been more if I had not spent the whole day limbering up. This is Prepeleac, 1,760m, and Omu cabana is at 2,505m, the highest in the Carpathians. The path goes straight up, with fixed cables and a lot of scrambling, for the first 50 minutes (although this time will be variable), through dwarf rhododendrons and then grass, with some chamois dotted around. There are also natural arches of conglomerate, and, higher up, views of other ridges and outcrops. From a marker pole on a ridge there is an easier quarter-hour's climb to a junction to the right down to Mălăieşti, and then after 20 minutes more you arrive at the summit of Bucşoiu (2,492m) from where there is a dip and then a fairly fast and level stretch for a total of 17 minutes more. A sign here claims that Omu is 45 minutes away, but eight minutes along a mossy ridge brings you to a sign claiming more accurately that it is only 200m away; in fact it took me two minutes to a junction right to Bran and, of course, Mălăieşti, and two more to the weather station and cabana, built up against the summit outcrop. It is a very basic cabana, with very little choice of food (unusually, it doesn't even have hens) — but when I settled for bread and cheese, with herbal tea, I actually got a lovely kind of fondu! It certainly has a better class of overnight visitor than most cabanas.

From here there is one route northwestwards towards Bran and Şimon (the route down the Gaura valley is particularly stunning, linking with the route described below), another to the southwest along the 'Borderguards' Road' to the western ridge of the Bucegi, which I crossed the next day as described below, a route directly down to Peştera via the Obîrşia Ialomiţei waterfall, another to the east down the lovely Valea Cerbului to Buşteni, and the most important southeastwards towards Babele and the eastern ridge. The ridges and glacial valleys that these routes take radiate like spokes from Omu, the focal point of the whole area. Many of the valleys have cliffs that look like Peak District Edges writ larger; however there are far more paths, and wider ones, than in most British National Parks.

The route southeast is initially marked by red, yellow and blue stripes, passing to the right of a hillock and down a slightly crumbly cliff to where the red and blue stripe routes branch right. Following the yellow stripes you drop to a saddle about 20 minutes from the cabana and continue to the left from a 4WD track, below an edge which even looks like Millstone Grit and after 20 minutes reach another saddle with a pile of bricks, where a path marked with red crosses forks left past the Vf Coştila TV tower to Vf Caraiman with its massive war memorial overlooking Buşteni. If preferred you can reach the winter route above the edge by a steep gully partially blocked by a gas pipe, of all things, or follow the 4WD track around to the right to avoid the gully. The main path continues south across level open moorland, pleasant walking except for the close proximity of the 4WD track and buried gas main, and the excessive number of marker poles for skiing in bad visibility.

Approaching Babele there are a few anthropomorphic outcrops, including one rather good likeness of an old woman bending down as in Millet's 'The Gleaners', and another known as the Sphinx. The complex of Babele cabana, broken-down wind turbine, weather station and cable-car terminals, at 2,206m, is reached in about 40 minutes from the pile of bricks. From here, fighting your way through the day-trippers, you can head left/east to the more intimate Caraiman cabana visible on the edge of the plateau at 2,025m just over one kilometre away (although the signs say it takes 30 minutes to get there) and then up to the huge monument to the heroes of 1916-18 or down the Valea Jepii to Buşteni, 1,300m below, or right/west to Peştera cabana in the Ialomiţa valley. There are also cable-cars down to both Buşteni and Peştera, except on Tuesdays.

Leaving here the yellow stripe route passes between the first and second pylons of the Buşteni cable-car on a stony track and heads south; again there are marker poles every 20 metres, as well as lots of semi-buried power cables to the various ski-drags dotted around the plateau. Although open moorland this is not a particularly attractive stretch with no real views. After 35 minutes there is a junction left (marked with red triangles) to Cantonul Jepi naturalists' cabana on the edge of the plateau at 1,960m, which when I first passed was polluting the whole area with a loud radio. After ten more minutes, now on a sandy track through dwarf pine, the path crosses a blue triangle path (beautifully graded and perhaps the easiest route up on to the plateau from the east, following the line of an old logging ropeway) from Buşteni to the east to the Piatra Arsă complex five minutes to the west at 1,950m. This includes a huge, ugly and unfinished hotel-style cabana and Romania's high-altitude sports training base, founded for the Mexico Olympics of 1968 and World Cup of 1970.

Piatra Arsă (Burnt Rock) itself is another 1½km south. To get here you can either go down to the cabana and then turn left to continue on the yellow stripe route, or keep to the bypass route and turn right at the running track and football pitch to join the yellow stripe route. After about eight minutes there is the first turning down to Sinaia (marked with blue stripes and passing via the Poiana Stînii where Ceauşescu had one of his many holiday homes and where a public cabana has now reopened), and after ten more minutes you pass on a sandy track to the left of a former stîna, where the yellow stripe route splits, going either up and over Vf Furnica by a badly eroded path or around it by a track to the left, with views over Sinaia. To reach the upper cable-car terminal and Miorita cabana you have to climb up from this track at some point. The cable-car is in two stages, the lower from Sinaia (Str Cuza Vodă) to the roadhead at the Hotel Alpin, also known as Cota 1400 (Altitude 1,400m), and the higher from there to Vf Furnica or Cota 2000 (more accurately Cota 1950). The cable-cars should run daily bar Mondays, but when I was there on a Sunday only the chairlift from Cota 1400 to Virfu cu Dor, five minutes to the south of Miorita, was operating. The Virfu cu Dor cabana, at 1,885m in the heart of the main skiing area of the Bucegi, has closed following a fire.

This would logically be the end of a hike south from Postăvaru or Omu, taking either the cable-car or 4WD track down to Cota 1400 and Sinaia; however, a slave to duty, I hypothetically returned from Sinaia and set off on another hike northwestwards to Peştera and Bran. This route, marked with red stripes and yellow crosses, follows a track up westwards over a saddle and then down to the new Valea Dorului (Valley of Desire) cabana at the foot of several ski-lifts. There is also a 'summer variant' of the red stripe route, unmarked but clear enough, following an enlarged sheep track along the open hillside to the right. This is a pleasant easy walk right around Vf Furnica, crossing two streams before turning left to cross the main Izvoru Dorului after 47 minutes in all, and rejoin the marked route. This is a very green and pleasant land, more like the Yorkshire Dales than the Omu area; there is an easy ten-minute climb up to Şaua Lăptici and the unmade road to Babele, easily visible from across the valley.

The next valley to the west is very different, full of trees and houses; the path drops to the right into fir trees, with some larch, forking right after 26 minutes at a sign and picnic table. After another eight minutes it crosses a *drum forestier* and stream and crosses a *poiana* recently planted with young conifers right across the path. Another eight minutes from the stream there is a left turn which you should take only if heading for Padina cabana; otherwise continue straight ahead to pick up the *drum forestier* north for ten minutes to the path (marked with a blue cross) left to Peştera Ialomiţei and back to Padina cabana. Continuing north you pass the present Peştera hermitage to the left, the Poiana Crucii fenced reservation of *Festucetum rubrae* and after five minutes in all Peştera cabana (more of a hotel than a cabana) to the right. Paths to Babele, Omu and Bran continue on up the *drum forestier*, past the cable-car terminal, while the blue stripe route to Piatra Arşa starts immediately behind and above the cabana.

The blue cross path leads around the south side of the hermitage to a side entrance, by which you are welcome to visit the small wooden church built in 1911, with a novel version of the Last Judgment painted inside the main door. The path continues down steps and a typically ropy boardwalk to cross the Ialomiţa just below the impressive but short Peşterii gorges. The Peştera cave is three minutes up a path to the right, under Mount Bătrîna, and the whole area is a reservation of 225 hectares with its luxuriant undergrowth of *Heracleum palmatum*, and sun-loving plants such as *Festucetum saxatilis* on the limestone slopes. The hermitage was originally, perhaps from 1509, in the mouth of the cave until it finally burnt down in 1956, and Mrs Gerard, like Sacheverell Sitwell, speaks evocatively of 'those solitary monks, snowed up during the greater part of the year in their cavern convent scooped out of the rock'. It is now planned to rebuild a hermitage in the cave mouth, as well as a bioenergy healing centre just below. The cave itself, 400m long with a 60m drop, was explored and opened up in 1897, and again in 1924 when the stream was diverted or diverted itself. The boardwalks, slippery and full of gaps, seem to date from 1924 or even 1897, the lighting is erratic and there is not a lot to see inside, although you may be shown the bones of cave bears that died there many centuries ago.

The blue cross path continues south along the right/west bank of the river for three minutes to run into a road in a beautiful circle of cliffs under Turnu Seciului. Where the road crosses to the left bank the path stays on the right and enters the Padina meadow, full of tents in the summer. The cabana has a bar with television and a few mod cons, but awful mattresses; there are nicer family rooms next door in the *canton*. From here the road runs south through the Coteanu and Tătarului gorges to the Scropoasa reservoir and Zănoaga cabana, reservation and gorges — mosquito-infested but very scenic.

I chose to head westwards to see the less frequented western wing of the Bucegi and to link to Bran and the Piatra Craiului and Leaota mountains. The route, marked with red dots and crosses, leaves by a stony track up behind the cabana and after nine minutes zigs to the right up a path marked with poles. The path flirts with the track to a stîna and after 20 minutes rises to a ridge (there is a more level route along the hillside behind the stîna to the right) and continues not too steeply up towards limestone outcrops above a conglomerate base. Fifteen minutes from the lower ridge the path arrives at the main ridge at the Şaua Strunga (1,904m); a short-cut route is planned but not, by 1991, marked (with red stripes) to pass over the 1,890m saddle just to the south and to lead to the Leaota mountains and the Piatra Craiului via the Curmătura Fiarelor.

The route north along the crest is also marked with red stripes (four hours to Omu): one variant starts just east of the saddle and goes steeply up over the rocks to the crest, while another takes a route to the east below the cliffs. Taking the higher route, I climbed for a quarter hour before levelling out and joining a shepherds' track which avoids the summit of Strungile Mari (2,089m), 24 minutes from the saddle. Here there are cliffs with a good view west and also northeast towards the Vf Coştila television tower; Omu seems to consistently attract clouds, if not crowds. The path drops quite steeply down to a saddle, still in open limestone moorland with attractive small flowers, and continues below the outcrops of Colţii Tapului before beginning to climb Vf Bătrîna about 53 minutes after leaving the saddle, still on a clear cart track. After 13 minutes the red triangle path directly from Peştera joins from the right and eight minutes later the path reaches signs just north of the summit. You can either continue along the ridge or drop down to the west, into a depression dotted with houses and fields in a most un-Romanian pattern. Whichever way you go, you will meet virtually no-one, either hikers or shepherds.

The path west is marked with red triangles, although not that well; after dropping to a beautiful shelf of meadow with outcrops of conglomerate above and limestone below, dwarf rhododendrons, lots of flowers and lots of flies, the path disappears to the left and zigzags down to the left of some very impressive outcrops, across scree below and into a wood, emerging into Poiana Guţanu 37 minutes from the top. Follow the top edge of the meadow right/north for five minutes to pick up the blue triangle markings; after about eight more minutes these head up to a ridge and into a spruce wood. It carries on easily northwards along the 1,600m contour below spectacular cliffs, crossing a ravine and stream and then dropping down through ash and elder and crossing a meadow littered with moraines, conglomerate boulders and tree stumps to reach the Gaura stream at a log bridge, just below a cowherd's hut, 24 minutes from the *poiana*.

From here there is a path down the valley to Şimon, marked with yellow triangles, and up the valley to Omu via Moara Dracului (Devil's Mill) waterfall not far above, marked with red crosses. The red triangles also continue across the stream to Bran three hours ahead; this path climbs steadily in spruce for seven minutes then goes up and down over some rather eroded stretches before climbing up to the Vf Pintecele ridge 28 minutes from the bridge (don't follow the sheep track left into the cleared area, which leads to Şimon). At the top is a clearing with a picnic table and signs, and a spring 60m to the left, although you pass plenty of water on the way up. Far below to the north the Birsenland depression is visible. The path heads to the left above young spruce and then steepish down through fine mature silver firs until after 50 minutes it reaches the end of a *drum forestier* with a camping place, and after seven minutes on the *drum* reaches the Valea Poartii forestry cabanas and then crosses to the right bank of the Poarta stream, with lots of lively white water. After about ten minutes you begin to enter the outskirts of Bran, with lots of half-completed houses (many apparently built by Securitate agents), but it takes almost half an hour from the forestry cabanas to reach the junction with the red stripe route from Omu (supposedly six hours away, although I don't believe it), and another 22 minutes to the road junction at the centre of the village. Braşov and the Han (Tourist Inn) are to the right, the castle and the cabana to the left (turn right at the bus stop and then left up a path to reach the cabana (closed Mondays) on the far side of the Turcu river). Private rooms are also available opposite the bus stop, and there is a new mini-hotel at the petrol station on the road north.

Moving on

The chief attraction of Bran, which brings in every coach party, Romanian or foreign, which comes to the Braşov area, is the castle relentlessly promoted as Dracula's, although this is certainly false: Vlad Ţepeş may have attacked the castle, built between 1395 and 1427 by Mircea cel Bătrîn and then held by the city of Braşov, but he never owned or lived in it. However it looks as though it *should* be Dracula's castle, and as Vlad's historic castle at Poienari, south of Lake Vidraru on the Trans-Făgăraş Highway, is largely in ruins and a very long climb from the car park, one can understand why this one has been promoted instead. (Ceauşescu was keen to set Vlad up as a model of Romanian nationalism, fighting off the Turks and so on, at a time when he was leading a very independent foreign policy himself.) The castle was closed for painstaking restoration for

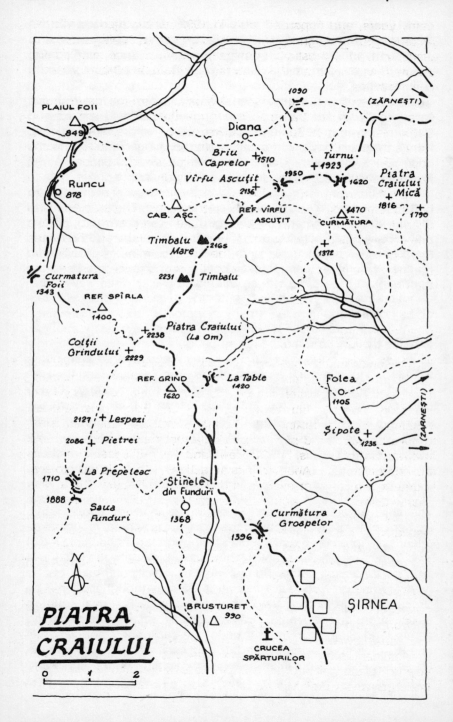

PIATRA
CRAIULUI

many years, and reopened early in 1992; as arranged by Queen Victoria's grand-daughter Marie it is a wonderful rabbit-warren of a place, with an interesting open-air museum of local architecture attached; well worth a visit if you can get there at 0900, before the coach parties.

Until the building of the road and railway through the Prahova valley via Sinaia, the Bran pass route was the only way through the Carpathians north of Bucureşti, used since Roman times at least. Hence the importance of the castle, and also of the *Vama* (customs post) just to its south, which houses a new and reasonably well presented museum, although only with Romanian captions.

From here you can continue south to the pass and Fundata to pick up the route into the Leaota mountains described in the section after next, hike west to the Piatra Craiului (see next section), or take one of the virtually hourly buses to Braşov — this is one of the routes that has been transformed since the revolution, as previously you had to take a far less frequent bus to Rîşnov and change to a train there.

PIATRA CRAIULUI

All the Romanian hillwalkers whose judgment I really respect say that the Piatra Craiului is their favourite, the choice of the discriminating hiker, and Bob Lancaster of High Places says of it 'There is a lot of verticality about... Crib Goch and Striding Edge plus some!'. Personally I prefer walking over moorland and find it mentally tiring to have to watch and plan every single footstep on a narrow and awkward ridge like this, but the views and the geological formations are indeed fantastic. Another of its attractions is that it is easy to see in one or two days, or even as a day trip from Braşov. It is a very clearly defined massif, a limestone ridge on crystalline schists 22km long with a very sharp crest and deep caves on the eastern side; geologically it is a continuation of the Bucegi, but in position it is connected to the Făgăraş range. It is recommended that you should not go alone or with a heavy pack due to the tricky rock-scrambling involved in places — but as usual I survived.

The northern and western slopes and main ridge are a natural reservation for chamois, *Rhododendron Kotschyi* and *Dianthus callizonus*, the Piatra Craiului pink, now found only here. There are the usual lower and upper mountain forest zones, with beech predominant in the lower zone and spruce in the upper zone, with yew in places at up to 1,200m, sycamore maple with thick undergrowth in dark valleys, and dwarf pine at about 1,770m to

1,900m. Fauna includes bear and lynx, as well as the chamois. The name means King's Stone (*Konigstein* in German; *Király-kö* in Hungarian).

Getting there

Although it is possible to reach the east side of the Piatra from Bran, the main access is via Zărneşti, at the end of a painfully slow branch line from Braşov; although absolutely flat and straight the train crawls along and tends to lose more time through lazy operating. There are not many buses directly from Braşov, although there are quite a few from the Bran direction; in any case the bus station (*Autocoloana*) is three kilometres out of town towards Braşov. The station is only about ten minutes from the centre where you can find a decent supermarket, a large hiking map of the massif and even a drinking fountain; but on the whole I feel that Zărneşti does very little for the hordes of hikers passing through it in the summer, and takes little profit from them at the moment. At the end of the main street the road left past the church (murals from 1782) leads to Gura Rîului cabana on the outskirts of town and to Curmătura cabana (which has a very good Saxon cabanier) and the eastern side of the Piatra, and the road right leads to Plain Foii cabana north of the Piatra which serves as a focus for routes to Iezer-Păpuşa and the Făgăraş ridge route (see relevant sections).

Hiking directions

If you leave Zărneşti by the route to the right and follow the signs left at once on to Str Tei and then left on to Str Vînătorii and right on to Str Topliţei, you rejoin the blue and yellow stripe routes to Curmătura, which turn left after another eight minutes (13 minutes from the start). This is in fact the main access to the northern and northwestern side of the Piatra, so you should turn off the Plaiul Foii road and follow this route, rising gradually above the unmade road to the right into fields dotted with small spruce trees and with the limestone cliffs looming ahead. After about 50 minutes, at a cross marked with a blue stripe, the path (marked with yellow stripes) turns left up the near side of a stream and into the woods; the assault begins. This is the Valea Crăpăturii, and after 14 minutes in the wood (with yew around the 1,200m level) you begin to climb up a rocky cleft; there is no more water from here on. It took me almost an hour of steady slog, interrupted by chamois spotting, to reach the ridge at 1,620m, 900m above Zărneşti.

From here the yellow stripes, with red and blue dots, continue down the other side for 15 minutes to Curmătura cabana (attractively set in meadows at 1,470m) which seems rather a waste of effort. The main ridge route south is marked with red dots and (after a brief diversion to a viewing platform) begins with some more rock-scrambling up and down among spruce trees. After six minutes there is a dip with a sign indicating an unmarked path down the valley to Curmătura, then the path goes up the edge of a scree patch to reach a cable and more rock-scrambling up and briefly down, which would be *very* tricky carrying a pack northwards. After just over half an hour it reaches the junction with a very steep blue cross route down northwards, and 120m or four minutes later the Turnu (Tower) peak at 1,923m.

The route continues on the crest before dropping left into trees and after 20 minutes coming up to the Şaua Padina Închisă at either 1,935m or 1,955m — higher than Turnu in any case. It crosses another route from Curmătura to the valley to the north, and another nine minutes on yet another steep path down northwards from Vf Padina Popii (1,970m). These peaks are more the ends of sections of ridge rather than real peaks, but they show the general rising trend. The path continues along the ridge with some complicated clambering over rocks, but one can equally well follow a parallel sheep track to the left/east through alpine meadows with dwarf bushes. After 38 minutes or so it reaches the blue triangle route from Curmătura to Plaiul Foii at Vf Ascuţit, with a polyhedral igloo as a basic refuge. From here there is some tricky climbing down to be done, mostly easier if you keep left, before following the ridge on upwards again and continuing over some awkward peaks and saddles, again frequently easier on the left-hand side, reaching La Om, the highest peak of the Piatra (2,238m), after 1¾ hours. Gradually the path becomes less rocky and more of an earth path, with dwarf rhododendrons.

From La Om the path does continue a long way along the ridge to the south but loses some of its interest, as well as being less well marked; most people either turn west here (in fact ten minutes south) to go down by *via ferrata* to Spîrla refuge and Plaiul Foii cabana, or at Şaua Funduri, 2½ hours south, to go to the Iezer-Păpuşa area, or else turn east as I first did to Grind refuge and the Leaota range. This path, marked with red stripes, continues south below the main ridge and turns left/east to cross some nasty slippery scree and the like, with some remarkably tame chamois, for 36 minutes, before going down across meadow marked with poles to the refuge, a tin hut visible from the ridge, with the nearest spring about ten minutes below. There are also interesting walks following blue triangles along the foot of the western cliffs, across scree slopes and to the Cerdacul Stancului, a rock arch blocked by a huge boulder which you can climb on to by a ladder.

From Grind the red stripe markings continue down the hill and left into the woods down a dry valley. After nine minutes take a fork to the right and zigzag down through the spruce woods for eight minutes more before again forking right on to a path marked with blue stripes to Brusturet cabana, at the north end of the Brusturet and Dîmboviciorei gorges. This path crosses a clearing above a line of trees with a stîna below and then around to the right down the left side of the valley, behind another line of trees. At the end, eleven minutes from the junction, follow the blue and yellow cross markings left down the shepherds' cart track by a stream that was dry when I was there in July. After four minutes it reaches a track from the left by another dry stream, and continues down to the right for eleven minutes to reach water by the junction of a *drum forestier* left to Şirnea and the Bran pass. I camped here, although Brusturet cabana is only another two kilometres on down the road.

It takes about 23 minutes along this very easy *drum* to the pass overlooking Şirnea; the view from here, with neat fields and scattered houses, with the sound of cowbells and the silhouette of the Bucegi massif beyond, seems very Austrian or, given the rudimentary drystone walls, like the Yorkshire Dales. The road goes to the right and zigs back left, so that you could easily take a short cut straight ahead to reach the first fringes of this very spread-out village. The vernacular architecture here is very attractive, with glazed verandahs and turreted first-floor rooms, often used in fact as hay lofts. It took me an hour from my camping place to reach the centre of the village, with post office and *alimentară* and then a *Bufet* with four camping cabins. There are occasional buses here, but I chose to walk on down the road to the main road, 40 minutes on; the rocks are mainly limestone and conglomerate, but there are odd moraine-like hillocks dotted all around this pleasant green countryside.

From the main road (DN 73) you could continue to the Bran pass 25 minutes south, and the junction to Fundata 15 minutes further on (see the next section), or head north to Bran and Braşov, probably by hitching as there are only about three buses a day as far as Bran.

THE LEAOTA MOUNTAINS

This hike is ideally part of a circuit from the Piatra Craiului (or Bucegi) to the Iezer-Păpuşa, beginning and ending, if desired, in Zărneşti. Of all the mountains in the immediate area these are the least known and the least frequented; this is a relief, but also means that navigation can be rather hit or miss at times, particularly in the lower, wooded, areas. Once up on the open moorland things become much simpler and more enjoyable. This area is not included in the *Invitation to the Romanian Carpathians*, but there is a new *Hartă Turistică* published in 1991 by Editura Pentru Turism, which includes the new roads, and in addition that of the Bucegi covers most of the Leaota area, with reasonable accuracy.

Getting there

We start from the DN 73 at Fundata, reached either from the Piatra Craiului as described in the previous section, or by road from Braşov and Bran to the north, or from Cîmpulung, where this part of the circuit ends up, to the south. There are about three buses a day from Braşov to Cîmpulung, and many more to Bran and the villages just south, from where you could hitch to Fundata. At the junction there is a post office and shops, although you should stock up before coming here. One minute down the side road you should go straight ahead, towards Fundăţica, where the road to Fundata turns left. Fundata proudly claims to be the highest village in Romania at 1,400m: this is in fact nothing special, when there are villages at over 4,000m altitude in the Himalayas and Andes, but nevertheless it is higher than Ben Nevis. Fundata is also well-known for the Nedeia of the Mountains, mentioned on page 110.

Hiking directions

From this junction the unmade road climbs briefly and then descends a dry valley to a T-junction, where you should turn left along a stream. After 11 minutes turn left where the stream and a track continue ahead, and climb just north of east for 12 minutes past a very good roofed-in spring and wonderful meadow flowers. Turn right on a left bend up a rough track for quarter of an hour and then curve right across a large *poiana* and stîna, continuing as a fenced track and swinging right along the edge of a spruce wood, just west of south. The route turns to the right/south and rises gently up a ridge, forking twice to the right and then, about 32 minutes from the stîna, swinging left in a level clearing and continuing up to the southeast. After five minutes it turns right at a spring and continues on a fairly level and easy path southwards until the path gets lost in the woods. I crossed a stream heading southwest, went over a ridge and southeast, still rising to come into the Sîntilia (Mică) *poiana*, with a stîna below to the right, about 45 minutes after passing the spring.

This route should be marked with red stripes but basically isn't; therefore it might be just as easy to continue ahead from the junction by the stream and follow that road and then a track

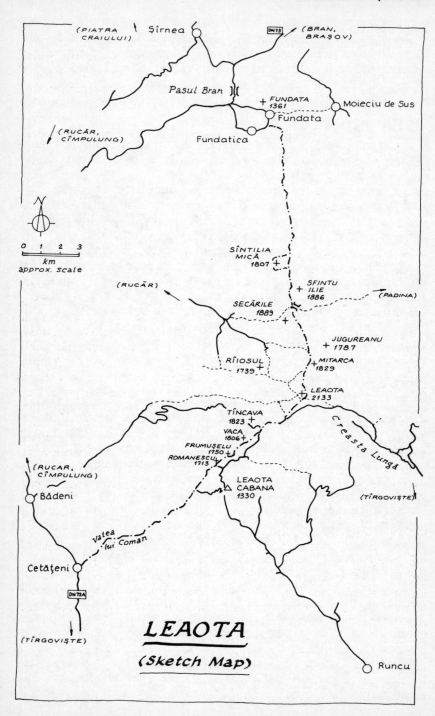

LEAOTA

(Sketch Map)

southeast up to Sîntilia.

It takes another six minutes to climb up through the meadow to reach a ridge with good views to the south; from here the route heads southeast along the top edge of the woods, on a sheep track passing below another small shepherds' hut and onwards into the spruce woods as the major track around the head of the valley to the right, and coming, 30 minutes from the ridge, into another *poiana*. After seven minutes the track reaches a saddle with one solitary red stripe mark, and continues south on sheep tracks climbing up the flank of Vf Sf Ilie (1,886m), also known as Sîntilia Mare, to the left and crossing its shoulder after ten minutes to continue more easily south-southeast to Curmătura Fiarelor (1,790m), eight minutes further. Here there are no markings, but the base of a signpost remains; this is where the red stripe route to Padina in the Bucegi is to turn left when completed.

The route on is theoretically marked with blue stripes, starting on a sheep track to the southwest for 12 minutes to a very sharp ridge, then up to the east for another 12 minutes to get above some dwarf shrubs and reach a minor saddle (clearly it would be quicker to go around the east side of the hill, if only there were a path) and on via a minor peak to a lower ridge. This is a particularly wide open, easy stretch of moorland walking, with logging in the valleys to the west. The route heads south, leaving a stîna to the left/east, and then southwest, finally turning southeast and dropping steeply to a sharp little saddle, about 26 minutes from the last minor saddle. Here, just northwest of Vf Jugureanu, there is a junction to the right, a good path going gently up into the spruce, and soon marked with blue stripes, although of course not at the junction itself. Passing a rather muddy spring, with newts, you are once again on the moors after nine minutes, climbing to a pole on a ridge with a stîna to the right, and then continuing on the level, mostly in spruce with more small springs, around the west side of Vf Mitarca (1,829m).

Seventeen minutes after coming back on to the moors, there is a brief climb to a high ridge with views south to Vf Leaota across the Mitărcii valley, and the path swings right to go around the head of the valley on clear sheep tracks to the left of the ridge. Having gone around the valley it climbs right around the shoulder of Vf Cumpărata and goes on up an easy sheep track, for a total of about 40 minutes, to a sign pointing vertically to the heavens southeast of the 2,133m summit of Leaota, having passed below the summit, which could easily be reached directly by following the ridge. This path continues to the southeast along the Creasta Lungă, but I turned right to a tarn and a cross on the ridge and found the scenery to the south desecrated by a major new unmade road leading to rigs similar to those prospecting for uranium in the

Apuseni.

I followed a sheep track (the red triangle route) to the right above this road, joining it after 34 minutes at a saddle with a junction to a stîna to the left/east. After 11 minutes on the road there is a turning to a rig to the east (although I suppose these things must be mobile) and after two minutes more the Tîncavei saddle and a junction to a road zigzagging down into a valley to the west leading to Bădeni. After two more minutes on the road to the left, the sheep track manages to escape from the new road, rising up and briefly losing it from sight; after 30 minutes it reaches another saddle with a cross and then goes over Vf Frumuşelu (1,750m). After about five minutes the road curves away to the southeast, and then (under Vf Românescu, 1,713m) the path marked with red triangles and blue stripes also turns away left to the southeast towards Leaota cabana at 1,330m. My sheep track curves away to the southwest, marked after a while with blue crosses, and after about 20 minutes more is joined by a cart track coming down on a ridge from the right.

After eight minutes this descends into spruce (to the right of the markings) and soon forks right to go down off the ridge to an old but usable hut after seven minutes. From here the path goes down south-southwest across a meadow and into the trees again, now silver birch and beech as well as spruce, with the route better marked on the trees than on the ground. With a final steep drop it reaches a valley and stream about 35 minutes after leaving the hut.

From here the next few minutes are tricky as there is no path through the nettles and you may have to constantly cross and recross the stream, but then a path appears, becoming a *drum forestier* and following the stream down the Valea lui Coman (with pleasant minor gorges, although the cliffs and waterfalls are mostly hidden by trees) to pass through some very sordid gypsy huts and reach the main road (DN 72A) after 1¼ hours at Cetăţeni, km 48 from Tîrgovişte, about one kilometre south of the Bădeni village limits. There seem to be plenty of buses to take you the 19km north to Cîmpulung Muscel, as it is properly known to distinguish it from Cîmpulung Moldovenesc in Moldavia.

Moving on

From the *Autogară* on Str IC Frimu on the east side of the river Tîrgului there is a footbridge to take you to the Cîmpulung Nord railway halt and via Str Nicu Leonard to the town centre; just north of the *Autogară* is a market and *cofetărie*, and on Str Dobrogeanu Gherea, a bit further north, a baker and *alimentară*, so that you can rapidly stock up before heading north to the Iezer-Păpuşa mountains, or west to the Trans-Făgăraş Highway or Cozia, or northeast to Bran and the Piatra Craiului.

Halfway to Bran is the village of Rucăr which I have not yet visited, but which Sacheverell Sitwell described as 'the ideal little mountain town' which was protected by the Dîmbovița gorges from Turkish intrusions and so 'has been left uncontaminated by Turkish influence and is typical of the purest strains of the Romanian race', going on to describe its Sunday market with men in 16th-Century Brueghel costumes and women in 19th-Century Ruritanian dress. Mind you, that was in the 1930s, but it should still be worth a look, for the setting if nothing else; there is a fairly new *han* or tourist inn. Georgina Harding says nothing about the village but talks of the shadowy Chinese crags in the clouds. Sitwell also said Cîmpulung was an 'ugly modern town, but enlivened by the costumes worn in the streets', which is still fairly true.

THE IEZER-PĂPUŞA RANGE

Situated just south of the Făgăraş range and connected to it by a thin ridge 2,000m high and ten kilometres long, the Iezer-Păpuşa mountains are one of the lesser-known Alpine regions of the Romanian Carpathians and are consequently less busy on the crest than the Făgăraş or Retezat areas. However the area around Voina cabana, at the heart of the basin surrounded by the U-shaped range, is very busy at weekends with campers from Cîmpulung, who rarely move far away.

Getting there

Access is almost always by the road from Cîmpulung to Lake Rîuşor dam and Voina cabana just beyond; there should be buses all the way, but in 1991 the condition of the road did not allow this. Instead there were eleven buses a day to the north end of Lereşti, a very linear village that begins at the main road outside Cîmpulung and continues for many kilometres. From here (where there is also a *Popas*) you should be able to get a lift to the dam and with luck to the cabana; the main road is the one to the east side of the lake. This lake is also the site of the Romanian chemical warfare school; as with our own Porton Down it is concerned with defence rather than offence, and the Romanians were very proud of having sent a chemical warfare defence unit as their contribution to the Gulf conflict alliance.

Other routes in, by foot, are from Plaiul Foii where my route finishes, from Rucăr and the Piatra Craiului to the east, from the Făgăraş by the ridge mentioned above, and by the continuation of

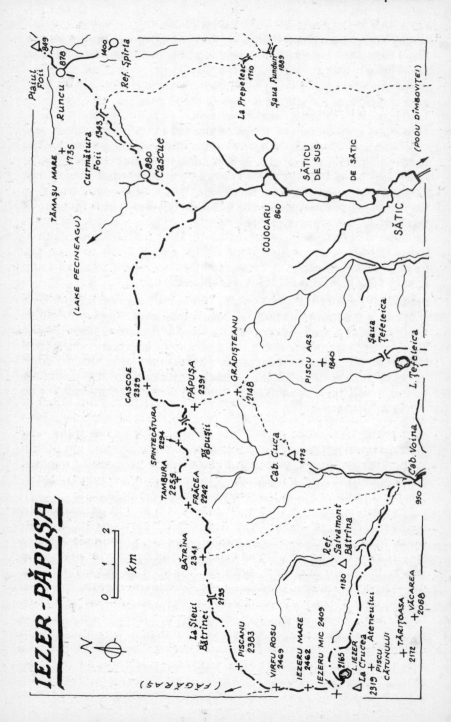

this red triangle route southwest to Slatina and Domneşti, west of Cîmpulung. The adventurous could also find a way up the largely disused forestry railway in the valleys just west of Cîmpulung to just south of Vf Iezer.

Hiking directions

The Voina cabana is basically a hotel, with bar and restaurant, and costing several times more than a mountain hut, but there is plenty of space here for camping, and also a *cabana sportiva* belonging to a Cîmpulung sports club where you might be allowed to stay and even perhaps use the weight training room. Voina is the centre of this great mountain basin, and although there are now two newer cabanas further north it is still the focal point for paths radiating to all sides. It is possible to take a path up by the stream just south of the cabana, marked with red stripes, for a ridge route to Iezer, but this takes about six hours rather than the four by the blue dot route through the *jepi* that everyone urged me to take.

From the cabana at 950m this runs north up a *drum forestier* towards Cuca cabana for nine minutes and turns left at a bridge to follow the Bătrîna stream for 2½km and almost half an hour to just short of Bătrîna cabana. If you reach the confluence with the Cătunu or Iezeru Mic and the sign left to Iezer by the blue dot and blue cross paths, you will probably have to backtrack slightly to cross by a footbridge over a weir, and then probably climb through the woods (spruce with sycamore maple and beech, with lots of small frogs) to avoid a flooded section behind the next weir. This also blocks off the start of the blue cross route. Four minutes after rejoining the now disused *drum forestier* you should take a rather slippery log bridge to the left/north bank, and then three times in the next 17 minutes use stepping stones, if the water is high enough, to continue along this bank before fording the stream back to the right bank.

The path leaves the stream and there is a sudden change from luxuriant waterside woods to spruce without undergrowth, through which the path climbs steeply for 30 minutes and then more easily for ten minutes to a clearing where there is at last a brief view of the hills to the north and east, if not yet ahead. After ten minutes the path rejoins the stream and climbs steeply up a moraine to cross the stream after 15 minutes and enter the famous *padurea de jepi* or dwarf pine forest somewhere just above 1,600m. This is soon passed and the climb continues up moraine with the stream cascading down to the left, to reach after 40 minutes the junction with the old blue cross path. Four minutes above this is the old Iezer refuge, now taken over and rendered uninhabitable by shepherds; a shame, as it is a good solid stone hut. Lake Iezer is just south in this cirque, a classic alpine setting. *lezer* in fact means a mountain lake or tarn.

From here there is a 12-minute climb following marker poles to the south to reach the main crest at La Crucea Ateneului; in fact this is quite flat and grassy, with a *drum* which heads southwest to curve down to Lake Rîusor. The path (marked with red stripes) heads north on the crest, passing Vf Iezeru Mic to the left and then going up a bit with a bit of rock-hopping to pass the grey and stony Snowdon-like Vf Iezeru Mare to the right after about half an hour and reach Vf Roşu (2,469m) with an easy grassy walk up after 50 minutes. From here the red triangle route turns left along the Culmea Mezea to reach the Făgăraş in about seven hours. The main red stripe route along the crest goes down to the northeast to a saddle where the marker poles are not particularly close to the actual path and on to the right side of some open moorland. There are three more saddles before a steepish climb up Vf Bătrîna (2,341m) reached one hour 23 minutes after Vf Roşu. Again there is an easy grassy walk to the summit itself; these mountains are intensively grazed by sheep all the way to the top, and the dogs are not particularly used to hikers.

There are three separate junctions leading to the red triangle route back to Voina; after descending for a quarter hour the red stripe route reaches a saddle and again continues east-northeast along an easy ridge at about 2,250m. It drops away to the right of the ridge to reach a steep saddle after 45 minutes, and then goes steeply up Vf Păpuşa (meaning doll or puppet). The path, marked by poles which may be slightly hard to spot against the rock, crosses to the left, eventually zigs up to the right and goes a long way south to reach, after 20 minutes, a junction with the blue stripe route running up the eastern wing of the massif. Heading north it passes to the west of the summit (2,391m) after about 12 minutes and crosses to the east side of the ridge, where there are truly stunning views to the Piatra Craiului with the Bucegi and Leaota massifs beyond. After 17 minutes along the ridge the path comes to a sign for the yellow triangle route right/east to Plaiul Foii via Plaiul Cascoe, but there is no need to go as far as the sign — just turn right towards the cairn and marker pole. The blue stripe route also continues to Plaiul Foii by a slightly longer route. From here there is a view north to the plains of Transylvania.

From the cairn, five minutes off the crest, the path follows the ridge down eastwards through dwarf pine and some very cushion-like moss. After 35 minutes you should keep left where the ridge splits and go on for another quarter hour to a stîna. From here the path cuts back to the right/west into spruce to cross a stream after six minutes and then turns down into common silver fir, with some larch and beech, and then just spruce again with an amazing variety of huge mushrooms and toadstools. After half an hour it swings right in a clearing and goes on down to cross a stream and meet the main Cascoe stream; you may need to head upstream a little to cross easily. From here, by a couple of forestry cabanas, a *drum forestier* runs down the right bank for almost half an hour to reach the Dîmboviţa valley and road at 880m — there is a daily bus at 1400 from Cîmpulung and Rucăr along this road to Pecineagu, the reservoir just south of the eastern end of the Făgăraş range, presumably returning in the late afternoon.

The final stage of this route goes over the Curmătura Foii, just west of the Piatra Craiului, to Plaiul Foii cabana and Zărneşti, where my five-day circuit through the Piatra Craiului, Leaota and Iezer-Păpuşa began. It is covered by Map 12 (Piatra Craiului) of the *Invitation*. Turn left up the valley for 20 minutes and then turn right over a bridge up the Tămaşu valley. Ignore two turnings to the left, even though the *drum forestier* is increasingly disused and becomes a rocky streambed. When it next splits the yellow triangle path goes steeply up between the two forks, then a bit more easily to the right through mature beeches to reach the Curmătura (1,343m) in half an hour, or almost an hour from the road. Here in spruce on the ridge are a bench and table and signs for paths between the Piatra Craiului to the right and Vf Comisu at the eastern end of the Făgăraş chain, four hours away to the left. The route to Plaiul Foii, marked with red and blue triangles, goes slightly to the left, rerouted above fallen trees, and after three minutes is joined by a blue stripe route from the left. From here it descends easily and then zigzags down to a clearing after 26 minutes and then a *drum forestier* which was blocked in 1991 by a cow yard with a sign in the middle. You can go through this or find a way across the stream to the left to a *drum forestier*.

From here it takes 15 minutes down the *drum* to a junction by a smithy at Plaiul Foii; in summer there are tents everywhere on these meadows, as Romanians love to camp by a stream. The cabana is across the Bîrsa Groşetului stream opposite this junction, and the Salvamont cabana to the right on the road to Zărneşti, just before some remarkable wooden statues by local sculptors. To the left is the main route to the end of the Făgăraş ridge route, but you will probably need to go to Zărneşti or even Braşov to stock up rather than carrying straight on, as the cabana here, though not bad, doesn't have bulk supplies of food for sale to hikers.

Practical information

The area is covered by the *Hartă Turistică* of the Făgăraş as well as by Map 11 of the *Invitation*.

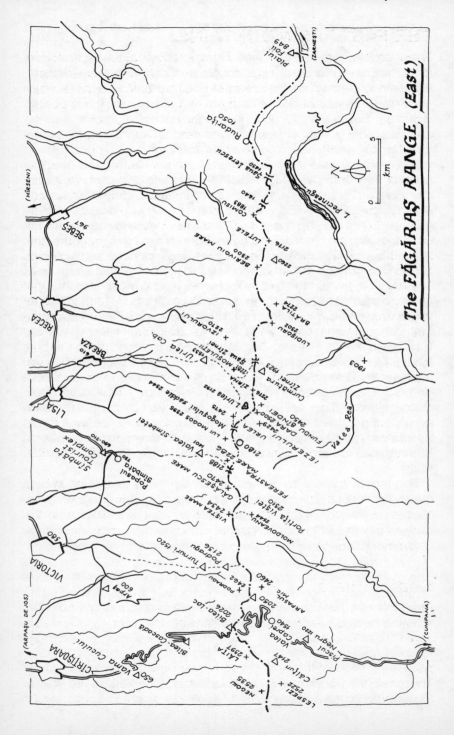

The FĂGĂRAŞ RANGE (East)

THE FǍGǍRAŞ MOUNTAINS

These are the mountains that you may already have heard referred to as the Transylvanian Alps (although, as it happens, their southern side is in Wallachia, and the town of Fǎgǎraş itself was traditionally ruled by Wallachian princes); there are other alpine ranges in Romania, but not as long nor as high, nor for the most part as spectacular. Romania's two highest peaks are Moldoveanu (2,544m) and Negoiu (2,535m) and the main crest or ridge route passes within a few minutes of the first (and 17 metres below), and over the second. I shall describe the basic ridge route from east to west, but there are many side trips to the many cabanas below on the north side, which I also mention. Whereas on my first visit I was able to walk the 70km crest in three days (it was cloudy and there wasn't a lot to look at), and the 'official' times add up to 37¼-41¾ hours, the Romanians usually take five to seven days, spending much of their time hiking down to cabanas and up to the crest again the next day. They usually aim to be in shelter by about 1600, due to the inadequacies of their equipment and the fact that it often starts to cloud over and perhaps rain at that time. There are refuges (rather than cabanas) on the ridge and although never exactly an easy walk it seems to me far less trouble to stick to the ridge than to spend extra time leaving and rejoining it. However you may wish to go via the Negoiu cabana to avoid the difficult stretch from Vf Negoiu to Vf Şerbota. The refuges are the simplest of shelters, and you are often better off camping there, but the cabanas are relatively well equipped and you will not need to carry a great deal of food. Whichever you choose you are at least almost certain to pass Bîlea Lac cabana, and the Podragu cabana is also very close to the ridge route.

The mountains are formed of metamorphic or crystalline rocks, mainly micaceous schists with quartz, in the classically jagged alpine shapes, with long ridges running south. There are more than 70 lakes of which Bîlea is the largest at 4.65 hectares, in a reservation of almost 100 hectares.

Getting there

Apart from my ridge route from the Birsenland depression to the Olt valley, access is mainly from the north side, which is relatively steep and straightforward whereas the south side features a seemingly endless row of parallel ridges running north from the Wallachian plains and allowing access only to excessively long forestry roads. Tourism in the Fǎgǎraş was developed almost entirely by the Saxon *Siebenbürgischen Karpatenverein*, so almost all the cabanas are to

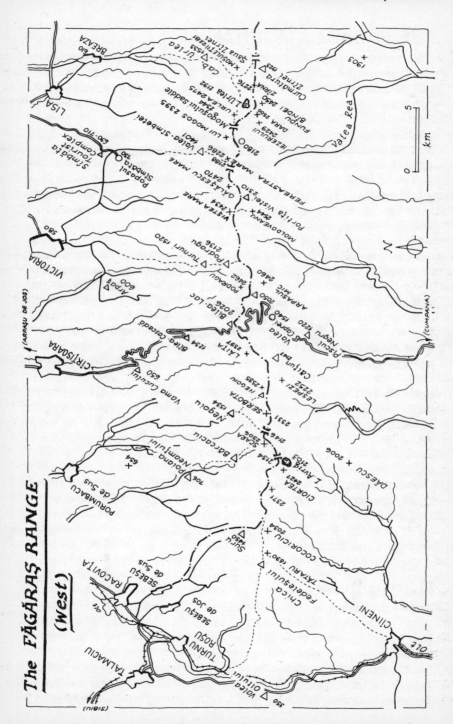

The FĂGĂRAŞ RANGE

(West)

the north.

In addition there is the Trans-Făgăraş Highway (DN 7C) of which the Romanians are inordinately proud, although it is only open for a few summer months each year. This leads from Curtea de Argeş (see page 123) past Poienari, the genuine Dracula's castle, and the Lake Vidraru reservoir where you find at 850m the only cabanas on the south side of the Făgăraş, to cross the range by a 887m tunnel at Bîlea Lac (2,045m) and go down under the cable-car to Bîlea Cascada and on to join the DN 1 at Cîrta, where there are the fine and relatively little-known ruins of a Cistercian abbey.

There should in theory be summer buses from Sibiu to Bîlea Cascada, and it might be possible to hitch here, although most cars will be full. Apart from a few deliveries, trucks are not allowed on this road. To the north the DN 1 and the Braşov to Sibiu railway run parallel to the mountains, and almost every station has signs marking a route to a cabana and the mountains. It only takes a few hours to get into the mountains, but if you want to cut your approach hike to the minimum, there are buses from the town of Făgăraş (an ugly town dominated by the chemical industry, although there is a fairly good museum in the Vaubanesque castle; fortunately the bus station is next to the rail station) to Victoria and the very basic *Complexul Turistic Sîmbăta*, where there is the Sîmbăta or Saturday monastery, built by Brîncoveanu in 1696, razed in 1785 and rebuilt in 1936 and 1962, and a bad cabana, with a better one two hours south and 710m higher at Valea Sîmbatei, itself only two hours and 787m climb from the main ridge at Fereastra Mare.

Hiking directions

My route begins at Zărneşti, reached as described in the section on Piatra Craiului; from here you should walk (or hitch) the 13km of unmade road to Plaiul Foii (849m), which should take about two and a half hours. This is a good jumping-off point, with other routes to the Piatra Craiului and Iezer-Păpuşa massifs, as described in those sections, but the *drum forestier* continues another ten kilometres to Rudariţa (1,050m), and forks here. There are forestry cabanas here, sometimes let to visitors, and some camping space; according to the *Invitation* it will take you 11-13 hours to reach the Urlea cabana, but according to signs here it will take 7-8 hours, while a sign half an hour closer to Urlea (ie westwards) claims it is now 9-10 hours away. At any rate it's about a days hiking, which is as accurate as one can be in Romania. (If I had taken the turning to Urlea, I think it would have taken me about eight hours.)

In any case, to the Romanians Rudariţa is the last outpost of civilisation and the last place to spend a night in safety from bears and the like; however I pushed on for another hour and a half, mad fool that I am. The main route west takes the left fork of the *drum forestier* and follows it upstream for almost half an hour before turning off to the left and crossing the stream to climb up on to Lerescu. It is also possible to take a more northerly route from Rudariţa via Văcăria Mare to Vf Comisu, marked with red dots. My route, marked with red stripes as befits the most important ridge route in the country, climbs steeply south for 25 minutes to the ridge where it meets the path, also marked with red stripes, from Curmătura Foii and Piatra Craiului to the left.

Already in the spruce level, the path west passes to the left of a camping place and along a hill to the left to go up the left side of a cleared area; you should ignore an arrow to the left in the woods after 18 minutes as there are, or at least were, too many fallen trees blocking the path. The path passes above a spruce nursery plantation and a turning to a stîna to the left; you can either go right over the open hilltop of Lerescu (1,690m) about 27 minutes from the clearing, or by a path around its left side, overlooking the stîna. The route passes into woods again, with a clearing and camping places, and then on to moorland and up to the Comisu stîna, 15 minutes from the previous hill, at the junction with the path from Rudariţa via Văcăria Mare and that north to Sebeş, as well as to a spring 300m away. After ten minutes the path west runs to the left/south of Vf Comisu (1,883m), 14 minutes later over another hill and then up Luţele (2,176m, also known as Buzduganu) after a steepish climb up to the ridge. The path continues more easily to a spring 40 minutes from Comisu, then passes above cliffs to the right. Sixteen minutes from the spring the path dips and then climbs past Berivoiu (or Berivoescu) Mare (2,300m) to the right/north; it takes another 13 minutes to reach the turning left to the Berivoiu refuge, a small Nissen-style hut by a pool at 2,260m.

Generally these eastern foothills are conveniently terraced, meaning that having gained some height one continues more or less on the level before climbing again, rather than instantly dropping into a valley and having to regain the height lost before starting to climb further. There can be navigational problems in this area in bad weather, especially fog, as the route is not as well marked as it might be. From Berivoiu the path continues on open moorland, mainly to the left of the ridge, passing two springs and also more cliffs to the right, to reach a pool after 38 minutes with Vf Brătila (2,274m) to the south. After 17 minutes more the path reaches another pool at Curmătura Brătilei (2,122m, a bit lower than the Berivoiu refuge) with the junction with the red triangle route from Vf Roşu in the Iezer-Păpuşa range (see previous section), which also maintains virtually the same height of 2,050m throughout. There is also a sign to drinking water five minutes down this route; there should be a route north, marked with red triangles, from here or just east to Recea, but I saw no sign of it.

Now comes one of the periodical climbs for quarter of an hour to the next level plateau, where the path then heads northwest for 13 minutes before swinging west. After 15 minutes the path swings almost to the north, passes four springs, then curves left with a waterfall opposite to drop to the Curmătura Zîrnei 20 minutes later. This is a broad saddle with another refuge, a small polyhedral igloo this time, with a double-deck sleeping platform; the *Invitation* typically gives its altitude as 1,970m and 1,915m within the space of ten lines, and as 1,923m on the map, which is the figure confirmed by other sources. Water can be found in the dwarf pine just to the southwest.

Ahead you can now see 'real' mountains, as opposed to this moorland scenery; two minutes from the refuge is the junction to Urlea cabana, about seven kilometres away to the right/north and marked with red dots, and after this the path becomes steeper and rockier, climbing for 40 minutes, with cliffs to the left this time, to reach the top of Vf Zîrna (2,216m), and swing northwest and then west to climb along the north side of Vf Fundu Bîndei. Twenty minutes from Zîrna there is a sign near the junction of an unmarked path west-southwest to Vf Dara (2,500m). After a tiny spring the path sets off along a narrow rocky ridge to the northwest, mainly just to the left of the crest itself. This is the route of which the *Invitation* rightly says 'It is an itinerary on the top and it is accessible only in summer to well-trained hikers!'. After 27 minutes there is a junction to the right with a path, not shown on maps but marked with blue dots, down some pretty impressive cliffs to Urlea Lake. The path continues above some sheep tracks to the left and in 15 minutes, at the Mogoşului saddle (2,344m), reaches the junction with the main blue triangle route from Urlea cabana.

After 22 minutes easy walking past Vf lui Mogoş (2,395m) the path comes to the red dot route to the right along the Caţaveiu ridge to the Valea Sîmbetei cabana, and 20 minutes later at Fereastra Mare (The Big Window, 2,180m), after the Colţul Bălăceni rocks, the main red triangle route to the same place, both being steep and fairly tricky descents. There is a good view north to the Sîmbăta Monastery at the edge of the Olt valley at 670m.

From here the ridge route climbs steeply for seven minutes to Vf Budru (2,268m, better known as Vf Slănina), drops for seven more to the Fereastra Mică saddle, marked with a cross, and again climbs steeply for ten minutes to a ridge with cliffs and crags to the north and a broad valley to the south. From here the path again climbs steeply for ten minutes, turning left up a rocky ridge — take care to turn right if doing this route in reverse, or you may reach the

Sîmbetei valley more quickly than planned. From this shoulder of Gălăşescu Mic you have good views of the route ahead to Moldoveanu; the path drops in about ten minutes to a sharp saddle at 2,311m and then climbs steeply up the south side of Gălăşescu Mare (2,470m), reaching a ridge after about 15 minutes, turning left on the ridge then zigging right, with the Iezerul Gălăşescului tarn to the left/south. Again there's a drop to a saddle and a traverse along the side of Vf Gălbanele (the Yellow Peak, 2,456m) to the right, another couple of minor saddles above more small tarns, a steeper climb to a ridge south of Hîrtopu Ursului, (the Bear's Cirque), 40 minutes from the Gălăşescu ridge, and then an eleven minute drop to the Portiţa Viştea or Valea Rea refuge, at 2,300m, with the Iezerul Valea Rea below in a classic cirque high above a deep valley to the south. This used to be named Moldoveanu refuge, down by the tarn, but was moved up to the ridge route in 1989 because of many problems with snow. It's a breeze-block box, rather stuffy.

Six minutes west and slightly higher at 2,310m at Şaua Portiţa Viştea the path crosses another marked with red triangles from Victoria five hours north to the old refuge and the Rîul Doamnei *drum forestier* to the south. From here there is a steep climb to reach the summit of Viştea Mare (2,527m) in anything between 17 minutes and twice that; from here it is just ten minutes to the summit of Moldoveanu, Romania's highest peak at 2,544m. From here you can see, as well as Negoiu and the rest of the Făgăraş chain, the prominent ridges and deep valleys stretching to the south, and the *Ţara Oltului* (Land of the Olt), the Făgăraş Depression and the hills of Transylvania to the north, weather permitting — it seems that there are often clouds on the northern side of the range, and changes in the weather always come from this direction. Paths marked with blue triangles and red crosses head south along the ridges from here to join forestry roads to the Vidra dam and Nucşoara.

There is a steep drop from here, of course, for 17 minutes, and then a narrow ridge across Şaua Orzănelei (2,305m), with impressive cliffs and the deep and broad Valea Orzăneaua Mare to the south. There should be a route marked with red triangles down into this valley from the saddle, but I have never seen it. Then the path traverses along the south sides of Vf Ucişoara and Ucea Mare, generally heading south of west before swinging more to the north after 40 minutes from the Saua Orzanelei, but still sticking to the southern slope. The path drops to a col after eight minutes, with cliffs to the right and a cirque to the left, then climbs steadily along the flank of Vf Tărîţa (2,414m) to reach the ridge after 20 minutes and after another 15 minutes the junction (at Şaua Podragului, 2,307m), with the red cross route north to Podragu cabana just 20 minutes below at 2,136m past a good spring and some lovely rose quartz, and a blue triangle route south to Lake Vidraru, again mainly on forestry roads.

The path, now much busier, drops southwest for 18 minutes to the left side of Lac Podu Giurgiului (2,250m), at the foot of Vf Podragu to the north, crosses the sizable exit stream and climbs steeply for another 18 minutes to cross the Vf Mircii ridge (2,461m) westwards and leave Arpaşul Mare (also known as Vîrtop) to the right. It drops for quarter of an hour to the Şaua Arpaşului (2,468m) and crosses for once to the north side of the ridge (a slightly tricky stretch, something like Striding Edge, I'm told) before passing over the minor peak of Paru de Fier above Lake Buda, in a cirque to the south, and on towards Arpaşul Mic ahead with sheep grazing right up to its 2,460m summit. Rather than climb this the path drops down to the right at the small Nerlinger Monument, below scree and up again, a ten minutes rock scramble in all, and ten minutes later, after crossing the ridge of the Muşeteica-Rîiosul (with an unmarked route north to the Arpaşul Mare valley), it crosses the Portiţa Arpaşului ridge (2,175m) and goes to the right around a very large cirque by a *via ferrata*, with chains and then unnecessary cables. After 25 minutes it reaches a junction, at Fereastra Zmeilor, left down to a Salvamont refuge (looking like a tin garage), then to km 79.6 on the Trans-Făgăraş highway and the Capra cabana, burnt down in 1992 (yellow triangles). The ridge route goes down steeply to a small spring and then after 11 minutes a better spring, and continues on around the cirque (with sun-loving flora that you would not normally find at this altitude), across scree, streams and snow patches, before climbing steeply to a ridge 30 minutes later, and dropping in ten minutes to Lacul Capra (Goat Lake, 2,241m), one of the most famous beauty spots in the Romanian Carpathians, in spite of the ugly white monument to its southeast. You now begin to meet crowds of walkers from Bîlea Lac.

From here a blue stripe route runs south to the former Capra hut, and another with a new sign to Cota 2000 cabana at the southern mouth of the tunnel; this is a private cabana belonging to *România Pitoreasca* (a hillwalkers' club) but you will probably be allowed to stay there in good company. The main route climbs relatively easily up to the Capra saddle (2,315m) in 11 minutes and down on very badly eroded rocky paths, marked mainly with blue triangles, to reach Bîlea Lac (2,034m) in 23 minutes. This is another famous beauty spot and tourist honey-pot, with a busy cabana on a virtual island in the lake. Now privatised, it shows its least attractive side, with piles of crates and rubbish, as you approach from the land, and keeps its picture-postcard aspect turned towards the lake. Breakfast is not served until 0830, and lunch not until 1330, with dinner from 1930 to 2100. Although the bar was smoky and fly-ridden, the food

and service were in fact good here. Beyond the lake is the upper
terminal of the cable-car from Bîlea Cascada (800m below at 1,234m
altitude), a former hunting lodge of Ceauşescu's, and the highway
and tunnel, only open for a few months from June to September or
October. From the lake it is possible to take a path to the northeast,
to reach Lacul Capra or head north via Vf Netedul (2,351m) on a
round-about route to Bîlea Cascada cabana, but it is not permitted
to continue eastwards into the Arpăşel valley from here.

From the cabana the route (not shown on Map 14 of the *Invitation*)
continues westwards following blue stripe markings, rising steadily
up the hill to the south side of the lake, passing under an outcrop
and zigzagging upwards (largely unmarked) for 25 minutes to a
junction with the red cross route which climbs more steeply from the
highway and then heads north to the Valea Doamnele (another
round-about route to Bîlea Cascada cabana, the direct route
naturally following the valley with the highway and cable-car). Your
path climbs up to the left, splitting into multiple pathlets for 15
minutes until the red stripe route from Şaua Caprei rejoins as a
minor path from the left at Şaua Paltinei (2,350m). The route goes
slightly down to the southeast and at once swings back to the
right/south to briefly cross some peaty moor and then head down
and south into some rocky waste with a spring, eight minutes from
the saddle, where a path marked with blue dots branches south to
Piscul Negru (Black Fish) cabana.

The red stripe ridge route turns right and climbs for a few minutes
before entering a rocky cleft, with a brief stretch of not particularly
necessary chain, to emerge on the north side of the ridge and climb
steeply on to moorland. The path continues climbing gently to the
southwest, crossing the ridge and running along its left/south side
with the help of cables. Thirty minutes from the cleft it climbs steeply
for 11 minutes to Vf Lăiţel (2,390m), a grassy peak with chamois all
lost in the cloud when I was first there. From here the path descends
steeply, with quite a bit of rock-scrambling, to the west, before after
18 minutes going up and then down on the left/south side of the
ridge for nine minutes. Then there is a five minute climb, with minor
rock-scrambling again, before a two minute drop to a spring and
signs by Lacul Călţun (2,147m), where there is a Salvamont refuge
in a basic Nissen hut with one sleeping platform and a tin dump
behind a dry-stone wall.

From here one path drops southeast to Piscul Negru and the
highway, and the main path west continues along the right or north
side of the lake, in its classic alpine cirque, and climbs the right-
hand side of the rockfall and then a scree of smaller rocks, before,
a quarter hour from the refuge, reaching an unmarked junction right
to the Negoiu cabana (almost hotel-style) following red cross

markings via Strunga Ciobanului. Another seven minutes up the red stripe route, with more loose stones, brings you to the junction of a yellow stripe path to the left; this is a longer and easier route to the top of Vf Negoiu via Strunga Doamnei. The red stripe route via Strunga Dracului climbs steeply up with chains (BEWARE — the last of the first set of chains may not be attached at the top, and this route should not be used downhill in wet weather) to reach the top ridge after 21 minutes. Turning right you meet the top of the yellow stripe path and reach the summit of Negoiu, Romania's second highest peak at 2,535m, after twelve minutes.

The next stage, from Vf Negoiu to Vf Şerbota (2,331m), is very difficult and only recommended for well-equipped hikers and in good weather. On Şerbota there is a sign, on the ground but seemingly referring to the eastbound crest route, which says (in Romanian) *STOP! Impassable path*, but there is no such sign on Negoiu. In any case there are no chains along this section and climbing down from Şerbota with a heavy backpack would be crazy. The alternatives are either to go northwards via Negoiu cabana, either avoiding the peak altogether on the red cross route or turning off the ridge at Şaua Cleopatrei 20 minutes west of the summit, or to go *prin caldarea*, via the cauldron or basin to the south. This route also begins at Şaua Cleopatrei, drops down into the basin and then slogs back uphill to Vf Şerbota.

The ridge route from Negoiu starts with a steep climb down on loose rocks for 15 minutes, followed by five easier minutes down to the Şaua Cleopatrei and the junction of the blue triangle path north to Negoiu cabana. From here it drops a bit, then climbs to the rocky ridge and along its north side before again dropping 22 minutes later to the junction of the route, marked with blue stripes, into the *caldarea* to the south. The hard work really begins here, with a tricky scramble down the north side of the ridge then up a rock cleft before continuing along the ridge. After 32 minutes it reaches another steep climb followed by some 'ferocious' rock-climbing for 18 minutes to the summit, with sheep grazing right to the top. Although I did so, you should not tackle this section of route alone or with a heavy pack; it would be madness to do so eastbound when there are safer routes available.

One minute to the west of Şerbota another route to the Negoiu cabana branches off, marked with blue stripes and following the Muchea Şerbotei ridge. The main route from here to Şaua Puha is also shown as dangerous on the panoramic 'wallchart' map but this is really not so, and to say so risks leading people to underestimate the very real problems of the Şerbota to Negoiu section; it heads left/southwest across easy moorland for 14 minutes down to a big stone windbreak, then up a bit more steeply to a minor peak of

2,212m and then two more, along an increasingly rocky and narrow ridge, then on its northern side, and then 27 minutes from the windbreak, along its southern side and down to the west-northwest to the Şaua Puha (or Scara) saddle (2,146m) with a Salvamont refuge (known as *refugiul Scara*) like a metal tent held down by guy-ropes, and the junction with the blue cross route north to the Negoiu cabana (and also in theory south to the Cumpăna cabana and a very long *drum forestier* to Sălătrucu, although I saw no sign of this and it is not shown on the 'wallchart' map).

From here there is a fairly 'normal slog' of 17 minutes up southwest to Vf Scara (2,307m) and then an easy descent on MEPs (multiple eroded paths) for 11 minutes to the sign at the junction of the red cross path right/north to the Bărcaciu (or Bîrcaciu) cabana. The route continues on the left/south side of the ridge, switching after 14 minutes at the Şaua Gîrbovei (2,134m) to the right and crossing two very eroded gullies before beginning to descend (with some hardly necessary chains at one point) to Lacul Avrig (2,011m) after 21 more minutes. There is no longer a refuge here, but it is an attractive cirque though with the usual collection of empty tins.

Crossing the stream to the north and passing the blue dot route to Bărcaciu cabana, the path then climbs 'normally' for 18 minutes to the Portiţa Avrigului (2,178m) on the rim of the cirque. From here on the route is mainly on open moorland with rocky outcrops, rising at first gently to the west-northwest and then more steeply, passing beneath a cairn on Vf Budislavu (2,375m) after almost half an hour, and then descending in rocky zigzags for 17 minutes to a saddle. From here it continues around the head of a broad cirque to the south, with a stîna below, crossing four streams and climbing very easily to reach a broad, grassy saddle on the far side of the cirque after 26 minutes. This is the Şaua Suru (2,133m), where I turned off the ridge route to reach the last of the cabanas on the northern slopes; the red stripe route continues westwards, together with various branches, all leading to the Olt valley and the Sibiu to Rîmnicu Vîlcea railway line.

Two minutes after crossing the saddle to the right/northwest there is the first sign for the red triangle route to Suru, but in fact both routes continue down together for another minute to a second sign. From here my red triangle route goes down and then to the left, with some zigzags, to a spring after eight minutes. It crosses other small streams, drops to some dwarf bushes and then climbs up, still on the left side of the valley, to the Gorganu ridge 24 minutes from the spring. From here the path zigs down rapidly to the cabana, soon visible just below the tree line at 1,450m, and reached in 27 minutes more. There is no level ground for camping at the cabana but it is quite a nice large building in the traditional style; although breakfast is at 0700, lunch is not until 1400, with dinner from 1930 to 2130.

The red triangles continue to mark the best route onwards, although there is also a red dot route to the west which goes via Morsei waterfall and then 11km of unmade road. The red triangle route goes down by a fence and on at a perfect gradient for both climbing and descending; the hiking equivalent of a motorway, through beautiful woods with benches, water points and even a cable used as a fence rather than for hauling oneself uphill. After 30 minutes there is the junction of a blue triangle path to the right/northeast to Avrig station; according to the *Invitation* this is confusingly also marked with red triangles, but surprisingly enough someone has got around to re-marking it. Avrig, incidentally, is one of the villages designated as a new town under the systematisation programme (see page 107), although there is little sign of this other than the fact that eight *accelerat* trains stop there; it has a Saxon church, plain and forbidding-looking, just east of the centre, and the grave of the poet and educationalist Gheorghe Lazăr (1779-1823) at an interesting Orthodox church to the west.

After another 34 minutes the main path reaches a small meadow and camping place and swings more to the west through silver birch and blackthorn to reach another meadow with a water trough in another 15 minutes. Here you should keep to the main ridge and avoid the temptation to drop to the left; in about 30 minutes the path finally drops off the end of the Muchia Moaşa ridge and joins the road at a bridge five minutes south of the village of Sebeşu de Sus, about 1½km long with only a *Magazin Mixt* and a *Magazin Forestier*. It took me 50 minutes (in the dark) from here to the main road, forking left at the Racoviţa junction. Unless hitch-hiking east you should turn left/west here for five minutes to the Sebeş Olt railway halt, where virtually nothing does halt, and two kilometres further west along the river the Podu Olt station, served by Sibiu to Braşov and Sibiu to Rîmnicu Vîlcea trains. Just a bit further west is Talmaciu, also designated as a New Town, with an encampment of spectacularly bearded gypsies on the way in from the east.

Practical information

There is a reasonable map in the *Invitation*, with enlargements of the most crowded sections, and a *Hartă Turistică* which is more detailed. You may also find at some cabanas a panoramic perspective map, often used as a wall-poster, which is useful although it should not be the only map you take. In 1992 there was a new coloured version of this, not as good as the original.

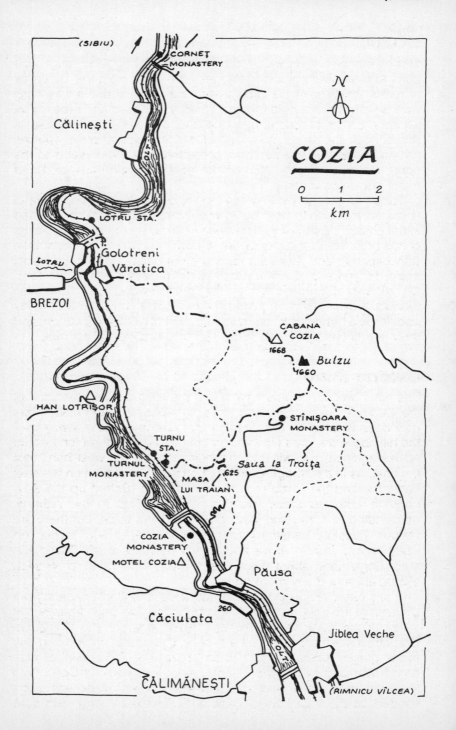

COZIA

This combines a short walk in the foothills of the Făgăraş range with visits to three Orthodox monasteries. The climb from the Olt valley at about 230m to Cozia cabana and summit at 1,668m was hard work on a hot and humid day, but given a light load and reasonable weather it should be more enjoyable. Cozia Nature Reserve is notable for the large numbers of Mediterranean plant species growing happily in this sun-trap, protected by the mountains to the north. Oak grows to 1,200m on the south-facing slopes, and wild roses are very common.

Cozia monastery is one of the best known and most important in Romania; founded in 1387 by Voivode Mircea the Old (who is buried in the church), it shows the influence of Byzantine styles, with bands of red brick set in the stonework, a porch (1704-10) by Constantin Brîncoveanu, and frescoes dating from 1390 (in the pronaos) onwards. There is also a museum with fine views across the river. On summer Saturdays it can be very crowded with Romanian tourists. Across the dam just to the north is a campsite with many cabins, by a rather spurious reconstruction of a Roman *castrum*, and there are hotels just south in the spa of Călimăneşti-Căciulata.

Getting there

The main problem in this area is that the road on the east bank of the Olt from Cozia dam north to Turnu monastery and station has now been flooded by the dam, so that unless you find a way over the hill above the dam (or through the railway tunnel, which I would advise against), you will find the monastery on the west bank (not the east, as in the *Rough Guide*) cut off from the station on the east bank. I visited the Cozia monastery first, then hitched up the west bank to Lotru to cross the river and hike up to the cabana, descending to Turnu and leaving by train from there; but there are various possible variations of this route depending mainly on whether you wish to arrive and depart by road or rail. There are, surprisingly, only about three buses a day from Sibiu to Rîmnicu Vîlcea, and not many more trains.

In any case, although there is road access to Cozia cabana from Dîngeşti to the east, you are almost bound to approach from the Olt valley to the west; this is the only point at which the Romanian Carpathians are breached by a river and, although not forming any major gorges or canyons, it is an impressive defile with its fast, broad river and mountains to either side. Just north of Cozia dam the road runs on a viaduct where the original route has been flooded, to the Han Lotrişor, now a Turkish truck stop, and then around a couple of bends that used to be navigational hazards until the dam tamed the river, to Brezoi where there are 18th-Century wooden houses and a road branches west to Voineasa, Obîrşia Lotrului, and Petroşani, providing access to the Căpăţînii, Lotrului, Parîng and Sebeş mountains. Just north of this is an old rail bridge now carrying pedestrians, and north of this a road over another dam, both leading to Lotru station; a bit further up the road on the west bank, beyond Călineşti (not to be confused with Călimăneşti just south of Cozia), is the monastery of Corneţ, noted for the tiles and the like decorating its external walls.

Hiking directions

From Lotru station I headed south along a track on the west side of the main railway line and then passed through an under-bridge to the east side; after a quarter hour or so the route turns left in the hamlet of Văratica, at house no 22 where a stream crosses the track, then turns sharp right and climbs up to the left into a meadow on a cart track marked with blue stripes. After another quarter hour there is a cunningly disguised right turn by some very mature beeches, and the path continues to climb mainly on the right bank of a stream. After 17 minutes there is another unmarked right turn and a *very* steep zigzagging climb for almost an hour (in addition I spent 20 minutes resting on this stretch). Then there is a sharp left turn just before reaching the ridge, leading to a small meadow on the ridge in two minutes. The path continues up in woods and then turns 90 degrees right in the next meadow, very soon running across the top of another meadow. About 45 minutes after reaching the ridge it comes to a good stream, climbs up and then down to reach another meadow with a disused stîna after eight minutes more. Here it turns 90 degrees left and climbs, mainly in meadow, before again turning 90 degrees left on to a path marked with red triangles and stripes from Turnu and Păuşa.

From here, on the ridge, you have a view of the cabana and two relay towers; the path continues in meadows for 15 minutes before passing through woods for a final ten minutes to the cabana. The scenery here is somewhat reminiscent of Darjeeling or Simla in the Himalayan foothills, with glorious views, weather permitting, of distant ranges and ridges stretching out below. The cabana is busy and popular, although it has outside toilets and seemingly no water at all beyond what you can beg from the kitchen. There is a meteorological station with friendly staff, keen to practise their English, in the dormitory block of the cabana.

From here I descended by the path marked with a blue stripe to the Stînişoara monastery and then picked up the red stripe markings to Turnu monastery and station; this starts along the road to the television tower, built in 1975, and continues straight ahead where this turns left at a hairpin bend. It passes to the right of the Bulzu rocks ahead (1,660m, virtually equal to Cozia itself), and descends steeply with the help of cables — this is shown as a road on map 10 of the *Invitation*, but this is clearly wrong. After 55 minutes it reaches a resting-place, with table, benches and cross, and continues down with various short cuts to cross a dry stream bed after 18 minutes. The path continues to the right, dropping down into very tall oak trees, and after ten minutes reaches a better stream, two minutes before a junction to the right, also two minutes before the fence of Stînişoara monastery. This was founded as a hermitage in 1671 and expanded in 1747; the galleried buildings around the church are simple and lovely, and the setting is glorious.

The path onwards starts from the main gates and goes straight down to a stream and then down its left bank before crossing it and climbing on a generally well-made track much used by Sunday picnickers who go no further than the monastery. After 23 minutes it meets the red stripe route from the cabana, and after another ten minutes I turned right at Şaua la Troiţă, with a grave and cross, onto this red stripe route to Turnu; the blue stripe route continues southwards to Păuşa, south of Cozia. To reach Cozia monastery by this route would entail a bit of a dog's leg of two kilometres north along the road to the dam, and then almost one kilometre back southwards on the west bank. The yellow stripe route, when completed, will lead by a *drum forestier* to the road just south of the dam, but this had not been done by the spring of 1991.

After nine minutes the red stripe route forks right at a curve and then after five minutes a bulldozed track comes in from the left. I could hear chanting soon after this point, and reached the Turnu monastery after descending this track for 13 minutes. Here there is an ugly modern church replacing a tiny but atmospheric church built in the 16th Century but rebuilt after being destroyed in the First World War and a fire in 1932. There are also some troglodyte cells in the cliff here. From here it is just five minutes walk to the station; there is an overnight train to Bucureşti and others to Sibiu and Craiova, as well as more local services.

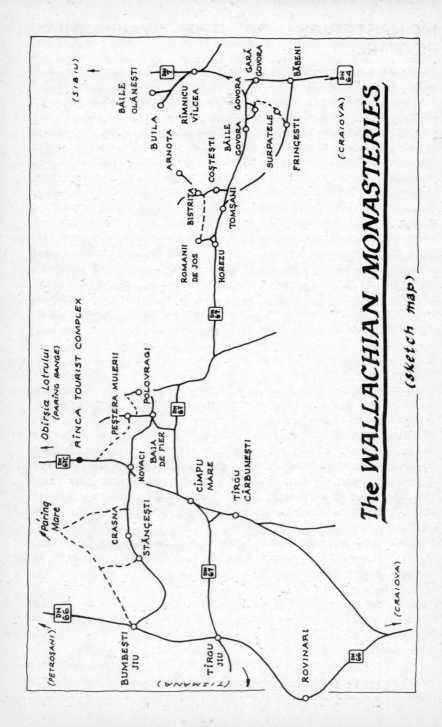

The WALLACHIAN MONASTERIES

(sketch map)

MONASTERIES OF THE WALLACHIAN FOOTHILLS

Along the southern fringes of the Carpathians from the River Olt to west of the River Jiu lies a chain of monasteries, many in the indigenous Wallachian style of architecture developed in the 18th Century by Constantin Brîncoveanu and named after him. To the east of the Olt are those covered in the section on Cozia, to the west is Tismana covered in the section on the Retezat Mountains, and in between are others such as Govora, Bistriţa, Arnota, Horezu and Polovragi. Although well-known and beautiful, these are working monasteries, without even the traces of commercialisation found in those of Bucovina; you can wander in and around freely and will be asked only to part with a couple of Lei if you visit the museums, which you should feel obliged to do even if sick up to the teeth with icons and vestments. The only hiking in this section is really an easy country stroll between Bistriţa, Arnota and the best of them all, Horezu, but I aim to give an outline of the entire route along the DN 67 from Rîmnicu Vîlcea to Tîrgu Jiu, as there are many interesting things along the way, and the public transport is not totally straightforward.

Getting there

From the Rîmnicu Vîlcea *autogară*, to the east of the main road south out of this modern town, frankly unattractive but with four museums, on the Sibiu to Craiova railway line, there are two buses a day west to Bistriţa, two to Polovragi and two to Tîrgu Jiu, as well as quite a few to Horezu (the town, several kilometres south of the monastery) by various routes. Town bus 4 runs to Gară Govora, about five kilometres before Govora monastery, the first stop along this route. The main road bypasses Govora to the north and you may have to walk a couple of kilometres back from the road junction, although there are more direct routes across the fields from the main road. This is a small nunnery built in 1496, where I heard a splendid *toaca* at 1700; however the main interest is the *biserica dintr'o lemn* or 'church made from one tree' three kilometres away at the Brîncoveanu monastery of Surpatele — turn left from the monastery gates and then right along a stream into the woods. It can also be reached on foot from the small spa of Băile Govora just west of Govora along the DN 67 (with a campsite at 360m), or by road via Gara Govora and Franceşti to the east and south.

From Govora there is a very scenic road to the Bistriţa junction at a bridge near Coşteşti five kilometres east of Horezu. The Bistriţa monastery is about ten kilometres north along a minor road which spends its first four kilometres escaping from Coşteşti. Buses are rare and it's not the easiest of roads to hitch on. The monastery was founded in 1492 and rebuilt in 1519-20 in the reign of Voivode Neagoe Basarab; the *Mică* or little church dates from 1611-23 and the *Mare* or great church from 1633. The rest of the present buildings date from 1846-56. There is also a *peştera* or cave through the arch opposite the main church porch and to the right; to the left is the original little church of 1520 with attractive murals.

Hiking directions

From a junction to the east of the monastery a road turns right to Arnota monastery, four kilometres away and high above on top of the cliffs to the north. Halfway up is a quarry, and it is supposedly possible to go up in a works bus at about 0600, 1400 and 2200. Alternatively on foot there is a short cut alongside a conveyor-belt to the lorry depot half-way up the road; on the road just above this is a junction left signposted to the monastery. Equally there is a path starting from the road beside the Bistriţa monastery, by the artificial water channel, crossing the stream by the footbridge and climbing up to the left past the cemetery gate to the first hairpin bend below the lorry depot; coming down from Arnota to Bistriţa by this route took me just over half an hour.

The Arnota monastery was founded in 1634 by Voivode Matei Basarab; the story is that he was hiding from the Turks in a chapel here while his faithful retainer Arnault went out in his master's clothes and was executed in his place. Therefore this monastery was founded in his memory, and Matei was buried here himself in the Carrara marble tomb just inside the door. Later Constantin Brîncoveanu added a porch and spire, as was his habit, and more buildings were added during 1852-56 by some unnamed foreign architects as an alternative to political prison. It is a very quiet and peaceful spot with two rabbits which they promise me are not for eating, and a splendid old white-bearded monk who translated *Paradise Lost* from Russian into Romanian. Although the monastery is not far from the grotto of Sf Grigore, this is in the Bistriţa gorges far below and the only way to get there is to return to Bistriţa and then follow the main route, marked with blue triangles, north into the gorges.

Returning to Bistriţa, the next stage leads west to Horezu monastery, in fact in the village of Romanii de Jos, north of the town of Horezu. This starts from the road just over one kilometre south of the monastery, by a bus stop and combined well and shelter, just south of kilometre post 5; from here you should go right/west and turn left at the end of the village after 15 minutes onto a muddy sunken farm track. After 11 minutes turn right at a junction just below a ridge on to a well-used path running west through lovely farmland with woods and orchards for about ten minutes, before running into a vague cart track to the left. After three minutes this crosses straight over another cart track, and after 19 minutes, after the first houses, you should fork right. This track continues downhill, increasingly built-up, and after 17 minutes turns right on to a similar unmade road, and two minutes later right again onto the asphalt road by a shop and an intriguing active water mill, leading to the Horezu monastery in seven minutes.

This is the greatest of Brîncoveanu's monasteries and the site of a school that he set up to create a style in architecture, painting, wood and stone carving, and to spread it elsewhere. It was built between 1691 and 1697, followed during 1697-9 by the *Bolniţa* or infirmary to the east. Then there is the Hermitage of the Holy Apostles (1698-1700) 500m away, St Steven's hermitage (1703) across the Romani river, and the church of the Archangel Michael built to the south of the gate in 1708 for the use of the villagers. Brîncoveanu's own chambers are now a museum. There are fine frescoes of the Last Judgment and Church Councils in the church porch and the nuns' refectory. From here the road leads past a junction, near kilometre post 2, to Romani de Sus to the north, and then about 500m south a junction right on an unmade road direct to Horezu town; the asphalt road continues to the main DN 67 a kilometre or two east of the town. The *autogară* is just south of the main east-west road, and a campsite just to the north.

Moving on

As you move west you might next wish to stop at Polovragi; this is on a minor road just north of the DN 67 and parallel to it, with plenty of interconnections (not very clearly shown on Map 8 of the *Invitation*). I believe that almost any bus from Horezu towards Tîrgu Jiu will stop there. From the stop, where the bus and the main road turn 90 degrees left to head west, you will have to continue a kilometre or so north on the asphalt to reach the monastery (in fact inhabited by 15 nuns); this was founded in 1504, but was taken over and rebuilt by Brîncoveanu in 1693, with frescoes painted from 1698 to 1705. Through a wooden porch to the north is the *Bolniţa* or infirmary church (1732-38) with especially fine frescoes. Outside the main entrance is a small *bufete* with some camping cabins in case of need; the road north (to be marked with blue stripes) continues into the Olteţ gorge, 1.5km of limestone cliffs, with the 9,250m long Polovragi cavern where Zalmoxis, the Dacian supreme god, is said to have taken refuge after their defeat by the Romans. 450m of the

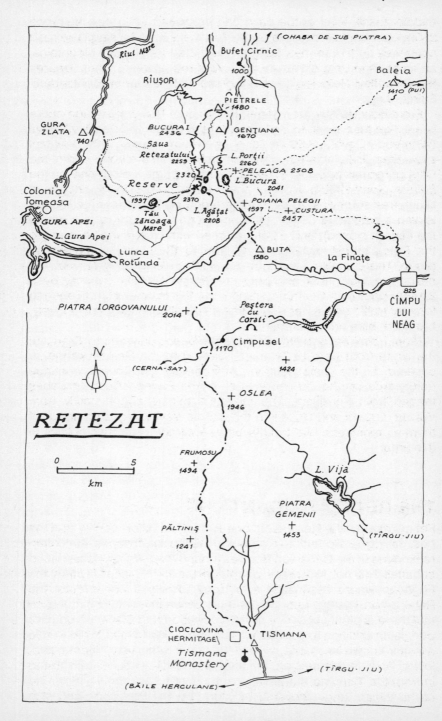

(OHABA DE SUB PIATRA)

Riul Mare

Bufet Cîrnic

RÎUŞOR

Baleia
△ 1410 (PUI)

PIETRELE
△ 1480

GURA
ZLATA   BUCURA I
△   2436
740   △   GENTIANA
Saua   1670
Retezatului
2259   L.Porţii
＋   2260
2320   ＋ PELEAGA 2508
Reserve   ＞ L.Bucura
Colonia   2041
Tomeaşa   1997   2370   ＋ POIANA PELEGII
GURA APEI   L.Agăţat   1597
L.Gura Apei   Tău   2208   ＋ CUSTURA
Zănoaga   2457
Mare
Lunca   △ BUTA
Rotunda   1580   La Finaţe
CÎMPU
LUI
PIATRA IORGOVANULUI ＋   825   NEAG
2014   Peştera
cu
Corali
N   Cîmpusel
＋ 1170   ＋
(CERNA-SAT)   1424

RETEZAT

＋ OSLEA
1946
0   5
km

FRUMOSU
＋   L. Vija
1494
PIATRA
GEMENII
＋
1453   (TÎRGU·JIU)
PĂLTINIŞ
＋
1241

CIOCLOVINA
HERMITAGE   △ TISMANA
Tismana
Monastery   (TÎRGU·JIU)
(BĂILE HERCULANE)

middle, fossil, level of the cave can be visited via a new entrance 250m upstream of the cave portal, but there is no lighting. The road continues north into the Căpăţînii (translated as 'Heady') Mountains, an empty and unspoilt area with a ridge route leading back towards the Olt valley. Polovragi is also the site of a *Nedeia* or Highlanders' Fair in July.

From Baia de Fier (Iron Mine), just west of Polovragi village, there is a 2.5km road north to Galbenu (Yellow) gorge and Peştera Muierii (Womens' Cave), 3,566m long of which 700m, with beautiful stalactites, is illuminated and open daily. (From the north end of the Olteţ gorge it is possible to take unmarked paths, shown only on the *Editura Sport-Turism* map of the Parîng range, for a couple of kilometres southwest to the southern end of Galbenu gorge.) There is also a cabana at 585m at the north end of the gorge (ask here if the cave is closed), and a path, marked with blue triangles, north to the Rînca tourist complex at 1,600m to the south of the Parîng range. There is also a road, the DN 67C, to Rînca from Novaci, the next town west; this continues to Obîrşia Lotrului cabana, by a 2,141m pass over the Parîng range, but this is only officially open to forestry traffic until it has finally been asphalted. It could be a lovely, but hard, bike ride until then.

From Polovragi and Novaci there are buses onwards to Tîrgu Jiu; the route from here to Tismana, leading to the Retezat range, is covered in the next section. Alternatively you could continue northwards up the Jiu valley to enter the Parîng, Vîlcan or Sebeş ranges from Petroşani. The infamous miners come mostly from Vulcan, Lupeni and Uricani in the Jiul de Vest valley; don't think of them as monsters, but it might be as well not to discuss politics in this area.

THE RETEZAT MOUNTAINS

For my money, the Retezat offers the most beautiful scenery and the best hiking in Romania — stunning alpine landscapes that often remind me of the Canadian Rockies, unspoilt woods and lakes, good cabanas but not too many people in the high places. Unlike the Făgăraş, where essentially everybody follows a ridge route, the Retezat consists of a network of routes between adjacent cirques, so that there is plenty of scope for improvisation and plenty of room for people. In addition to the main crystalline alpine massif, there is also a lesser-known limestone ridge to the south with a very different sun-loving flora. In this section, I include a preliminary day spent hiking in from the Tismana monastery to the south, over the western end of the Vîlcan range (covered by Map 7 in the *Invitation*), and also continue north to include the Romans' capital of Sarmizegetusa and the fascinating church at Densuş, all well worth visiting. As usual, you can vary this to suit yourself.

The National Park, Romania's first, created in 1935, covers an area about 80km by 60km, of which 3,700 hectares to the west is a Scientific Reservation, closed to all but specially authorised visitors. Ceauşescu used to regard this as a handy private shooting reserve, but now it is once again safe for genuine scientific research.

The main massif is Quarternary crystalline rock, mostly micaschist with granite intrusions, and is the most heavily glaciated area in Romania, with waterfalls up to 300m high and many beautiful alpine lakes. The southern ridge is Mesozoic limestone, with karst caves. There are 20 peaks over 2,300m and 40 more over 2,200m, giving an average altitude in the central zone higher than that of the Făgăraş range. They rise 2,000m above the Haţeg basin to the north.

Judging from fossils, this was once a sub-tropical zone; nowadays it has only two or three really warm and sunny months each summer, when the vegetation is exuberant. However there is less variety than in the Bucegi or Ceahlău, with only 320 species, of which 46% are European and Eurasian in origin, 22% Alpine and Arctic, 16% Balkan and Mediterranean, 12% endemic to Romania, and 4% endemic specifically to the Retezat. Much as elsewhere the main trees are beech from about 750m to as high as the summit of Vf Buta (1,560m), and spruce from 800m to 1,800m, or in dwarf form to 1,900m, with dwarf pines from 1,530m to 2,285m on the north slope of Vf Custura, associated with Arolla or Zîmbra pine (*Pinus Cembra*) to almost 2,000m on Vf Bîrlea and around Lacul Gemenele; there are also many other species such as birch, hornbeam, alders (*Alnus glutinosa, A. incana, A. viridis*), sycamore, rowan, Silesian willow (*Salix salesiaca*) and red-berried elder (*Sambucus racemosa*), together with flowering ash (*Fraxinus ornus*) on the sheltered banks of the Rîul Mare, and small-leaved lime (*Tilia cordata*) by Gura Apii reservoir. The shrubs are fairly familiar, such as juniper and *Bruckenthalia spiculifolia*.

The most valuable plants, apparently, are the endemic *Hieracium* species, mostly in the Scientific Reservation around Lac Gemenele and by the Zlătuia river, as well as in the spruce forests of the Pietrele and Rea valleys and in the dwarf pine zone above. Other endemics include *Barbarea lepusnice* on the stony floor of the Lăpuşnic valley, the grass *Poa lepusnica Nyár* on Vf Custura, and *Draba dorneri* on Vf Colţului.

On the limestone massif between the Lăpuşnic and Jiu de Vest valleys, the richest vegetation is in the chimneys on Vf Piule, Vf Albele and Piatra Iorgovanului, notably orchids and lilies (such as

Lilium jankae), and *Carduus csürösi, C. lobulati* and *Festuca pachyphylla*.

The fauna is less exotic, although it seems that bears are thriving in the area, with a population of 115 a few years ago, together with wolves, boar, lynx, marten, and about 2,000 chamois, partly around Gemenele in the Scientific Reservation, but also on the limestone ridge. Retezat chamois have, it seems, bigger horns than other *Rupicapra rupicapra*, although the difference is not that noticeable. The viper *Vipera berus* is found here, together with *Vipera ammodytes* whose range stretches from here to the Volga.

Large groups of golden eagles (*Aquila chrysaëtos*) can be seen especially on the limestone Drăgşan ridge, and white-headed and black vultures (*Gyps falcus* and *Aegypius monachus*) are also to be seen, together with capercaillie (*Tetrao urogallus*) in the coniferous forests.

There are trout in the Lăpuşnic and Bărbat rivers, and they have been artificially introduced into five of the largest lakes (Bucura, Ana, Zănoaga, Gemenele and Galeş).

Getting there

There are various fairly long walks in from places along the road and railway line from Petroşani to Haţeg, such as Pui or Ohaba de sub Piatra, or from Sarmizegetusa, described as my route out at the end of this section; it is also possible to walk in, in a couple of days, from Muntele Mic or Băile Herculane to the west (see the final section, on the Banat). However the road which comes closest to the heart of the Park is that through Vulcan and Lupeni to Cîmpu lui Neag (Neag's Field), where there is a cabana a couple of kilometres south of the town and bus-stop. From a point about three kilometres further upstream (west) there is a *drum forestier* marked with red crosses to the right to Buta cabana (see below), and a bit further on a more direct path up the Buta valley, which should in theory be marked by blue crosses or blue stripes. The main route continues up the Jiul de Vest valley for another 15km through the Scocul Jiului gorges to Cîmpuşel, and in fact continues right on to the Cerna valley and Băile Herculane, although only as a forestry road with virtually no through traffic; it would be an interesting route to cycle.

I in fact chose to reach Cîmpuşel by spending a preliminary day hiking north from the Tismana monastery, over the western end of the Vîlcan mountains (Map 7 in the *Invitation*). This is a continuation of the previous section on the Wallachian Monasteries, which brought me to Tîrgu Jiu; here, although the bus station is next to the rail station, you ought to take the time to wander around and look at the monumental statues of Constantin Brancuşi (1938). Perhaps the most famous, the Endless Column, is echoed in the porch pillars of all the half-completed 'modern vernacular' houses of the area; this is known as the 'Pillar of Heaven' motif. From Tîrgu Jiu there are buses west first to Runcu, at the southern end of the Runcu or Sohodol gorges, through which an unmade road runs north to Sohodol cabana and tourist complex, and on between the two halves of the Vîlcan range to Cîmpu lui Neag; and then on to Tismana via Brancuşi's birthplace of Hobiţa.

Tismana has a major festival on the Feast of the Assumption of the Virgin on August 15 — a good opportunity for buying arts and crafts. There are camping cabins at Hobiţa, at a motel at the south end of Tismana village (by a narrow-gauge level-crossing) and about one kilometre south of the monastery, north of the village, and just north of the monastery is Tismana Nord touristic complex and cabana, which I found ridiculously overpriced for a place without water or lights bright enough to read or write by. Nor will they serve breakfast before 1000, which gives time to visit the monastery first. However it has the advantage that some if not all of the buses terminate here. It is also possible to reach Tismana from the west, from Băile Herculane via Baia de Arama, from where one can also reach some of Romania's finest karst caves, such as Topolniţa, near Cireşu, Ponoare and Cloşani.

The Tismana monastery (or rather nunnery) is Romania's oldest, founded in 1378, with murals painted in 1564 and 1732. The buildings now seem very white and clean and modern, and indeed a new porch to the church has just been completed; like most Romanian monasteries it is walled, with a Baronial gate tower, and served as the headquarters of the revolutionary Tudor Vladimirescu in 1821.

Hiking directions

Just north of the tourist complex is a logging camp with post office and *alimentară*, with particularly unreliable opening hours; five minutes north of here, after crossing a bridge, I was shown a small unmarked path up to the left, which crosses a *drum forestier* after ten minutes and forks right after three minutes more, all in good beech woods. After 14 minutes (crossing a good stream halfway) the path reaches the Schitu Cioclovina; this is a serene and beautiful hermitage with a tiny chapel barely bigger than the wooden porch along its side.

From here the path goes up steadily and easily to the north almost all day, contouring around the hilltops. It starts by going up to the left behind the chapel, then immediately right at a fork. After about seven minutes there is a track straight ahead and another to the left, but the path keeps firmly to the right, with some very basic blue triangle markings, without the normal white base. It crosses two streams and after ten minutes turns right on to a *drum forestier* to climb steadily up, through ash, elder and mountain rose, to reach a clearing after 13 minutes. Here the path turns left and then swings up to the right, ie not taking the fork to the left, into the first conifers, and then on in shady beech woods. After nine minutes it reaches another clearing above a stîna to the left, with a view to lots of other stînas ahead to the northwest, and the Godeanu mountains beyond. The path continues upwards and northwards, passes up the right side of a clearing after 20 minutes, and after ten minutes more enters another clearing, from where it climbs for 18 minutes up to a ridge leading west-southwest to the stînas, which, I presume, would also lead towards the Cloşani cave.

Ten minutes after this ridge there is a path leftwards up to the top of Păltiniş (1,241m), while the main track (unmarked) goes around the right/east side, with views of the forested Piatra Gemeni twin peaks to the east. There is a good spring on this open section of track, and after 18 minutes the path rejoins that via the summit and heads down into beech woods. It passes a saddle, planted with young beech, and goes up Vf Carpineiul — there is an alternative cart track above where the path is blocked, and then again there is an unmarked path to the right avoiding the summit. The paths are reunited, half an hour from entering into the beech woods, before a hut, covered with graffiti but with a sound roof, at the start of another major ridge running west. Like the start of the other ridge west, this is a lovely spot for a rest.

Four minutes from here, fork left into conifers to another junction 11 minutes further on. Again there is a path, marked with blue triangles with a pinkish centre, to the right for 11 minutes around Vf Frumosu (Beautiful Peak, 1,494m). After reunion with the path over the summit, the route crosses over the Lespezel stream (where I passed a couple of travelling women fast asleep, with a pair of tethered donkeys, which are quite unusual in this country), and swings right to the northeast, passing briefly through a conifer plantation. Sixteen minutes from the stream it reaches a saddle, also cleared with good views ahead. After another nine minutes the path again comes up into a meadow and heads to the right of an outcrop at the end of the Boului ridge (1,671m), before zigzagging around its left/west side, with good views to the west and north. There are some intriguing old culverts here made from slabs of field stone. After a quarter hour the path enters beech woods again from the meadow, and after another quarter hour reaches a ridge and swings left at its end, leaving the woods after ten minutes. After five minutes the path leaves the upper edge of the woods, beginning a long steady climb up into moorland, passing around a buttress after about 13 minutes, and reaching the main ridge west of Vf Oslea after another 13 minutes. There were a lot of beautiful horses grazing loose in this area, although not many sheep or shepherds.

From here the route goes straight across the ridge and to the left or northwest, and then down past a red cross marker pole and down a side ridge to meet a zigzag cart track. Marked with red crosses and a few blue triangles, the path goes down the end of the ridge in a clear strip between woods and in under half an hour reaches a *drum forestier* by a picnic shelter. From here it is 40 minutes walk east along the road to Cîmpuşel, where there is nothing but a hunters' cabana on the right with a camping place and picnic table to the left just before a bridge. From here, as mentioned above, it is possible to go west to Băile Herculane or east to Cîmpu lui Neag and Petroşani.

Although it is possible to reach the Buta cabana more directly from Cîmpu lui Neag, the more interesting route starts here and climbs steeply up to Piatra Iorgovanului, Iorgovan's Rock, said to have been split in two by the dragon-killer Iorgo Iorgovan to test his sword. This path starts without markings along the track behind the camping place, across the stream and right in the field behind to a marker pole. The path climbs up the first tiny side valley to the right, steeply at first and then more easily, quite recently and well marked with red triangles, which always seemed to be climbing above whenever I thought I'd reached a level stretch. After 38 minutes (net) I reached a ridge, as the conifers gave way to dwarf pines. The path continues up to the northwest in scenery that reminded me of the Alpes Maritimes — very dry, stunningly white limestone, with dwarf bushes and lizards. After 35 minutes there is a marker pole on a prominent outcrop which you can in fact bypass to the left, and the climb is then easier for 17 minutes to a sign on the ridge. You can ignore a pole higher to the left which is on the ridge route to Băile Herculane; the summit of Piatra Iorgovanului (2,014m) is a quarter hour to the left on this route.

Although the maps both show this ridge route marked as usual with red stripes, it in fact seems to be marked with blue triangles to the east and red triangles to the west. The route to Buta goes to the right/east; the first marker pole is hidden behind bushes but if you head straight for the best-looking patch of grass you should find it without trouble. The path goes up and to the right around Vf Albele (2,005m) and then down along a stream bed to the confluence of three streams. Although the *Invitation* map is correct here, the *Hartă Turistică* wrongly shows a deviation to the right around the head of the main stream. The path crosses just below the confluence, 48 minutes after reaching the ridge, and continues above the right bank of the stream on the far side. From here it's fifteen minutes to a ridge in open moorland, with a good view of a deep trench valley to the left. This was the Lăpuşnic glacier, 14km long in its prime, and presently you will have to cross this valley.

The path continues for now along the ridge eastwards, to the north of Vf Drăgşanu, where there may be golden eagles to be seen. After about 25 minutes it crosses a stream and after 16 more goes down to the left to find a way through a particularly thick patch of dwarf pines and reach the Şaua Plaiul Mic (1,879m) after another 20 minutes. From here the blue triangles continue along the limestone ridge to Vf Custura and Vf Păpuşa at the head of the valley; the route from Custura east to a point between Lupeni and Uricani is particularly recommended by the Buta *cabanier*, although the yellow cross markings have apparently been defaced by shepherds who don't want hikers in the area. To the right is the path, now marked with blue stripes and red crosses (and blue triangles painted out) to Buta cabana (1,580m), which took me 27 minutes down and 36 up. From Buta there is now a *drum forestier* to Cîmpu lui Neag, about four hours away. The cabana is very simple and pleasant, with its own cows but very little food available for visitors. There is a derelict hydroelectric waterwheel but no electricity. I gather there is now a private cabana a little way below this one.

The path north down into the Lăpuşnic valley is also marked with blue stripes and red crosses (and blue dots painted out); after 15 minutes it crosses a broad stream through rocks to the right, and eight minutes later reaches Gura Bucurei, the mouth of the Bucura valley, at 1,500m. There is a usable hut here at the end of the *drum forestier*, marked with red crosses, down the valley to Gura Apei dam 20km away, and a very beautiful pool where the river has been blocked with a wooden dam. This would periodically have been opened by loggers to wash their felled trees down the river to be retrieved somewhere below. Having clambered across on logs or just waded, you climb up into the Poiana Pelegii camping place, supposedly 97m above the river, where there is the Refugiul Diana, little more than a wooden tent, with an earth floor and no door or glass windows. Any port is welcome in a storm, though.

The path sets off northwards up the Bucura valley, mostly over buried boulders with a cascading stream to the left, through spruce and then dwarf pines; it is much moister on this side of the limestone ridge, and more reminiscent of Canada than of southern France. The path climbs steadily but not too steeply up a moraine dam, passing three marker poles before reaching the ridge 52 minutes from Gura Bucurei. At this point you are already past Lac Lia (1,930m), the first of the many lovely alpine lakes dotted around this great cirque. From here there is another climb up a moraine for about ten minutes to reach the shore of Lac Bucura (2,041m), the largest of the Retezat lakes at either 8.9 or 11 hectares, depending which source you believe. In summer there should be a Salvamont tent refuge (*Tabăra Mobilă*) here; in any case it is a very popular camping spot, understandably, even though there are *Camping Verboten* signs in German and Romanian and a L1,000 fine, and there is the usual dump of tin cans here. Sheep, and thus sheepdogs, are also *verboten*, which is excellent news; this is one of the most peaceful and beautiful spots I know, although possibly if all the snow melted there would be more bare rock than the ideal. It would, just, be possible to go from Cîmpuşel to Pietrele in one day via Bucura, but it would be a shame to rush.

The path to the Baleia cabana, well to the east on the way out to Pui, goes to the right/east of the lake; my route to Pietrele, still marked with blue stripes, goes to the left/west, and after seven minutes passes the junction left, marked with yellow dots and blue crosses, to the Slăveiu ridge, and then three minutes further on, after a small tarn to the left, another junction left, marked with red dots and yellow stripes, to Tău (the local word for a tarn) Porţii almost 200m above; there it links with the route I took the next day back from Pietrele to Gura Zlata, which offers a different view of this Bucura cirque.

Seventeen minutes later I reached the Curmătura Bucurei, the narrow ridge at 2,206m between the Bucura and Pietrele cirques; as in the Făgăraş the weather on the north side of the ridge can be totally different to (and worse than) that on the south side. As late as June 20 I found heavy snow blocking the path here and about ten metres visibility; eventually I slid down the snow on the first steep section into the fog, and then simply followed the trend of the valley downwards to the north. The marked path starts by veering to the right and zigzags down to the bottom of the valley; then it winds through rocks and dwarf bushes, crossing lots of parallel streams and passing Lac Pietrele (1,990m) to the west. About 50 minutes after leaving the ridge the path crosses two streams from the right/east bank to the left/west, and two minutes later crosses back again; a couple of minutes later you can safely ignore a marker pole back on the left bank. The *Hartă Turistică* is inaccurate here, as it shows the path following the left bank of the stream throughout. The route continues through a mess of moraine and dwarf pine, getting a bit steeper before crossing to the left bank by a broken footbridge after another 23 minutes. It passes through a stony meadow and after nine minutes arrives at the Genţiana refuge (1,670m), which was locked and out of use when I passed.

The path continues into taller trees between scree-covered slopes, with a considerable amount of rock-hopping at first. After 18 minutes it reaches a covered bench at the junction of a path marked with yellow triangles east to Valea Rea and Baleia cabana; this crosses the Pietrele river by a pair of slippery tree trunks two minutes below and continues as a fairly minor path. The path north, marked with both blue stripes and yellow triangles, reaches Pietrele cabana in 15 minutes. This is in fact quite a complex, with a fairly large cabana and also cabins with four rooms opening on to a verandah. Here as at Buta there is a disused hydroelectric waterwheel; there are light fittings but naturally no bulbs. From here there is a road northwards to Ohaba de sub Piatra station about six hours away; there is a *magazin forestier* four kilometres north at Poiana Cirnic, beyond Lolaia waterfall, but as usual there's no telling when it will be open. The cabana does offer decent meals, though.

Instead of the tedious hike north you might choose to return to the central area by an alternative route to the Baleia or Gura Zlata cabanas; there is a fairly direct route to Gura Zlata to the north of the Scientific Reservation, but I chose to skirt right around it to the east and south to enjoy the views of the Bucura lakes from above. Because of the snow still cluttering the upper valleys I took the route along the Lolaia ridge which turned out to be rather hard work; in normal summertime circumstances I suspect the Stînişoara valley route would be better, and I hope to check before too long. Meanwhile I can only describe the route I used.

Heading west from Pietrele, across the lesser stream, the yellow stripe markings at once proved very hard to follow in the light and shade of the woods, blending nicely with the lichen. The path then climbs across and then up a rockfall — do not take the tempting path by the stream (this is NOT the Stînişoara). At the far side of the rockfall the markings, such as they are, cut back a bit to the right and reach the top about half an hour after leaving the cabana; after a brief zigzag up through conifers it climbs up the left side of another steeper rockfall, reaching the top after another 14 minutes. There are great views here down to the cabana, still only a few hundred metres away, and north to Vf Bucura and the main ridge. From here you can make your own way to the ridge just north of Şaua Ciurlia, a saddle covered with grass, rocks, dwarf bushes and dead branches. About seven minutes from here you will meet a path marked with blue crosses, leading down to the Stînişoara valley to the left/east and to the Rîuşor cabana, on a *drum forestier* leading north towards Rîu de Mori, to the right/west. This is probably an easier route up to the ridge. The path onwards starts off to the right, then climbs, mainly on granite rocks, to reach after 26 minutes La Zimbrii Arşi, a rocky summit with a deep cleft to the east and a very narrow grassy saddle.

Another 24 minutes brings you to Vf Lolaia Nord (2,180m) and another 16 minutes to Vf Lolaia Sud (2,275m) before dropping quite a way to the Lolaia saddle; this is almost all over bare rocks, alive with ants and spiders. From here the rock scrambling is somewhat faster, with mini-cairns rather than painted markings; after about 25 minutes there is a gully to the right with views to Lac Ştevia, as well as smaller tarns below to the east, and very soon after this the path begins to trend to the left of the cliffs ahead. However this soon disintegrates to little more than a chamois track — quite passable but without markings. It takes you around the east side of Vf Retezat, with views of the Stînişoara cirque and lake; I took half an hour to get to the junction with the much better path from Gura Zlata and Vf Retezat marked with blue triangles and a red square, which marks the edge of the Scientific Reservation and means *no entry* — the boundary of the Reservation is further north than shown in the *Invitation*. From here the path continues down for another ten minutes (through what the *Invitation* describes as 'the famous slope of granodiorite rocks') to the Şaua Retezat (2,251m) where the blue triangles turn left down to Lac Stînişoara and the path south continues marked with yellow and some red stripes.

The going is faster now, with some rock-hopping, and after 15 minutes passes around the west side of Vf Bucura I, with one section badly eroded. Another thirty minutes brings you to the saddle at 2,320m above Tău Porţii; the path down to the tarn, the highest in the Retezat at 2,240 or 2,260m, depending which page of the *Invitation* you believe, is badly eroded and takes about ten minutes. From here one path goes down to Lac Bucura, as mentioned above, and the other to Gura Zlata, marked with red dots, climbs up the cliff-face for half an hour to Şaua Judele (2,370m). The route continues mostly just south of the Bîrlea ridge and the Reservation, now on open moorland with some rocks; after half an hour it starts to zigzag down for 15 minutes to Lac Zănoaga at about 1,973m, the deepest of the lakes at 29m. This is a lovely spot, and it's a shame camping is not allowed here. The path around the left/south side is largely unmarked, until another marked with blue crosses appears from the south on the east side of the Zănoaga stream and climbs up to the west to regain the fine open moorland again in 15 minutes. Twelve minutes further west, just before a ridge curving south around the Zănoguţa basin, the blue cross route heads southwest to the Gura Apii reservoir. After another five minutes you reach two signs about 100m apart and follow the red stripe route to the right or northwest. After 22 minutes through rocks and dwarf pine the path descends into meadow and follows marker poles to the left of a spring and the Radeş stîna (c1,800m), with views of the Rîul Mare (Big River) and the Ţarcu mountains to the west.

The path zigzags down into conifers, levels out and even rises slightly to reach the end of the ridge 23 minutes from the stîna; again it zigzags down, now with the hill of Cioaca Porumbelului (1,453m) to the left, into silver birch, ash, sycamore, elder and ferns, to gradually approach the Radeşu Mare stream to the north. The woods here are a humid mix of beech and tall conifers. One hour from the end of the ridge the path crosses the stream (into the Reservation, as it happens) by a jumble of fallen trees, crosses a side stream by a better bridge after six more minutes, and after nine more crosses back to the south; for some reason the footbridge is hidden about ten metres upstream from the path. After four minutes the path, now used by horses as well, crosses back to the right bank and soon passes the park gate and some private cabanas at La Cirjiţe — a road leads to the asphalt and a bridge across the Rîul Mare to the main road and Gura Zlata cabana a couple of minutes south at 740m altitude. Here they tried to charge me an immense sum for a room, but camping was quite cheap at L10 per square metre of tent.

This is the end of the Retezats as such; from here you can go south to Gura Apii dam and either hike for a couple of days west into the Ţarcu mountains to Muntele Mic or Băile Herculane, or southeast towards Piatra Iorgovanului, Cîmpuşel or Buta, or you can go north by road. Dam construction work is scheduled until 1993, so until then it should be fairly easy to hitch a lift as far as Brazi, 15km north along this lovely valley, where an underground power station is being built, fed by a tunnel 18.5km long. You can either continue from Brazi through Rîu de Mori to Haţeg for trains and buses, or turn left just before Brazi to reach Roman Sarmizegetusa.

From the junction it is two kilometres to Clopotiva, passing a grandstand, helipad and mock Trajan's column built for the 'opening' of the incomplete hydroelectric project by Ceauşescu before the revolution. In Clopotiva turn left, signposted six kilometres to Sarmizegetusa, and then right, unsignposted, past the church (which contains Roman remains) and on along a dirt road. After about one kilometre, just before the top of the only hill, there is a possible short cut left along a vague cart track; this doesn't really save much time, but is more pleasant, with less dust and many meadow flowers.

In any case you will reach the main road from Haţeg to Caransebeş and turn left; after the motel you come to the museum on the right and the Roman remains on the left. Colonia Ulpia Traiana Augusta Dacica Sarmizegetusa was founded by Trajan in AD108 as the capital of Roman Dacia, controlling the main route through the Iron Gates of Transylvania to the rest of the Empire; it takes its name from the Dacians' own capital of Sarmizegetusa in the

Sebeş mountains, dealt with in the next section. The museum, closed on Mondays, has some remarkably well-preserved inscriptions and lamps and a map of the remains to orientate you. The area around the amphitheatre, across the road, is well preserved although used for growing hay; down a lane behind and to the right is the less tidy Forum complex.

From here you can go east or west along the main DN 68 road (note that there are no passenger trains along the railway west of Sarmizegetusa, and only two mixed trains — freight trains with a coach tagged on the end — per day east to Subcetate), but it is well worth taking the easy stroll north over minor hills to the fascinating little church at Densuş. This starts by turning north along a tree-lined track about 300m east of the Sarmizegetusa motel to the village of Breazova; here you can turn left at the church up a sheep track, or continue a bit further and turn left up a farm track. The track peters out by a spring; continue to the northwest to the lowest point of the ridge and turn right along it. Half an hour from the main road cross the ridge and go into young mixed forestry (conifers, beech, oaks), and after seven minutes turn left just before reaching a meadow into a similarly overgrown path. After five minutes it goes into mature beech, takes a big zig left and goes down north across a meadow to a stile. From here the path goes right to another stile, crosses the stream to the north, and turns right along an unmade road after nine minutes.

From here it's a quarter hour northeast up the Peşteniţa village street with the stream now on the left and houses on the right. Take the first left turn, at a green cross, opposite green gates without a number, turn right across the ford and after three minutes cross a cart track; follow a line of fruit trees northwards down to the stream and climb straight up the other side to a saddle. Of the two villages visible ahead Densuş is the one to the left; go down to the left across fields in what could be the Sussex Downs, follow a hedge north and cut across the end of a field to a stile into an orchard and then another stile out at the other end. One path goes to the right around the head of a ravine, down to a grassy track and (45 minutes from the line of fruit trees) out on to a dirt road from Peşteana, by a well at house no 179; the main road is just below to the left and the *alimentară* is to the left here. The other route from the orchard goes down the ravine and emerges on the west side of the *alimentară*, which unusually is open from 0700 to 1100 and 1700 to 2100, although the staff were presumably still in the fields the evening I was there.

To reach the church, turn right at the bus stop, just beyond the shop, past the statue of the village's favourite son, the etymologist and historian of the Romanian language Ovid Densuşianu, and across the river bridge. The church is thought to be largely made from the 4th-Century mausoleum of a Roman army commander, probably remodelled in the early 13th Century and with frescoes from 1443. The south aisle is now open, while the interior is dark and simple, with what seems like a four-poster in the centre supporting the heavy tower. In 1991 the key was at No 15 (the fifth house on the left going east from the statue on the main road) but I doubt if he'll be able to take the pace once tourists start to flood in. There is another interesting church in Ciula Mare, due north straight over the hill behind the church, but Densuş is a better place to catch the occasional bus to Haţeg. There are similar churches nearby in Sîntămaria-Orlea, just south of Haţeg, and in Strei, just south of Călan.

Practical information

There is a good *Hartă Turistică* of the *Trasee Turistice în Masivul Retezat*, and the area is covered by Maps 5-6 of the *Invitation*.

THE SEBEŞ AND ŞUREANU MOUNTAINS

The greatest attraction of the Sebeş mountains is the opportunity to visit the ancient citadels of the Dacians, but both the Sebeş (also known as the Orăştie) and the Şureanu mountains (more open moorland just to the east) are unspoilt hills with a few rather grotty cabanas and remarkably few hikers. Although the Dacians left archaeological remains all over Transylvania and beyond, it is in this area that they left an entire network of remarkable citadels, as well as long walls and civil remains, surrounding their capital of Sarmizegetusa Regia. After two hard-fought campaigns, the Romans were justifiably pleased with themselves when they finally beat the Dacians in AD106, as commemorated on Trajan's Column in Rome. The Romanians are also proud to claim them as their ancestors.

Getting there

There is now a road, the DN 67C, to the east of the massif, from Sebeş to the Obîrşia Lotrului crossroads and cabana (see pages 251 and 273), with occasional bus service as far as Oaşa cabana. The main hiking route runs south from Orăştie on the *drum forestier* through Sibişel and on to Prislop cabana (which doesn't have the best of reputations) and Şureanu cabana (see below).

However this entirely misses the Dacian citadels, which are a bit harder to reach; your first objective is the village of Costeşti, reached

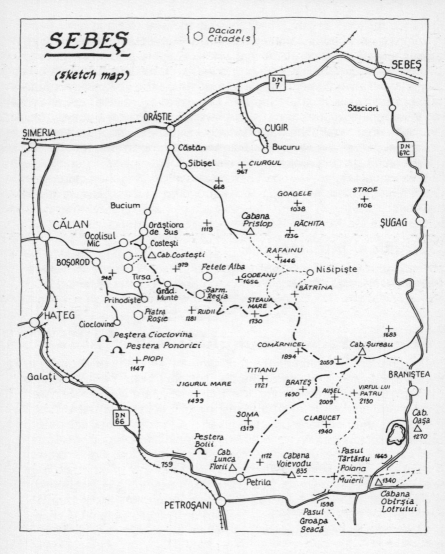

by occasional buses from Orăştie. However I walked over the hill from Călan, on the Haţeg to Simeria road and railway and linked by frequent buses to Hunedoara, site of a stunning and intact Gothic castle (1409), base of the great hero Iancu de Hunedoara, and also unfortunately of a large steelworks which rather spoils the view, although it has been there since 1750. Just south of Călan on the main road is the village of Strei, with a lovely ancient church; the Călan *autogară* is near another steelworks at the main road junction, while the town itself and former Roman spa (Aquae Callidae, 231m) is across the river to the east. There are nine buses a day through the town (mostly modern blocks, with reasonable shops, and another lovely 11th-Century church in Strei Sîngeorgiu to the south) to Boşorod; get off after six kilometres at the Ocolişu Mic junction and walk up this dirt road, to the left/east, through the typical but unlovely village (which also has the occasional bus), to reach the ridge after six kilometres.

From here the road goes down to Orăştioara de Sus, but you can take cart tracks down to the right directly to Costeşti village. Turn right/south along a level dirt road by a stream, then left on footbridges across this stream and then the main Apa Grădiştie to reach the main road south of the village just before a double bend. Just over one kilometre south is the Popas Salcîmul campsite and then a grand ceremonial gateway and Costeşti cabana on the left at the end of the asphalt. Although there is a bus stop here, I am told the bus no longer runs beyond the village.

Hiking directions

The first of the Dacian citadels, Cetatea Costeşti, is an easy sidetrip to the west — cross the river by the bridge towards some cabins, turn right (passing a sign to the citadel after about 100m) and then left to climb up the left side of the valley and turn sharp left again at an isolated farm where you can buy postcards or a guide book to the area with English summary. It took a total of 35 minutes to reach the citadel, three rows of fortifications with three bastions and a double palisade, on a 561m hilltop now largely hidden in trees. This is cow country, with silver birch, cherry trees, and blackberries, and of course lots of hay being scythed in small fields on the hillsides. Returning to the bridge, you have the option of following the southern fork for about an hour and a half to the slightly less impressive Cetatea Blidaru (703m); unfortunately it is not possible to get from one to the other across country. From Blidaru it should however be possible to follow a ridge route parallel to the *drum forestier* to Sarmizegetusa Regia or to reach (by an awkward roundabout route) the citadel at Piatra Roşie, the 2.5km Dacian wall at Cioclovina and the Cioclovina and Ponorici caves not far from the main Haţeg to Petroşani road, the DN 66.

The Costeşti meadows are a very popular picnic spot at weekends, and some very full cars continue south on the *drum forestier*; however it is best to try hitching on working days when there are a few forestry trucks passing. This would be an ideal place to have a mountain bike; otherwise it might mean a rather tedious walk in. The tiny logging settlement of Grădiştea de Munte is roughly eight kilometres south and has a *magazin forestier* and a bakery. There is also an archaeologists' cabana where you are likely to be made welcome in the summer. Several kilometres further southeast is a turning left up the Pîrîul Alb valley to approach Sarmizegetusa Regia from behind by a rough road, as well as the Fetele Alba citadel; keeping right along the main Apa Grădiştie valley, parallel to the remains of a narrow-gauge forestry railway, brings you to Cetate *cabana forestier* at the confluence of the Timpului river, about eight kilometres from Grădiştea de Munte below Vf Rudii (1,281m).

From here you should walk up the left-hand (northern) valley for ten minutes to a concrete culvert by telegraph pole no 28 and take a small steep path up to the left/north into the beech woods; after about fifteen minutes you will reach an archaeologists' cabana just to the right in a small clearing, and three minutes above that, the citadel of Sarmizegetusa Regia itself at 1,058m or 1,200m. To the right, as you emerge into a clearing, are the foundations of various temples, round and square, with a solar calendar, and to the left a litter of strange preformed concrete objects — the habits of *Homus archaeologistus* are at least as strange as those of the Dacians. However it is the majesty of the tall and straight beeches all around rather than this junk that sticks in the mind. From here one follows an amazingly well made stretch of stone road uphill to the citadel, with its fine stone walls somewhat lower than in their prime surrounding remains of both Dacian and Roman buildings and more fine beech trees. At the opposite gate is the end of the road. It is easy to imagine characters rather like Astérix and his friends living in this setting.

To continue eastwards into the mountains, return down the path to the *drum forestier* and turn left up the valley. After about 15 minutes this reaches an old cabana and then a new dam, before beginning to climb steeply up to the north-northeast in a very impressive gorge. About 30 minutes from the dam is a junction; our route crosses the river to the right to Godeanu cabana (private) and a steep climb up to the ridge of the Culmea Şesului, while a new road continues ahead to cut back sharply left up to Vf Godeanu (1,656m). After 30 minutes of steady zigzagging up a fairly recently bulldozed track, you reach the ridge and turn left on to an older track, broad and sandy, with a bench and table two minutes to the left, with water just below.

Continuing northeast from here you should keep left at two junctions with forestry tracks and then curve right and up to the southeast to reach a ridge after 25 minutes, and emerge from conifers on to open moorland. On a hill to the left is a circle which I hoped was Dacian but is probably the remains of a stîna. The track goes to the right, past a junction from the left and then past the Steaua Mica (Little Star) stîna at 1,675m to the left/east. One could turn left here through this stîna and continue east, but I in fact kept to the track and turned off after 18 minutes to the Steaua Mare stîna at 1,730m. This is a remarkably solid and permanent settlement, with women in residence, unlike those at higher altitudes which are usually men-only. The spring is also unusually close.

Beyond the stîna I turned left on to the same track as before, which had taken a great sweep around the head of the valley. This climbs east to a ridge after ten or more minutes, and after four more minutes runs into a track from the right at a spring, and drops to the northeast to some huts by a stream and a road from the left and presumably Steaua Mica. This route is slightly more direct but involves a slightly greater drop and then climb. The path continues northeast up a meadow, becoming a clearer cart track after a spring six minutes from the huts and then after four more minutes meeting a path marked with red triangles coming from the left at an illegible sign; this is the main route from Prislop cabana which we follow to Şureanu. It continues on rather tussocky open moorland, with no one clear route, swinging left around the head of a major valley to the south and reaching after 20 minutes the Sinca saddle between this and another major valley to the north, from where a path marked with red dots heads north to Cugir station, along the west side of the valley and over Vf Bătrînă (1,792m).

The path continues southeastwards, following marker poles, and then unobtrusively turns left over the ridge as the more obvious shepherds' path continues south towards Vf Neagru (Black Peak, 1,862m), so called because of the dark dwarf pines covering its summit. The route to Şureanu is very unclear here, but it doesn't matter too much as long as you turn left before Vf Neagru and continue along its rocky east flank, through scattered conifers. The path drops a bit to a cross and then climbs a bit to an arrow sign 45 minutes from the Sinca saddle. The path continues for 15 minutes to the head of the valley, more or less on the level above the bulk of the trees, and swings left over another of the saddles between valleys to the north and south that characterise this route. The path climbs to the east-northeast, past a stîna to the left, to a ridge 27 minutes from the saddle, with good views of open downs country all around, and the Parîng mountains beyond to the south. It then goes around the head of another valley to the south, reaching a ridge after 28 minutes and then dropping for ten minutes to another high saddle with a small stone shelter, too small to sleep in but a useful windbreak; from here it climbs to one saddle and then a higher one at right angles to it, running east-west, 19 minutes from the shelter. The path turns left along the side of the Şureanu ridge, climbing and then dropping towards the Şureanu saddle below to the right with a stîna on the far side; however it does not cross but keeps to the left, going down into spruce 21 minutes from the highest saddle, and reaching Şureanu cabana (1,734m), after another three minutes.

I was not impressed by the cabanier here, who was clearly more interested in his livestock than in tourists, and had nothing in the shop apart from wine and tinned meat, and nothing else to offer but *mămăligă*. I gather Prislop cabana is similar. There is a lovely walk beyond the cabana to Lac Şurian (1,790m), surrounded on three sides by tall *Adenostyletalia* flowers, with dwarf pine and spruce beyond. The fine sand is made from the crushed shells of diatomites, trapped here since the Ice Age. From here there is a *drum forestier* northwards, marked with red triangles to Cugir and with blue triangles to Sebeş, as well as a red cross route eastwards to the Sebeş to Obîrşia Lotrului road and the Cindrel mountains.

However I went south to Petrila following the blue triangle markings; this route turns right/south off the *drum forestier* after eight minutes but then runs parallel to it for 12 minutes to the Şureanu saddle. Here the blue cross route to Voievodu cabana and the blue stripe route to Obîrşia Lotrului cross to the left/southeast, and the blue triangle route follows the *drum forestier* into the woods, emerging above the trees after ten minutes. After 13 minutes the path turns to the left but very soon rejoins the track, after a branch turns off uphill to the right. Then after another 23 minutes the path really does turn off to the left — you may miss the turning, but look out for an arrow sign visible to the left soon after. Even if you do miss it, the track via Vf Brateş will eventually bring you down to the same route. The path goes down, briefly across a meadow and then for half an hour through spruce, zigzagging down the steep hill to reach the Auşel valley and a very underused *drum forestier*, by a bench and an illegible sign opposite a ruined hut.

The road runs down the right bank of this surprisingly small stream in its deep, steep-sided valley; after 13 minutes it reaches Auşeu hunters' cabana, and after 30 more minutes the junction with a *drum forestier* from Vf Brateş to the west, just upstream of a couple of small cabanas. The valley widens, with meadows by the stream, and after exactly another 30 minutes the road reaches some forestry cabanas with an *alimentară forestier*, at the junction with a valley from the west. After eight minutes there is a bridge to two forestry roads on the east bank, and 15 minutes after that the road itself crosses to the left/east bank six minutes before the turning right, back across the river, to Lunca Florii cabana (850m), at the top of Map 8 of the *Invitation*. From here it is five kilometres to Petrila, which took me 55 minutes through a short gorge with a couple of caves, cliffs where soldiers were being taught rock-climbing, and a small barrage. The final three kilometres across the plain are very industrial and dusty and not at all pleasant. Arriving at the main road from Voievodu to the east, there is a city bus stop just to the right/west at the technical school to go straight into Petroşani.

Practical information

I found no generally available hiking map of this area, therefore I have attempted to give a detailed route description comprehensible in both directions.

THE PARÎNG, LOTRU AND CINDREL MOUNTAINS

The Parîng mountains are one of the lesser known parts of the so-called Transylvanian Alps, between the Făgăraş and Retezat massifs, offering a sight of very lovely alpine scenery in a very concentrated area that is easy to get to and see in a limited amount of time. The western end, close to Petroşani, is well developed with cabanas, a ski-lift and television tower, but the eastern end, just 10km east, will remain quieter at least until the DN 67C from Rînca to Obîrşia Lotrului has been asphalted and officially opened to public traffic. From the Obîrşia Lotrului cabana my route continues into the much quieter and less spectacular Lotru and Cindrel ranges to the northeast, but it is also possible to go northwest into the Şureanu and Sebeş mountains (see previous section) or southeast into the Latoriţei and Căpăţînii mountains, which I do not cover. In particular when the DN 67C and the east-west DN 7A are fully opened there will be all sorts of possibilities for linking them together: the routes I describe are, as usual, starting points for your own variations. In addition I shall describe the route west from Păltiniş and the Cînaia refuge to Oaşa cabana on the DN 67C north of Obîrşia Lotrului, for access to the Şureanu and Sebeş ranges.

The Parîng massif is steep to the north and slopes gently away to the south; the north side shows signs of typically alpine glaciation, with sharp crests or *arêtes* and the two massive cirques of Roşiile and Cîlcescu, full of lakes, while the south shows carpatic glaciation, with flattened ridges between rivers and isolated conical peaks. It is mostly composed of crystalline schists as well as mesozoic sediments such as limestone, breccia, microconglomerates and clays, and Flysch or Turbidite to the southeast. Deciduous forests grow from 500m to 1,400m on the southern slopes and from 500m to 1,200m on the northern slopes, and conifers, almost entirely spruce, from 1,200m to 1,800m to the south and from 1,000m to 1,750m to the north. Above this are alpine meadows with dwarf bushes and flowers such as edelweiss, and above this the rocky

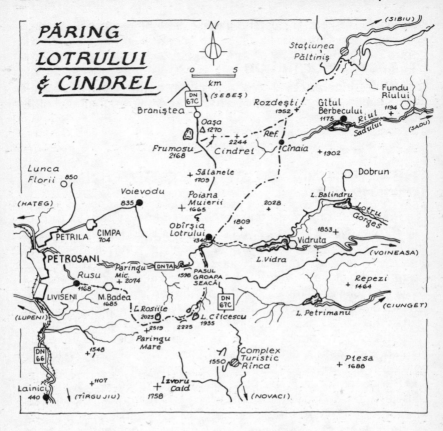

zone with lichen and saxifrage. Chamois can be seen in the Roşiile and Ghereşu cirques.

The Cindrel (or Cibin) mountains are easily accessible and pleasant hills without any particularly threatening peaks or steep uphill slogs; when the *Invitation* calls them 'barren' it simply means they are not tree-covered. While in no way exceptional they make a convenient excursion for a couple of days from Sibiu, as described by Mrs Gerard in the last century. Nowadays you can do this most easily by taking a bus from Sibiu to the ski resort of Păltiniş.

Getting there

The main access point is likely to be Petroşani, although there are also routes in from the area of the Wallachian monasteries to the south. Petroşani is the centre of the Jiu valley mining area, with mostly modern shops and hotels. From here, at 600m or just below, you need to make your way to the lower terminal of the *Telescaun* or chair-lift at 1,073m, either by a road looping to the north with occasional workers' buses and the like, or by a steep path marked with red stripes from the *Institutul de Mine* (Mining Institute) in the centre (about two hours walking). There is also a path from the suburb of Livezeni to the south, but the blue stripe markings are old and intermittent. At the road's end, perched above the terminal, is Rusu cabana (1,168m), more a youth hotel than a mountain hut; to get a good start next day you would be best advised to take the *Telescaun* to an intermediate platform at 1,581m and find a bed in the Salvamont refuge, in fact in the *Baza Sportif* of the Hidromin factory. There is another private cabana next door which offers more in the way of food and drink, and a friendly weather station beyond. The chair-lift (2.5km and a climb of 612m in 25 minutes) operates from 0930 to 1630 Mondays excepted and charges more than most at L100.

To start from Pǎltiniş there is first a 32km bus ride from a grey kiosk on the corner of Str 9 Mai near the Sibiu *autogarǎ*. The tram line from Sibiu to Rǎşinari has now closed, so buses tend to be very full for the first 12km. Departures in 1991 were at 0700, 0900, 1100, 1300 and 1530; this last arrives at 1700 and forms the last service back at 1730, taking the staff of all the shops with it — clearly no-one actually lives in Pǎltiniş if they can help it, but it's not actually an unpleasant spot, strung along a loop of road in a spruce forest. From the bus stop by the post office and rather limited *alimentarǎ* you can either go back to the right to the *Casa Turiştilor*, or turn left up a slight hill to the terminal of a chair-lift up to Vf Onceşti and under a low bridge to reach the cabana, somewhat cheaper than the *Casa Turiştilor*. With three new hotels planned, the resort is due to expand considerably.

Hiking directions

From the upper terminal of the chair-lift above Petroşani at 1,685m, with the prominent television tower and a mess of other huts, set off up the track up Parîngu Mic and after *very* roughly ten minutes turn right to begin a traverse, rising gently and following red stripe markings, across a grassy slope to turn left around a shoulder and reach the main ridge after 33 minutes. This ridge continues eastwards, almost all at 2,000m or above, and almost all without water, for 40km into the Cǎpǎţînii range. From here Petroşani is hidden, but there is a fine view west to the Retezat and east into the cirque; the hills here, as in the Cindrel and Şureanu massifs, are covered with dwarf bushes of *Rhododendrum Kotschyi (smîrdar)* with clusters of rosepink tubular flowers which are gathered for tea from May to July, when the whole hill seems to glow. The path passes to the right of a small hilltop of 2,202m and then zigzags up to Vf Cîrja

(2,405m) almost an hour from arriving on the ridge. The path now gets faster, continuing southeast over Stoiniţa (2,421m) and Gemănarea (2,426m) and turning left after another 55 minutes on to the final eight minute approach to Parîngu Mare. Here you have already reached the highest point of the massif at 2,519m, so it's all downhill from here on (if only it were so simple).

From here there are routes to the south, with red crosses to the Lainici campsite, monastery and station in the narrow, winding Jiu valley, and red crosses to Stănceşti, both across broader open moorland ridges. The main ridge route winds down to the Gruiu saddle in 16 minutes, then goes around the south side of Vf Gruiu (2,345m) to another saddle in 18 minutes, and turns sharply left around Vf Pîcleşa (2,335m) after 13 minutes more. The ridge is now heading north around the eastern side of the Roşiile cirque, with great views of lakes still frozen in late June; the path climbs for another quarter hour above scree to Vf Ieşu (2,375m) and then drops for 20 minutes to the Ghereşu saddle before climbing for 18 minutes to the Piatra Tăiată saddle, from where a side ridge and a path to be marked with blue stripes run north to Groapa Seacă pass on the DN 7A.

From here you can continue eastwards on the red stripe route for many kilometres, but my chosen route, marked with red crosses, drops down into the Cîlcescu cirque and heads north to the Obîrşia Lotrului cabana. To begin with this path is slow, on a loose surface, and once at the bottom of the cliffs it keeps well to the right under low crags rather than going into the dwarf pine. The path is unclear when it does enter the bushes to go around Lac Cîlcescu, as there are many small camping places and pools dotted around the floor of the cirque, with the usual mess of empty cans. This snow-melt water is so perfectly clear that a wasp didn't see the surface of a pool at all and flew straight into it.

The path reaches the outlet stream from Lac Cîlcescu (1,935m) after 45 minutes; a path marked with red triangles goes up to the southeast to rejoin the ridge route, and the red crosses continue north, crossing briefly to the right/east bank and then back to the left bank to go down a moraine covered with dense dwarf pines for 20 minutes. It then crosses the stream (the young Lotru river) again and after six minutes reaches a sign with two arrows both pointing the same way: in fact the path to the left, back across the stream, leads quite directly to the *drum forestier* while the other heads right across a small stream, goes up and then left into a meadow and then follows the left bank of another stream. This path vanishes altogether but then reappears with shiny new metal red cross marker plates fixed to trees, presumably after joining the path down from Lac Iezer to the southeast. This route involves some fairly primitive bushwalking, but the reward, apart from the relief of getting away from route markings for a change, is the wild white water of this stream, very reminiscent of the Canadian Rockies. After more than half an hour the path crosses the stream on a fallen tree at a very steep angle, and after two more minutes reaches a *drum forestier* (at about 1,600m) which goes down for 15 minutes to the right bank of the Lotru where it joins the main grassed-over track along the bank.

The clear river flowing over stones reminded me again of the foothills of the Rockies; it would be ideal for swimming on a hot day. After six minutes the track crosses a bridge to the left bank, then climbs up to a small bluff and then down to the Găuri or Huluzu forestry cabana, ten minutes before meeting the DN 67C, at this point an unmade forestry road, from a bridge to the right (at just below 1,400m altitude). It takes another 30 minutes virtually on the level to reach another forestry cabana at the junction with the DN 7A to Petroşani, 27.5km west. Another quarter hour of plodding along this road finally brings you to the Obîrşia Lotrului junction, where the DN 7A turns right/east to Lacu Vidra, a reservoir with a developing resort, and the Olt valley. The cabana here (without any sign to indicate its location) serves as bar and social club for the loggers, but there is good enough accommodation across the road in camping cabins with electric light.

From here my route continues northeast into the Lotru and Cindrel ranges to reach Păltiniş and Sibiu; alternatively you can, if very patient, attempt to hitch east or west on the DN 7A, or walk four kilometres north up the DN 67C to the turning left to Poiana Muierii and the Şureanu range, or continue up the DN 67C to Oaşa cabana by Lac Oaşa, from where there are occasional buses to Sebeş (see below).

This section of my route, largely unmarked but very easy walking, starts five minutes east of the Obîrşia Lotrului cabana on the DN 7A; marked with red crosses it strikes north and turns right to climb into conifers up a forestry track parallel to the road and river. After 13 minutes it forks left and after five minutes more forks right, both badly marked. It crosses a very small cleared area and climbs up to the left for 11 minutes. From here the path is mainly an enlarged sheep track, largely unmarked, in open meadow with plenty of springs; this is lovely open downs country, rather Home Counties with shepherds in ARO four-wheel drive vehicles, but looking more like Austria when you look back to the Parîng range or to Lac Vidra to the southeast.

The path passes through some conifers above a stîna and then heads northeast through meadow, more to the north to cross the small Tîmpel valley, and on to the northeast along the shoulder of a hill to the left. Finally, 45 minutes after leaving the forest, it passes over the left side of a hill of 1,802m and invisibly joins a red stripe ridge route from Vf Tîmpa to the left. Continuing as multiple sheep tracks it passes through some conifers after 15 minutes and bashes on steadily to the northeast, going up a longish hill and then around to the right of its summit after 40 more minutes. It continues to the northeast towards Vf Piatra Alba about three kilometres ahead and goes left around the head of a wooded valley; after another quarter hour it passes between two small sheep pens and up a stony cart track just north of east for five minutes to reach a ridge and then go slightly down to a saddle. Here you should not take the obvious cart track down to the left but rather continue upwards along the edge of the dwarf pines; to the right is an unmarked but fairly clear route to Lac Vidra by a cart track along a ridge. After 15 minutes you reach a marker pole, no less, and curve right before continuing northeastwards towards Piatra Alba. The grass is much poorer up here, and the atmosphere is very peaceful or very lonely, depending on your point of view. In fact I was never alone up here as I had a huge cloud of flies following me throughout. There are stones marked with red stripes but in snow it would be impossible to follow this route. (On the other hand one would be free from flies.)

The path keeps climbing up the left side of the hill and 38 minutes from the lone marker pole reaches a large sign that looks as if it has escaped from a motorway verge; unfortunately it carries no useful information at all. From here you can follow marker poles for 25 minutes east and then just east of north to a major saddle between deep valleys to east and west. Now climb northwards for 11 minutes to an outcrop with a logan or rocking stone, to the left of the rocky summit that gives Piatra Alba (White Rock, 2,178m) its name. The path continues, marked with red crosses replacing red stripes, around the left side of Vf Ştefleşti (2,242m), and at last drops down a horrible stony stretch through mainly dead dwarf pine to reach the Şaua Ştefleşti after 47 minutes. Here the path crosses an unmade minor road with virtually no through traffic from Rîu Sadului and the Gîtul Berbecului cabana in the east to Tărtărau on the DN 67C in the west.

The path crosses the saddle into the Cindrel range and forks to the right to climb not too steeply northwards on to a cart track and to a disused hut after 26 minutes. Five minutes above this there is a new sign at a junction right to the Cînaia refuge, marked with red triangles; this path is well marked, going along the southeastern flanks of Vf Cindrel, quite wonderful with the evening sun on the pink rhododendron flowers and the many rocky outcrops. After 25 minutes it drops gently around the Caldarea Iujbea, a large but unremarkable cirque, and reaches the refuge at 1,775m after 50 minutes. This very friendly hut is a cabana in all but name, though without any food or drink available.

From here the route to Păltiniş runs along a cart track rising steadily to the northeast for half an hour to the Şerbănei saddle (1,861m) where it joins the red stripe route along the ridge from Vf Cindrel. It is possible to go straight ahead here on a path marked with red crosses north to Fîntînele (Fountains) cabana and the small village of Sibiel, well known for its collection of icons painted on glass. The route to Păltiniş follows the main cart track across moorland to the right, over Vf Rozdeşti (1,952m) after 27 minutes, and on to the northeast for 27 minutes again to reach the junction of a red cross path left: take this across the saddle and then to the right above a valley to the left, on the level between trees to the left and dwarf bushes to the right. After 27 minutes once again turn downhill to the left and into woods after five minutes. The path zigs down and then heads right; after 22 minutes cross a stream and turn up to the right off the *drum forestier* on to a path following the hillside around to the right for 11 minutes, to reach the unmade road from Vf Onceşti just a couple of hundred metres from the Păltiniş cabana, to the left at about 1,430m. The Vf Onceşti television tower, incidentally, was the scene of some fierce fighting at Christmas 1989.

I later returned in thick cloud to the Cînaia refuge and then via Vf Cindrel to Oaşa cabana. Climbing from the woods it is easy to turn right too soon; if you reach a spring marked *Heil Quelle* you've gone wrong. It took me two hours 40 minutes to get back to the refuge, and I then took the path up to the left behind the cabana, marked with red triangles, crossing a cart track and reaching the Cînaia saddle in 32 minutes. It would of course be possible to follow the ridge route directly from the Şaua Şerbănei to here, which would make it possible to hike from Păltiniş to Oaşa in one day. Blue triangle markings continue ahead to the Fîntînele cabana via Niculeşti forestry cabana, where there may be some accommodation for tourists. The route west follows the crest to the left, marked with red stripes, dipping slightly to the south-southwest and then zigzagging up to a ridge and reaching Vf Cindrel (2,244m) after 33 minutes. Here I rejoined the red cross route from Obîrşia Lotrului and Şaua Ştefleşti, as well as blue stripes to Fîntînele.

This is tussocky moorland with rock outcrops, rather like Dartmoor but less boggy and with cliffs to the right dropping into two cirques with tarns in them. The path is well marked to keep you well away from the cliffs in cloud and fog, for which I was very grateful. After 25 minutes, more or less level, I reached Vf Frumosu (Beautiful Peak, 2,168m) where the blue stripes branch north; it would, I think, be a rather unexciting walk taking the best part of a day. The red crosses continue west, still well marked, crossing a cart track after four minutes and then beginning to drop to the first dwarf pines after 34 minutes more. The path now follows a cart track for 45 minutes and then swings right/northwest to pass a stîna to the left and swing back to the left. After 15 minutes fork right and go west-southwest for four minutes to reach spruce woods and a *drum forestier*. After 20 minutes this reaches a meadow where the track is less clear — swing right a bit to go west-southwest up to a forked tree on Oaşa Mare (1,731m), from where marker poles take over until you re-enter the trees after 20 minutes in the clearing. After eight minutes go steeply down to the left/west-southwest, not south on the more important-seeming track, and fork left after 20 minutes again. Four minutes further on the path is lost where the trees have been felled — go northwest across the cleared area, and ten minutes later turn left when you reach the edge of another cleared area. This is a sign that you are close to civilisation; after another 11 minutes you drop down to the DN 67C just south of Oaşa cabana (1,280m), 62km south of Sebeş and 72km north of Novaci, although much of this section to the south is officially closed to public traffic.

The cabana has now been rebuilt on the east side of Lac Oaşa reservoir, 1.2km south of the dam; opposite it is a childrens' holiday colony. The red cross markings continue west to Şureanu cabana (see previous section) from a bend in the road between the dam and the colony. A bus leaves the colony at 1640, at least on summer Sundays, and calls at the cabana before heading north at 1715 to Sebeş, arriving two and a half hours later at the *autogară* and adjacent railway station. Southbound it leaves Sebeş at 0715. Sebeş was one of the original *Siebenbürgen*, under the name of Mühlbach, and still has a fine church, 'the most remarkable Gothic building in Transylvania' (1240-1382) and a museum in the former Voivodes' Palace (15th Century). Three kilometres from the town is the Rîpa Roşie (Red Precipice) natural monument, a 456m cliff with weird buttress formations of red clay and gritstone and rare fossils.

Practical information

The Lotru mountains, the least frequented and worst marked of these ranges, are not covered by any available map. The Parîng and Cindrel mountains are both covered by the *Invitation*, and there is also a *Hartă Turistică* of the Parîng published by Editura Sport-Turism, which is an excellent map, but wasn't available in Petroşani when I was there.

SIBIU

Sibiu, known as Hermannstadt to the Saxons and Nagy-Szeben to the Magyars, was the home of Dr Faustus and the traditional capital of the Siebenbürgen or Transylvanian Saxons, although it has been rather over-shadowed by Braşov (Kronstadt) since that town's post-war industrial development. Being sited at the north end of the main Olt valley route through the Carpathians, it was sacked by the Mongols in 1241, but then, fortified with three ring walls and forty towers, repelled attacks by the Turks in 1432, 1438 (when Sultan Amurad was killed by an arrow) and 1442. Now the defences are largely gone, but Mrs Gerard, who came here as wife of a Hungarian cavalry officer in 1883, describes Sibiu as a largely medieval city: 'The top-heavy overhanging gables, the deserted watch towers, the ancient ramparts, the crooked streets...all combine to give the impresssion of a past which has scarcely gone and of a present which has not yet penetrated.' Streams flowed down the centre of each street, and after summer thunderstorms 'for an hour or so Hermannstadt becomes Venice — minus the gondolas'.

Getting there

Sibiu is reached by two non-electrified railway lines from Bucureşti, the main one via Braşov and the other via Rîmnicu Vîlcea and the Olt valley; although most international trains take the electrified line via Sighişoara, one train a day to Budapest runs via Sibiu. To the west, Vinţu de Jos is the junction for Cluj; to the north there is a line towards Mediaş and Sighişoara, but if you wish to avoid the ecological hell-hole of Copşa Mică it is best to take a bus, from the main *autogară* next to the rail station. There is another *autogară* to the west on Str Lemnelor, for services towards Sebeş.

Where to stay and eat

The three main hotels, all I think rather out of the backpacker's price bracket, are the Împăratul Romanilor (Str N Bălcescu 4), the Bulevard (Piaţa Unirii 10) and the Continental (Calea Dumbrava 2). A new hotel is the Manitas at Str V Cîrlova 26 in the Ştrand quarter (tel 414 797).

In addition there are a campsite and *han* in the Pădurea Dumbrava (or Jungwald) oak wood to the southwest of town, on trolley bus route T1 and the bus route to Paltiniş, jumping-off point for the Cindrel mountains (see previous section). I cannot recommend the campsite, but the *han* does have a good restaurant and sells some maps at reception. Not far away at Str Rogojinei 13 is the Valea Aurie cabana, rather small with just 38 beds, but worth trying. There

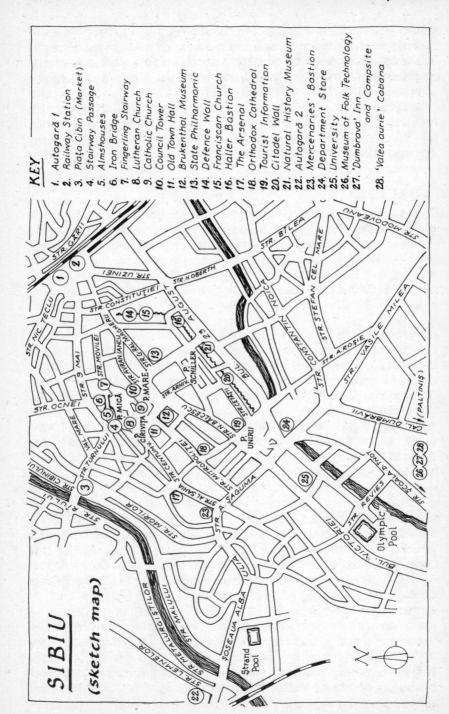

SIBIU
(sketch map)

KEY

1. Autogară 1
2. Railway Station
3. Piața Cibin (Market)
4. Stairway Passage
5. Almshouses
6. Iron Bridge
7. Fingerling Stairway
8. Lutheran Church
9. Catholic Church
10. Council Tower
11. Old Town Hall
12. Brukenthal Museum
13. State Philharmonic
14. Defence Wall
15. Franciscan Church
16. Haller Bastion
17. The Arsenal
18. Orthodox Cathedral
19. Tourist Information
20. Citadel Wall
21. Natural History Museum
22. Autogară 2
23. Mercenaries' Bastion
24. Department Store
25. University
26. Museum of Folk Technology
27. 'Dumbrava' Inn
    and Campsite
28. 'Valea aurie' Cabana

is also a campsite at the spa of Ocna Sibiului, 18km to the northwest by road or rail. Sibiu is now a university town, with student rooms available in the summer on Bdul Victoriei, and private rooms are available through EXO at Str Doljului 2, near the station (tel 821 960), or an agency on Str N Bălcescu.

The best feeding places are on the central squares and in the main hotels, as well as the Pizza Tîrgu Piscului in the lower town not far from the Stairway Passage, which serves a pretty good approximation to real pizza.

What to see

The centre of the old town lies around the interconnecting squares of Piaţa Mare, Piaţa Mică and Piaţa Griviţa, dominated by the Lutheran 'cathedral' (good strong Gothic from c1370-1520, with a beautiful font from 1438, open Tuesdays to Saturdays 0900-1300, with organ concerts on Wednesdays at 1800) and a Jesuit Catholic church from 1733 (with an 'undistinguished' Baroque interior), and rows of solid 16th- and 17th-Century houses with typically German dormer windows, like winking eyes in the roofs, and courtyards that are worth exploring. On Piaţa Mare are restaurants and cafés and the Brukenthal Palace (1788; according to Mrs Gerard 'a stately building... of which even the Grand Canal at Venice need not be ashamed') which still houses the superb art collection of Baron Samuel von Brukenthal, the first Saxon governor of Transylvania under Maria-Theresa, which has been open to the public since 1817.

Between Piaţa Mare and Piaţa Mică stands the Council Tower (1366, rebuilt in 1588), now closed to visitors. On Piaţa Mică is the arcaded Old Market Hall (15th Century), now used for art exhibitions, and Ethnographic and Pharmaceutical Museums. Piaţa Griviţa is reached across the Iron (or Liars') Bridge (Podul Minciunilor), built in 1859 across Str Ocnei, cut through the old fortifications; here are the great Evangelical (Lutheran) church, the Baroque buildings of the German school, and a 13th-Century tower. There are two stairways from the old town down to the lower town; first the Stairway Passage from Piaţa Griviţa down to Str Turnului, and the Fingerling Stairway, a vaulted passage, rebuilt in 1567, from Piaţa Mică to Piaţa Aurarilor (Goldsmiths' Square or Fingerlingsplatz), at the end of Str Movilei.

Str Mitropoliţiei, running southwest from Piaţa Griviţa, has the Primaria Vecche (Old Town Hall, 1470-1545, containing a museum of history and weapons), the Baroque Caryatids Palace at no 13, and the Orthodox cathedral, in the familiar neo-Byzantine style with overtones of railway station, but unusually built in 1906 before the unification of Transylvania with Romania.

The area around Piaţa Schiller, south of Piaţa Mare along Str Arhivelor, is very quiet and attractive, leading down to Str Cetaţii (Citadel Street) with a stretch of 14th-Century wall and three towers, and the Natural History Museum at no 1.

Elsewhere in the lower town, north of the centre, are other remains of fortifications, and out in the Dumbrava Forest the Museum of Popular Technology, perhaps the best of Romania's open air museums, near the country's oldest zoo, founded in 1929.

Practical Information

There have been some changes to street names since the revolution: Piaţa Republicii is again Piaţa Mare, Piaţa 6 Martie is Piaţa Mică, Str Karl Marx is Str Ocnei, Str 1 Mai is Str Mitropolitiei, Str Gh Gheorghiu-Dej is Str Vasile Milea, and Str Lenin is Str Andrei Şaguma.

Str N Bălcescu is the main business area of Sibiu, with the ticket offices of CFR at no 6, TAROM at no 10 and the tourist office (now Prima Ardeleana) at no 53, on the corner of Piaţa Unirii (tel 924 12140). A good private garage specialising in foreign cars is on Str Cîmpului (tel 430 833) beyond the market on Piaţa Cibin.

Excursions

Sibiu is surrounded by Saxon villages, many of which are well worth visiting; immediately to the south, and linked to Sibiu by no less than 34 buses a day, is Cisnădie (Heltau) with a fortified church built in the 13th to 15th Centuries with a four-turreted bell tower rebuilt in 1590, and a textile museum. About three kilometres west is the smaller village of Cisnădioara (Michelsberg), with perhaps the oldest Romanesque church in Romania, dating from 1223, on top of a high rock overlooking the village. Twelve kilometres further west, on the DN 106A from Sibiu to Păltiniş, is the Romanian village of Răşinari, where there is an ethnographic museum in a 14th-Century building, including some of the icons painted on glass that are a local speciality.

On the DN 1/7 and the railway line west of Sibiu lie Cristian (Grossau), with a village museum and a village citadel or fortified church from the 13th to 16th Centuries, and Sălişte, the centre of the area known as the Mărginimea Sibiului, with a *han*, camp site, ethnographic museum and a 'national camp of wood sculpture'. Just south of Sălişte is Sibiel, with the best collection of icons on glass in the country, and the remains of a Dacian fortress; it is now possible to stay in 'two star private homes' here, and there are regular visits by coach parties from Sibiu.

A narrow gauge railway runs from Sibiu northeast to Agnita (Agnetheln) through Saxon villages with fortified churches such as Hosman (Holzmengen) and Nocrich (Leschkirch); Marpod (Marpod), southeast of Nocrich, has a good church (1300-1423) with a *Speckturm* and *Fanen* or banners, normally only unrolled for festivals. A branch line runs to Vurpăr (Burgberg), with a Romanesque church (about 1200), from where one could walk west over the hills for about 14km to Slimnic (Stolzenburg), on the DN 14 north of Sibiu, where there are the spectacular remains of a very large 14th Century church.

Finally it is worth mentioning the lovely ruins of the Cistercian abbey of Cîrţa (Kerz), on the Olt between Sibiu and Făgăraş, conveniently situated at the north end of the Trans-Făgăraş Highway.

THE SAXON VILLAGES

The heartland of the Transylvanian Saxons is the triangle between Braşov, Sighişoara and Sibiu known as the 'Alteland', meaning not the old land but the land of the Olt river; here every valley has a row of smaller valleys off it, and each of these has still smaller valleys opening off it; and each valley has a small settlement guarding its entrance. Each Saxon settlement is a world in itself, with its own church, school and shop, and in fact each home is self-contained with its own baking oven, kitchen garden, wine making equipment and so on. If you have any interest in seeing this culture, now vanishing after 850 years, you can combine this with easy pleasant walking between these villages through the lush, fertile scenery of the Transylvanian plateau. The greatest attraction of the countryside here is not that it is in any way exotic, but that it is exactly how western Europe was until modern agricultural techniques changed it for ever; so the meadows are full of wonderful flowers and butterflies, foxes and deer cross your path, and there are jays, buzzards and other birds in far greater numbers than in the west.

However the greatest attraction for me is the chance to visit the many different fortified churches, also known as 'peasant citadels' or 'village citadels' in the language of communist era tourist leaflets, or as *Kirchebürgen* in German (as opposed to *Bürgkirchen* which are castle chapels), and to talk to the remaining Saxons about their life there. Although the churches began to be built from the mid-12th Century, in Romanesque and then in Gothic styles, they were not fortified until the second quarter of the 15th Century when the Turks took over from the Tartars as the main threat; those in the east were surrounded with solid walls and towers, while those in the west are simple fortified buildings. There was always a tower for the storage

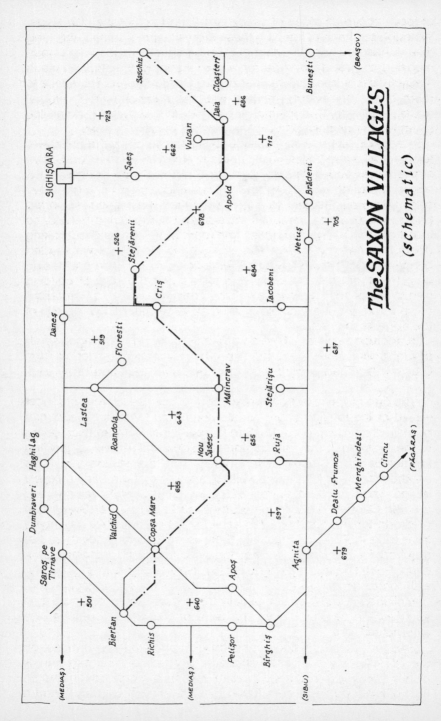

The SAXON VILLAGES
(schematic)

of food, above all sides of *speck* or bacon fat, in case of a siege. Although the habit of keeping these stores lasted a remarkably long time, it has now virtually died out, but in some villages it has been modified to provide a store for a year's supply of *speck* for each family. A pig is killed every year before Christmas and the *speck* is hung in the *speckturm*, marked with the number of the owners' house, and every Sunday morning the tower is unlocked and a slice taken for the next week. Surplus *speck* is made into soap.

In addition it is usually possible for visitors to climb the bell tower to see clocks and bells, mostly made in Germany, and to look down at the lovely and distinctive roofscape of the Saxon houses; each house is end-on to the street, with two windows and a large heavy cart gate opening on to the street, and has been extended backwards over the centuries towards the outbuildings behind, so that they form a long thin house one room wide, often without linking doors between the rooms. The courtyard is almost always shaded by vines, and there is always a wine-cellar below. The end facing onto the street bears the owner's initials and the date of building with symbols such as flowers or fruit in paint or plaster; a Romanian-owned house will always carry a cross either painted or on top of the ridge of the roof.

In addition to my real hike from Biertan through the villages south of Sighişoara, I also describe two other minor circuits not far from Braşov which can easily be covered by public transport or by bike.

1. The first of these is from Braşov to the best preserved and most visited of the fortified churches at Hărman and Prejmer, which can be visited *en route* to the Eastern Carpathians. Hărman (Honigberg to the Germans), the rail junction to Întorsura Buzăului, is just ten kilometres from Braşov; unfortunately from the station you have another couple of kilometres walk to the centre of this fairly unlovely village. The church dates from 1293, with 15th-Century vaulting and an 18th-Century organ donated by King Ludwig XII of Sweden in gratitude for the first Lutheran service he heard on his way home from exile in Turkey. Unusually there is no gallery other than that required for the organ. In the ring wall, above an ice-cellar, is a chapel with fine frescoes showing late medieval costumes. The ring wall contains food stores for all the families of the village (some were demolished in 1803) and unusually there were stores for single men such as the teacher above the aisle of the church, reached by external ladders.

Prejmer (Tartlau) is another seven kilometres further northeast on the DN 10; this is a more attractive village than Hărman and is clearly better organised for tourism, having the only Saxon church with official opening hours (0900 to 1700, except Sundays) and a porter's lodge. The church dates from the 13th Century with a complex of walls and courtyards begun in 1421 (the year after the first Turkish invasion) and 17th-Century storehouses, with a locally painted altarpiece and an octagonal tower both from 1460-1. Again the only gallery is for the organ, so the men sit to the right of the nave and the women to the left, with children in the north transept and old women in the south transept. However the most memorable sight here is the inside of the ring walls, with 272 storage rooms reached by parallel staircases and galleries. From the top of the stairs over the entrance to the inner precinct you can reach the defence passage with an early version of a Gatling gun, five barrels on one plank which can be loaded and fired in turn.

From here you can continue north or east, or return to Braşov via Sîn Petru (Petersberg), a small Saxon village just six kilometres north of the city which has a 14th-15th Century fortified church and a remarkably lively community with quite a few young people and a Saxon Folk Dance troupe which has toured to Germany and actually returned.

2. From Braşov I also took a train north on the Sighişoara line through Feldioara, Măieruş and Apaţa, all of which also have fortified churches, to Staţia Rupea, where trains are met by a bus to Rupea via the outskirts of Homorod. You could also take a bus from Braşov to Rupea along the DN 132 over the Bogata pass in the Perşani hills, where there is a cabana at 980m. The Homorod (Hamruden) church key can be found at no 29, in the square by the church; it was built about 1270, with 15th-Century walls and a massive 16th-Century tower, with later additions. Internally this has the standard layout for this area, with the organ set above the altar and a gallery for the men of the congregation; the women sit in the body of the church in strict order of seniority behind Frau Pfarrer, the Pastor's wife, with the children in front for her to keep an eye on, and those preparing for confirmation usually in the chancel. On the choir walls there are three layers of paintings, all pre-Reformation. Externally the church seems to be almost touching the wooden galleries of the ring walls crowded around it. Six kilometres further north is Caţa (Katzendorf), reached by walking on through Homorod and turning left after the level crossing; the church key was at no 279, opposite the church, but the occupants may well have emigrated. The church here is simpler, more like a Methodist chapel, but the wooden galleries on the towers and ring walls are elaborate if tatty. There is also a station to the left at the north end of the village; seven kilometres to the right is Drăuşeni (Draas) where there is a 13th Century fortified church with painted furniture and murals.

Rupea (Reps) is a much larger town, with shops, restaurants, a hotel, an *autogară* and an ethnographic museum, as well as mineral springs. Instead of a fortified church there is here a proper 13th-Century fort on top of a basalt hill, left and left again from the museum on the main square. You may be able to find a key at the last house but if not it's possible to slide the bar back to open the gate. From here it is seven kilometres to Dacia (Stein) where there is an onion-domed church behind low walls which I didn't visit, although I know the curate's house (for the key) is the green house on the left over the crossroads. From Dacia it is seven kilometres to everywhere, including Viscri (aptly called Deutsch Weisskirch or German White Church), reached up a dirt road by a bus leaving Rupea at 1615. It is well worth making the effort to get here, as this is a truly spectacular complex set on its hilltop, with an attractive village around it.

The church has two Romanesque capitals, although the present buildings are Gothic; the church tower was built in 1494 and the walls from 1500, with three towers in 1630, 1649 and 1715. There is a pilot project being set up by the European Council to attempt to maintain both the social and the physical fabric of the village and to find alternative uses for the empty houses (the population is a fraction of what it was in 1989). The key is available from no 141, and if you write in advance you may be able to rent the cottage at the church gates.

From here it is another 7km north on a dirt road (no buses) to rejoin the main DN 13 from Braşov and Rupea to Sighişoara at Buneşti (Bodendorf) where there is a lovely fortified church, later than most, with a double gallery and a *speckturm* still in use. Another 3.5km north is the small village of Criţ (Deutsch-Kreuz, not to be confused with Criş), with a side road to Meşendorf (Meschendorf), six kilometres west, of which I have heard many good things.

Between here and Sighişoara the main village is Saschiz (Keisd) which had a population of 1,300 Saxons and now has 250. Traditionally the village was noted for its blue and white ceramics. It has a castle on the hill to the west and one very strong tower with obvious earthquake damage by the church. The key can be obtained from the *Kirchenvater* at no 301, down the lane by the church.

The road to Sighişoara runs through Albeşti (Weisskirch bei Schässburg), the site of a battle in 1849 during the crushing of the bourgeois revolutions of 1848 where Hungary's great Romantic poet, Petöfi, was killed. As his body was never found, this gave rise to myths of his Arthur-like return to save the nation. There is a monument by a spring, and a small museum, as well as the late-Romantic Heller-Boiu palace one kilometre away.

Sighişoara (Schässburg) is undoubtedly (especially since the attack on Dubrovnik) one of the greatest medieval cityscapes in the world, with a skyline as evocative of Camelot as you could wish for. Georgina Harding compares it with a Dürer engraving, and Claudio Magris with Prague, speaking of 'the mystery of its stones and the gateways opening on to some other and secret space, on to an unexpected side of things. The slender, pointed iron banners which surmount the towers are silhouetted clearly against the sky, intrepid in the wind, fearless knights in the arena, waiting for the tourney and an unknown destiny'. Although a beautiful town, it is not as useful a base as Braşov or Sibiu. It was initially a Dacian and a Roman settlement before the Saxons arrived there in 1191, fortifying it in the 13th and 14th Centuries; it's hardly changed since then, but incredibly the architect of the Bucureşti Centru Civic still has plans to demolish large areas of the lower town, including a church and a leper hospital, for redevelopment. The area across the river from the Orthodox Cathedral was cleared before the 1989 revolution.

The hilltop citadel is a walled town rather than a fortress, with buildings from the 14th Century on, including the clock tower guarding the main gate, the house where Vlad Ţepeş (Vlad the Impaler or 'Dracula') was born in 1431, the 14th-Century *Bergkirche* (Church on the Hill) at the top of a wooden staircase, and a 13th-Century Dominican church. More practical things such as the post, CFR and tourist offices and the Steaua Hotel are on Str Gh Gheorghiu-Dej (probably renamed) in the Lower Town, and north across the Tîrnava Mare river are the Orthodox cathedral and behind that a preserved narrow-gauge steam locomotive that operated the tram line to Agnita until it closed in 1965 (the Agnita-Sibiu section still operates with diesel power), and beyond that the bus and rail stations, both of which have singularly little information on display — allow time to plan your onward travel here. Accommodation is either at the Steaua Hotel, at a campsite on the hill behind the station, or at the Hula Daneş campsite four kilometres west at km 88 on the DN 14 to Mediaş (Mediasch), an ideal jumping-off point for the main hike through the Saxon villages to the south.

3. Biertan (Birthälm) lies nine kilometres south of Şaroş pe Tîrnava (Scharosch bei Mediasch), on the DN 14 near Dumbrăveni (Elizabethstadt), and can be reached by bus from Sighişoara; its church was for many years a bishop's seat and it has now had a lot of money spent on its restoration. It is a big church built as late as 1516, with aisles, and two ring walls from 1558, with a covered staircase through them. In the bases of the towers are some of the bishops' tombstones and some defaced paintings; on the First World War memorial and elsewhere is the thumb and two fingers

symbol of the village. In this area the organ is set in the gallery at the west end of the church.

Hiking directions

Leaving here on foot, your first stop is the neighbouring village of Copşa Mare (Grosskopisch, *not* to be confused with the far larger Copşa Mică (Kleinkopisch), the most polluted town in Romania whose carbon-black works should be closed down at some point soon); the path starts to the right of house no 87 to the east end of the village. Go through the gate and up the hill, looking back to enjoy the view of the church and village set in the valley with the *weinbergen* or vine terraces stepped up the hills behind. It takes just ten minutes to go up to the wooded ridge and five to go down to the unmade road in the next valley; turn right onto this (in the other direction you should look for a very small path about 100m north of a bend ten minutes from a very minor pass). Following the road on from this pass it takes about 15 minutes (via an obvious short cut down into the village itself) to reach Copşa Mare, where the church is better out than in; the key was at no 124 but I am sure they will have left by now.

The path on to Nou Săsesc (Neudorf bei Schässburg) turns left at no 159 at the south end of the village, up a farm track churned up by cattle, and when this ends after 17 minutes turns left up a side valley to the ridge and down the other side to a road in at most 20 minutes. This climbs to the right/east to another minor pass and swings south into a new valley system. Where a track drops down to the left after 200m I kept going to the southeast to arrive after two and a half hours to the south of Nou Săsesc; it would be quicker to go left and continue eastwards as far as the Laslea (Lasseln) valley to reach the north end of the village.

However I will describe my route for those who would rather be safe than sorry; it traversed along the hillside to the southeast, on a very faint path across a field, overgrown along the edge of a wood, before running into a beech ride after almost 30 minutes. After eight minutes this forks right along the ridge and after another eight minutes passes a methane wellhead by a junction from the right. Another track comes in from the left, then another from the right by a house and wellhead, and another from the left as what is now a decent-sized lane emerges into meadows (as all these paths are unmarked details of junctions are essential for anyone to find their way in the other direction). This gravel lane runs along the plateau for just over an hour, curving around to the left around the head of the Lapşea valley before beginning to drop to the northeast, with a road coming in from the left. After more than half an hour the road finally arrives at the south end of the village by no 119A.

There were 800 Saxons here in 1989, and by the end of 1991 this was down to 200, of whom almost half go to church on Sunday morning. (All Saxon villages have very detailed parish records, which are invaluable for proving the right to German citizenship.) There are also plenty of Romanian and Țigane families here, and the village is big enough to have a bus to Sighişoara at 0600 on weekdays. The church is small and simple, with a separate bell tower but no fortifications.

From here you need once again to cross the ridge to the next valley and the village of Mălîncrav (Malmkrog); take the road up to the east below the church, crossing the ridge after 30 minutes by multiple cart tracks, then making your own way to the left of power lines to find the bridge across the stream and climb to another ridge after another 25 minutes. Here you find the tiny village ahead nestling in trees in a narrow valley; the road swings to the north but there is a path directly down through an orchard to go down the right side of the church, just over an hour from Nou Săsesc. This church was built in the late 14th Century and surrounded by low walls in the 15th Century; it is noted for its lovely paintings from the end of the 14th Century and the second half of the 15th Century. The tower is excellent both inside and out, with bell ropes passing through the hubs of old cartwheels.

The next stop is Criş (Kreisch); the route goes left from Mălîncrav church, then right across a bridge and left by another bridge at the end of the village, to climb up to a sandstone cutting and then on very slippery clay in a beech wood to reach a ridge after 23 minutes. It goes down across meadow and a forestry road, and up to the north-northeast by a sunken road in a beech wood, reaching another ridge after 24 more minutes. Again it goes down across meadow to the right, with a track coming in from the left just before a bridge over the Felţa stream; after eight minutes it goes east into woods (with two tracks coming in from the right) and curves left/north at the ridge before forking right. The main track keeps left as a couple of duplicate tracks go to the right and emerges into meadow after 23 minutes; after five minutes you can swing left through fields to the village, or go straight ahead to the road and then left. What is interesting here is not a Saxon church but a Hungarian castle, built by the ruling Bethlen family in 1559-89 and the 1670s, in a late Renaissance style. Apparently this survived intact until the Second World War, but then fell into ruin, and the arboretum was cut down for firewood; it would be quite feasible to camp in the courtyard if that took your fancy; in any case there are plenty of Latin plaques to study.

From here you can go on to Stejăreni (Peschendorf) by road; go about one kilometre north up the road to Daneş (Dunesdorf) and turn right/east at the crest of a small hill on to an unmade road which goes over a ridge after about half an hour and down to the village. Forking left at the ridge I came down to a shop near no 200, and then right across a bridge to the church; this was built in 1913 and is not very attractive. From here you can go directly east to Şaeş (Schaas), which also has a fairly uninteresting church from 1820 (although it does have pre-Reformation altar paintings which show the Virgin Mary, unusually for a Lutheran church, and three apostles like the three monkeys seeing, hearing and speaking nothing while Christ prays on the Mount of Olives).

However I followed the ridge (up to 678m altitude, the highest on this route) further to the southeast to Apold (Trappold); the path starts at a drinking trough at the south end of the village, going left up a farm track and then across a field to the top. It goes left up a track to the east and along a ridge on a sheep track in lovely beech wood with occasional marker stones. After almost two hours this emerges into fields and takes a vague cart track to the left/east down the valley to Apold. This is very badly churned up by cows, but you can go through the fields alongside; after 40 minutes turn left at a T-junction and into the village. The church is quite small and simple, but it has an excellent tower which also gives access to the inside of the roof; although the timbers are not original it still has all the atmosphere of a medieval tithe barn. There is also a *Speckkammer* with 30 sides of pig fat hanging, although I was told there were only ten families out of 200 left. In 1938 the ring wall was used to build a *Kulturhaus* or community hall.

Here you are on the bus route from Sighişoara to Agnita; Şaeş is six kilometres to the north, while the villages along the road south to Agnita are all rather ugly and dusty, although the churches have good strong central towers. Agnita (Agnetheln) is also a dusty unattractive town with one hotel; the church (late 15th Century) has aisles and pews like an English church, and a gallery in Strawberry Hill Gothic style. It also has good strong fortified towers, incorporated into the adjacent school (education has always been fundamental to the Saxons and there is a school within almost every church precinct). The key is at the *Pfarrhaus*, no 14, above the church. On the road to Voila and Făgăraş (Fogarasch) are the villages of Dealu Frumos (Schönberg), Merghindeal (Mergeln), Cincu (GrossSchenk) and Cincşor (KleinSchenk) which are all very attractive with strong impressive fortified churches.

From Apold it is possible to walk on to the east to the Braşov to Sighişoara road; this starts with eight kilometres of road to Daia, passing a turning north to Vulcan (Wolkendorf), which was always a poor village of serfs and has now been totally depopulated of

Saxons and has gone badly downhill with a largely Ţigane population. Here too however there are ambitious plans for renewal. The church dates from 1182 and was fortified in 1521.

Daia (Denndorf) had 42 Saxons left in 1991 out of 700; the church dates from 1457 but seems mainly 18th Century, with some nice naïve paintings of fortified churches. Here too the *Speckkammer* was still in use, and the church key could be found at no 72. From here I went over the hill to Saschiz, up a muddy road by the church to reach the ridge after 35 minutes. Turn right at a T-junction, near a state farm and a lake, and follow the farm road for a couple of hours down the Flosa valley to Saschiz (see above). Equally it is possible to follow the Şaeş valley southeast from Daia and then turn left over Dealul Cloaşterf (686m) to reach Cloaşterf ((Klosdorf) two kilometres from the DN 13, five kilometres south of Saschiz. The Saxons have almost all left so that although the church is in good condition, the fortifications and churchyard are now fairly decrepit. There is some very good woodwork in the church, which sits in a dominant position on a hillock. The key should still be at no 99, at the eastern end of the village.

Practical information

There are Braşov, Sibiu and Mureş Judeţ (county) maps available which while not completely accurate are better than anything published in Bucureşti; naturally, they only give the Romanian place-names (see also the previous section on Sibiu and the surrounding villages).

A wooden church, Ieud, Maramureş

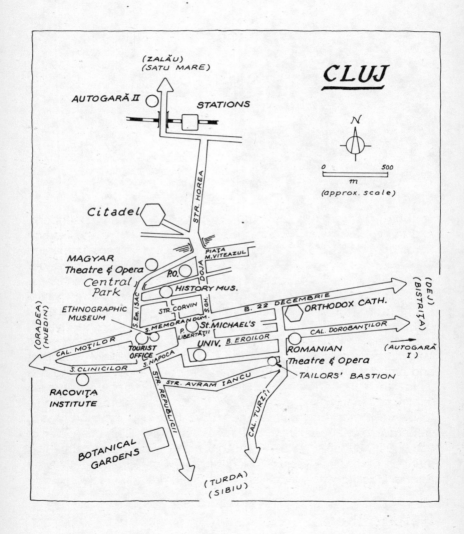

Chapter 8

The West

CLUJ

To the Hungarians it is Kolozsvár, to the Germans it is Klausenberg, and to Romanians it is generally just Cluj — on maps the Roman name of Napoca is suffixed to remind everyone of Daco-Romanian continuity, but if you call the place Cluj-Napoca you will only pander to the worst Romanian chauvinists and annoy the Hungarians. Certainly it is the leading Magyar city of Romania, the winter capital of the Transylvanian aristocracy in the days of Mrs Gerard and even of Patrick Leigh-Fermor, and traces of the elegance and style of those days can still be seen; about 25-30% of the population is still Magyar, but the mayor is Gheorghe Funar, of the rabidly chauvinist and anti-Magyar PUNR or Romanian National Unity Party, who has for instance banned Hungarian-language signs. It is now also the aid capital of Transylvania, where every second car sometimes seems to be from the West, and home to the country's best orchestra. Generally the appearance is that of any tatty Romanian city of 300,000 inhabitants, but every so often you come upon something that can perhaps be described as Brighton Pavilion meets Charles Rennie Mackintosh, a local version of Jugendstil.

Getting there

Cluj is on one of the two main rail routes from Bucureşti to Budapest, that via Oradea, with regular through trains; it also lies on the main cross-country route from Timişoara to Suceava. In addition to the main long-distance station (*Lung Parcors*), there is also a local station (*Scurt Parcurs*) to the east, with its own booking hall. From the station you can take a trolley-bus into the city centre, or walk down Stradă Horea in about 15 minutes. There are two *autogarăs*, no 2 just across the tracks northwest of the railway station, which serves the area to the north and northwest of the city (a little-known but attractive area of hills with tiny villages and wooden churches) as well as Abrud to the southwest of Cluj, and three buses a week to Budapest, and no 1, 1.5km east of the centre, serving everywhere else.

Where to stay and eat

Cluj has some classy Belle Epoque hotels in the centre, such as the Continental and the Central, others slightly further out and slightly cheaper, such as the Delta (at *autogară* 2), the Pax (opposite the railway station), the Transilvania (in the ruins of the 15th Century citadel), the Sport, Napoca, Siesta, Astoria, and the Vladeasa. The Hotel Victoria on Bdul 22 Decembrie, just west of the Orthodox cathedral, was formerly reserved for party officials but is now open as possibly the best hotel in town.

There are also a surprising number of cabanas in the immediate vicinity of the city, the Făget and Făget-Pădure cabanas, about 15 minutes walk from the Făget campsite at km 473 on the main DN 1 road south to Feleacu and Turda (bus 10, 10A or 46), the Cheile Baciului at Baciu on the DN 1F and the railway to the west of the city, and the Colina Han and campsite and the Făget-Izvor cabana off the DN 1 to the southwest. It would be well worth enquiring at the Tourist Office before deciding which one to head for.

The main restaurants are on Pţa Libertăţii and in the main hotels; being a student town there are also cafés and lacto-vegetarian restaurants on Str Napoca and Str Universitaţii.

What to see

The centre of the city is Piaţa Libertăţii, with the great Catholic hall church of St Michael in the centre, dating from the 14th-16th Centuries. Around the square are the main hotels, the University Bookshop, the CFR booking office and the Art Museum in the Bánffy Palace at no 30. At Str Memorandumului 21, on the main east-west street, is the Ethnographic Museum, and just off Str Memorandumului at Str Gh Doja 2 is yet another Pharmaceutical Museum in a building dating from 1573. To the south of the centre are the puppet theatre and University (born of a shotgun marriage in 1959 between the Romanian Babeş and Magyar Bólyai universities, which of course resulted in the Magyar elements being lost), with a mineralogical museum left and left again inside the main entrance, and the well-known Botanical Gardens beyond; to the east are the Tailors' Bastion (*Bastionul Croitorilor*, the remains of a 15th-Century city gate, where a park and Unitarian church are planned), the Romanian language theatre and opera house and the Romanian Orthodox cathedral, built in 1923 when similar cathedrals were being built in every city of the newly Romanian Transylvania, but in an even more massively Byzantine style than usual.

Just north of the centre, but south of the citadel and the river, is a pleasant area of old backstreets including the birthplace of Matthias Corvinus, the great Renaissance king of Hungary, the Museum of Transylvanian History (on Piaţa Muzeului) and the Magyar language theatre and opera house. To the west are the Racoviţa Institute of Speleology (see page 99) and the Zoological Museum, and at Str Moţilor 84 the 'Cock Church', a rather wonderful Hungarian Calvinist church built in 1913 by Kós Károly, and to the northwest the excellent open-air section of the Ethnographic Museum, housing examples of vernacular buildings and wooden churches.

Practical Information

Here too there have been some changes to street names since the revolution: Str 30 Decembrie is now Str Memoramdumului, Bdul Lenin is Bdul 22 Decembrie, Str 6 Martie is Str Iuliu Maniu, Str Petru Groza is Bdul Eroilor, and Str 1 Mai is Str Emil Isac.

The Tourist Office (now Turism Feleacul SA) is on Calea Moţilor (technically Str Gh Şincai 2, tel 951-17778), and the CFR office for rail tickets is on Piaţa Libertaţii, across Str Napoca from the Hotel Continental. The Post Office and main department store are almost opposite each other on Str Gh Doja, with just to the east the main market on Piaţa Mihai Viteazul and a cycle shop on Str Voiteşti.

APUSENI

The Apuseni massif is one of the terms used to describe the whole rather confused area of hills closing off the western end of the Transylvanian plateau; although not especially difficult or wild scenically, the inhabitants are wild enough. This area, with Maramureş never conquered by the Romans, was the heartland of revolutionaries such as Horea in 1784 and Avram Iancu in 1848, and the present inhabitants, the *Moţi*, seem to have moved from the valleys in the 18th Century, to escape the creeping colonisation of Maria-Theresa. They may be descended from the Celts (who originally crossed Europe from Asia), and seeing their affinity with

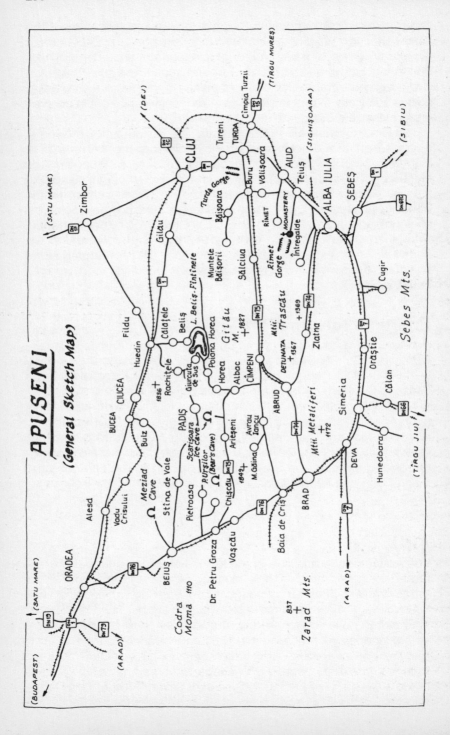

APUSENI
(General Sketch Map)

cats (or vice versa) I can accept this. Until relatively recently they still trapped particles of gold with sheep fleeces nailed to boards and laid in the streams of the Arieş basin in the spring thaw. This technique gave rise to the legend of the Golden Fleece from Colchis, now western Georgia, across the Black Sea. Nowadays they are noted for their woodworking, and particularly for the large barrels that they load onto their distinctive hooped carts and then take all around the country until they have sold them all. They live in scattered villages (called *crînguri* or groves) of simple huts, traditionally all thatched, at altitudes of up to about 1,300m, higher than any fixed settlements in Romania other than Fundata (see page 221). They also have some highly characteristic festivals (see page 112).

However for the tourist the main attraction of the Apuseni is the karst scenery of the central Padiş plateau and nearby areas. It is a pot-holer's paradise, and offers the walker an opportunity for generally undemanding hiking, through green and pleasant scenery, with the opportunity to dive into weird and majestic caves and tunnels — it's best to have a torch (flashlight). Streams appear and vanish again, and it's hard to keep track of them all. This area is to be created a National Park, although there are conflicts with mining and logging interests.

In addition to the karst limestone of the Padiş plateau, the Codru Moma (or Moneasa) and Trascău ranges, and gorges such as Rimeţ and Turda, there are also the volcanic peaks of Vf Vlădeasa to the north and the Munţii Metaliferi (Metal-bearing Mountains) and the twin basalt pillars of Detunata to the south. The Muntele Mare (or Gilău) mountains and, to the south of the Mureş river, the Poiana Rusca mountains are typical of the older crystalline schists, with radial valleys.

This section deals with the central Padiş and Scarişoara area: see also the following sections on the Turda and Rimeţ gorges, and page 99 on caving.

Getting there

This is a route from the main Cluj to Oradea road and railway along the Crişul Repede valley to the north, to the DN 75 from Turda to the town of Dr Petru Groza (due for renaming, being named after a communist) and the narrow-gauge line from Turda to Abrud along the Arieş valley to the south. Access is also possible from the west, by bus from Beiuş to the ski resort of Stîna de Vale (The Sheep Fold in the Valley, 1,102m) (or to the Meziad cave and then by a path marked with blue triangles to Stîna de Vale, taking six to eight hours), or from Beiuş to Pietroasa and on by *drum forestier* to the

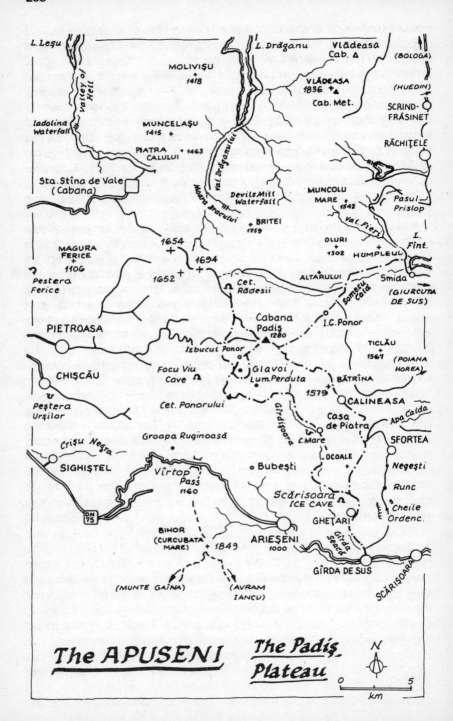

The **APUSENI**   *The Padiş*
                    Plateau

Focu Viu cave or Padiş, which would be an ideal cycling route.

From the north there are two parallel roads, one from Bucea and Bulz down the Valea Iadului or Valley of Hell, so called because of its weird karst scenery, to Lac Leşu and Stîna de Vale, and the other to the east from Poieni down the Valea Drăganului (Dragon's valley) to Lac Drăganu from where you can walk to Stîna de Vale. However the Stîna de Vale to Padiş road is now so bad that it is used for motocross racing, and the best approach by bus to Padiş from the north is by the 1630 (**not** Wednesdays or Thursdays) from Huedin to Giurcuţa de Sus at the west end of the artificial Lac Beliş-Fîntînele, or failing this a bus to Răchiţele and on by foot or forestry truck.

Huedin is a prosperous Hungarian town, also known as Banffyhunyad, with its bus station five minutes walk west of the rail station. The centre, five minutes south, has a modern hotel and 'one of the most remarkable Hungarian churches of the area', 15th Century with a fine painted ceiling (key from the parish office opposite, closed by 1700). In the small villages to the north, for example Fildu de Sus, are wooden churches, 'among the most perfect realisations of Romanian wooden architecture', with squatter spires than those in Maramureş. The road south to Răchiţele, mostly asphalted, is quite lovely, through small Romanian villages. From Răchiţele the road continues south as a *drum forestier* over the Prislop pass (most Romanian passes are called Prislop) through beautiful mature forests to the west end of the lake.

From here, if not before, you will almost certainly have to walk west up the Someş Cald valley; after about four kilometres you pass the turning right to Radeş, after another two kilometres the turning left to Poiana Horea and then after another kilometre the forestry complex of IC Ponor, known usually as Icponor. From here it takes an hour and a quarter, past two turnings to the left, to a stîna at the head of the valley. From here, if going to Padiş cabana, you can go straight up a short cut by, and in, the stream bed, taking 12 minutes to the watershed; if going south to Scărişoara, you should take the road to the left/south and turn off on the bend right (see below). From the watershed it takes just ten more minutes, dropping slightly on to the plateau, to reach the cabana. This is a friendly but rather messy compound by the road, with camping cabins further away in very attractive meadows. The Apuseni area is perfect camping country, as long as your stream doesn't suddenly vanish into a hole in the ground. There has been a water shortage in some of the higher villages for some time, of which you should be aware.

Hiking directions

From here I describe the basic hike south to the famous Scărişoara

ice cave and the Arieş valley at Gîrda de Sus, and also a return loop
from Scărişoara up the Gîrdişoara or Gîrda Seacă valley to the west
to the Ponor and Radeş 'citadels' (underground karst complexes)
and back to Padiş cabana, as well as the direct route from Ponor to
Padiş. In such an area, without a dominant ridge, it is possible to
make up almost any itinerary that takes your fancy.

1. From the cabana it takes ten minutes back to the watershed and
nine more to the bend where you go straight on past a stîna to the
right; after three minutes the blue triangle route to the Gîrdişoara
valley goes over the hill to the right and you should continue ahead
following blue stripe markings. These go straight up to the ridge
ahead, just left of the saddle, in about 17 minutes, and swing left
around the head of the next valley before going left/southeast from
the ridge along the right side of another valley. After six minutes turn
right at an unmarked T-junction on to a messy *drum forestier* which
emerges out of firs and spruce into a meadow after five minutes. Go
left uphill and along the right side of the next valley before turning
right/south over a rocky ridge at its end and dropping into a grassy
basin that was full of loose horses the first time I was here. Again go
slightly left uphill to another rocky ridge (about 33 minutes from
entering the meadow) then right to pass through conifers, to the left
of a hut and then half right at a stîna, to drop to the southeast to a
very ramshackle collection of Moţi huts in a valley, ten minutes from
the ridge. From here the path, unmarked, goes straight up the other
side to a marked tree on the skyline, past scattered cows each with
a woman in attendance. This hilltop is the site of the Călineasa *Tîrgu
de Dat* or Festival of Trading, both gifts and blows (see page 112).
　　From here the path heads for a marker pole just left of a survey
tripod (or tetrapod) on the ridge and left around a karstitic valley to
the right, with views to the right/west into the Bihor plains, and the
television tower on Vf Bihor (or Curcubata Mare, 1,848m) to the
southwest. The track gets stonier and after about 25 minutes
crosses to the left side of the hill and goes down into conifers; 13
minutes further on it crosses a small meadow and continues beside
a muddy *drum forestier*, up through spruce to very attractive
meadows, with a wonderful display of wild flowers in mid-July. A
minor *drum forestier* turns off to the left/east and the track on
becomes a drier fenced-off road, and in seven minutes reaches the
road from Gîrda de Sus. From here it takes almost an hour, walking
to the right/south through the scattered Moţi settlement of Ocoale,
to reach the village of Gheţari. The cabana, ten minutes south of the
village, has been closed and demolished for some time, but there is
a new private campsite at the south end of Ocoale. How long it will
survive so far from a decent road is anyone's guess.

The 'ice-cave' (Peştera Gheţarul, one of about ten in Europe) of Scărişoara is in fact just west of Gheţari, along the obvious track from the centre — when it was discovered and named, the nearest village was Scărişoara, below Gîrda de Sus in the Arieş valley. Since then the Moţi people have moved from the valley to settle the hills. The cave is first recorded at the end of the 18th Century, when it was fitted with wooden steps; Racoviţa explored it in 1923, and it is now a tourist attraction of sorts, although as no one is paying the caretaker its future is uncertain. The entrance is by the stairs in the doline or sinkhole; as you go down the atmosphere gets noticeably more humid and you can see the flora change. At the bottom there is normally snow and the *Doronicum nivalis*, usually found only in alpine regions. Inside the cave is almost filled with a 75,000-cubic metres block of ice 15m thick. Monthly measurement since 1965 of the four microclimates in the cave and analysis of the layers of ice built up over at least 4,000 years are helping to build up a picture of climatic cycles over the centuries; below the ice block there are two lower galleries, only discovered in 1950, which are scientific reservations with strange ice stalagmites in a steady temperature of 1°C. There's no way down here without your own wire ladder, but tourists can visit 'the church' at the back of the cave, so called because of its ice pillars. The caretaker should have a torch, if he's still there, but take your own to be sure.

2. To get from Gheţari to Gîrda de Sus, you could of course take the road north for five kilometres and then all the way back south again for another 13km, but there are more direct routes. The red stripe markings lead south past the site of the cabana (1,108m), swinging right to pass a good covered spring and continue as a muddy farm track, just like a West Country lane. A quarter of an hour from the cabana site the path passes down the left side of one meadow and the right side of the next and goes up through young beech to a ridge after six minutes more. It goes down through alternate woods and fields, all very lush and pastoral, for eight minutes and at a stile by a spring turns sharp right — **not** the obvious route ahead. A rocky path leads around the far side of a farm to the left, goes right in woods and then drops in virtual freefall to reach another lane, seven minutes from the stile. If coming up, you should look for a path to the right on a left-hand bend just after a small spring; there are red stripes painted on trees on both sides of the lane, but no arrow to indicate a turning. Going down, turn left and zig down steeply for seven minutes to reach the main Gîrda Seacă valley at a bridge and houses. Turning left and going downstream for 13 minutes you reach the road from Gheţari coming in from the left/east, and the main Arieş valley road after eight minutes more. To the right is an

18th-Century wooden-roofed church, to the left some reasonable
shops (the *alimentară* is closed on Tuesday and open on Sunday,
unusually) and a bus shelter with a good fruit stall in it if you're
lucky. From here there are about 40km of very scenic road east to
Cîmpeni, where you can catch a train to Turda.

3. Alternatively, the route from the ice-cave to Ponor (not IC Ponor)
starts around the right-hand side of the doline, following blue
triangles, and within a couple of minutes turns left up a small path
through beech, firs and sycamore. Turn right at a fence and then
almost at once left across a stile (all very badly marked) to cross a
meadow full of lovely flowers and piles of stones gathered up into
piles as in western Ireland. The path drops through a beech wood
and another meadow to go down a very overgrown path to reach a
major valley. However the path does not go straight into the main
valley but turns right along the hillside, up through woodland for a
long unmarked stretch. After a total of 40 minutes it drops down
through a Moţi settlement, making a hairpin bend left at a home-
made wooden sign, and then another to the right, dropping down
and up the other side to more huts with good springs under wooden
lids. After 12 minutes you cross a *drum forestier* leading down into
the valley; the path in fact goes straight ahead across the angle of
this hairpin bend and zigzags down for six minutes to reach the road
along the Gîrda Seacă valley at a bridge seven minutes south of
some cabanas. Two minutes north of this there is a sign left to a
spring; after another 40 minutes, past various bridges and side
tracks, you reach the forestry settlement of Casă de Piatra ('Stone
House' although I saw no such thing). After seven more minutes you
reach a turning left to the Coiba Mare cave, only three minutes away.
As with many of these caves, the narrow passages are blocked with
tree trunks washed in by floods. The Coiba Mică cave, just above,
is still active, ie with a stream running through and still changing its
shape, and it is also blocked by logs. This stream can be heard as
a distant hum flowing beneath the Coiba Mare.
  Another 45 minutes north of here is a very rough *drum forestier*
which you should take up to the northwest, just after a cave with the
main stream pouring out of it and just before a disused but very
usable hut; if you reach a sign to Padiş at the end of the valley road
you have overshot and should return for five minutes. At this point
you leave the marked route to Padiş to cross a ridge to the Valea
Seacă; the route sets off just north of west, turns right and then
climbs west-southwest from beech wood into firs. After ten minutes
turn right at a junction before curving left and then taking a hairpin
bend left on to an easier track used by sheep and horses. It
continues just west of south to meet the ridge 11 minutes from the

junction.

From here you can go any way you like down into the valley, but I chose to turn right and go northwest through newly planted conifers and then left around the head of the valley before following a stream down to the *drum forestier*, in under thirty minutes. After a quarter hour another branch of the *drum forestier* comes in on the left, all the way from the ridge to the southeast where it almost certainly links to the Gîrda Seaca valley; especially if doing this route in reverse this would be a very risk-free short cut and I would appreciate details from anyone who tries it. The route now passes just to the south of the area known as the *Lumea Perduta* (Lost World), an area of mysterious pits and sinkholes such as the Avenida Negru, Avenida Acoperit and Avenida Germanata. After 13 minutes you meet the red triangle route from Arieşeni, on a 'tractor road' to the left just before the Căput *cabana forestier*. Seven minutes on you reach the paths from Padiş cabana to the right and the turning left to our objective, the Cetăţile Ponorului.

Although the sign says this is 90 minutes away it in fact only took me ten minutes to the top of the stairs down into Dolina I, the first of the three huge sinkholes. The stairs are no better than you would expect and the rock below can be very slippery; at the bottom you find an arch leading to passages to the other dolines, practicable only by cavers with the right equipment; however there is a path to the left from the bottom of the stairs to Dolina III, the most impresssive with its 150m high cliffs and steaming pit. From here the blue dot route continues up scree and then through luxuriant undergrowth to climb out of the doline and turn right on to a forestry track to pass right around the doline via four clifftop viewing balconies and a junction left (marked with yellow dots) to Galbenei gorge and paths west to Pietroasa or the DN 75. The path around the cliffs takes 15 minutes, in and out of typical karst depressions, to reach a *drum forestier* and turn right for 15 minutes to regain the main *drum* from the Valea Seacă, just before Canton Glavoi forestry cabana. This is a very popular camping spot with lots of open meadow; to the right is the direct path to Padiş (see below), and to the left a path (also marked with yellow dots) to the Focul Viu cave and the paths west.

Less than two kilometres north of here the road should cross a red stripe path but in the open meadow it was impossible to spot it. I chose to go up to the junction with the Pietroasa to Radeş road where there is an excellent map of the area, but in any case it would be easy to turn right across the Poiana Bălileasa to pick up this road and then simply follow it north for about four kilometres across the karst plateau, mostly lush meadow but dotted with strange pits with bushes or trees in them which get normally calm cavers squeaking with excitement — every one offers the hope of some tiny cavity leading to a larger cave system.

Seven minutes after a pass, where the road (marked with red stripes to Stîna de Vale and blue stripes to, ultimately, the Vlădeasa cabana) turns 90 degrees left to the west, it may just be possible to see a marker pole on the ridge to the north, beyond a stub of road and space to camp. In any case the initially unmarked red dot path to the Cetaţea Radeşii passes to the right of this pole and goes down into spruce to the left. It crosses up to six tiny streams, most of which are likely to be dry, to a map on a tree (one of the few in Romania to show where you are) where the stream passes through a cave below. From here you go down by a tricky bit of path and a ladder with one rung missing, and into the entrance of Radeş citadel 15 minutes from the road. You can go quite a way by daylight alone, but immediately beyond this are more stairs down with some missing rungs at the bottom and then ramshackle boardwalks above the stream itself which get progressively worse as you proceed; although there are some natural skylights you should not try this route without a torch. It took me 15 minutes to emerge into the gorge below, from where you can continue on downstream all the way to IC Ponor, or turn left for 50m up another gorge to a small waterfall, or return to the road either through the citadel again or over the top by a path climbing up between the two gorges. Taking this path, ignore the first arrow to the left after four minutes and then take the second past one of the skylights and then down to the left to reach the sign near the entrance of the citadel in eight more minutes.

To reach Padiş from the camping spot by the road, follow the road back over the pass, past a lake and a cabana to an unmarked junction 24 minutes from the pass, where the road bends right. After four minutes along this cart track to the left, and again after three minutes, turn right at unmarked forks and climb through spruce woods, up for nine minutes and down for another nine to reach forestry cabanas on the major *drum forestier* to IC Ponor; Padiş cabana is just to the left/east across a bridge, with a BTT youth camp to the left.

4. The route here from Canton Glavoi (or Ponor), initially unmarked, follows the obvious track northeast uphill for five minutes and on in meadow. After five minutes it reaches the Ponor stream at Poiana Ponor, a quite lovely camping spot upstream of the point where the stream plunges underground to the Citadel. The track continues up the right bank of the stream and after five minutes crosses a twin-log bridge over a stream that appears from the foot of a cliff just a couple of minutes to the left. The route continues up the main valley,

following red triangle markings from Căput and blue and yellow dots from Ponor. The track ends and continues as a path up the left side of the valley, into beech and spruce woods, and is joined by yellow cross markings from the Lumea Perduta to the right. Seventeen minutes from the bridge it reaches a small clearing at the ridge and soon comes down into the now familiar karst plateau pockmarked with dips and hollows. The path is rather vague, keeping to the right of a stîna and *drum* until it finally joins the road 12 minutes from the ridge at the edge of a small wood ten minutes before Padiş cabana. If, going from Padiş to Ponor, you miss the marked path here and keep going along the road, you can take a path to the left at the ridge and make your own way down to the road north of Glavoi.

THE TURDA AND RÎMEŢ GORGES

In this section I describe two short walks along gorges on the edge of the Apuseni massif. They can easily be linked by the Arieş valley railway line, but unless you are interested in rock-climbing you may well feel that one is enough.

1. TURDA

The Turda Gorges (Cheile Turzii) are probably the most famous in the country, among climbers, botanists and tourists pure and simple. They are indeed spectacular, with 300m limestone cliffs over a length of 2.9km, but they have also suffered both from normal tourist litter and from the climbers who have painted the gradings of the various climbs on to the cliffs. After seeing them in 1883 Mrs Gerard summed them up as 'one of the most remarkable natural phenomena which the country presents. It is nothing else but a gaping unexpected rift of 3-4 English miles in length, right through the limestone rocks which rise about 1200 feet at the highest point. Deep and gloomy caverns, formerly the abode of robbers, honeycomb these rocky walls, and a wild mountain torrent fills up the space between them, completing a weirdly beautiful scene; but on our first view of it from the railway carriage it resembled nothing so much as a magnified loaf of bread severed in two by the cut of a gigantic knife'.

They are also of great interest to naturalists, being essentially a sun-trap and providing ideal conditions for plants and butterflies that are otherwise found only on the shores of the Mediterranean or indeed nowhere else at all. The whole gorge is a reservation, with sun-loving steppe plants on the left side and moisture-seeking plants on the shadier right side. Among the 13 endemic plant species are

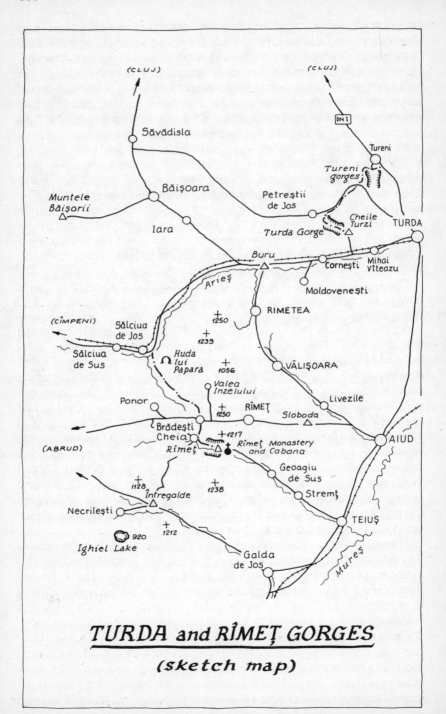

TURDA and RÎMEŢ GORGES
(sketch map)

Aconitum fissurae, Carduus fissurae, Dianthus integripetalus and *Hieracium tordanum.* Other rarities are *Dianthus spiculifolius, Dianthus carthusianorum ssp. saxigenus, Sempervivum schlehani, Ferrula sadleriana,* otherwise only found in Hungary, and *Allium obliquum,* the Turda gorge garlic, found in Turkestan and the Tian Shan, but only here in Romania. Birds include the rock sparrow and the rock vulture, at opposite extremes of the pecking order.

Getting there

Most visitors simply approach from the Arieş valley to Cheile Turzii cabana at the southern end of the gorge, have a look and return the same way. However I have put together an itinerary from the Cluj to Turda road, past the Tureni gorges to the north and through the whole length of the Turda gorges to the cabana and the Arieş. Your decision whether to walk to or from Tureni will probably hinge on whether you wish to start or finish at the cabana.

There are now 29 buses a day between Cluj and Turda, so it should be no problem getting to the village of Tureni (Tordatúr in Hungarian), 21km from Cluj. If not coming from Cluj, you will probably arrive at the station of Cîmpia Turzii and find that the rail link to Turda (Torda), nine kilometres west, is now freight only; however city bus no 2 runs frequently from the station forecourt to Pta Republicii, the main street of Turda (unusually, you buy tickets on the bus, perhaps due to Hungarian influence). The *autogară* proper is on Str Gheorghe Lazăr, through the excellent market just east of Pta Republicii, and the *Gara Mici* ('small station'), for the three narrow-gauge mixed trains daily (one at 0325) west along the Arieş to Abrud, is about 25 minutes walk south (signposted *Zona Industriala*) from a bus-stop opposite an *alimentară* on the Cîmpia Turzii road (from the centre walk down to the main roundabout and across the bridge). After a long hike through the cement works take the first left and then the first right, down what seems a sordid dead-end but really will lead you to the station.

Turda is ringed with dirty and ugly industrial plants but the core of this historic Magyar town is still very pleasant, with Protestant and Catholic churches from about 1500 and a museum in the former seat of the Transylvanian Diet, as well as some good *cofetărie*. There is a hotel at the top of Pta Republicii and a campsite near the Roman saltmines at Turda-Bai two kilometres to the northwest; Stejeris *Han* and campsite is just off the main DN 1 road 12km south but only has a couple of direct buses per day. In any case it's only eight kilometres to Cheile Turzii cabana following red and blue cross markings from the DN 75 Cîmpeni road, west from the main roundabout; there are also buses every hour or so along this road to Corneşti — get off at the unmarked turning to Cheia two kilometres after Mihai Viteazu and walk five kilometres up the road to the cabana, as described below in reverse.

Hiking directions

Starting from the south end of Tureni on the main road, take an unmade road across the fields to the west, with the main part of the village to your right, with a large hall church and another with a wooden belfry, both very common in this area. After 18 minutes cross a bridge by a watermill, follow the road left up above the right/west bank of the stream and carry on along the clifftop following some yellow triangle markings.

At various points I was shown ways down into the gorge and assured there was a path along the bottom, but there never was. However there is a very luxuriant flora by the water, together with frogs and magnificent blue and green dragonflies; there are also caves, which I never reached. An hour and a quarter after leaving the village I reached a road running south to a quarry. The one real success of environmentalists under Ceauşescu was in defeating plans for this quarry to expand and simply destroy the entire gorge. As it is though, it is still a safe distance to the west. You can either follow the road to its junction by the quarry, or follow the markings along the clifftop and then return along the power line to the road, where blue triangle markings fork left across a field towards Turda town in the plains below. To reach the Turda gorge, turn right at the road junction just before the quarry and follow the asphalt DJ 107L west and then southwest around the side of a hill. Almost at once the blue stripe markings turn left to go directly to the cabana, but if you want go straight down the gorge from the north you should follow the road for five kilometres (50 minutes to an hour on foot) to the first left turn in the village of Petreştii de Jos at house no 7. (The village is called Peşteri de Jos in the *Rough Guide*, which would be appropriate, meaning 'Lower Caves', but sadly is wrong.)

This village street becomes a farm track, then a path marked by red stripe markings from the Cluj-Făget cabanas and red crosses from Băişoara cabana in the hills 40km to the west (there's an evening bus from Turda if you fancy the circuit) which leads into the gorge; at first it is not ideally suited to carrying a pack, but it improves as you go on. After 20 minutes you cross the first bridge to the right/west bank, by the first of the caves walled up to provide refuge from the Tartars, and later shelter for *haiducs* or outlaws.

Caves here have also revealed traces of prehistoric habitation and the most spectacular, the Cetăţeaua Mare (65m deep, on the right bank) and the Cetăţeaua Mica (43m deep, on the left bank) were once one huge chamber later cut in half by the river as it carved out the gorge. Now as you cross the river three more times you pass the most impressive climbing cliffs, rising over 300m from the river which drops from 460m to 420m. After half an hour or so, the path, by now virtually motorway standard, takes you slightly up to the southeast to the cabana. It is a pleasant spot with camping space under fruit trees and various routes on to Turda and other villages in the Arieş valley including Buru and Corneşti. There is also a circular walk of four to five hours along the clifftops on either side of the gorge, marked with red dots.

I took the route marked with blue crosses to Cheia which, apart from a brief initial cut-off to the left, turned out to follow the road all the way down, meeting an asphalt road from the right/west after 33 minutes and passing through the village to meet the main road after exactly one hour in all, nine kilometres west of Turda.

From here you can return to Turda by bus or car, or head west up the Arieş valley to the Rîmeţ gorge (see below), into the Apuseni massif (see previous section) or to the Munte Găina Girl Fair (see page 112).

Practical information

Although the general relationship of Turda, Tureni and the gorges is shown on the *Hartă Turistică* of Cluj *judeţ*, this does not show any of the paths. There is a map outside Cheile Turzii cabana, but apart from that you'll have to trust my efforts.

2. RÎMEŢ

In the southeastern corner of the Apuseni massif, the Trascău mountains are a limestone extension of the Metaliferi mountains to the west and offer spectacular karst caves and gorges, as well as another tranquil monastery and small farming communities largely untouched by modern life. However, while all this is particularly accessible and close to trunk routes, what makes this route particularly bizarre is the nature of the marked route through the Rîmeţ gorge, which runs through the stream itself, at times up to chest deep in the water. There is a goat track high on the cliffs above which I would not recommend to the nervous, and if neither appeals you can go around easily by road. Thus, although I describe a north-south through route, if the idea of wading down the gorge particularly attracts you, you should go first to Rîmeţ cabana at the southern end of the gorge to leave luggage and then tackle the hike.

Getting there

My route starts at the Sălciua de Jos halt, 42km west of Turda on the narrow-gauge rail line to Abrud and the DN 75 to Cîmpeni and Dr Petru Groza. There are plenty of buses and cars, and three trains each way per day. It ends with a bus from Valea Mînîsterea, near Rîmeţ, to Teiuş station and Aiud *autogară*, as opposed to the local *autobaza* at the railway station ten minutes walk away. Teiuş is the junction between trains from Cluj to Sighişoara and Braşov, and to Deva, and has several Gothic churches; Aiud is a bigger town with an old Hungarian church and museum within the walls of one of Transylvania's oldest castles, dating from 1302.

Hiking directions

Apart from the Sălciua de Jos rail halt, there is a large village limits sign here, with a springy pedestrian suspension bridge which you should take across the Arieş (badly polluted here by industry in Cîmpeni) and go left and right to continue southwards, turning left after five minutes and almost at once right where the red cross routes continue straight ahead to the Aiud gorge and Colţii Trascăului. The route climbs steadily southwards on a gravel road through gorges and a small farming village for 37 minutes to Huda lui Papară cave (567m). The path to the cave passes behind the breeze-block ticket shed and into the cave by a relatively decent walkway above the cascading stream (why the *Invitation* should say access is by boat I can't imagine!). There may be a closed gate but the Racoviţa Institute is quite happy for careful cavers to climb over or under this. It is very impressive but not all that long; although the stream goes right through the hill you will have to return to the ticket hut, cross the stream to a good picnic shelter and follow a steep and stony farm track, marked with blue crosses, up through beech wood dotted with limestone boulders, and then across meadow to the ridge after 22 minutes.

From here it goes down the left/east side of the valley for 18 minutes, then forks right and down into a Moţi settlement with little thatched huts that look like hay ricks, with poles sticking out of the top. The red soil here can be very sticky in places, and the area is almost reminiscent of west Dorset about 200 years ago, with small orchards and vegetable gardens among the meadows. Continue up the valley for 45 minutes, turning left at a small ford in Valea Poienii and continuing more steeply (past an unmarked junction where a *drum* comes in from the left) for 23 minutes to Brădeşti on a sharp ridge — the *Invitation* is wrong in showing a stream flowing south through the village, rather than north through Huda lui Papară.

The road to Rîmeţ (or Remete) goes to the left here; the path to the gorge, mostly unmarked, goes down to the left of the small shop and church and very shortly turns twice to the left, and then three times to the right to end up on an overgrown and unmarked path to a beech wood. From here it follows the stream, crossing frequently from one side to the other, to Cheia, one hour from Brădeşti. Cut left through the grounds of the Muntele cu Flori school groups cabana to cross the stream by a bridge (or continue to the sign at the junction and then get your feet wet). From here you can continue south-southwest (blue triangles) for about three hours to Întregalde cabana, near more scenic gorges, and on to the Ighiel lake (920m), noted for its rare species of newts (!), and ultimately to another narrow-gauge railway from Zlatna to Alba Iulia.

However the main route turns left into the Rîmeţ gorges (there is emphatically no road here, as shown on the *Invitation* map) for five minutes and then splits after a camping spot with a sign spelling out the perils of the alternative routes, either over the Strunga Caprei cliffs (marked with blue triangles) or through the water (blue crosses). The route through the water would be enjoyable without a pack on a warm day; there are plenty of patches of woodland in the bends of the river, so it's a matter of picking the shallow or slower-flowing side of the stretches between. At the lower end there is some cable, but it's also needed further upstream.

The upper route starts inconspicuously several metres west of a rock painted with junction markings and takes about an hour and ten minutes to regain water level at the far end of the gorge. It is almost all on a narrow goat track, with a couple of stretches of cable, definitely not suitable for mass tourism, and the final sections are quite difficult carrying a pack down and would be harder carrying one up. The final drop down is greatly helped by the memorial cross to one Pinca Ioan, to whom I'm grateful. You will have to ford the river here in any case before following a path through beech trees down the right bank, reaching a road after about 13 minutes and carrying on past private chalets for 37 minutes to reach the big modern tourist cabana (440m) across the river to the left, just above a gap cut by the river in a saw-toothed limestone ridge. There are camping cabins and plenty of space for camping here; the main building seemed to be under restoration in 1991, having recently been privatised and taken over by the Rîmeţ monastery.

This monastery (again, a nunnery in fact — see back cover) lies 13 minutes further down the valley. Its 14th-Century church is small and peaceful, with frescoes dating from 1377 to the 19th Century. Due to floods and damp damaging these frescoes, the church was raised by 2 metres in 1988; there is still a cool sweet well beneath it. There is also a new church, begun in 1984, but still being finished, and a

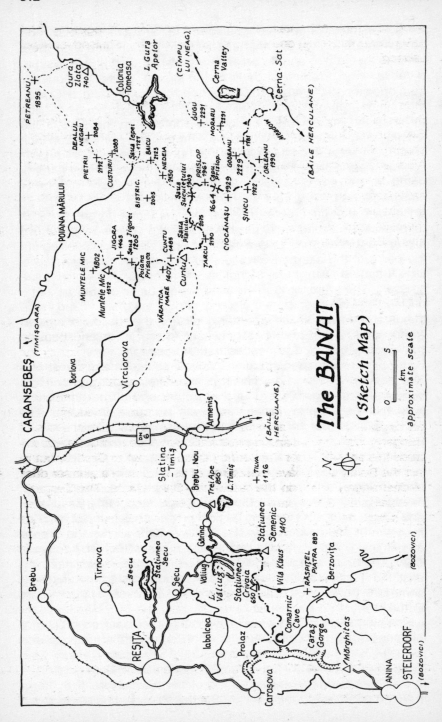

small museum with interesting exhibits of Moţi ethnography and naïve icons, including one of the Virgin cunningly disguised as Nigel Lawson.

Moving on and practical information

Buses leave here at 0500, 1230 and 1630 to Teiuş and Aiud, passing Geoagiu de Sus, where there is a 16th-Century Orthodox Bishop's church. There are also paths to the cabanas at Sloboda (above Aiud) and Întregalde. Map 3 of the *Invitation* is not particularly good, being a very cramped map of an area overcrowded with tiny settlements, quite apart from the various errors noted above such as the absurd notion of a road along the Rîmeţ gorge. However it's all there is apart from my efforts. Note that the Turda gorge is just above Buru cabana in the top right-hand corner.

THE BANAT

The Banat is the name generally applied to the whole area of Romania to the west of the Carpathians, although strictly speaking the name only applies to the southwestern corner and the contiguous areas of Yugoslavia (Vojvodina) and Hungary. It was directly ruled by the Turks, and then by the Hapsburgs until 1918, so that the towns are full of *Jugendstil (art nouveau)* architecture, and the folk music reflects strong Serbian influences. The countryside is mostly an extension of the *Alföld* (Great Plain of Hungary), well drained and agriculturally developed; most visitors will cross this as they enter the country through Arad or Oradea, but in fact the Banat does have mountains of its own, with a warmer drier Mediterranean feel than the rest of the Carpathians. The Semenic mountains are 800 square kilometres of limestone with karst gorges and caves, and a 3,217m underground river at Buhui, just outside the town of Anina which also has the deepest coal mine in Europe at 1,107m. There is a particularly spectacular railway from Anina to Oraviţa, with 30 viaducts and 14 tunnels in its 34km length. To the east the Ţarcu-Godeanu ranges are largely open moorland with some high peaks offering excellent walking. Thirdly Mount Domogled in the Mehedinţi range east of the Roman spa of Băile Herculane was Romania's first nature reserve in 1932 and is now set to become a 60,000-hectare National Park, as is the area of the Iron Gates on the Danube nearby. The south side of the Mehedinţi is also a karst zone, with many caves such as the 10,330m Topolniţa system.

I will swiftly guide you through the Semenic range, from Reşiţa through the Caraş gorge to the Comarnic cave, the ski resort of

Semenic and the German villages of Trei Ape and Brebu Nou, and then in more detail from the ski resort of Muntele Mic south to Vf Ţarcu and the Cerna valley above Băile Herculane, through an area of moorland where ancient shepherds' paths have crossed for centuries.

Getting there

Stage one starts at Caraşova, between Reşiţa and Anina; Reşiţa is a metal-bashing town, formerly the centre of the Romanian locomotive-building industry. There is a static display of steam locomotives near the Nord station, but you will eventually need to get to the terminus at the Sud station, by a very good market. From here you should head south and then east to reach the *autogară*, a little way from the centre on the road to Valiug. Caraşova is 16km south, and you should get dropped off as close as possible to the big modern viaduct at the northern end of the bypass to the east of the town. (There is also a daily bus from Reşiţa to Crivaia, Trei Ape, Semenic, then back to Reşiţa via Trei Ape again.)

Hiking directions

1. The path up the Caraş gorges runs under this bridge, on the left/south bank; it's a good path with some rather slimy limestone in parts, and the views of the cliffs are often obscured by trees. After an hour and a quarter I reached a big camping place with a few farm houses across the river (a place known as Prolaz); although the best bit of the gorge is just a bit further on, after that the route becomes *nerecomendabil* unless you take a boat (rather reminiscent of Rîmeţ). You should in fact cross the river just below the camping place by a pair of cables, one for the feet and one to hang on to — it's really quite safe and easy. Rather than the obvious track leading up to a farm, you should take a path to the left and follow blue stripe markings up to an clear saddle, through woods of southern oaks, thorns and alder, quite unlike anything in Transylvania proper. At the top, fork right across hayfields and follow a generally unmarked but reasonably well trodden path southeast, passing to the right of a house with a fenced paddock. This path turns right on to a stony farm track and runs through an orchard of plum trees, with the path well marked on the trees. At the end it turns left through a wood and on by a most attractive path to drop down to a *cabana forestier* just before a bridge (1½ hours from Prolaz) and beyond it the steps up to the Comarnic cave, which still has one active level, and the familiar stalagmitic columns and veils. The last visit is at 1500, and you might have to pay for a group of five if no one else turns up.

The guide is to be found at a hut just to the right on the *drum* towards Anina.

From the bridge (by a good spring) the path to Semenic goes up the right bank of the stream, crossing by a log after seven minutes and climbing up a *drum forestier*, still well marked with blue stripes, for quite a steep slog through beech trees to go virtually over the top of the hill after 40 minutes. (The map in the *Invitation* gets it wrong here.) From here the path runs down to the northeast through what could be very tatty English parkland, and then down to the left (not easy to find) into beech wood to reach a major *drum forestier* along the Birzava valley at a good camping spot where there is even a log perfectly placed for foot washing. From here it is just 1.5km downstream to Crivaia, at 650m at the end of Lac Văliug, where there are two cabanas which somehow manage to have both their restaurants closed on Sundays. There should be a route to Semenic via Villa Klaus to the south, but I was unable to find the red cross markings; it's my belief that commercial interests at Crivaia have removed them.

The blue stripe route up to Semenic starts at the left bend between the two cabanas, going through an unmarked gateway in a concrete wall and forking left at once. After this it is fairly clear and decently marked all the way up to a (perhaps temporarily) derelict ski-lift terminal, 80 minutes from Crivaia. The ski resort is above to the right, with a large modern cabana below a chapel. From here there is a route south, marked with red crosses, to Pătaş and Topleţ near the Danube; however the blue dot route east to Teregova seems almost impossible to follow. The blue cross route to Trei Ape is also unmarked, although it's a clear *drum forestier* turning east off the road north from Semenic to the Prislop pass. Trei Ape (Dreiwasser or Three Waters) cabana is very lively, with watersports on the lake. The village of Brebu Nou, just beyond, is, or rather was, the Böhme German village of Weidental, which looks nothing like the villages of the Transylvanian Saxons, with its white houses with red tiled roofs scattered around low sandy hills. There is an unmade road over the pass east from here, which had a bus service until the German population departed to the Munich area. This comes down to Slatina-Timiş, 19km south of Caransebeş in the Timiş valley.

2. Caransebeş is on the main rail line from Bucureşti and Craiova to Timişoara, and is in fact the main junction to Reşiţa. From the *autogară* just south of the river there are one or two buses a day to the Telescaun Muntele Mic chair-lift, with more to Borlova, halfway to the chair-lift terminal, and two a day to Poiana Marului to the north of Muntele Mic. The road to the chair-lift terminal, Str Muntele Mic, is not at all easy to find, but it runs east to the north of the Sebeş river

past two churches in the Austro-Hungarian ochre and onion-dome style. Again there is a dam being built here, a surprising distance into the plains, but the Valea Craiului leading into the hills is largely unspoilt. After 25km this reaches the lower terminal of the chair-lift at about 800m; from here the chair-lift (1000-1700, except Tuesdays) takes you in 35 minutes almost north to the ski resort, from where my route then returns south, so you might prefer to take a more direct route continuing eastwards up the *drum* to the Şaua Jigorei (1,205m) on my north-south route. I confess I took the chair-lift to the resort at 1,573m. Here there is one main hotel (a ten-storey block), several wooden cabanas, and a chapel as at Semenic. However there's not actually a lot to stop for other than accommodation. The path to Vf Ţarcu follows poles marked with red stripes south from the ridge above the resort across lovely moorland with Ţarcu visible ahead, dropping down and just to the west of Vf Jigora (1,463m). It goes down an old cart track between beech woods to the left/east and the new zigzag road to the right/west, to reach the Jigorei saddle by the Dacia private cabana in 45 minutes. From here it climbs slightly, between the woods and the road as before, crossing after nine minutes the yellow stripe route from the lower chair-lift terminal to Poiana Marului. After 22 minutes more, now following the track itself through beech and spruce woods, there is an excellent viewpoint in the small hilltop meadow of Poiana Şeroni (1,399m), and after another five minutes another link to the lower chair-lift terminal. Now the track is mainly level, arriving after 12 minutes just above the tree line at Cuntu weather station, a large four-storey stone building that acts as base for the real weather station on the peak above. There is another private cabana here, belonging to the *Prieteni Munţilor* (Friends of the Mountains), where you might get accommodation at weekends.

The route up Ţarcu sets off up the track to the left/northeast of the cabanas and goes straight on where this takes a hairpin to the right, climbing up steeply past three marker poles to a cairn on the shoulder of the hill to the right. It continues steeply up (with the track linking the weather stations just to the east) over very plain moor with no bushes or flowers other than half-buried lichen, and reaches a bigger cairn on the main shoulder after 30 minutes. Continuing upwards, after 15 minutes you reach the edge of the great cirque on the north side of the summit; one path takes a lower route left across the cirque to the Şaua Plaiului, the *drum* runs to the right/west with marker poles on the ridge itself, and the path follows the top of the cliff, swinging left until it joins the *drum* and reaches the weather station just before the summit of Vf Ţarcu at 2,190m.

From here it takes under 20 minutes to go down to the Şaua Plaiului (2,075m) to the northeast; the path continues to the east-northeast and then due east for 45 minutes to an illegible sign at the start of the broad Şaua Şuculeţului (1,909m), where you should keep right on the ridge (now supposedly marked with red dots) rather than following the red stripes left into the valley. The main path follows the ridge southwards, although I took a worse path below to reach a stream, and took an hour and a half to cover about seven kilometres to the 1,664m saddle at the south end of the Prislop ridge. The red dot route turns left here down the valley to Vf Godeanu and the south side of the Retezat, while I continued on an unmarked path to the south, uphill and to the left of the peaks of Vf Ciocănaşu (1,929m) and Vf Şincu (1,922m).

After half an hour this curves left above a stîna, crosses twin streams by obvious tracks and continues parallel to a stream to the left/north, with two other valleys, the further deeply eroded, to the right. This stream reminds me of the Yorkshire Dales, with rather tea-coloured water over white stones; after following it for about 35 minutes I reached an obvious saddle in the ridge from Vf Godeanu (2,229m) to the left to Vf Orleanu (or Olanelor, 1,990m) to the right; to the right the ridge runs down to Băile Herculane 40km away, and you should in fact go left to the next gap in this ridge to reach another along the left side of the next valley, running south-southeast to the Cerna. This ridge is much steeper and sharper than the moorland thus far; the path weaves left and right of minor peaks before passing to the right side of Oslea Romănă (1,781m) after another hour. You should keep high on fairly plain hillside past two side ridges to the right before curving right past a geodesic marker and dropping to the southeast, towards the Mehedinţi massif beyond the Cerna, which looks very like the Piatra Craiului.

The path passes to the right of a stîna, with a glimpse of Cerna reservoir to the left, and down a broad ride between beech woods and then through hayfields to a saddle an hour from Oslea Romănă. Here it takes a level path to the left by a pile of stones, forking left after three minutes and going down with woods to the left and fields and fruit trees to the right, to a valley on the right. From a spring in beech trees the path goes down the left side of this valley to reach a stream at the bottom and turn left down this to reach the Cerna valley road, with a tiny *alimentară* (closed on Thursdays) down to the right. Cerna-Sat is a tiny settlement but it does have a *Popas Turistic*, really a cabana with a field for camping. From here it is about ten kilometres through impressive gorges down to the much better road from Baia de Arama, and another 22km to Băile Herculane. In the other direction, to the northeast, there is a *drum forestier* to Cîmpu lui Neag (see the section on the Retezat) which should at some point be metalled. There should be a couple of buses a day to Cerna dam, just above Cerna-Sat.

Băile Herculane, the Baths of Hercules, at 160m, has been a spa since Roman times, and was particularly stylish and popular in the 18th and 19th Centuries. A military band still plays on the bandstand on summer mornings, and there is a small museum in the former casino. There are plenty of reasonably marked walks into the hills on both sides, to the nature reserve on Vf Domogled (1,105m) to the east, and to the lower ridge route to Vf Godeanu to the west (this should be marked with a red stripe but isn't, as far as I can tell), including shorter walks to the Munk spring, the Vf Ciorici viewpoint and the Steam Cave where steam hisses out at 56°C.

There are several hotels and four campsites, the first six kilometres north at the Şapte Izvoare Calde (Seven Hot Springs) Ştrand or bathing place, very crowded and rather sordid (near a hydroelectric power station dating back to 1893), another, the Popas Flora, just south of the centre, then the Pecinişca in the southern suburbs but near the only decent shops, and the Plopii Fara Sat at the station five kilometres south. There are buses every 20-30 minutes from the CFR *Agenţia* on the Piaţa Hercules to the station for trains between Craiova and Timişoara.

Practical information

The Semenic mountains, but not the Muntele Mic/Ţarcu mountains, are covered in the *Invitation*; they are both covered by two books in the *Munţii Nostrii* series which were widely available, at least in 1991. The Semenic book's map is very inadequate and the Muntele Mic/Ţarcu one, though better, does not extend all the way to the Cerna valley. In Băile Herculane you may find an English language booklet of walks which includes a decent map of the Cerna valley and Mehedinţi massif; there is also a special supplement to *România Pitoreasca* magazine available at the tourist office which includes a map of the area and some walks described in Romanian.

INDEX

Explore Eastern Europe with Bradt

If you enjoy hiking and want to explore the less crowded areas of eastern Europe we have three books for you:

Guide to Czechoslovakia by Simon Hayman
The emphasis here is on outdoor pursuits: hiking, skiing, river-running, caving. There are also sight-seeing suggestions for the many towns and villages of historic interest, and information on accommodation, public transport, self-drive ... everything the adventurous traveller needs for a trouble-free stay.

Guide to East Germany by Stephen Baister and Chris Patrick
This guide covers all the areas of cultural, historical or scenic interest.

Eastern Europe by Rail by Rob Dodson
Everything the rail traveller needs to know, from where to stay near the station to suggested itineraries making the most of your rail pass. Each major town has a plan showing station facilities such as luggage lockers, information desks and restaurants, to avoid unpleasant surprises. **To be published late 1993**.

* * *

We also publish a wide range of guides to other continents with the emphasis on natural history, hiking and backpacking. We also have an expanding rail guide series. Send for a catalogue:

Bradt Publications, 41 Nortoft Road, Chalfont St Peter, Bucks SL9 0LA. Tel: 0494 873478.

NOTES

NOTES